MCA
914.7
1996

Fodor's 96

Moscow, DISCARD
St. Petersburg,
Kiev

"When it comes to information on regional history, what to see and do, and shopping, these guides are exhaustive."

—USAir Magazine

"Usable, sophisticated restaurant coverage, with an emphasis on good value."
—Andy Birsh, *Gourmet Magazine* columnist

"Valuable because of their comprehensiveness."
—*Minneapolis Star-Tribune*

"Fodor's always delivers high quality...thoughtfully presented...thorough."

—*Houston Post*

"An excellent choice for those who want everything under one cover."

—*Washington Post*

Fodor's Travel Publications, Inc.
New York • Toronto • London • Sydney • Auckland

19
Bro

Fodor's Moscow, St. Petersburg, Kiev

Editor: Christopher Billy

Contributors: Steven Amsterdam, Robert Blake, David Brown, Fionn Davenport, Lauri del Commune, Bevin McLaughlin, Sam Lardner, Linda K. Schmidt, M.T. Schwartzman, Katherine Semler, Juliette Shapland.

Creative Director: Fabrizio La Rocca

Cartographer: David Lindroth

Cover Photograph: Jeffrey Aaronson/Network Aspen

Text Design: Between the Covers

Copyright

Special Sales

CONTENTS

ON THE ROAD WITH FODOR'S

A GOOD TRAVEL GUIDE is like a wonderful traveling companion. It's charming, it's brimming with sound recommendations and solid ideas, it pulls no punches in describing lodging and dining establishments, and it's consistently full of fascinating facts that make you view what you've traveled to see in a rich new light. In the creation of *Moscow, St. Petersburg, Kiev '96*, we at Fodor's have gone to great lengths to provide you with the very best of all possible traveling companions—and to make your trip the best of all possible vacations.

About Our Writer

The information in these pages has been compiled by an extraordinary writer. **Lauri del Commune** has lived in Moscow since 1993. She previously worked for 12 years in U.S. book publishing, the last six years in the international department of Alfred A. Knopf in New York.

What's New

Big things are happening at Fodor's—and in Moscow, St. Petersburg, and Kiev.

A New Design

If this is not the first Fodor's guide you've purchased, you'll immediately notice our new look. More readable and easier-to-use than ever? We think so–and we hope you do, too.

Travel Updates

Just before your trip, you may want to order a Fodor's Worldview Travel Update. From local publications all over Ireland, the lively, cosmopolitan editors at Worldview gather information on concerts, plays, opera, dance performances, gallery and museum shows, sports competitions, and other special events that coincide with your visit. See the order blank in the back of this book for more information, call 800/799–9609, or fax 800/799–9619.

And in Moscow, St. Petersburg, and Kiev

Events have moved on a long way since the world watched in fascination at the fiery attack on Moscow's parliament building in October 1993. A vocal and energized Boris Yeltsin defiantly braved the conservative backlash and won a great political—and moral—victory. Two years later, the image of Yeltsin the revolutionary democrat has been replaced by that of Yeltsin the stumbling autocrat, battling increasing popular dissatisfaction with the pace of his reforms, the disastrous campaign to subjugate Chechnya, his insistence on governing by decree, and a personal illness that has left him a shadow of the man who catapulted himself and his reformist supporters onto the international stage. Paradoxically, the pace of change has been both remarkable and nonexistant; while the monolith of communist rule has been radically overhauled, the fledgling market system that has replaced it has not resulted in the widespread improvement of living conditions it had so vociferously promised. Indeed, while reforms and the introduction of a crude market system have brought tangible increases in the lifestyles of entrepreneurs and market players, most ordinary Russians and Ukrainians have been unable to escape the poverty and economic confinement they suffered during the Soviet years.

While the economic reforms begun by Mikhail Gorbachev and continued by Yeltsin have met with dubious success, one area where the improvements have been dramatic is the tourist industry. In the past five years, dozens of new hotels, many of them foreign-owned and -managed, have opened in the major cities, reintroducing, for the first time since the Bolshevik Revolution, the concept of luxury accommodations. The tourist industry has also shifted its focus from group to individual travel. If in the past the Soviet tourist industry frowned upon individual tourists, encouraging foreigners to travel in groups by giving them preferential treatment and discount rates, today the situation has been reversed. In 1996 tourists will discover that there is now a direct correlation between what you pay for and what you get.

What is certain, however, is that the economy will continue to remain in a state of flux for the time being, at least until the hotly anticipated elections in 1996, when conservatives opposing Yeltsin are expected to offer a genuine threat to the current government. In typical Russian fashion, however, it is not yet clear whether these elections will actually take place at the appointed time, or whether strategic delays by the government will put the elections back while they attempt to shore up the support that once brought them to power but is now threatening to confine them to, in the words of a bygone era, "the dustbin of history."

Moscow

In this, the most Russian of all Russian cities, change is a question of perspective. For most, life continues as it always did, despite additions to the skyline of new, flashing neon advertisements encouraging the purchase of domestic and foreign goods (and one that shows the dollar exchange rate). The mayor has made radical municipal changes, turning buildings that once housed the labyrinthian Soviet bureaucracy into new agencies charged with accelerating economic reform. Indeed, economic activity is in evidence literally everywhere, from the small-time entrepreneurs hawking folk art on nearly every street corner to massive international ventures that have resulted in the construction of business centers and hotels, as well as the emergence from out of the woodwork of an extremely well-organized—and often ruthless—industry of organized crime. There is no one in Moscow who does not have a take on the activities of the Mafia; the problem has gotten so bad that many Muscovites have thrown up their hands in despair, unable to distinguish between what is a legitimate business venture from what has been obtained by extortion, bribery, and violence.

St. Petersburg

The **50th anniversary** of the end of World War II was celebrated in 1995, amid much pomp and circumstance (including the presence of many world leaders at the official celebrations) and much emotion, as citizens looked back fifty years to the devastating siege of their beloved city by the Nazis that symbolized the struggle of all of the Soviet Union during the War. Today, St. Petersburg's struggles continue, albeit in a different way: Like its urban counterparts in Russia and Ukraine, the city has mobilized itself to make the market system work for its citizens. Although it continues to lag behind Moscow in terms of general prosperity, the positive growth resulting from the introduction of a market economy has had tangible effects. Like the capital, St. Petersburg is full of new projects for hotels and business centers, and it has been relatively successful in attracting foreign business. Prices are lower in this genteel city, and the nouveau riche that are very much in evidence in Moscow seem to be absent here, even if the plague of organized crime is as widespread—some say more so—as in Moscow.

Kiev

The rebirth of Kiev as the capital of a sovereign state has led to the establishment of foreign embassies and an influx of businesspeople from Eastern and Western Europe. Although tourist facilities are still relatively limited, restaurants catering to the growing foreign community are opening, and hotels are being refurbished to approach Western standards. Tense relations between Russia and Ukraine are having a direct impact on the struggling Ukrainian economy. Oil and gas are in short supply, and public buildings tend to be poorly heated in winter.

How to Use this Book

Organization

Up front is **The Gold Guide,** comprised of two sections on gold-colored paper chock-full of information about traveling in general and specifically at your destination. Both are in alphabetical order by topic. **Important Contacts A to Z** gives you addresses and telephone numbers of organizations and companies that offer detailed information and publications, plus information about getting to Russia and Ukraine and back again. **Smart Travel Tips** gives you specific tips on how to get the most out of your travels as well as information on how to accomplish what you need to in your destination.

Stars

Stars in the margin denote the most highly recommended sights, attractions, hotels, and restaurants.

Hotel Facilities

Note that in general you incur charges when you use many hotel facilities; we wanted to let you know what facilities the hotel has to offer, but don't always specify whether or not there's a charge, so when planning a resort vacation that entails a stay of several days, it's wise to ask what's included in your rates.

Credit Cards

The following abbreviations are used: **AE,** American Express; **DC,** Diners Club; **MC,** MasterCard (called Access in Ireland and Northern Ireland), and **V,** Visa. Discover is not accepted outside the U.S.

Please Write to Us

Everyone who has worked on *Moscow, St. Petersburg, Kiev '96* has worked hard to make the text accurate. All prices and opening times are based on information supplied to us at press time, and the publisher cannot accept responsibility for any errors that may have occurred. The passage of time will bring changes, so it's always a good idea to call ahead and confirm information when it matters—particularly if you're making a detour to visit specific sights or attractions. When making reservations at a hotel or inn, be sure to speak up if you have a disability or are traveling with children, if you prefer a private bath or a certain type of bed, or if you have specific dietary needs or any other concerns.

Were the restaurants we recommended as described? Did our hotel picks exceed your expectations? Did you find a museum we recommended a waste of time? Positive and negative, we would love your feedback. If you have complaints, we'll look into them and revise our entries when the facts warrant it. If there's a special place you've happened upon that we haven't included, we'll pass the information along to the writers so they can check it out. So please send us a letter or post card (we're at 201 East 50th Street, New York, New York 10022). We'll look forward to hearing from you. And in the mean time, have a wonderful trip!

Karen Cure
Editorial Director

European Russia and Ukraine

KEY
— Rail Lines

0   300 miles
0   400 km

Barents Sea

NORWAY
Nike
Murmansk
Kozhva
Pechora

SWEDEN

White Sea

Arkhangelsk
Vendenga
Mikun
Syktyvkar

Yushkozero
Kimasozero

Gulf of Bothnia

FINLAND

Severnaya Dvina

Petrozavodsk

Kotlas

Lake Ladoga

RUSSIA

Kirov

Helsinki
Tallinn
Gulf of Finland
St. Petersburg
Vologda
Vyatka

Cherepovets

Baltic Sea
ESTONIA
Novgorod
Yaroslavl
Nizhniy Novgorod
Kazan

Gulf of Riga
Pskov
Volga

Riga
LATVIA
Tver
Vladimir
Simbirsk
Saransk

LITHUANIA
Kaunas
Vitsyebsk
Moscow
Oka

Kaliningrad
RUSSIA
Vilnius
Smolensk
Kaluga
Ryazan
Penza

Minsk
Mahilyow
Tambov
Saratov

Warsaw
BELARUS
Bryansk
Oka
Lipetsk
KAZAKHSTAN

Homyel
Orel
Kursk
Voronezh

POLAND
Belgorod
Don
Volga

L'viv
UKRAINE
Kiev
Kharkiv
Volgograd

SLOVAKIA
Dnieper
Donets

Vinnytsya
Dnipropetrovsk

HUNGARY
MOLDOVA
Rostov na Donu

Chisinau
Kherson
Sea of Azov
Stavropol

Odesa
Krasnodar

ROMANIA

Bucharest
Sevastopol

Black Sea
GEORGIA

Danube
BULGARIA

Reykjavik
ICELAND

NORWAY
Bergen

SCOTLAND
Edinburgh

North Sea

Skagerrack

NORTHERN IRELAND

DENMARK

IRELAND

Belfast

Irish Sea

Dublin

UNITED KINGDOM

WALES

ENGLAND

NETHERLANDS

Hamburg

Cardiff

London

The Hague

Amsterdam

Rotterdam

GERMA

ATLANTIC OCEAN

English Channel

Brussels

BELGIUM

Bonn

Frankfurt

Paris

LUXEMBOURG

F R A N C E

Zürich

Munich

Bern

SWITZERLAND

Lyon

LIECHTENSTEIN

Milan

Venice

Lju

Monte Carlo

Nice

MONACO

PORTUGAL

Madrid

ANDORRA

Marseille

Florence

Lisbon

SPAIN

Barcelona

Corsica

Seville

Granada

Balearic Islands

Sardinia

Tyrrhenian S

Gibraltar

Mediterranean Sea

MOROCCO

ALGERIA

0   400 miles

0   600 km

TUNISIA

x

Numbers below vertical bands relate each zone to Greenwich Mean Time (0 hrs.).
Local times frequently differ from these general indications,
as indicated by light-face numbers on map.

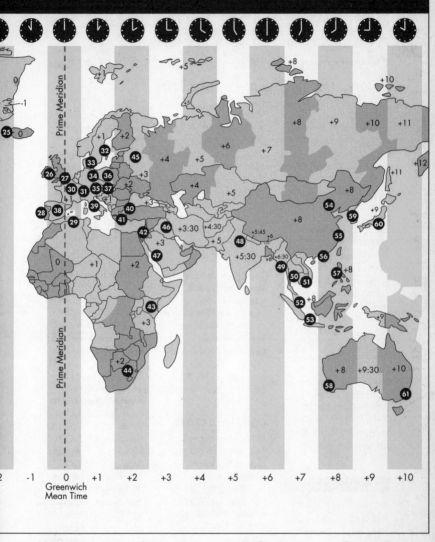

IMPORTANT CONTACTS A TO Z

An Alphabetical Listing of Publications, Organizations, and Companies That Will Help You before, during, and after Your Trip

No single travel resource can give you every detail about every topic that might interest or concern you at the various stages of your journey—when you're planning your trip, while you're on the road, and after you get back home. The following organizations, books, and brochures will supplement the information in *Fodor's Moscow, St. Petersburg, and Kiev '96*. For related information, including both basic tips on visiting the area and background information on many of the topics below, study Smart Travel Tips A to Z, the section that follows Important Contacts A to Z.

A

AIR TRAVEL

The major gateways to Moscow, St. Petersburg, and Kiev are **Sheremetovo II Airport** in Moscow (☎ 578 75 18/78 16), **Pulkovo II Airport** in St. Petersburg (☎ 104 34 44), and **Borispol Airport** in Kiev. Flying time is 8½ hours from New York, 10–11 hours from Chicago, and 12 hours from Los Angeles.

CARRIERS

Carriers serving Russia and Ukraine include **Aeroflot** (630 5th Avenue, New York, NY 10111, ☎ 212/332–1050 or 800/995–5555), **Air France** (☎ 800/237–2747), **British Air** (☎ 800/247–9297), **Delta** (☎ 800/221–1212), **Finnair** (☎ 800/950–5000), **KLM** (☎ 800/374–7747), **Lufthansa** (☎ 800/645–3880), and **SAS** (☎ 800/221–2350).

To register complaints about charter and scheduled airlines, contact the U.S. Department of Transportation's **Office of Consumer Affairs** (400 7th St. NW, Washington, DC 20590, ☎ 202/366–2220 or 800/322–7873).

CONSOLIDATORS

Established consolidators selling to the public include **BET World Travel** (841 Blossom Hill Rd., Suite 212-C, San Jose, CA 95123, ☎ 408/229–7880 or 800/747–1476). **FLY-ASAP** (3824 E. Indian School Road, Phoenix, AZ 85018, ☎ 800/359–2727) isn't a discounter, but gets good deals from among published fares, and gets discount tickets from consolidators.

PUBLICATIONS

For general information about charter carriers, ask for the Office of Consumer Affairs' brochure **"Plane Talk: Public Charter Flights."** The Department of Transportation also publishes a 58-page booklet, **"Fly Rights"** ($1.75; Consumer Information Center, Dept. 133B, Pueblo, CO 81009).

For other tips and hints, consult the Consumers Union's monthly **"Consumer Reports Travel Letter"** ($39 a year; Box 53629, Boulder, CO 80322, ☎ 800/234–1970) and the newsletter **"Travel Smart"** ($37 a year; 40 Beechdale Rd., Dobbs Ferry, NY 10522, ☎ 800/327–3633); *The Official Frequent Flyer Guidebook,* by Randy Petersen ($14.99 plus $3 shipping; 4715-C Town Center Dr., Colorado Springs, CO 80916, ☎ 719/597–8899 or 800/487–8893); *Airfare Secrets Exposed,* by Sharon Tyler and Matthew Wonder (Universal Information Publishing; $16.95 plus $3.75 shipping from Sandcastle Publishing, Box 3070-A, South Pasadena, CA 91031, ☎ 213/255–3616 or 800/655–0053); and *202 Tips Even the Best Business Travelers May Not Know,* by Christopher McGinnis ($10 plus $3 shipping; Irwin Professional Publishing, 1333 Burr Ridge Parkway, Burr Ridge, IL 60521, ☎ 800/634–3966).

B

For local contacts in the home town of a tour operator you may be considering, consult the **Council of Better Business Bureaus** (4200 Wilson Blvd., Arlington, VA 22203, ☎ 703/276-0100).

C

Major car-rental companies represented in Moscow include **Avis** (☎ 800/331-1084, 800/879-2847 in Canada) and **Hertz** (☎ 800/654-3001, 800/263-0600 in Canada, 0181/679-1799 in the U.K.). Rates in Moscow begin at $43 a day and $238 a week plus 36¢ per kilometer. This price does not include 21.5% tax.

INSURANCE

Ingosstrakh (12 Pyatniskaya ulitsa, Moscow, ☎ 095/231-1677, FAX 095/230-2518, telex 411144).

FLYING

Look into **"Flying with Baby"** ($5.95 plus $1 shipping; Third Street Press, Box 261250, Littleton, CO 80126, ☎ 303/595-5959), cowritten by a flight attendant. **"Kids and Teens in Flight,"** free from the U.S. Department of Transportation's Office of Consumer Affairs, offers tips for children flying alone. Every two years the February issue of **Family Travel Times** (*see* Know-How, *below*) details children's services on three dozen airlines.

GAMES

The gamemeister, Milton Bradley, has games to help keep little (and not so little) children from getting fidgety while riding in planes, trains, and automobiles. Try packing the *Travel Battleship* sea battle game ($7), *Travel Connect Four*, a vertical strategy game ($8), the *Travel Yahtzee* dice game ($6), the *Travel Trouble* dice and board game ($7), and the *Travel Guess Who* mystery game ($8).

KNOW-HOW

Family Travel Times, published four times a year by Travel with Your Children (TWYCH, 45 W. 18th St., New York, NY 10011, ☎ 212/206-0688; annual subscription $40), covers destinations, types of vacations, and modes of travel.

The **Family Travel Guides** catalogue ($1 postage; Box 6061, Albany, CA 94706; ☎ 510/527-5849) lists about 200 books and articles on family travel. Also check **Take Your Baby and Go! A Guide for Traveling with Babies, Toddlers and Young Children,** by Sheri Andrews, Judy Bordeaux, and Vivian Vasquez ($5.95 plus $1.50 shipping; Bear Creek Publications, 2507 Minor Ave., Seattle, WA 98102, ☎ 206/322-7604 or 800/326-6566). **Innocents Abroad: Traveling with Kids in Europe,** by Valerie Wolf Deutsch and Laura Sutherland ($15.95 hardcover, $5.95 paperback plus $2 shipping; Penguin USA, 120 Woodbine St., Bergenfield, NJ 07621, ☎ 201/387-0600 or 800/253-6476), covers child- and teen-friendly activities, food, and transportation.

TOUR OPERATORS

If you're outdoorsy, look into tours from the **American Museum of Natural History** (79th St. and Central Park W., New York, NY 10024, ☎ 212/769-5700 or 800/462-8687).

U.S. CITIZENS

The **U.S. Customs Service** (Box 7407, Washington, DC 20044, ☎ 202/927-6724) can answer questions on duty-free limits and publishes a helpful brochure, "Know Before You Go." For information on registering foreign-made articles, call 202/927-0540.

CANADIANS

Contact **Revenue Canada** (2265 St. Laurent Blvd. S, Ottawa, Ontario K1G 4K3, ☎ 613/993-0534) for a copy of the free brochure **"I Declare/Je Déclare"** and for details on duties that exceed the standard duty-free limit.

U.K. CITIZENS

HM Customs and Excise (Dorset House, Stamford St., London SE1 9NG, ☎ 0171/202-4227) can answer questions about U.K. customs regulations and publishes **"A Guide for Travellers,"** detailing standard procedures and import rules.

D
FOR TRAVELERS WITH DISABILITIES

COMPLAINTS

To register complaints under the provisions of the Americans with Disabilities Act, contact the U.S. Department of Justice's **Disability Rights Section** (Box 66738, Washington, DC 20035, ☎ 202/514–0301, TTY 202/514–0383, FAX 202/307–1198).

ORGANIZATIONS

FOR TRAVELERS WITH HEARING IMPAIRMENTS➤ Contact the **American Academy of Otolaryngology** (1 Prince St., Alexandria, VA 22314, ☎ 703/836–4444, FAX 703/683–5100, TTY 703/519–1585).

FOR TRAVELERS WITH MOBILITY PROBLEMS➤ Contact the **Information Center for Individuals with Disabilities** (Fort Point Pl., 27–43 Wormwood St., Boston, MA 02210, ☎ 617/727–5540, 800/462–5015 in MA, TTY 617/345–9743); **Mobility International USA** (Box 10767, Eugene, OR 97440, ☎ and TTY 503/343–1284, FAX 503/343–6812), the U.S. branch of an international organization based in Belgium (*see below*) that has affiliates in 30 countries; **MossRehab Hospital Travel Information Service** (1200 W. Tabor Rd., Philadelphia, PA 19141, ☎

215/456–9603, TTY 215/456–9602); the **Society for the Advancement of Travel for the Handicapped** (347 5th Ave., Suite 610, New York, NY 10016, ☎ 212/447–7284, FAX 212/725–8253); the **Travel Industry and Disabled Exchange** (TIDE, 5435 Donna Ave., Tarzana, CA 91356, ☎ 818/344–3640, FAX 818/344–0078); and **Travelin' Talk** (Box 3534, Clarksville, TN 37043, ☎ 615/552–6670, FAX 615/552–1182).

FOR TRAVELERS WITH VISION IMPAIRMENTS➤ Contact the **American Council of the Blind** (1155 15th St. NW, Suite 720, Washington, DC 20005, ☎ 202/467–5081, FAX 202/467–5085) or the **American Foundation for the Blind** (15 W. 16th St., New York, NY 10011, ☎ 212/620–2000, TTY 212/620–2158).

IN THE U.K.

Contact the **Royal Association for Disability and Rehabilitation** (RADAR, 12 City Forum, 250 City Rd., London EC1V 8AF, ☎ 0171/250–3222) or **Mobility International** (Rue de Manchester 25, B–1070 Brussels, Belgium, ☎ 00–322–410–6297), an international clearinghouse of travel information for people with disabilities.

PUBLICATIONS

Several free publications are available from the U.S. Information Center (Box 100, Pueblo, CO 81009, ☎ 719/948–3334): **"New Horizons for the Air Traveler with**

a Disability" (address to Dept. 355A), describing legally mandated changes; the pocket-size **"Fly Smart"** (Dept. 575B), good on flight safety; and the Airport Operators Council's worldwide **"Access Travel: Airports"** (Dept. 575A).

The 500-page **Travelin' Talk Directory** ($35; Box 3534, Clarksville, TN 37043, ☎ 615/552–6670) lists people and organizations who help travelers with disabilities. For specialist travel agents worldwide, consult the **Directory of Travel Agencies for the Disabled** ($19.95 plus $2 shipping; Twin Peaks Press, Box 129, Vancouver, WA 98666, ☎ 206/694–2462 or 800/637–2256).

TRAVEL AGENCIES AND TOUR OPERATORS

The Americans with Disabilities Act requires that travel firms serve the needs of all travelers. However, some agencies and operators specialize in making group and individual arrangements for travelers with disabilities, among them **Access Adventures** (206 Chestnut Ridge Rd., Rochester, NY 14624, ☎ 716/889–9096), run by a former physical-rehab counselor. In addition, many general-interest operators and agencies (*see* Tour Operators, *below*) can also arrange vacations for travelers with disabilities.

FOR TRAVELERS WITH MOBILITY IMPAIRMENTS➤ A number of operators specialize in working with travelers with mobility impairments: **Flying Wheels Travel** (143 W. Bridge St., Box 382, Owatonna, MN 55060, ☎ 507/451–5005 or 800/535–6790), a travel agency that specializes in European cruises and tours; **Hinsdale Travel Service** (201 E. Ogden Ave., Suite 100, Hinsdale, IL 60521, ☎ 708/325–1335 or 800/303–5521), a travel agency that will give you access to the services of wheelchair traveler Janice Perkins; and **Wheelchair Journeys** (16979 Redmond Way, Redmond, WA 98052, ☎ 206/885–2210), which can handle arrangements worldwide.

FOR TRAVELERS WITH DEVELOPMENTAL DISABILITIES➤ Contact the nonprofit **New Directions** (5276 Hollister Ave., Suite 207, Santa Barbara, CA 93111, ☎ 805/967–2841), as well as the general-interest operators above.

DISCOUNT CLUBS

Options include **Entertainment Travel Editions** (fee $28–$53, depending on destination; Box 1068, Trumbull, CT 06611, ☎ 800/445–4137), **Great American Traveler** ($49.95 annually; Box 27965, Salt Lake City, UT 84127, ☎ 800/548–2812), **Moment's Notice Discount Travel Club** ($25 annually, single or family; 163 Amsterdam Ave., Suite 137, New York, NY 10023, ☎ 212/486–0500), **Privilege Card** ($74.95 annually; 3391 Peachtree Rd. NE, Suite 110,

Atlanta, GA 30326, ☎ 404/262–0222 or 800/236–9732), **Travelers Advantage** ($49 annually, single or family; CUC Travel Service, 49 Music Sq. W, Nashville, TN 37203, ☎ 800/548–1116 or 800/648–4037), and **Worldwide Discount Travel Club** ($50 annually for family, $40 single; 1674 Meridian Ave., Miami Beach, FL 33139, ☎ 305/534–2082).

E

ELECTRICITY

Send a self-addressed, stamped envelope to the **Franzus Company** (Customer Service, Dept. B50, Murtha Industrial Park, Box 142, Beacon Falls, CT 06403, ☎ 203/723–6664) for a copy of the free brochure "Foreign Electricity Is No Deep Dark Secret."

G

GAY AND LESBIAN TRAVEL

ORGANIZATIONS

The **International Gay Travel Association** (Box 4974, Key West, FL 33041, ☎ 800/448–8550), a consortium of 800 businesses, can supply names of travel agents and tour operators.

PUBLICATIONS

The premier international travel magazine for gays and lesbians is *Our World* ($35 for 10 issues; 1104 N. Nova Rd., Suite 251, Daytona Beach, FL 32117, ☎ 904/441–5367). The 16-page monthly *"Out & About"* ($49 for 10 issues; ☎ 212/645–

6922 or 800/929–2268) covers gay-friendly resorts, hotels, cruise lines, and airlines.

TOUR OPERATORS

Toto Tours (1326 W. Albion, Suite 3W, Chicago, IL 60626, ☎ 312/274–8686 or 800/565–1241) offers group tours worldwide.

TRAVEL AGENCIES

The largest agencies serving gay travelers are **Advance Travel** (10700 Northwest Freeway, Suite 160, Houston, TX 77092, ☎ 713/682–2002 or 800/695–0880), **Islanders/Kennedy Travel** (183 W. 10th St., New York, NY 10014, ☎ 212/242–3222 or 800/988–1181), **Now Voyager** (4406 18th St., San Francisco, CA 94114, ☎ 415/626–1169 or 800/255–6951), and **Yellowbrick Road** (1500 W. Balmoral Ave., Chicago, IL 60640, ☎ 312/561–1800 or 800/642–2488). **Skylink Women's Travel** (746 Ashland Ave., Santa Monica, CA 90405, ☎ 310/452–0506 or 800/225-5759) works with lesbians.

H

HEALTH ISSUES

FINDING A DOCTOR

For members, the **International Association for Medical Assistance to Travellers** (IAMAT, 417 Center St., Lewiston, NY 14092, ☎ 716/754–4883; 40 Regal Rd., Guelph, Ontario N1K 1B5, ☎ 519/836–0102; 1287 St. Clair Ave., Toronto, Ontario M6E 1B8, ☎ 416/652–0137;

57 Voirets, 1212 Grand-Lancy, Geneva, Switzerland; membership free) publishes a worldwide directory of English-speaking physicians meeting IAMAT standards.

MEDICAL-ASSISTANCE COMPANIES

Contact **International SOS Assistance** (Box 11568, Philadelphia, PA 19116, ☎ 215/244–1500 or 800/523–8930; Box 466, Pl. Bonaventure, Montréal, Québec. H5A 1C1, ☎ 514/874–7674 or 800/363–0263), **Medex Assistance Corporation** (Box 10623, Baltimore, MD 21285, ☎ 410/296–2530 or 800/573–2029), **Near Travel Services** (Box 1339, Calumet City, IL 60409, ☎ 708/868–6700 or 800/654–6700), and **Travel Assistance International** (1133 15th St. NW, Suite 400, Washington, DC 20005, ☎ 202/331–1609 or 800/821–2828). Because these companies also sell death-and-dismemberment, trip-cancellation, and other insurance coverage, there is some overlap with the travel-insurance policies sold by the companies listed under Insurance, *below.*

PUBLICATIONS

The Safe Travel Book, by Peter Savage ($12.95 plus $2 postage; Lexington Books, 866 3rd Ave., 22nd Floor, New York, NY 10022, ☎ 212/702–4771 or 800/223–23485, FAX 212/605–4872), and *Traveler's Medical Resource,* by William W. Forgey

($19.95; ICS Books, Box 10767, Merrillville, IN 45410, ☎ 219/769–0585 or 800/541–7323), are authoritative.

WARNINGS

The **National Centers for Disease Control** (Center for Preventive Services, Division of Quarantine, Traveler's Health Section, 1600 Clifton Rd., MSE03, Atlanta, GA 30333, automated hot line 404/332–4559) provides information on health risks abroad and vaccination requirements and recommendations.

I

INSURANCE

Travel insurance covering baggage, health, and trip cancellation or interruptions available from **Access America** (Box 90315, Richmond, VA 23286, ☎ 804/285–3300 or 800/284–8300), **Carefree Travel Insurance** (Box 9366, 100 Garden City Plaza, Garden City, NY 11530, ☎ 516/294–0220 or 800/323–3149), **Near Travel Services** (Box 1339, Calumet City, IL 60409, ☎ 708/868–6700 or 800/654–6700), **Tele-Trip** (Mutual of Omaha Plaza, Box 31716, Omaha, NE 68131, ☎ 800/228–9792), **Travel Insured International** (Box 280568, East Hartford, CT 06128–0568, ☎ 203/528–7663 or 800/243–3174), **Travel Guard International** (1145 Clark St., Stevens Point, WI 54481, ☎ 715/345–0505 or 800/826–1300), and **Wallach &**

Company (107 W. Federal St., Box 480, Middleburg, VA 22117, ☎ 703/687–3166 or 800/237–6615).

IN THE U.K.

The **Association of British Insurers** (51 Gresham St., London EC2V 7HQ, ☎ 0171/600–3333; 30 Gordon St., Glasgow G1 3PU, ☎ 0141/226–3905; Scottish Provident Bldg., Donegall Sq. W, Belfast BT1 6JE, ☎ 01232/249176; and other locations) gives advice by phone and publishes the free **"Holiday Insurance,"** which sets out typical policy provisions and costs.

L

LODGING

APARTMENT AND VILLA RENTAL

Among the companies to contact is **Property Rentals International** (1008 Mansfield Crossing Rd., Richmond, VA 23236, ☎ 804/378–6054 or 800/220–3332).

HOME EXCHANGE

Principal clearinghouses include **Loan-a-Home** ($35–$45 annually; 2 Park La., Apt. 6E, Mount Vernon, NY 10552-3443, ☎ 914/664–7640), which specializes in long-term exchanges.

M

MONEY MATTERS

ATMS

For specific foreign **Cirrus** locations, call 800/424–7787; for foreign Plus locations, consult the **Plus** directory at your local bank.

CURRENCY EXCHANGE

If your bank doesn't exchange currency, contact **Thomas Cook Currency Services** (41 E. 42nd St., New York, NY 10017, or 511 Madison Ave., New York, NY 10022, ☎ 212/757–6915 or 800/223–7373 for locations) or **Ruesch International** (☎ 800/424–2923 for locations).

WIRING FUNDS

Funds can be wired via **American Express MoneyGram**^{SM} (☎ 800/926–9400 from the U.S. and Canada for locations and information) or **Western Union** (☎ 800/325–6000 for agent locations or to send using MasterCard or Visa, 800/321–2923 in Canada).

U.S. CITIZENS

For fees, documentation requirements, and other information, call the **Office of Passport Services** information line (☎ 202/647–0518).

CANADIANS

For fees, documentation requirements, and other information, call the Ministry of Foreign Affairs and International Trade's **Passport Office** (☎ 819/994–3500 or 800/567–6868).

U.K. CITIZENS

For fees, documentation requirements, and to get an emergency passport, call the **London Passport Office** (☎ 0171/271–3000).

The country code for Russia is 7; for the Ukraine, 380. For local access numbers abroad, contact **AT&T** USA-Direct (☎ 800/874–4000), **MCI** Call USA (☎ 800/444–4444), or **Sprint** Express (☎ 800/793–1153).

The **Kodak Information Center** (☎ 800/242–2424) answers consumer questions about film and photography.

EDUCATIONAL TRAVEL

The nonprofit **Elderhostel** (75 Federal St., 3rd Floor, Boston, MA 02110, ☎ 617/426–7788), for people 60 and older, has offered inexpensive study programs since 1975. The nearly 2,000 courses cover everything from marine science to Greek myths and cowboy poetry. Fees for two- to three-week international trips—including room, board, and transportation from the United States—range from $1,800 to $4,500.

ORGANIZATIONS

Contact the **American Association of Retired Persons** (AARP, 601 E St. NW, Washington, DC 20049, ☎ 202/434–2277; $8 per person or couple annually). Its Purchase Privilege Program gets members discounts on lodging, car rentals, and sightseeing.

For other discounts on lodgings, car rentals, and other travel products, along with magazines and newsletters, contact the **National Council of Senior Citizens** (membership $12 annually; 1331 F St. NW, Washington, DC 20004, ☎ 202/347–8800) and **Mature Outlook** (subscription $9.95 annually; 6001 N. Clark St., Chicago, IL 60660, ☎ 312/465–6466 or 800/336–6330).

PUBLICATIONS

The 50+ Traveler's Guidebook: Where to Go, Where to Stay, What to Do, by Anita Williams and Merrimac Dillon ($12.95; St. Martin's Press, 175 5th Ave., New York, NY 10010, ☎ 212/674–5151 or 800/288–2131), offers many useful tips. **"The Mature Traveler"** ($29.95; Box 50400, Reno, NV 89513, ☎ 702/786–7419), a monthly newsletter, covers travel deals.

HOSTELING

Contact **Hostelling International–American Youth Hostels** (733 15th St. NW, Suite 840, Washington, DC 20005, ☎ 202/783–6161) in the United States, **Hostelling International–Canada** (205 Catherine St., Suite 400, Ottawa, Ontario K2P 1C3, ☎ 613/237–7884) in Canada, and the **Youth Hostel Association of England and Wales** (Trevelyan House, 8 St. Stephen's Hill, St. Albans, Hertfordshire AL1 2DY,

THE GOLD GUIDE / IMPORTANT CONTACTS

☎ 01727/855215 or 01727/845047) in the United Kingdom. Membership ($25 in the U.S., C$26.75 in Canada, and £9 in the U.K.) gets you access to 5,000 hostels worldwide that charge $7–$20 nightly per person.

I.D. CARDS

To be eligible for discounts on transportation and admissions, get the **International Student Identity Card** (ISIC) if you're a bona fide student or the **International Youth Card** (IYC) if you're under 26. In the United States, the ISIC and IYC cards cost $16 each and include basic travel-accident and illness coverage, plus a toll-free travel hot line. Apply through the Council on International Educational Exchange (*see* Organizations, *below*). Cards are available for $15 each in Canada from **Travel Cuts** (187 College St., Toronto, Ontario M5T 1P7, ☎ 416/979–2406 or 800/667–2887) and in the United Kingdom for £5 each at student unions and student travel companies.

ORGANIZATIONS

A major contact is the **Council on International Educational Exchange** (CIEE, 205 E. 42nd St., 16th Floor, New York, NY 10017, ☎ 212/661–1450) with locations in Boston (729 Boylston St., 02116, ☎ 617/266–1926), Miami (9100 S. Dadeland Blvd., 33156, ☎ 305/670–9261), Los Angeles (1093 Broxton Ave., 90024, ☎ 310/208–3551), 43 other

college towns nationwide, and the United Kingdom (28A Poland St., London W1V 3DB, ☎ 0171/437–7767). Twice a year, it publishes *Student Travels* magazine. The CIEE's Council Travel Service is the exclusive U.S. agent for several student-discount cards.

For air travel only, contact **TMI Student Travel** (100 W. 33rd St., Suite 813, New York, NY 10001, ☎ 800/245–3672).

In Canada, also contact **Travel Cuts** (*see* I.D. Cards, *above*).

TOUR OPERATORS

Among the companies selling tours and packages to Moscow, St. Petersburg, and Kiev, the following have a proven reputation, are nationally known, and offer plenty of options.

GROUP TOURS

Super-deluxe escorted tours to Moscow, St. Petersburg, and Kiev are available from **Abercrombie & Kent** (1520 Kensington Rd., Oak Brook, IL 60521, ☎ 708/954–2944 or 800/323–7308) and **Travcoa** (Box 2630, Newport Beach, CA, 92658, ☎ 714/476–2800 or 800/992–2003). For deluxe programs, try **Maupintour** (Box 807, Lawrence KS 66044, ☎ 913/843–1211 or 800/255–4266). For first-class programs, contact **Caravan Tours** (401 N. Michigan Ave., Chicago, IL 60611, ☎ 312/321–9800 or 800/CARAVAN), **Delta Dream Vacations** (☎

800/872–7786), **General Tours** (53 Summer St., Keene, NH 03431, ☎ 603/357–5033 or 800/221–2216), **Isram World of Travel** (630 Third Ave., New York, NY 10017, ☎ 212/661–1193 or 800/223–7460), **Rahim Tours** (12 S. Dixie Hwy., Lake Worth, FL 33460, ☎ 407/585–5305 or 800/556–5305), **Russian Travel Bureau** (225 E. 44th St., New York, NY 10017, ☎ 212/986–1500 or 800/847–1800), **Trafalgar Tours** (21 E. 26th St., New York, NY 10010, ☎ 212/689–8977 or 800/854–0103), and **Uniworld** (16000 Ventura Blvd., Suite 200, Encino, CA 91436, ☎ 818/382–7820 or 800/733–7820).

PACKAGES

Independent vacation packages are available from major tour operators and airlines. Contact **Abercrombie & Kent** (*see* Group Tours, *above*), **General Tours** (*see* Group Tours, *above*), **Five Star Touring** (60 E. 42nd St., New York, NY 10165, ☎ 212/818–9140 or 800/792–7827), **ITS Tours & Travel** (1055 Texas Ave., Suite 104, College Station, TX 77840, ☎ 409/764–9400 or 800/533–8688), **MIR Corp.** (85 South Washington, Suite 210, Seattle, WA 98104, ☎ 206/624–7289 or 800/424–7289), **Rahim Tours** (*see* Group Tours, *above*), and **Russian Travel Bureau** (*see* Group Tours, *above*).

New Solutions (912 S. Juanita Ave., Redondo Beach, CA 90277, ☎

310/543–9829 or 800/768–9535) specializes in custom-designed tours organized around a religious, historical, academic or genealogical theme.

THEME TRIPS

ART➤ For tours of Moscow and St. Petersburg's art and architecture, look into **Esplanade Tours** (581 Boylston St., Boston, MA 02116, ☎ 617/266–7465 or 800/628–4893), **Five Star Touring** (*see* Group Tours, *above*), and **Russian Travel Bureau** (*see* Group Tours, *above*).

CRUISES➤ For a cruise on the Volga River between Moscow and St. Petersburg, contact the operators listed above. Also contact **EuroCruises** (303 W. 13th St., New York, NY 10014, ☎ 212/691–2099 or 800/688–3876), which represents more than 20 European-based cruise lines and 60 ships, ranging from 32-passenger yachts to 2,500-passenger ocean liners.

HOMESTAYS➤ To stay with a Russian or Ukrainian family, contact **Bolshoi Adventures** (311 Turner St., Suite 303, Utica, NY 13501, ☎ 315/793–0074), **Home & Host International** (2445 Park Ave., Minneapolis, MN 55404, ☎ 612/871–0596 or 800/SO-VIET-U), or ITS (*see* Packages, *above*).

MUSIC➤ For packages that include tickets to the ballet, opera and classical concerts, call **Dailey-Thorp Travel** (330 W. 58th St., New York, NY 10019, ☎ 212/307–1555; book through travel agents).

RAIL➤ Abercrombie & Kent (*see* Group Tours, *above*) operates a five-passenger private railcar, the Anna Karenina, between Moscow and St. Petersburg. Sumptuous meals, champagne and personal attendants are part of the ride.

ORGANIZATIONS

The **National Tour Association** (546 E. Main St., Lexington, KY 40508, ☎ 606/226–4444 or 800/755–8687) and **United States Tour Operators Association** (USTOA, 211 E. 51st St., Suite 12B, New York, NY 10022, ☎ 212/750–7371) can provide lists of member operators and information on booking tours.

PUBLICATIONS

Consult the brochure **On Tour** and ask for a current list of member operators from the National Tour Association (*see* Organizations, *above*). Also get a copy of the **"Worldwide Tour & Vacation Package Finder"** from the USTOA (*see* Organizations, *above*) and the Better Business Bureau's **"Tips on Travel Packages"** (publication No. 24-195, $2; 4200 Wilson Blvd., Arlington, VA 22203).

TRAVEL AGENCIES

For names of reputable agencies in your area, contact the **American Society of Travel Agents** (1101 King St., Suite 200, Alexandria, VA 22314, ☎ 703/739–2782).

U

U.S. GOVERNMENT TRAVEL BRIEFINGS

The U.S. Department of State's Overseas Citizens Emergency Center (Room 4811, Washington, DC 20520; enclose SASE) issues **Consular Information Sheets,** which cover crime, security, political climate, and health risks as well as embassy locations, entry requirements, currency regulations, and other routine matters. (Travel Warnings, which counsel travelers to avoid a country entirely, are issued in extreme cases.) For the latest information, stop in at any U.S. passport office, consulate, or embassy; call the interactive hot line (☎ 202/647–5225 or fax 202/647-3000); or, with your PC's modem, tap into the Bureau of Consular Affairs' computer bulletin board (☎ 202/647–9225).

V

VISITOR INFORMATION

Intourist-USA, Inc. (620 5th Ave., New York, NY 10111, ☎ 212/757–3884) can provide information about traveling in Russia and assist with some travel arrangements. The **Russian Consulate General** (9 E. 91st St., New York, NY, ☎ 212/348–0926; in Canada, 3655 Ave. du Musée, Montréal, Québec H3G 2E1, ☎ 514/843–5901; in the U.K., 5 Kensington Palace Gardens, London W8, ☎ 0171/

229–8027) can also provide some assistance with travel plans. For information about Kiev, contact the **Ukrainian Consulate** (3350 M St., NW, Washington, D.C. 20007, ☎ 202/333–7507; in Canada, 331

Metcalfe St., Ottawa, Ontario K2P 1S3, ☎ 613/230–8015 or 613/235–8214).

WEATHER

For current conditions and forecasts, plus the

local time and helpful travel tips, call the **Weather Channel Connection** (☎ 900/932–8437; 95¢ per minute) from a touch-tone phone.

SMART TRAVEL TIPS A TO Z

Basic Information on Traveling in Moscow, St. Petersburg, and Kiev and Savvy Tips to Make Your Trip a Breeze

The more you travel, the more you know about how to make trips run like clockwork. To help make your travels hassle-free, Fodor's editors have rounded up dozens of tips from our contributors and travel experts all over the world, as well as basic information on visiting Moscow, St. Petersburg, and Kiev. For names of organizations to contact and publications that can give you more information, see Important Contacts A to Z, *above*.

A
AIR TRAVEL

If time is an issue, **always look for nonstop flights,** which require no change of plane. If possible, **avoid connecting flights,** which stop at least once and can involve a change of plane, although the flight number remains the same; if the first leg is late, the second waits.

CUTTING COSTS

The Sunday travel section of most newspapers is a good source of deals.

MAJOR AIRLINES➤ The least-expensive airfares from the major airlines are priced for round-trip travel and are subject to restrictions. You must usually **book in advance and buy the ticket within 24 hours** to get cheaper fares, and you may have to **stay over a Saturday night.** The lowest fare is subject to availability, and only a small percentage of the plane's total seats are sold at that price. It's good to **call a number of airlines, and when you are quoted a good price, book it on the spot**—the same fare on the same flight may not be available the next day. Airlines generally allow you to change your return date for a $25 to $50 fee, but most low-fare tickets are nonrefundable. However, if you don't use it, you can apply the cost toward the purchase price of a new ticket, again for a small charge.

CONSOLIDATORS➤ Consolidators, who buy tickets at reduced rates from scheduled airlines, sell them at prices below the lowest available from the airlines directly—usually without advance restrictions. Sometimes you can even get your money back if you need to return the ticket. Carefully read the fine print detailing penalties for changes and cancellations. If you doubt the reliability of a consolidator, **confirm your reservation with the airline.**

ALOFT

AIRLINE FOOD➤ If you hate airline food, **ask for special meals when booking.** These can be vegetarian, low-cholesterol, or kosher, for example; commonly prepared to order in smaller quantities than standard catered fare, they can be tastier.

JET LAG

To avoid this syndrome, which occurs when travel disrupts your body's natural cycles, try to maintain a normal routine. At night, **get some sleep.** By day, move about the cabin to **stretch your legs, eat light meals, and drink water—not alcohol.**

SMOKING➤ Smoking is banned on all flights within the United States of less than six hours' duration and on all Canadian flights; the ban also applies to domestic segments of international flights aboard U.S. and foreign carriers. On U.S. carriers flying to Russia, Ukraine, and other destinations abroad, a seat in a no-smoking section must be provided for every passenger who requests one, and the section must be enlarged to accommodate such passengers if necessary as long as they have complied with the airline's deadline for check-in and seat assignment. If smoking bothers you, request a seat far from the smoking section.

Foreign airlines are exempt from these rules but do provide no-smoking sections; some nations have banned smoking on all domestic flights, and others may ban smoking on some flights. Talks continue on the feasibility of broadening no-smoking policies.

WITHIN RUSSIA AND UKRAINE

The airline industry in the former Soviet Union is in a state of flux bordering on chaos. Aeroflot, once the Soviet Union's only airline, is still the leading carrier within Russia and the CIS, but much of its fleet has been nationalized by the various republics. Russia has inherited Aeroflot, while the new republican airlines sport such names as Air Ukraine and Air Uzbekistan. They all offer the same outdated aircraft and abominable service for which Aeroflot is famous.

Since the collapse of the Soviet Union, many routes have been abandoned, smaller airports have been closed permanently, and the scheduled flights that remain are often canceled due to fuel shortages. Because of unpredictable service, many tour operators are now chartering flights for their groups. Seasoned business travelers frequently choose to fly circuitous routes on international carriers (i.e., Moscow–Helsinki–Kiev), which

often proves faster and certainly more reliable than flying direct on Aeroflot.

If you are flying as an independent traveler within the CIS, **purchase your ticket in hard currency before you leave home.** Foreigners are not allowed to fly on tickets purchased in rubles; hard-currency tickets are available in-country, but purchasing one is often a long and frustrating endeavor. Be forewarned that delays and outright cancellations are common, and you should **reconfirm your booking in person as soon as you arrive in the country.**

On the day of your departure, **get to the airport early to avoid being bumped.** Bring some snacks and beverages with you—after a meal on Aeroflot, Western airline food will seem gourmet. On flights shorter than four hours the only refreshment served is vile-tasting mineral water. Planes are usually boarded with no regard for assigned seats; passengers either take a bus or walk en masse across the runway to their waiting plane and then push and shove their way aboard. If you are traveling with a group of foreign tourists, you may be granted the courtesy of boarding ahead of the Russian passengers. If you are traveling independently, it is likely that you will be completely ignored and left to your own defenses. If you encounter any

difficulties, assert your rights and make it clear to everyone that you paid for your ticket in hard currency.

The rules regulating carry-on luggage are strict but often disregarded. Since checked luggage is frequently lost and/or pilfered, **pack as much as you can in your carry-on,** including all of your valuables. Many airports have a special section set aside for foreign travelers, a holdover from the days when foreigners received preferential treatment by Soviet authorities. These sections are usually more comfortable and often have a hard-currency shop or café where you can buy snacks and refreshments.

B
BUSINESS HOURS

State banks are usually open 9:30–1, and the many new private banks are normally open 10–6. Private exchange offices and those in hotels are usually open 9–6 daily, with an hour break for lunch between 1 and 3 PM. Museums keep varying hours; many are closed on Mondays and Tuesdays. Last entry is usually an hour before closing time, and museums often close an hour earlier the day before their closed day. Stores likewise keep varying hours, with grocery stores normally opening at 8 or 9 AM and department stores opening at 11 AM. Closing times also vary; stores are rarely open past 8 or 9 PM. Many shops are closed on Sunday, and almost every store closes for an hour at lunchtime between 1 and 3 PM. Restaurants usually open around noon and often close by midnight, although many are staying open later these days. Many restaurants, especially those that are state-run, close for a "dinner" break somewhere between 4 and 6 PM.

C

CAMERAS, CAMCORDERS, AND COMPUTERS

LAPTOPS

Before you depart, **check your portable computer's battery,** because you may be asked at security to turn on the computer to prove that it is what it appears to be. At the airport, you may prefer to **request a manual inspection,** although security X-rays do not harm hard-disk or floppy-disk storage. Also, **register your foreign-made laptop with U.S. Customs.** If your laptop is U.S.-made, call the consulate of the country you'll be visiting to find out whether or not it should be registered with local customs upon arrival. You may want to **find out about repair facilities at your destination** in case you need them.

PHOTOGRAPHY

If your camera is new or if you haven't used it for a while, **shoot and develop a few rolls of film** before you leave.

Always **store film in a cool, dry place**—never in the car's glove compartment or on the shelf under the rear window.

Every pass of film through an X-ray machine increases the chance of clouding. To protect it, carry it in a clear plastic bag and **ask for hand inspection at security.** Such requests are virtually always honored at U.S. airports, and usually are accommodated abroad. Don't depend on a lead-lined bag to protect film in checked luggage—the airline may increase the radiation to see what's inside.

VIDEO

Before your trip, **test your camcorder, invest in a skylight filter to protect the lens, and charge the batteries.** (Airport security personnel may ask you to turn on the camcorder to prove that it's what it appears to be.) The batteries of most newer camcorders can be recharged with a universal or worldwide AC adapter charger (or multivoltage converter), usable whether the voltage is 110 or 220. All that's needed is the appropriate plug.

Videotape is not damaged by X-rays, but it may be harmed by the magnetic field of a walk-through metal detector, so **ask that videotapes be hand-checked.** Videotape sold in Russia and Ukraine is based on a standard different from that of videotape sold in the United States. You will not be able to view your

tapes through the local TV set or view movies bought there in your home VCR. Blank tapes bought in Russia and Ukraine can be used for camcorder taping, but they are pricey. Some U.S. audiovisual shops convert foreign tapes to U.S. standards; contact an electronics dealer to find the nearest.

CHILDREN AND TRAVEL

BABY-SITTING

For recommended local sitters, **check with your hotel desk.**

DRIVING

If you are renting a car, **arrange for a car seat when you reserve.** Sometimes they're free.

FLYING

Always **ask about discounted children's fares.** On international flights, the fare for infants under age 2 not occupying a seat is generally either free or 10% of the accompanying adult's fare; children ages 2 through 11 usually pay half to two-thirds of the adult fare. On domestic flights, children under 2 not occupying a seat travel free, and older children currently travel on the lowest applicable adult fare.

BAGGAGE➤ In general, the adult baggage allowance applies for children paying half or more of the adult fare. Before departure, **ask about carry-on allowances,** if you are traveling with an infant. In general, those paying 10% of the adult fare are allowed one carry-on bag, not to exceed

70 pounds or 45 inches (length + width + height) and a collapsible stroller; you may be allowed less if the flight is full.

SAFETY SEATS➤ According to the Federal Aviation Administration (FAA), it's a good idea to **use safety seats aloft.** Airline policy varies. U.S. carriers allow FAA-approved models, but airlines usually require that you buy a ticket, even if your child would otherwise ride free, because the seats must be strapped into regular passenger seats. Foreign carriers may not allow infant seats, may charge the child's rather than the infant's fare for their use, or may require you to hold your baby during takeoff and landing, thus defeating the seat's purpose.

FACILITIES➤ When making your reservation, **ask for children's meals or freestanding bassinets** if you need them; the latter are available only to those with seats at the bulkhead, where there's enough legroom. If you don't need a bassinet, **think twice before requesting bulkhead seats**—the only storage for in-flight necessities is in the inconveniently distant overhead bins.

LODGING

Most hotels allow children under a certain age to stay in their parents' room at no extra charge, while others charge them as extra adults; be sure to **ask about the cut-off age.**

CUSTOMS AND DUTIES

ON ARRIVAL

Upon arrival, you first pass through passport control, where a border guard will carefully examine your passport and visa, and retain one sheet of your Russian visa. The procedure in Ukraine is similar, except that the Ukrainian visa is actually stamped in your passport.

After retrieving your luggage, you fill out a customs form that you must keep until departure, when you will be asked to present it again. You may import free of duty and without special license any articles intended for personal use, including clothing, food, tobacco and cigarettes, alcoholic drinks, perfume, sports equipment, and camera. One video camera and one laptop computer per person are allowed. Importing weapons and ammunition, as well as opium, hashish, and pipes for smoking them, is prohibited. The punishment for carrying illegal substances is severe. You should **write down on the customs form the exact amount of currency you are carrying** (in cash as well as traveler's checks); you may enter the country with any amount of money, but you cannot leave the country with more money than you had when you entered. You should also **include on your customs form any jewelry (particularly silver, gold, and amber) as well as any electronic goods (cameras, personal tape recorders, computers, etc.) you have.** It is important to include any valuable items on the form to ensure that you will be allowed to export them, but beware that you are expected to take them with you, so you cannot leave them behind as gifts. If an item included on your customs form is stolen, you should obtain a police report to avoid being questioned upon departure.

BACK HOME

IN THE U.S.➤ You may bring home $400 worth of foreign goods duty-free if you've been out of the country for at least 48 hours and haven't already used the $400 exemption, or any part of it, in the past 30 days.

Travelers 21 or older may bring back 1 liter of alcohol duty-free, provided the beverage laws of the state through which they reenter the United States allow it. In addition, 100 non-Cuban cigars and 200 cigarettes are allowed, regardless of your age. Antiques and works of art more than 100 years old are duty-free.

Duty-free, travelers may mail packages valued at up to $200 to themselves and up to $100 to others, with a limit of one parcel per addressee per day (and no alcohol or tobacco products or perfume valued at more than $5); outside, identify the package as being for personal use or an unsolicited gift, specifying the contents and their retail value.

Mailed items do not count as part of your exemption.

In Canada➤ Once per calendar year, when you've been out of Canada for at least seven days, you may bring in C$300 worth of goods duty-free. If you've been away less than seven days but more than 48 hours, the duty-free exemption drops to C$100 but can be claimed any number of times (as can a C$20 duty-free exemption for absences of 24 hours or more). You cannot combine the yearly and 48-hour exemptions, use the C$300 exemption only partially (to save the balance for a later trip), or pool exemptions with family members. Goods claimed under the C$300 exemption may follow you by mail; those claimed under the lesser exemptions must accompany you.

Alcohol and tobacco products may be included in the yearly and 48-hour exemptions but not in the 24-hour exemption. If you meet the age requirements of the province through which you reenter Canada, you may bring in, duty-free, 1.14 liters (40 imperial ounces) of wine or liquor *or* 24 12-ounce cans or bottles of beer or ale. If you are 16 or older, you may bring in, duty-free, 200 cigarettes, 50 cigars or cigarillos, and 400 tobacco sticks or 400 grams of manufactured tobacco. Alcohol and tobacco must accompany you on your return.

An unlimited number of gifts valued up to C$60 each may be mailed to Canada duty-free. These do not count as part of your exemption. Label the package "Unsolicited Gift— Value under $60." Alcohol and tobacco are excluded.

In the U.K.➤ From countries outside the EU, including Russia and Ukraine, you may import duty-free 200 cigarettes, 100 cigarillos, 50 cigars or 250 grams of tobacco; 1 liter of spirits or 2 liters of fortified or sparkling wine; 2 liters of still table wine; 60 milliliters of perfume; 250 milliliters of toilet water; plus £136 worth of other goods, including gifts and souvenirs.

D
DINING

IN HOTELS

If you are traveling on an organized tour, you can **expect your hotel meals to be hearty and ample but far from gourmet.** If you depend on coffee to wake you up in the morning, **bring a small jar of instant coffee with you;** sometimes only tea is available in the morning and sometimes hotel restaurants use "coffee-flavored drink" instead of genuine coffee.

EATING OUT

When you tire of the traditional hotel cuisine, you can explore the many new private restaurants and joint-venture establishments that have recently opened in all three cities. You should

always **make reservations in advance.** Even if the restaurant is half-empty, you may be refused a table if you don't have a reservation. Be prepared to **set aside an entire evening for your restaurant meal**; Russians and Ukrainians consider dining out to be a form of entertainment, and table turnover is virtually an unknown concept.

Drinks are normally ordered by grams (100 or 200) or by the bottle. An average bottle holds about three-quarters of a liter. In foreign-run establishments you will often find an impressive wine list with imported wine and foreign liquors, but the state-run restaurants and smaller cooperatives usually have only vodka and wine available. Georgian wine is excellent, although supplies have become limited (distribution has been disrupted by the ongoing ethnic strife in that country).

Getting a quick snack on the go is not an easy feat in any of the cities and is particularly difficult in Kiev. State-run cafés and *stolovayas* (cafeterias) abound, but the quality of the food and service often leaves a lot to be desired. If you're sightseeing on your own, you'd be smart to **arrange your day around the place where you'll have lunch.** If you find yourself suddenly suffering from hunger pangs in the middle of the day, you can always stop by a *khleb* (bread) store.

Russia and Ukraine are famous for their delicious bread, which makes an inexpensive and filling snack.

FOR TRAVELERS WITH DISABILITIES

Provisions for disabled travelers in Russia and Ukraine are extremely limited. Traveling with a nondisabled companion is probably the best solution. Some of the new, foreign-built hotels in Moscow offer wheelchair-accessible rooms, but beyond that special facilities at public buildings in all three cities are rare. Public transportation is especially difficult for the disabled traveler to maneuver.

When discussing accessibility with an operator or reservationist, **ask hard questions.** Are there any stairs, inside *or* out? Are there grab bars next to the toilet *and* in the shower/tub? How wide is the doorway to the room? To the bathroom? For the most extensive facilities, meeting the latest legal specifications, **opt for newer accommodations,** which more often have been designed with access in mind. Older properties or ships must usually be retrofitted and may offer more limited facilities as a result. Be sure to **discuss your needs before booking.**

DISCOUNT CLUBS

Travel clubs offer members unsold space on airplanes, cruise ships, and package tours at as much as 50% below regular prices. Membership may include a regular bulletin or access to a toll-free hot line giving details of available trips departing from three or four days to several months in the future. Most also offer 50% discounts off hotel rack rates. Before booking with a club, **make sure the hotel or other supplier isn't offering a better deal.**

DRIVING

Due to poor and sometimes even dangerous conditions, you should **avoid driving in the former Soviet Union.** Even the main highways are potholed and in poor condition. Repair stations are few and far between, and there is a severe shortage of gasoline. In addition, you should not underestimate the risk of crime; highway robbery and car theft are on the rise, and foreign drivers are number-one targets. Russian drivers routinely remove their window blades, side mirrors, and anything else removable when parking their car for the evening, since theft of these items is common. Also, you should never **leave anything of value inside your car.**

GASOLINE AND REPAIRS

The gasoline shortage in Russia, and especially in Ukraine, is severe. You should **fill up your tank at every opportunity.** In rubles, gasoline is very inexpensive, but you will have to wait in long lines; often drivers line up hours before an expected delivery of gasoline. In all three cities you can find foreign-currency gasoline stations, where lines are much shorter, but even these are not immune to the local shortages. It's also difficult to find unleaded gasoline. Finally, since repair stations are few and poorly stocked, tourists are advised to **bring a complete emergency repair kit,** including a set of tools, a towing cable, a pressure gauge, a pump, a spare wheel, a repair outfit for tubeless tires, a good jack and one or two tire levers, gasoline can, a spare fan belt, spare window-screen blades, and spark plugs. You should also have a set of lamp bulbs and fuses, a set of contact-breaker points for the ignition distributor, a spare condenser, a box of tire valve interiors, and a roll of insulating tape.

POLICE

Traffic control in Russia and Ukraine is exercised by traffic inspectors (GAI) who are stationed at permanent posts; they also patrol in cars and on motorcycles. They may stop you for no apparent reason other than simply to check your documentation. Information on rules and road conditions can be obtained from them; they will also supply directions to motels, campsites, restaurants, and filling and service stations.

REQUIREMENTS

Tourists driving in Russia or Ukraine will need an international driver's license and an international certificate of registration of the car in the country of departure. You will also need a certificate of obligation promising to take the car out of the country, to be registered with customs at the point of entry.

RULES OF THE ROAD

Driving regulations are strict, but they are often broken by local drivers; a good rule of thumb is to **drive defensively.** Traffic keeps to the right. The speed limit on highways is 90 kph (56 mph); in towns and populated areas it is 60 kph (37 mph), although on the wide streets of Moscow few people observe this rule. You can proceed at traffic lights only when the light is green—this includes left and right turns. You must wait for a signal—an arrow—permitting the turn, and give way to pedestrians crossing. Wearing front seatbelts is compulsory; driving while intoxicated carries very heavy fines, including imprisonment. Do not consume any alcohol at all if you plan to drive. You should also **keep your car clean**—drivers can be fined for having a dirty car.

H
HEALTH
CONCERNS

The Russian and Ukrainian medical systems are far below world standards. Anyone visiting these countries runs the risk of encountering the horrors of their medical facilities, and individuals in frail health and those who suffer from a

chronic medical condition should take this risk into careful consideration. You may want to **purchase traveler's health insurance,** which would cover medical evacuation. Sometimes even minor conditions cannot be treated adequately in-country due to the severe and chronic shortage of basic medicines and medical equipment.

These warnings aside, as long as you don't get sick, a visit to Russia or Ukraine poses no special health risk. The U.S. government affirms that the fallout from the 1986 Chernobyl nuclear accident no longer poses any risk to either short- or long-term visitors to Kiev.

You should **drink only boiled or bottled water.** The water supply in St. Petersburg is thought to contain an intestinal parasite called Giardia Lamblia, which causes diarrhea, stomach cramps, and nausea. The gestation period is two-three weeks, so that symptoms usually arise after the traveler has already returned home. The condition is easily treatable, but be sure to let your doctor know that you may have been exposed to this parasite. Avoid icecubes and use bottled water to brush your teeth. In Moscow and St. Petersburg, imported, bottled water is freely available in hardcurrency shops, but this is not always true in Kiev. You may want to **consider bringing a small supply of bottled water with you.** Hotel floor attendants always

have a samovar in their offices and will provide boiled water if asked.

Food poisoning is common in Russia and Ukraine, so **be wary of dairy products and ice cream that may not be fresh.** The pirozhki (meat and cabbage-filled pies) sold everywhere on the streets are cheap and tasty, but they can give you a nasty stomach ache.

I
INSURANCE

Travel insurance can protect your investment, replace your luggage and its contents, or provide for medical coverage should you fall ill during your trip. Most tour operators, travel agents, and insurance agents sell specialized health-and-accident, flight, trip-cancellation, and luggage insurance as well as comprehensive policies with some or all of these features. Before you make any purchase, **review your existing health and homeowner's policies** to find out whether they cover expenses incurred while traveling.

BAGGAGE

Airline liability for your baggage is limited to $1,250 per person on domestic flights. On international flights, the airlines' liability is $9.07 per pound or $20 per kilogram for checked baggage (roughly $640 per 70-pound bag) and $400 per passenger for unchecked baggage. Insurance for losses exceeding the terms of your airline ticket can be bought directly from the airline at check-in for about $10 per $1,000 of coverage; note that it excludes a rather extensive list of items, shown on your airline ticket.

FLIGHT

You should **think twice before buying flight insurance.** Often purchased as a last-minute impulse at the airport, it pays a lump sum when a plane crashes, either to a beneficiary if the insured dies or sometimes to a surviving passenger who loses eyesight or a limb. Supplementing the airlines' coverage described in the limits-of-liability paragraphs on your ticket, it's expensive and basically unnecessary. Charging an airline ticket to a major credit card often automatically entitles you to coverage and may also embrace travel by bus, train, and ship.

HEALTH

If your own health insurance policy does not cover you outside the U.S., **consider buying supplemental medical coverage.** It can cover from $1,000 to $150,000 worth of medical and/or dental expenses incurred as a result of an accident or illness during a trip. These policies also may include a personal-accident, or death-and-dismemberment, provision, which pays a lump sum ranging from $15,000 to $500,000 to your beneficiaries if you die or to you if you lose one or more limbs or your eyesight, and a medical-assistance provision, which may either reimburse you for the cost of referrals, evacuation, or repatriation and other services, or may automatically enroll you as a member of a particular medical-assistance company. (*See* Health Issues in Important Contacts A to Z, *above.*)

FOR U.K. TRAVELERS

You can buy an annual travel-insurance policy valid for most vacations during the year in which it's purchased. If you go this route, make sure it covers you if you have a preexisting medical condition or are pregnant.

TRIP

Without insurance, you will lose all or most of your money if you must cancel your trip due to illness or any other reason. Especially if your airline ticket, cruise, or package tour is nonrefundable and cannot be changed, it's essential that you **buy trip-cancellation-and-interruption insurance.** When considering how much coverage you need, look for a policy that will cover the cost of your trip plus the nondiscounted price of a one-way airline ticket should you need to return home early. Read the fine print carefully, especially sections defining "family member" and "preexisting medical conditions." Also **consider default or bankruptcy insurance,** which protects you against a supplier's failure to deliver. However, such policies often do not cover default by a travel agency, tour operator, airline, or cruise line if you bought your tour and the coverage directly from the firm in question.

L

LANGUAGE

Russian and Ukrainian are closely related East Slavic languages. Russian is still spoken widely in Ukraine, although its use has become a controversial political issue. With the rise of Ukrainian nationalism, Russian street signs are being replaced and public announcements are now recorded in Ukrainian. But if you speak Russian, you will have no problem getting by in Kiev. Both languages use the Cyrillic alphabet, which makes them particularly intimidating for English-speakers.

If you make an effort to learn the Russian alphabet, you will be able to decipher many words; with just a rudimentary knowledge of the alphabet you will be able to navigate the streets and subways on your own. You may want to **learn a few basic words** in both languages, but don't expect to become conversant overnight. Hotel staff almost always speak good English, and the many restaurants and shops catering to foreigners are also staffed with English-speakers. Outside these places a good grasp of English is uncommon, though most people know at least a few words and phrases since they all took English in grade school. German is the second most common language in both countries.

LODGING

Detailed information about the hotels available can be found in the individual city chapter. In most instances you can book reservations (and request visa support for your Russian visa) directly with the hotel (in the past, all hotel reservations had to be made through Intourist, the official state tourist agency of the Soviet Union). But it is difficult to communicate with the CIS. In addition to the language barrier, placing a call to Russia or Ukraine can be extremely time-consuming. International telephone lines are often overloaded and once you get through, you may find that no one answers the phone. To save time and avoid language problems, **book your hotel through a travel agent or sign on for an organized tour.**

Until the early 1990s, hotels catering to foreign tourists were controlled by Intourist and Sputnik, a branch of the Komsomol specializing in youth tourism. Most of the hotels built and owned by Intourist and Sputnik are now operating as independent establishments, but capitalism is catching on slowly, and service and accommodations have improved only slightly. If you are traveling with an organized tour, you will probably land in one of the old Intourist hotels, most of which are bleak, modern high rises. Accommodations at these hotels are adequate but far from luxurious. Standard items found in most Western hotels, such as soap, shampoo, and even sink stoppers, are rarely provided. Rooms usually come with telephone and televisions, but don't expect room service or in-room movies. The hot-water supply may be interrupted, a problem that occurs most frequently in summer.

Many hotels still have key attendants on each floor to whom you are supposed to relinquish your room key every time you leave the hotel. Since only one key is given out for a double room, you may find this a convenient system. But the key attendant often leaves the key unattended (in an open box on the desk in front of the stairwell), so if you can coordinate your schedule with your roommate, you're better off "attending" to the key yourself. The key attendants—usually rather stern elderly women—can be quite friendly and helpful, however. They can provide extra blankets or help get a leaky faucet fixed. They almost always have a samovar in their office and will provide hot water for tea or coffee.

APARTMENT AND VILLA RENTALS

If you want a home base that's roomy enough for a family and comes with cooking facilities, **consider a furnished rental.** It's generally cost-wise, too, although not always—some rentals are luxury properties (economical only when your party is large). Home-exchange directories do list rentals—often second homes owned by prospective house swappers—and some services search for a house or apartment for you (even a castle if that's your fancy) and handle the paperwork. Some send an illustrated catalogue and others send photographs of specific properties, sometimes at a charge; up-front registration fees may apply.

HOME EXCHANGE

If you would like to find a house, an apartment, or other vacation property to exchange for your own while on vacation, **become a member of a home-exchange organization,** which will send you its annual directories listing available exchanges and will include your own listing in at least one of them. Arrangements for the actual exchange are made by the two parties to it, not by the organization.

HOME STAYS

Visa restrictions make it virtually impossible for Western tourists to make their own arrangements to stay in a private home. In order to obtain a Russian visa, you must first have a confirmed hotel reservation or an official invitation from a Russian organization.

But if you're interested in a more native experience, home-stay options are now available as part of package tours. If you opt for this choice, **ask lots of questions when arranging your home stay.** How are the families chosen and screened? What are the living conditions? Will you have your own room? Do your hosts speak English? If you book a tour through a travel agency, the Russian visa should be included as part of the package.

HOSTELS

Accommodations at Sputnik hotels, the Soviet Union's answer to youth hostels, vary tremendously but are often just as good as the more expensive Intourist hotels. Rooms are usually doubles or triples with only the basic necessities provided (bath and bed but little else). Sputnik hotels are most commonly found on the city outskirts.

M
MAIL

Postal rates increase at nearly the same rapid pace as inflation, but again the advantageous exchange rate vis-à-vis the dollar keeps rates low for foreigners. You can **buy international envelopes and postcards at post-offices and in hotel-lobby kiosks.** Beware that the postal system in the former Soviet Union is notoriously inefficient and mail is often lost. DHL and Federal Express have offices in Moscow and St. Petersburg if

you need to send something important back home. Postcards generally have a better chance of reaching their destination than letters.

RECEIVING MAIL

Mail from outside the CIS takes approximately four weeks to arrive, sometimes longer, and sometimes it never arrives at all. If you absolutely must receive something from home during your trip, **consider using an express-mail service, such as DHL or Federal Express.**

MEDICAL ASSISTANCE

No one plans to get sick while traveling, but it happens, so **consider signing up with a medical assistance company.** These outfits provide referrals, emergency evacuation or repatriation, 24-hour telephone hot lines for medical consultation, dispatch of medical personnel, relay of medical records, cash for emergencies, and other personal and legal assistance.

MONEY AND EXPENSES
IN RUSSIA

The national currency in Russia is the ruble, which is divided into 100 kopecks. There are paper notes of 1,3,5, 10, 25, 50, 100, 200, 500, 1,000, 5,000, 10,000, and 50,000 rubles. Until the early 1990s, the highest denomination was the 100-ruble note; new, larger notes were added recently to keep up with inflation. Inflation is so

high these days that kopecks are no longer in circulation, and 1-, 3-, and 5-ruble notes have become the equivalent of small change.

Rubles cannot be obtained outside Russia, and it is illegal to import or export them. There is no limit, however, on the amount of foreign currency you may bring in with you. The ruble is not a freely convertible currency; many establishments (hotels, stores and restaurants) do not accept rubles but instead trade exclusively in foreign or "hard" currency. You will also find that street artists and vendors often prefer payment in dollars. You should **never change more money than you expect to need immediately,** since, in addition to the ruble's limited acceptance, it is often difficult to change unspent rubles back into dollars; this can be done only at the airport and only if you have saved your original exchange receipts. Russia is a cash society; traveler's checks can be cashed at only a limited number of banks and hard-currency establishments. Major credit cards (American Express, Diners Club, Eurocard, JCB, MasterCard and Visa) are more widely accepted, but often the only accepted form of payment is cash. Of course it is safest to carry your money in traveler's checks, but you will want to have at least $100 in cash (in tens and twenties). If you don't mind the risk of theft or loss, bring more; you are bound to need it. Worn or torn bills are often refused by Russian merchants, so **make sure your bills are crisp and clean.**

IN UKRAINE

As in Russia, Ukraine has a two-tiered, predominantly cash economy. Dollars (cash) and major credit cards are accepted at many restaurants, stores and hotels; as in Russia, many establishments accept only foreign currency. Traveler's checks are almost impossible to cash. The Russian ruble—once the only currency throughout the former Soviet Union—is gradually being replaced by the Ukrainian "coupon." The coupon was originally introduced as a ration card to prevent the sale of Ukrainian goods to non-Ukrainian residents and has gradually acquired the status of a national currency. Its value decreases on a daily basis, and you should never exchange more money than you expect to need in the next day or so. The inflation rate in Ukraine has outpaced Russia's, and by press time (fall 1995), one ruble would buy approximately 46 coupons. You can exchange rubles or dollars for coupons at banks and all major hotels. As in Russia, the black market is a thriving business, and again you are advised to stay away from it.

ATMS

Cirrus, Plus and many other networks connect-ing automated-teller machines operate internationally. Chances are that you can **use your bank card at ATMs** to withdraw money from an account and get cash advances on a credit-card account if your card has been programmed with a personal identification number, or PIN. Before leaving home, **check in on frequency limits** for withdrawals and cash advances. Also **ask whether your card's PIN must be reprogrammed** for use in Russia and Ukraine. Four digits are commonly used overseas. Note that Discover is accepted only in the United States.

On cash advances you are charged interest from the day you receive the money, whether from a teller or an ATM. Although transaction fees for ATM withdrawals abroad may be higher than fees for withdrawals at home, Cirrus and Plus exchange rates are excellent because they are based on wholesale rates only offered by major banks.

COSTS

Russians talk about prices in much the same way Americans talk about weather. The inflation rate is mind-boggling, but so far the exchange rate vis-à-vis the dollar has kept pace. In November 1989, when the Soviet government relaxed the strict regulations controlling exchange rates, one ruble was worth approximately $1.50; by the summer of 1993, one dollar was worth more than 1,000 rubles. You can find some incredible bargains for rubles, but you will have to **search for ruble-priced values.**

Goods and services aimed at foreigners are as expensive as anywhere in Western Europe. A cup of coffee in a foreign-run hotel will cost around $3; in a stand-up café dealing in rubles, around 10¢. A ride on the subway is less than a penny and a pass for the entire month costs around a dollar. Taxi rates are also incredibly low, but as soon as the driver realizes that you are a foreigner, the rate goes up, and you will most likely be asked to pay in dollars. Some museums, such as the Armory Palace in the Kremlin and St. Basil's Cathedral on Red Square, have instituted special, hard-currency fees for foreign tourists, but tickets for Russians, in rubles, are incredibly inexpensive. An evening of classical music at one of Russia's many concert halls can cost less than a dollar if you buy the tickets in rubles, but if you order them through a tourist agency, the cost rises significantly. The price discrimination against foreigners is particularly prevalent in Moscow.

EXCHANGING CURRENCY

Official state-run or bank exchange offices are few and far between in Russia and Ukraine, though more unofficial exchange offices open all the time. The best places to change money are the service bureaus of hotels. You can exchange your money at banks and at all the major hotels. You will be constantly approached by people on the streets, in your hotel, and particularly by waiters in state-run restaurants, offering to exchange money at more advantageous rates. These unofficial currency-exchange activities, commonly referred to as the black market, are now legal under Russian law, but only the foolhardy engage in them. Your chances of being short-changed are extremely high, and the savings are hardly worth the risk.

TRAVELER'S CHECKS

Whether or not to buy traveler's checks depends on where you are headed; **take cash to rural areas and small towns, traveler's checks to cities.** The most widely recognized are American Express, Citicorp, Thomas Cook, and Visa, which are sold by major commercial banks for 1% to 3% of the checks' face value—it pays to **shop around.** Both American Express and Thomas Cook issue checks that can be countersigned and used by you or your traveling companion. So you won't be left with excess foreign currency, **buy a few checks in small denominations** to cash toward the end of your trip. Record the numbers of the checks, cross them off as you spend them, and keep this information separate from your checks.

WIRING MONEY

You don't have to be a cardholder to send or receive funds through MoneyGram[SM] from American Express. Just go to a MoneyGram agent, located in retail and convenience stores and in American Express Travel Offices. Pay up to $1,000 with cash or a credit card, anything over that in cash. The money can be picked up within 10 minutes in the form of U.S. dollar traveler's checks or local currency at the nearest Money-Gram agent, or, abroad, the nearest American Express Travel Office. There's no limit, and the recipient need only present photo identification. The cost runs from 3% to 10%, depending on the amount sent, the destination, and how you pay.

Money sent from the United States or Canada will be available for pickup at agent locations in 100 countries within 15 minutes. Once the money is in the system, it can be picked up at any one of 25,000 locations. Fees range from 4% to 10%, depending on the amount you send.

P
PACKAGES
AND TOURS

A package or tour to Moscow, St. Petersburg, or Kiev can make your vacation less expensive and more convenient. Firms that sell tours and packages purchase airline seats, hotel rooms, and rental cars in bulk and pass some of the savings on to you. In addition, the best operators have local representatives to help you out at your destination.

A GOOD DEAL?

The more your package or tour includes, the better you can predict the ultimate cost of your vacation. Make sure you know exactly what is included, and **beware of hidden costs.** Are taxes, tips, and service charges included? Transfers and baggage handling? Entertainment and excursions? These can add up.

Most packages and tours are rated deluxe, first-class superior, first class, tourist, and budget. The key difference is usually accommodations. Remember, tourist class in the U.S. might be a comfortable chain hotel, while in Russia or Ukraine you might share a bath and do without hot water. If the package or tour you are considering is priced lower than in your wildest dreams, **be skeptical.** Also, **make sure your travel agent knows the hotels** and other services. Ask about location, room size, beds, and whether it has a pool, room service, or programs for children, if you care about these. Has your agent been there or sent others you can contact?

BUYER BEWARE

Each year consumers are stranded or lose their money when operators go out of business—even very large ones with excellent reputations. If you can't afford a loss, take the time to **check out the operator**—find out how long the company has been in business, and ask several agents about its reputation. Next, **don't book unless the firm has a consumer-protection program.** Members of the United States Tour Operators Association and the National Tour Association are required to set aside funds exclusively to cover your payments and travel arrangements in case of default. Nonmember operators may instead carry insurance; look for the details in the operator's brochure—and the name of an underwriter with a solid reputation. Note: When it comes to tour operators, **don't trust escrow accounts.** Although there are laws governing those of charter-flight operators, no governmental body prevents tour operators from raiding the till.

Next, **contact your local Better Business Bureau and the attorney general's office** in both your own state and the operator's; have any complaints been filed? Last, **pay with a major credit card.** Then you can cancel payment, provided that you can document your complaint. Always **consider trip-cancellation insurance** (*see* Insurance, *above*).

BIG VS. SMALL➤ An operator that handles several hundred thousand travelers annually can use its purchasing power to give you a good price. Its high volume may also indi-

cate financial stability. But some small companies provide more personalized service; because they tend to specialize, they may also be experts on an area.

USING AN AGENT

Travel agents are an excellent resource. In fact, large operators accept bookings only through travel agents. But it's good to **collect brochures from several agencies,** because some agents' suggestions may be skewed by promotional relationships with tour and package firms that reward them for volume sales. If you have a special interest, **find an agent with expertise in that area;** the American Society of Travel Agents can give you leads in the United States. (Don't rely solely on your agent, though; agents may be unaware of small-niche operators, and some special-interest travel companies only sell direct.)

SINGLE TRAVELERS

Prices are usually quoted per person, based on two sharing a room. If traveling solo, you may be required to pay the full double-occupancy rate. Some operators eliminate this surcharge if you agree to be matched up with a roommate of the same sex, even if one is not found by departure time.

PACKING FOR MOSCOW, ST. PETERSBURG, AND KIEV

No matter what time of year you visit, **bring a sweater.** St. Petersburg

especially can be unexpectedly cold in summer. A raincoat and fold-up umbrella are also musts. Since you will probably be doing a lot of walking outdoors, bring warm, comfortable clothing, and be sure to pack a **pair of sturdy walking shoes.**

Russians and Ukrainians favor fashion over variety in their wardrobes, and it is perfectly acceptable to wear the same outfit several days in a row. Be sure to **pack one outfit for dress-up occasions,** such as theater events. Coat-check attendants at theaters and restaurants will scold you if you do not have a hook sewed into the back of your coat for hanging. The layer system works well in the unpredictable weather of fall and spring; wear a light coat with a sweater that you can put on and take off as the weather changes. If you visit in winter you will of course need to prepare for the cold. Take heavy sweaters, warm boots, a wool hat, a scarf and mittens, and a heavy coat. Woolen tights or long underwear are essential during the coldest months. Russian central heating can be overly efficient, so you'll use the layer system again to avoid sweltering in an overheated building or train.

MISCELLANEOUS

Local shortages are common. The hard-currency stores (especially those in Moscow) are well stocked, but certain items still disappear periodically and may be hard for passing tourists to find. To avoid running out of the essentials, **bring all your own toiletries and personal hygiene products with you.** Women should bring a supply of sanitary napkins or tampons. Of course you'll want to pack as light as possible, but consider whether you might want any of the difficult or impossible-to-find items: ball-point pens, insect repellent (in summer and fall mosquitoes can be a serious problem), film, camera batteries, laxatives, antidiarrhea pills, travel-sickness medicine, aspirin, and any over-the-counter medicine or prescription drug you take regularly.

Toilet paper is plentiful in hotels but less so in restaurants and public buidlings, so **bring small packages of tissue paper** to carry around with you. If you're a stickler for cleanliness and you are staying in one of the old Intourist hotels, bring disinfectant spray for the bathroom. Premoistened cleansing tissues will also come in handy, especially if you are traveling by train. A small flashlight may also prove useful, since streets are often dimly lit at night. Laundry facilities in hotels are unpredictable, so you will probably end up washing some clothes by hand. Bring your own laundry detergent and a round sink stopper (not always provided in hotel rooms). If you're a coffee drinker,

bring some instant coffee with you; when the restaurant runs out of coffee, you can ask for a cup of hot water and make your own.

If you meet any Russians, chances are they will give you something; Russians tend to give small gifts even on short acquaintance. You may want to be prepared to reciprocate with souvenirs from your hometown or state, such as postcards, pens, or pins.

Bring an extra pair of eyeglasses or contact lenses in your carry-on luggage, and if you have a health problem, **pack enough medication** to last the trip or have your doctor write a prescription using the drug's generic name, because brand names vary from country to country (you'll then need a prescription from a doctor in the country you're visiting). **Don't put prescription drugs or valuables in luggage to be checked,** for it could go astray. To avoid problems with customs officials, carry medications in original packaging. Also don't forget the addresses of offices that handle refunds of lost traveler's checks.

ELECTRICITY

To use your U.S.-purchased electric-powered equipment, **bring a converter and an adapter.** The electrical current in Russia and Ukraine is 220 volts, 50 cycles alternating current (AC); wall outlets take continental-type plugs, with two round prongs.

If your appliances are dual voltage, you'll need only an adapter. Hotels sometimes have 110-volt outlets for low-wattage appliances marked "For Shavers Only" near the sink; don't use them for high-wattage appliances like blow-dryers. If your laptop computer is older, carry a converter; new laptops operate equally well on 110 and 220 volts, so you need only an adapter.

LUGGAGE

Free airline baggage allowances depend on the airline, the route, and the class of your ticket; ask in advance. In general, on domestic flights and on international flights between the United States and foreign destinations, you are entitled to check two bags—neither exceeding 62 inches, or 158 centimeters (length + width + height), or weighing more than 70 pounds (32 kilograms). A third piece may be brought aboard; its total dimensions are generally limited to less than 45 inches (114 centimeters), so it will fit easily under the seat in front of you or in the overhead compartment. In the United States, the FAA gives airlines broad latitude to limit carry-on allowances and tailor them to different aircraft and operational conditions. Charges for excess, oversize, or overweight pieces vary.

If you are flying between two foreign destinations, note that baggage allowances may be determined not by piece but by weight—generally 88 pounds (40 kilograms) in first class, 66 pounds (30 kilograms) in business class, and 44 pounds (20 kilograms) in economy. If your flight between two cities abroad *connects* with your transatlantic or transpacific flight, the piece method still applies.

SAFEGUARDING YOUR LUGGAGE➤ Before leaving home, **itemize your bags' contents** and their worth, and label them with your name, address, and phone number. (If you use your home address, cover it so that potential thieves can't see it.) Inside your bag, **pack a copy of your itinerary.** At check-in, **make sure that your bag is correctly tagged** with the airport's three-letter destination code. If your bags arrive damaged or not at all, file a written report with the airline before leaving the airport.

PASSPORTS AND VISAS

If you don't already have one, **get a passport.** While traveling, **keep one photocopy of the data page** separate from your wallet and leave another copy with someone at home. If you lose your passport, promptly call the nearest embassy or consulate, and the local police; having the data page can speed replacement.

U.S. CITIZENS

All U.S. citizens, even infants, need a valid passport to enter Russia or Ukraine for stays of up to 90 days. New and renewal application forms are available at any of the 13 U.S. Passport Agency offices and at some post offices and courthouses. Passports are usually mailed within four weeks; allow five weeks or more in spring and summer.

U.S. citizens traveling to Russia and Ukraine are also required to obtain a visa for each country. For a Russian visa, you will need to submit the following items to the Russian Consulate at least 14 days before departure: a completed application, a copy of the signed page(s) of your passport, three photos, reference numbers from the hotels you'll be staying at (to prove that you have confirmed reservations), a self-addressed stamped envelope, and a $20 application fee. The fee is higher if you need a faster turnaround time ($30 for 2–14 days, $60 for 48 hours). Requirements vary slightly if you'll be staying as a guest in a private home or if you're traveling on business. Contact the Russian Consulate General (9 E. 91st St., New York, NY 10128, ☎ 212/348–0926) for application forms and more details.

The requirements for obtaining a visa to Ukraine are similar: an application form, copy of your passport, three photos, confirmation of hotel bookings, and the fee ($20 for a single-entry visa, $40 for a double-entry visa, and $100 for a multiple-entry visa). Contact the Ukrainian Consulate (3350 M St., NW Washington, D.C. 20007, ☎ 202/333–7505) for more information.

CANADIANS

You need a valid passport to enter Russian or Ukraine for stays of up to 90 days. Application forms are available at 28 regional passport offices as well as post offices and travel agencies. Whether for a first or a renewal passport, you must apply in person. Children under 16 may be included on a parent's passport but must have their own to travel alone. Passports are valid for five years and are usually mailed within two to three weeks of application.

Canadian citizens are required to obtain a visa to enter either Russia or Ukraine. Requirements are very similar to those outlined above for U.S. citizens. For application forms and details, contact the Russian Consulate General (3655 Avenue du Musée, Montréal, Québec, H3G 2E1, ☎ 514/843–5901) and the Ukrainian Consulate in Ottawa (☎ 613/230–8015 or 613/235–8214).

U.K. CITIZENS

Citizens of the United Kingdom need a valid passport to enter Russia or Ukraine for stays of up to 90 days. Applications for new and renewal passports are available from main post offices as well as at the passport offices located in Belfast, Glasgow, Liverpool, London, Newport, and Peterborough. You may apply in person at all passport offices, or by mail to all except the London office. Children under 16 may travel on an accompanying parent's passport. All passports are valid for 10 years. Allow a month for processing.

To obtain application forms and details about visa requirements for Russia, contact the Russian Consulate General (Kensington Palace Gardens 5, London W8, ☎ 0171/ 229–32–15). For information about visas to Ukraine, contact the Ukrainian Consulate (☎ 0171/727–6312).

R
RAIL TRAVEL

In Russia and the Ukraine, **take the train for the most reliable and convenient transportation.** Remarkably, most trains leave exactly on time; there is a broadcast warning five minutes before departure, but no whistle or "all aboard!" call, so be careful not to be left behind.

Trains are divided into four classes.The highest class, "deluxe," is usually only available on trains traveling international routes. The deluxe class offers two-berth compartments with soft seats and private washrooms; the other classes have washrooms at the end of the cars. The first-class service is called "soft-seat," with spring-

cushioned berths; there are two berths in each compartment. There is no segregation of the sexes and no matter what class of service you choose, chances are good that you will find yourself sharing a compartment with someone of the opposite sex. The second, or "hard-seat," class has a cushion on wooden berths, with four berths to a compartment. The third class—wooden berths without compartments—is rarely sold to foreigners unless specifically requested. Most compartments have a small table, limited room for baggage (including under the seats) and a radio that can be turned down, but not off. In soft class there is also a table lamp. The price of the ticket may or may not include use of bedding; sometimes this fee (which increases daily with the inflation rate) is collected by the conductor.

All the cars are also equipped with samovars. Back in the days of communism, the conductor would offer tea to passengers before bedtime. These days the train is often out of tea and sometimes even out of water, so **bring your own snacks and beverages onto the train.** Most conductors run their own small businesses selling champagne and caviar, so don't be surprised if you're approached with such an offer. The communal bathrooms located at both ends of each car are notoriously dirty, so

bring premoistened cleansing tissues for washing up and water for brushing your teeth. Definitely pack toilet paper. Also be sure to pack a heavy sweater. The cars are often overheated and toasty warm, but sometimes they are not heated at all, so in winter it can get very cold.

There are numerous day and overnight trains between St. Petersburg and Moscow and between Moscow and Kiev. There is also train service between Kiev and St. Petersburg, but the trip is a long one (over 30 hours). The past few years have witnessed increased crime on the overnight trains; the safest option for travel between Moscow and St. Petersburg is the high-speed day-train *Avrora*, which makes the trip in just under six hours. If you are traveling alone on an overnight train, you should take extra security precautions. The doors to the compartments can be locked, but the locks can be picked, so you might consider bringing a bicycle chain. You may also want to buy out the entire compartment so as not to risk your luck with unknown compartment-mates.

Train travel in Russia may be primitive by Western standards, but it offers an unrivaled opportunity to glimpse the quaint Russian countryside, which is dotted in places with colorful wooden cottages. If you are traveling by overnight train, be sure to set your alarm and get up an hour or so before arrival so that you can watch at close hand the workers going about their morning rounds in the rural areas just outside the cities.

Purchasing a domestic train ticket outside the CIS can be difficult, but tickets are easily purchased within the country. Tickets go on sale 10 days prior to departure. As of fall 1993, train tickets sold to foreigners for travel within Russia must be paid for with foreign currency. This is now being strictly enforced. A one-way ticket between Moscow and St. Petersburg on an overnight train now costs just under $25.

RENTING A CAR

CUTTING COSTS

To get the best deal, **book through a travel agent and shop around.** When pricing cars, **ask where the rental lot is located.** Some off-airport locations offer lower rates—even though their lots are only minutes away from the terminal via complimentary shuttle. You may also want to **price local car-rental companies,** whose rates may be lower still, although service and maintenance standards may not be up to those of a national firm. Also **ask your travel agent about a company's customer-service record.** How has it responded to late plane arrivals and vehicle mishaps? Are there often lines at the rental counter, and, if - you're traveling during a holiday period, does a

confirmed reservation guarantee you a car?

Always **find out what equipment is standard** at your destination before specifying what you want; **do without automatic transmission or air-conditioning** if they're optional. In Europe, manual transmissions are standard and air-conditioning is rare and often unnecessary.

Also in Europe, **look into wholesalers—** companies that do not own their own fleets but rent in bulk from those that do and often offer better rates than traditional car-rental operations. Prices are best during low travel periods, and rentals booked through wholesalers must be paid for before you leave the United States. If you use a wholesaler, **know whether the prices are guaranteed** in U.S. dollars or foreign currency, and if unlimited mileage is available; find out about required deposits, cancellation penalties, and drop-off charges; and confirm the cost of any required insurance coverage.

INSURANCE

Insurance is required of foreign motorists. As many foreign insurance companies are unwilling to insure cars touring Russia and Ukraine, or will charge very high premiums, you may wish to insure with a Russian firm Ingosstrakh (*see* Car Rental *in* Important Contacts A to Z).

When you drive a rented car, you are generally responsible for any

damage or personal injury that you cause as well as damage to the vehicle. Before you rent, **see what coverage you already have** under the terms of your personal auto-insurance policy and credit cards. For about $14 a day, rental companies sell insurance, known as a collision damage waiver (CDW), that eliminates your liability for damage to the car; it's always optional and should never be automatically added to your bill.

REQUIREMENTS

In Russia and Ukraine, your own driver's license is not acceptable. An International Driver's Permit, available from the American or Canadian Automobile Association, is necessary.

SURCHARGES

Before picking up the car in one city and leaving it in another, **ask about drop-off charges or one-way service fees,** which can be substantial. Note, too, that some rental agencies charge extra if you return the car before the time specified on your contract. To avoid a hefty refueling fee, **fill the tank just before you turn in the car.**

S

SENIOR-CITIZEN DISCOUNTS

To qualify for age-related discounts, **mention your senior-citizen status up front** when booking hotel reservations, not when checking out, and before you're seated in restaurants, not when

THE GOLD GUIDE / SMART TRAVEL TIPS

paying your bill. Note that discounts may be limited to certain menus, days, or hours. When renting a car, **ask about promotional car-rental discounts**—they can net lower costs than your senior-citizen discount.

STUDENTS ON THE ROAD

To save money, **look into deals available through student-oriented travel agencies.** To qualify, you'll need to have a bona fide student I.D. card. Members of international student groups also are eligible. *See* Students in Important Contacts A to Z, *above.*

T
TELEPHONES

At present, most coin-operated telephones in Moscow take the new one-ruble coin (as opposed to the old Soviet version) or special tokens. (The tokens, available at kiosks, currently cost about 10 rubles, but the price is likely to rise.) A sign above the telephone indicates whether it takes coins (*monety*) or tokens (*zhetony*). In St. Petersburg, public telephones take subway tokens. In both cities, however, you may still find public phones that operate on 15-kopeck coins; these coins are no longer in general circulation, but are sometimes found on sale at kiosks.

In Ukraine, where rubles in general are no longer in circulation, public telephones work without any coin at all.

This situation is likely to change, however, as soon as the Ukrainian government introduces a bona fide Ukrainian currency complete with metal coins.

LONG-DISTANCE

The long-distance services of AT&T, MCI, and Sprint make calling home relatively convenient and let you avoid hotel surcharges; typically, you dial a local number. Before you go, **find out the local access codes** for your destinations.

Most hotels offer satellite telephone booths where for several dollars a minute you can make an international call in a matter of seconds. If you want to economize, you can visit the main post office and order a call for rubles (sometimes there is a wait of up to 3 days). The per-minute rate increases frequently to keep pace with inflation but in recent years has never exceeded more than a dollar a minute. From your hotel room or from a private residence, you can dial direct. To place your call, dial 8, wait for the dial tone, then dial the country code (for the United States, 101) followed by the number you are trying to reach. In the new joint-venture hotels, rooms are often equipped with international, direct-dial (via satellite) telephones, but beware that the rates are hefty.

TIPPING

In the postcommunist era, tipping is rapidly

becoming an accepted practice, so **when in doubt, tip.** Cloak-room attendants, waiters, porters, and taxi drivers will all expect a tip, preferably in foreign currency. Add an extra 10% to 15% to a restaurant bill or taxi fare. Some restaurants are now adding a service charge to the bill automatically, so double-check before you leave a big tip. If you're paying by credit card, leave the tip in cash—the waiter will never see it if you add it to the credit-card charge.

W
WHEN TO GO

The climate in Russia and Ukraine changes dramatically with the seasons. All three cities are best visited in late spring or early autumn, just before and after the peak tourist season. The weather is always unpredictable, but you are most apt to encounter pleasantly warm and sunny days in late May and late August. In Moscow summers tend to be hot, although thunderstorms and heavy rainfall are common in July and August. In St. Petersburg, on the other hand, it rarely gets very hot, even at the height of summer. If this maritime city is your only destination, try to **visit St. Petersburg during the White Nights** (mid-June to early July), when the northern day is virtually endless.

The Ukrainian climate is milder than the Russian one; spring comes earlier to Kiev than to Moscow and St. Petersburg, and summer lasts longer. In winter months all three cities are covered in an attractive blanket of snow. But only the hardiest tourists should visit between late November and early February, when the days are short and dark, extremely so in St. Petersburg, and the weather is often bitterly cold.

Climate in Moscow

Below are the average daily maximum and minimum temperatures for Moscow.

Jan.	16F	– 9C	May	67F	19C	Sept.	61F	16C
	4	–16		47	8		45	7
Feb.	22F	– 6C	June	70F	21C	Oct.	49F	9C
	7	–14		52	11		38	3
Mar.	32F	0C	July	74F	23C	Nov.	36F	2C
	18	– 8		56	13		27	– 3
Apr.	50F	10C	Aug.	72F	22C	Dec.	23F	– 5C
	34	1		54	12		14	–10

THE GOLD GUIDE / SMART TRAVEL TIPS

THE RUSSIAN PARADOX

SUCH EXTREMES CHARACTERIZE Russia—extremes of geography, of politics, of temperament, and even of weather—that it ultimately defies characterization. Winston Churchill's observation that "Russia is a riddle wrapped in a mystery inside an enigma" is itself a masterfully Russian pronouncement, adamant in its opaqueness. And if it was accurate in 1939, it is no less so now, when the situations that "characterized" Russia then—devotion under Stalin to the communist purpose, a centralized economy, a nation-state comprising 15 republics welded into the monolith of the USSR—have been overturned as radically as they themselves overturned what had come before.

Today, after perestroika and glasnost, many in the West had hoped that Russia would stand revealed, that it would be comprehensible and accessible. Eager to embrace her, engage and understand her, perhaps even indulge her, we visit wondering if we may finally decipher that mysterious, fabled "Russian-ness." While there is indeed a new kind of Russian daily world, it is not the one we were expecting. It is likely to surprise us; some will be disappointed, others exhilarated. No one will go away unstimulated.

Stretching across 10 time zones, from the Pacific Ocean to the Baltic Sea, Russia remains the world's largest country. Even as a single ex-republic, its realms extend to the Arctic Circle and to subtropical resorts. Its western border is Europe; its eastern, the Orient. In between them the Russian people comprise over 100 distinct ethnic groups. How, then, can we speak in sweeping generalizations of a monolithic empire?

It helps to understand that Russia's power, as well as its charm, resides in paradox, and perhaps never before has its dual nature been so evident. Extremes and contrasts—these will form the bulk of your impressions as you tour these three cities.

The first, very difficult transitions are already far behind, but the path ahead can still look rocky. Sweeping changes in politics and economics, as well as in media, law, and entertainment, have transformed the lives of most Russians. Those left disenfranchised by the demise of the communist system have been set adrift for at least two generations, with no relief in sight.

Russia exists as if in a time warp. White-aproned clerks still calculate change on a wooden abacus; eggs are sold on the street; gas is peddled from trucks on the side of the road. Clothes are still washed mostly by hand; scythes are the Russian lawnmowers. Meanwhile, at least in the cities, sales of fax machines and personal computers outstrip nearly all others; there is a booming market for Mercedes-Benzes and Volvos. You see more cellular phones on the street than anywhere except Los Angeles. In Moscow, beneath a giant neon sign flashing the dollar-exchange rate, the very Soviet *gai* (traffic police) signal the tinted-glass limousine and the battered Lada laden with refrigerators, cigarettes, juice, and crates of possessions. On the corner a young mother taking her child to school waits to cross the busy intersection, along with recent arrivals from Armenia or Azerbaijan (a wave of immigration has convulsed Russia), an old man in a shabby suit laden with war medals and ribbons, a teenager in black leather and sneakers listening to a Walkman, and a kerchiefed grandmother in for the day from the village, struggling with a rusted cart filled with potatoes (or carrots or jars of homemade sour cream) to sell at the market.

Special words are reserved for Kiev's nation, Ukraine. Inextricably bound up in Russia's history during the last 70 years as an integral part of the Soviet Union, Ukraine has struck off in determined pursuit of its own destiny. While the two nations share many post-Soviet struggles, they are different, too. In their intertwined genealogy, it is Kiev that is said to have given birth to Russia. It was in Kiev, more than 1,000 years ago, that the Kievan-Rus civilization is considered to have begun. Eventually, power shifted

1 Destination: Moscow, St. Petersburg, Kiev

to the north, but the Ukrainian capital continued to thrive and grow on its own cultural, religious, and political terms. It is a separateness that it has now proclaimed wholly on its own.

Explored together, these cities will enrich and fascinate. Their monuments and people will command your interest, attention, and respect—and perhaps win your affection, too. In 1919 the American journalist Lincoln Steffens, back from a trip to the young Soviet Union, said to Bernard Baruch, "I have been over into the future, and it works." Perhaps it did, at least for a while. As you witness the future that is unfolding in Russia and Ukraine, judge for yourself if one could say the same today. But remember that, if the collapse of the empires here proves anything, it is that anything about this part of the world is averse to prediction. Welcome to the enigma. Enjoy the surprises.

WHAT'S WHERE

Moscow

The end of communism has undoubtedly affected the ancient capital of Russia. The central streets have largely reverted to their old pre-revolutionary names, and the number of places named after Lenin has been drastically reduced. The new advertising billboards, many in English as well as Russian, point to real and profound economic change. Western investment and cooperative agreements have led to a rash of new building, notably of hotels and business complexes. Yet for all this, the face of Moscow appears curiously impervious to change. Its Stalinist physionomy, born in the 1930s, continues to brazen it out; the Gothic skyscrapers of the old Ukraine Hotel and the Foreign Ministry look contemptuously down on the modest Western-style shops down below. Building after building, made redundant by the demise of communism with its vastly over-swollen bureaucracy and now taken over by new organizations, refuses to budge. Although Moscow has now much in common with its great Western counterparts—Paris, London, New York— it still has a stubbornly Russian stamp.

St. Petersburg

Planned from the first brick as a great capital, St. Petersburg has not fallen short of Peter the Great's original vision. It has not been the capital of Russia since the Bolshevik Revolution, but it still carries itself as though it were. Indeed, the imposing grandeur of its most important landmarks—Palace Square and the Winter Palace—and the stylish sophistication of its residences make this 300-year-old city one of the great urban centers in the world. Czar Peter's intention was to reorient Russia to the West by making the city a "window looking into Europe," and indeed the geometric elegance of its layout and the perfect planning of its architecture owe more to the grand cities of Europe than to its Russian counterparts to the east. It has also been called the northern Venice, for it is a city built on more than a hundred islands cradled in the watery lap of the winding Neva and the intricate network of canals carved into the soft ground at the mouth of the Gulf of Finland.

Kiev

Although it is the capital of the recently-independent Ukraine, Kiev is known as the Mother of Russia, for it was here in the 9th century that Russian civilization began and Rus, the land of the eastern Slavs, was founded. For centuries it was an important cultural, political, and economic center until it was razed to the ground by Mongol invaders in 1240. The city has seen its fair share of violence and tragedy: in this century alone, it witnessed a bitter struggle at the time of the Bolshevik Revolution, an 800-day occupation by the Germans during World War II, and, most recently, in 1986, the tragedy of Chernobyl, only 60 miles away. It is perhaps this combination of ancient glory and modern disaster that best define Kiev's struggle to re-establish itself as an urban center of importance; one need visit for only a few days to become aware of this dual identity, as the city proudly displays the elegance of its glorious past alongside the uncertain fervor of a newly independent capital tackling the problems inherited from 70 years of bureaucratic rule.

PLEASURES AND PASTIMES

Ballet

There have been few *corps de ballet* to match the Russians over the last 150 years. The Bolshoi and Kirov ballets have produced some of the world's greatest dancers; indeed, the names Pavlova, Nijinsky, Nureyev, Barishnikov, and Diaghilev, all home-grown talents, are synonymous with ballet excellence. Unfortunately, faltering standards due to chronic underfunding and the attraction of the West led to a seemingly unstoppable hemorrhaging of Russia's greatest dancers, beginning with the defection of Rudolf Nureyev in 1961. The demise of communism has exposed decades of complacency and lack of innovation, and has done little to stop the bleeding—the British Royal Ballet poached Russia's current great, Irek Mukhamedov, in 1991. Despite such problems, a night at the Kirov or the Bolshoi can be a unique experience for those wishing to take a peek at the heart of some of the world's greatest dance venues.

Bath Houses

A visit to the Russian *banya,* or bath, should not be missed. It has been part of the national culture for centuries; indeed, the bath houses of Moscow and St. Petersburg were once the last word in luxury. Yegerov's in St. Petersburg, for example, had a tented disrobing room, decked out in Moorish style with cushions and settees, and a swimming pool traversed by a grotto-like bridge and rockery, classical-style statues, and trailing greenery.

Bring a towel, shampoo, and plastic shoes or sandals. You may be given a plastic bathing robe and offered a *venik,* the bundle of birch twigs without which no visit to the bath is complete. By brushing the soaked twigs lightly across the body, striking more boldly with each turn, one stimulates the circulation of the blood and draws out toxins. Most Russians finish with a glass of tea or water or even a shot of vodka, but be careful not to overindulge: sip, don't gulp, any liquids.

Dining

The dining scene in all three cities has changed dramatically in the past few years. In terms of sheer numbers and types of restaurants, Moscow is far ahead of St. Petersburg and Kiev, but in all three cities you'll find a variety of cuisines and price ranges.

In Russia, Breakfast is often a familiar omelet or fried eggs, but don't be surprised if the meal includes cabbage salad, fish, or hot dogs (served with cold peas), which are all standard breakfast fare. The main meal of the day is served in mid afternoon and usually consists of a starter, soup, and a main course. Supper is traditionally a lighter meal, with just an appetizer and a main course. The main course will be either meat or fish; the fish you are most likely to be served are sturgeon, halibut, or herring. A favorite meat dish is beef Stroganoff, beef stewed in sour cream and served with mushrooms and fried potatoes. The soup is likely to be borscht, a beet soup, or *shchi,* cabbage soup. Other national dishes include piroshki, fried rolls filled with cabbage or meat, and blini, small, light pancakes rolled and filled with caviar, fish, melted butter, jam, or sour cream.

In Ukraine, you may be lucky enough to be served a well-cooked chicken Kiev—fried chicken breast filled with melted butter that shoots forth when you pierce the chicken with your fork. Another Ukrainian specialty is *vareniky,* sweet dumplings filled with fruit or cheese.

Nature

If you ask Russians what they think most identifies them as Russian, do not be surprised to hear that it is their close association with nature. At the turn of the century, it was estimated that 90 percent of the population was rural, and while this figure has dropped over the course of the century, the Russian attachement to the natural world has not. Every major city has at least one large park where citizens can spend entire days enjoying the greenery in the company of friends and family. At weekends, families stream out of the cities to their countryside *dachas* or to a low-budget hotel complex. There they can indulge one of the greatest of Russian pastimes, *mushrooming.* From early June to mid-October, the countryside is awash with genuflecting men and women picking mushrooms, which are then eaten at a *shashlik,* or barbecue.

Sports and Outdoor Activities

Skiing and hunting packages to Moscow and St. Petersburg are available, some through Intour Service. Cross-country skiing is a particularly popular sport in Russia and Ukraine, and all three cities have acres of wooded parkland perfect for it. Outdoor skating rinks also abound, and there are downhill skiing facilities just outside of Moscow. Rentals of skis and skates are available only sporadically, so you should bring your own equipment or make prior arrangements. If you plan to go hunting, you may bring your own hunting gun provided you carry a voucher issued by an accredited travel agent attesting to the fact that you intend to hunt. All sporting rifles must be presented for customs inspection and the serial numbers declared on the customs form.

Vodka

The Russian national drink is an inseparable part of Russian social life. It is drunk literally everywhere, with the effect of breaking down inhibitions and producing a state of conviviality that the Russians refer to as *dusha-dushe* (heart-to-heart). When a Russian taps his throat, beware: It's impossible to refuse this invitation to conviviality.

Vodka is often flavored and colored with herbs and spices. *Limonaya*, lemon-flavored vodka, is particularly popular with American tourists, as is *pertsovka*, pepper-flavored vodka. Other varieties include *starka* (a dark, smooth "old" vodka), *pshenichnaya* (made from wheat), *ryabinovka*, in which ashberries have been steeped, and *tminaya* (caraway-flavored vodka). Be wary of the *krepkaya* vodka, which at 110 proof is the strongest variety. In Ukraine, try *khorilka s pertsem* (with hot peppers).

Normally served from an ice bucket, vodka is drunk neat in one gulp and "chased" with a mouthful of food. It goes down particularly well with *zakuski* (hors d'oeuvres)—smoked salmon, salted herring, marinated mushrooms, salami, caviar, etc. To quell the fiery taste, some Russians advise exhaling before gulping, while others recommend deep inhalation. Many Russians swear by a shot of vodka with a dash of pepper as a cure for the common cold.

FODOR'S CHOICE

No two people will agree on what makes a perfect vacation, but it's fun and helpful to know what others think. We hope you'll have a chance to experience some of Fodor's Choices yourself while visiting Moscow, St. Petersburg, and Kiev. For detailed information about each entry, refer to the appropriate chapters within this guidebook.

Churches and Monasteries

★ **Alexander Nevsky Lavra, St. Petersburg.** One of only four highest-ranking monasteries in Russia and the Ukraine, the burial place of St. Alexander Nevsky—and many other famous names—was built in 1710 by Peter the Great.

★ **Donskoy Monastery, Moscow.** The once secret archives at this 16th-century monastery are a fascinating memorial to Russian architecture and art.

★ **Monastery of the Caves, Kiev.** An entire day should be set aside for discovering the intricate mazes of this 11th-century monastery, which was once the center of the Ukranian Orthodox Church.

★ **New Maiden's Convent and Cemetery, Moscow.** This immaculately preserved ensemble of 16th- and 17th-century architecture borders a fascinating cemetery where some of Russia's greatest literary, political, and miliatry figures are buried.

★ **St. Andrew's Cathedral, Kiev.** The green, blue, and gold cupolas of this magnificent cathedral high on a bluff overlooking the Dnieper River, are a fine example of the Ukrainian baroque.

★ **St. Sophia's Cathedral, Kiev.** The city's oldest church was consecrated in 1037 and is richly decorated with mosaics and frescoes dating from the 11th and 12th centuries.

★ **Smolny Convent and Cathedral, St. Petersburg.** This magnificent five-domed, blue-and-white masterpiece by Bartolomeo Rastrelli seems to have leapt off the pages of a fairy tale.

★ **Zagorsk (Sergyev Posad), Moscow.** Pilgrims have been worshipping at the monastery here, Russia's most important center of pilgrimage, for over 500 years.

Historical Buildings and Sites

★ **Armory Palace, Moscow.** A wide selection of imperial regalia and historical artifacts is stored in the vast galleries of the Kremlin's oldest and richest museum.

★ **Babi Yar, Kiev.** The Nazi's execution of over 100,000 Jews and partisans at this pretty ravine during World War II is commemorated by a dramatic monument that is a moving testament to the victims' suffering.

★ **Catherine Palace, Pushkin.** This dazzling example of Russian baroque architecture was the summer residence of the imperial family from the days of Peter the Great.

★ **Kremlin, Moscow.** There are few buildings in the world that can match the historical importance of the Kremlin, *the* symbol of Russia's mystery and power since the 15th century.

★ **Maria's Palace, Kiev.** This delightful mixture of Russian and Ukranian baroque has a magnificent facade with balustrades decorated with vases and sculptures of lions that lead down majestically to the formally landscaped park.

★ **Pavlovsk, St. Petersburg.** High on a bluff overlooking the river and a 1,500-acre park, the Great Palace was built as a summer residence for Paul I.

★ **Petrodvorets, St. Petersburg.** This former imperial palace on the shores of the Baltic sea, complete with lush parks, monumental cascades, and gilded fountains, will leave a lasting impression.

★ **Red Square, Moscow.** Surprisingly, the Bolshevik Revolution did not give this magnificent and beautiful square its name; the Russian word for "beautiful," strangely enough, comes from the word "red."

★ **Strelka, St. Petersburg.** The easternmost tip of Vasilievsky Island, lined with brightly colored houses, affords a dazzling view of the city and its glorious architecture.

★ **Winter Palace, St. Petersburg.** Created by Bartolomeo Rastrelli for the Empress Elizabeth I, the former imperial residence has over 1,000 rooms replete with works of art and historical objects.

Museums

★ **Chernobyl Museum, Kiev.** The somber display here commemorates the victims of the devastating nuclear explosion at the infamous power plant.

★ **Hermitage, St. Petersburg.** One of the world's richest repositories of art will be found here, with the Italian Renaissance, Spanish, and Dutch masters well represented.

★ **Kolomenskoye Estate Museum, Moscow.** This estate, once a favorite summer residence of Moscow's grand dukes and czars, has been turned into an impressive open-air museum that includes a Siberian prison tower and Peter the Great's cottage.

★ **Museum of Historical Treasures, Kiev.** The highlight of the impressive collection here is a massive gold pectoral, or chest ornament, decorated with scenes from Scythian life in the 4th century BC.

★ **Pushkin Museum of Fine Arts, Moscow.** After St. Petersburg's Hermitage, this is the largest museum of fine art in Russia, with a veritable smorgasbord of world-class art.

★ **State Museum of Russian Art, St. Petersburg.** The scores of Russian masterpieces on display here have made this one of the country's most important art galleries.

★ **Tretyakov Art Gallery, Moscow.** Russia's largest and most important repository of its national art is housed in a fanciful building designed in the Russian art nouveau style.

Parks and Gardens

★ **Gidro Park, Kiev.** This pretty park on an island near the left bank is a popular spot in summer for boating and bathing.

★ **Gorky Park, Moscow.** The 110-acre park is Moscow's most popular, and in summer families throng to its many attractions, including a giant Ferris wheel.

★ **Kirovsky Park on Yelagin Island, St. Petersburg.** An open-air theater, boating stations, and a beach are among the attractions at this park, which covers an entire island.

★ **Summer Gardens, St. Petersburg.** Pavilions, ponds, and an intricate network of fountains, along with sculptures and statues from all over the world, make up this brainchild of Peter the Great, who wanted to create the Russian Versailles.

Monuments

★ **Bronze Horseman, St. Petersburg.** This city landmark, depicting Peter the Great astride a rearing horse, is a symbol of Russia rising up to crush its enemies, shown here as a serpent.

★ **Egyptian Sphinxes, St. Petersburg.** It may have taken the Russians over a year to transport them from Thebes, but it was worth it, if only for the magnificent view of the old city from the supporting quay.

★ **Monument to the Baptism of Russia, Kiev.** A 66-foot bronze of Prince Vladimir holding a cross in his right hand dominates a hilltop overlooking the Dnieper.

Hotels

★ **Grand Hotel Europe, St. Petersburg.** The service shines in the midst of pre-revolutionary splendor, making it the finest hotel in town. $$$$

★ **Metropole, Moscow.** One of the capital's most elegant hotels, it successfully combines the opulence of its 19th-century decor with the efficiency of its late 20th-century service and amenities. $$$$

Restaurants

★ **Europe, St. Petersburg.** The opulent dinner served at this elegant restaurant is fit for a czar. $$$$

★ **Glazur, Moscow.** The subdued atmosphere and exquisite cuisine at this upscale establishments are geared toward the city's foreign community. $$$$

★ **Savoy, Moscow.** This might be the only restaurant where you can truly eat like a czar: It features a recreation of one of the menus served at the coronation of Czar Nicholas II in 1896. $$$$

★ **U Pirosmami, Moscow.** The service and the food are astonishingly good at this popular cooperative. $$$

Special Moments

★ **Red Square at night.** The best time to view the impressive square is when the red stars of the Kremlin towers light up the night and the entire area is floodlit.

★ **Your first glimpse of St. Basil's Cathedral.** The eight onion-shaped domes of this distinctive cathedral are one of the great architectural symbols of Russia and will not disappoint.

★ **An evening of classical music at the Tchaikovsky Conservatory.** Fine performances can be enjoyed at this auditorium named after one of Russia's greatest composers.

★ **A midnight cruise along the Neva River during the White Nights.** In June and July, when the northern day is virtually endless, the imperial palaces sparkle along the embankments and the colorful facades of the riverside estates glow gently as you wind your way around this northern Venice.

★ **Kiev in spring.** The climate is milder than in Moscow, and the end of winter means the shutters can reopen, the trees are in bloom, and all of the colors of this beautiful city come to life.

HOLIDAYS AND FESTIVALS

With the demise of the Soviet Union and the accompanying religious revival, church holidays are now more widely celebrated than the traditional political holidays. These days November 7, the anniversary of the Bolshevik Revolution, merits only a minor military parade in Moscow. The date goes by virtually unnoticed in Kiev, while in St. Petersburg November 7 is now celebrated as the anniversary of the city's renaming from Leningrad back to St. Petersburg. Listed below are the current major holidays celebrated in Russia and Ukraine.

mas is celebrated on January 7.

FEB.➤ February 23, **Soviet Army Day,** is somewhat similar to Father's Day in the United States. Since just about every male ends up in the army, the holiday traditionally honors all men, not just members of the military. In recent years the holiday—whose name has not changed despite the fact that the Soviet Army no longer exists—has acquired political significance for Communists and nationalists who want the Soviet Union back. The day is celebrated with fireworks in the evening.

Moscow Stars, a music and dance festival, is held in Moscow May 5 to 13.

SUMMER

JUNE➤ In Kiev, **Ivan Kupallo Day** (June 6) is a celebration of Mid-Summer's Night that dates from the city's pagan days. June 12 is **Russian Independence Day.** In St. Petersburg, the **White Nights Music Festival** is held during the last two weeks of June.

AUG.➤ August 24 is **Ukrainian Independence Day.**

WINTER

DEC.➤ **New Year's Eve** is a favorite holiday marked by merrymaking and family gatherings. Friends and family exchange small gifts, putting them under a New Year's tree, a tradition that began when Christmas and other religious holidays were not tolerated by the Soviet authorities. December Nights is a month-long festival of music, dance, theater and art held in Moscow.

JAN.➤ **New Year's Eve** is celebrated twice—first on December 31, with the rest of the world, and then again on January 13, "Old" New Year's Eve (according to the Julian calendar used in Russia until the revolution). Russian Orthodox Christ-

SPRING

MAR.➤ March 8, **International Women's Day,** is a popular holiday similar to Mother's Day.

MAR.–APR.➤ **Orthodox Easter** is a major national holiday in both Russia and Ukraine. Visitors should attend the festive services, which begin at midnight and run through the night.

MAY➤ May 1, formerly **International Labor Day,** has in recent years turned into a celebration of spring (in Russian, *Prazdnik Vesny*). May 9, **Victory Day,** is one of the country's most important holidays; World War II veterans appear on the streets decked out in their medals and are honored throughout the day at open-air festivals and parades.

AUTUMN

NOV.➤ November 7 and 8, the **Anniversary of the Bolshevik Revolution,** were, at press time, still public holidays in Russia.

2 Moscow

By Lauri del
Commune

IT IS DIFFICULT FOR WESTERNERS TO COMPREHEND what an important place Moscow holds in the Russian imagination as a symbol of spiritual and political power. Through much of its history the city was known as Holy Moscow and was regarded by Russians as a place of pilgrimage not unlike Jerusalem, Mecca, or Rome. Founded more than 850 years ago as the center of one of several competing minor principalities, Moscow eventually emerged as the center of a unified Russian state in the 15th century. One hundred years later it had grown into the capital of a strong and prosperous state, one of the largest in the world. Although civil war and Polish invasion ravaged the city in the early 17th century, a new era of stability and development began with the establishment of the Romanov dynasty in 1613.

The true test for Moscow came under Peter the Great. Greatly influenced by his exposure to the West, Peter deliberately turned his back on the old traditions of Moscow, establishing his own new capital— St. Petersburg—on the shores of the Baltic Sea. Yet Western-looking St. Petersburg never replaced Moscow as the heart and soul of the Russian nation. Moscow continued to thrive as an economic and cultural center, despite its demotion. More than 200 years later, within a year of the Bolshevik revolution in 1917, the young Soviet government restored Moscow's status as the nation's capital. In a move just as deliberate as Peter the Great's, the new communist rulers transferred their government back to the Russian heartland, away from the besieged frontier and away from Russia's imperial past.

Moscow thus became the political and ideological center of the vast Soviet empire. And even though that empire itself has now broken apart, the city retains its political, industrial, and cultural sway. Although the several republics are now politically independent, no one challenges Moscow's status as capital of Russia or as the effective if not official center of that loosely defined political formation known as the Commonwealth of Independent States. With a population of more than 9 million, Moscow is Russia's largest city and most popular place of residence. It is home to the country's most renowned theaters, film studios, and cultural institutions. It is its most important transportation hub (even today most flights to the former Soviet republics are routed through Moscow's airports). And it is still the center of the continuing power struggles in the Russian government.

During the Soviet years, when all things foreign were regarded with deep suspicion, Moscow was the embodiment of the extreme isolationism of the Russian communist regime. Sweeping political changes have dramatically changed this. To salvage and propel its giant economy, the Russian government and business community are actively pursuing foreign investment, even turning to foreign governments for assistance and advice, and everywhere setting their own economic plans and agendas into action.

Nowhere in Russia are the dramatic contrasts of this new era more evident than in Moscow, where the newly rich live among the newly poorer. Mercedes-Benzes race past decrepit buses lurching over streets riddled with potholes (equal foe to both kinds of transport). The omnipresent paeans to Soviet achievement—statues and monuments to heroes, street and station names, exhibition halls and museums—have fallen, changed, or been closed. In their place are restaurants, advertising offices, dance clubs, and supermarkets. Churches destroyed or closed in the previous 70 years are being lovingly refurbished or rebuilt. Electronic billboards atop Stalinist-era socialist-realist buildings broadcast an eclectic array of messages, including the daily exchange rate, and the site adjacent to Red Square is under excavation for the construction of an indoor shopping mall. Capitalism has not come lightly here, or cheaply, as Moscow prices skyrocket, but the city's streets and squares bustle with the activity and color of commerce. In stores and on endless rows of makeshift tables on some streets are a mix and breadth of products unthinkable in years past. A huge swelling in the number of cars means that traffic jams and their attendant noise—not to mention exhaust fumes—form a constant backdrop to the lively new street life. But all of it vividly reflects the commotion and excitement (as well as the pain and struggle) involved in the ongoing transition from a centralized economic system to a fluid free market.

EXPLORING

Tour 1: The Kremlin and Red Square

Numbers in the margin correspond to points of interest on the Kremlin and Moscow maps.

★ ❶ The logical place to begin your exploration of Moscow is at its oldest part and its heart, the **Kremlin,** situated at the very center of the city, atop Borovitsky (Pine Grove) Hill. The first wooden structure was erected on this site sometime in the 12th century. As Moscow grew, it followed the traditional pattern of Russian cities, developing in concentric circles around the elevated fortress at its center (the Russian word *kreml* means citadel or fortress). After Moscow emerged as the center of a vast empire in the late 15th century, the Kremlin came to symbolize the mystery and power of Russia. In the 20th century the Kremlin became synonymous with the Soviet government, and "Kremlinologists," Western specialists who studied the movements of the politicians in and around the fortress, made careers out of trying to decipher Soviet Russian policies. Much has changed in the last decade, as the former Soviet Union has unraveled. But despite the dramatic changes, the Kremlin remains mysteriously alluring. You'll find many signs of the old—and new—Russian enigma as you tour the ancient Kremlin grounds, where, before the black-suited men of the Bolshevik Revolution took over, czars were crowned and buried.

You can buy tickets for the Kremlin grounds and cathedrals for rubles at the kiosk in the **Aleksandrovsky Sad** (Alexander Garden) outside the Kremlin walls. There is a two-tiered price system; foreigners pay significantly more than Russians. There are separate fees for seeing the Kremlin, each of its churches, the Armory Museum, and the Diamond Fund, and you pay accordingly, or tell the clerk that you want "fsye bil-YE-ti" (all tickets). Although you can purchase the Armory and Diamond Fund tickets inside as well, tickets to the cathedrals are only sold here, so be sure to get all the tickets you need now and save yourself the trip back. Also, for entrance to the **Armory and Diamond Fund,** foreigners must pay in hard currency, a rule that is strictly enforced. Beware of scalpers offering tickets to the Armory at reduced prices; they are usually invalid for foreigners. There are four tours daily, at 10, noon, 2:30, and 4:30. Join the line that forms outside the Armory entrance about 15 minutes before the tour. If you don't want to tackle all of this solo, you should consider a tour of the Kremlin grounds that includes the Armory, available from virtually any tour service that you prefer in Moscow. The Kremlin grounds and Cathedrals are open every day 10–6 except Thursday. The Armory and Diamond Fund are also closed on Thursday.

The tour can start at the **Aleksandrovsky Sad** subway stop itself, or you may begin from the **Teatralnaya** station, in order to visit a few sights on your way to the Kremlin gates. Emerging from the **Teatralnaya** stop, you will find yourself behind the red brick **History Museum** (*see* Tour 2). To its right are the Kremlin's battlemented walls. In some places 65 feet high and 10 to 20 feet thick, they have stood in their present form practically unchanged since the end of the 15th century. Walk to them, to the northernmost point of the Kremlin, the so-called **Sobakina (Arsenal) Tower,** the first of the Kremlin towers you will see. The Sobakina Tower, more than 180 feet high, was an important part of the Kremlin's defenses. Its thick walls concealed a secret well, which was of vital importance during times of siege.

Adjacent to the Sobakina Tower is the monumental, wrought-iron gate that marks the entrance to the **Aleksandrovsky Sad.** Laid out in the 19th century by the Russian architect Osip Bove, the garden stretches along the northwest wall of the Kremlin, where the Neglinnaya River once flowed. The river now runs beneath the garden, through an underground pipe. Just beyond the garden entrance, situated to your left against the Kremlin wall, is the **Tomb of the Unknown Soldier.** It was dedicated on May 9, 1967, the 22nd anniversary of the Russian victory over Germany. The body resting under the red granite slab is that of an unidentified Soviet soldier, one of those who, in the autumn of 1941, stopped the German attack at the village of Kryukovo, just outside Moscow. To the right of the grave there are six urns holding soil from the six "heroic cities" that so stubbornly resisted the German onslaught: Odessa, Sevastopol, Volgograd (Stalingrad), Kiev, Brest, and Leningrad (St. Petersburg). Very likely, no matter what time of year you are visiting, you'll see at least one wedding party. The young couple in full wedding regalia, along with friends and family, customarily stops here after getting married, leaving behind flowers and snapping photographs along the way. The gray obelisk just beyond the Tomb of the Unknown Soldier was erected in 1918 to commemorate the Marxist theoreticians who contributed to the Bolshevik Revolution. It was created out of an obelisk put up three years earlier, in honor of the 300th anniversary of the Romanov Dynasty. The arched "ruins" along the Kremlin wall, opposite the Obelisk, were designed by Osip Bove when he created the park. In the 19th century it was fashionable to include authentic-looking ruins in a landscaped park.

Looking up from the garden to the Kremlin walls, you see a large yellow building, the Arsenal. Begun in 1701 by Peter the Great, it was finished only at the end of the 18th century; its present form dates from the early 19th century, when it was reconstructed by Bove (the same architect who designed the Alexander Garden), after it was partially destroyed in the 1812 fire. The simple yet impressive two-floored building was originally commissioned by Peter the Great as a weapons arsenal; today it houses government offices.

Continuing along the garden's path, you reach a double bastion lined by a stone bridge on nine pillars. The white, outer bastion defended the approach to the bridge, which once functioned as a drawbridge over the Neglinnaya River. The outer tower is called **Kutafya,** which in Old Slavonic means "clumsy" or "confused," so called because it differs so in shape and size from the other towers of the Kremlin. The Kutafya Tower leads to the massive **Troitskaya Bashnya** (Trinity Tower), the tallest in the Kremlin wall. It rises 240 feet above the garden. Its deep, subterranean chambers were once used as prison cells. It is said that Napoleon lost his hat when he entered the Kremlin through this gate in 1812.

To reach Kutafya continue through the garden and walk beneath the bridge. Up to the right is the exit for the Alexandrovsky Sad subway stop, and further up, as you ascend around to the right toward the tower, you will find the kiosk where you purchase tickets to the Kremlin grounds and cathedrals. After you have your tickets, go back to the path and continue through the garden to its end at the western corner of the Kremlin. To your left a path leads up a steep incline to the pyramid-shaped **⑥ Borovitskaya Tower,** the main entrance to the Kremlin. It rises to more than 50 meters (150 feet). At its foot a gate pierces its thick walls, and you can still see the slits for the chains of the former drawbridge. Black Volgas carrying government employees to work go whizzing through the vehicular entrance. Uniformed security guards stand at the separate pedestrian entrance, which opens promptly at 10 AM every day except Thursday. Tourists are usually admitted a few, or a group, at a time. The guards may ask where you are from and check inside your bags; sometimes there is a small security checkpoint to walk through, similar to those at airports.

★ ⑦ The yellow building to your immediate left as you enter the Kremlin houses the **Oruzheynaya Palata** (Armory Palace), the oldest and richest museum in the Kremlin. It was originally founded in 1806 as the Imperial Court Museum, which was created out of three royal treasuries: the Court Treasury, where the regalia of the czars and ambassadorial gifts were kept; the Stable Treasury, which contained the royal harnesses and carriages used by the czars during state ceremonies; and the Armory, a collection of arms, armor, and other valuable objects gathered from the country's chief armories and storehouses. The Imperial Court Museum was moved to the present building in 1851. It was further enhanced and expanded after the Bolshevik Revolution with valuables confiscated and nationalized from wealthy noble families as well as from the Patriarchal Sacristy of the Moscow Kremlin. It now contains some 4,000 exhibits dating from the 12th century to 1917, including a rare collection of 17th-century silver. The museum tour begins on the second floor, which may cause some confusion if you visit the Armory on your own. Halls VI–IX are on the first floor, and Halls I–V are on the second floor.

Halls I and II display works of goldsmiths and silversmiths of the 12th through 19th centuries. Hall II contains a collection of 18th- to 20th-century jewelry. One of the most astounding exhibits is the collection of Fabergé eggs on display in Hall II (case 23). Among them is a silver egg whose surface is engraved with a map of the Trans-Siberian Railroad. The "surprise" inside the egg, which is also on display, was a golden clockwork model of a train with a platinum engine, windows of crystal, and a headlight made of a tiny ruby.

Hall III contains Oriental and Western European arms and armor, including heavy Western European suits of armor of the 15th to 17th century, pistols, and firearms.

Hall IV has a large collection of Russian arms and armor from the 12th to early 19th century, with a striking display of helmets. The earliest helmet here dates from the 13th century and is ascribed to Prince Yaroslav, father of Alexander Nevsky. Here, too, you will find the helmet of Prince Ivan, the son of Ivan the Terrible. The prince was killed by his father at the age of 28, an accidental victim of the czar's un-

14

Moscow

15

Tsentralny Muzey V.I. Lenina, **36**

Tserkov Bolshovo Vozneseniya, **51**

Tserkov Georgiya na Pskovskoy Gorke, **29**

Tserkov Nikoly v Khamovnikakh, **66**

Tserkov Simeona Stolpnika, **59**

Tserkov Troitsy v Nikitnikakh, **30**

Tserkov Velikomuchenitsy Varvary, **26**

Tserkov Voskreseniya, **39**

Tverskaya Ploshchad, **40**

Vakhtangov Theater, **58**

Yeliseyevksy's, **42**

Zaikonospassky Monastery, **23**

Znamensky Sobor, **27**

Zoological Museum, **48**

The Kremlin

predictable rage. The tragic event has been memorialized in a famous painting by Ilya Repin (now in the Tretyakov Gallery; *see* Tour 7, *below*) showing the frightened czar holding his mortally wounded son. Russian chain mail, battle-axes, maces, harquebuses, ceremonial armor, and Russian and Oriental sabers are also in this hall. A highlight of the collection is the large Greek quiver belonging to Czar Alexei, his Oriental saber, and a heavy golden mace presented to him by the Persian Shah Abbas. Among the sabers on display here are those of Kuzma Minin and Dmitry Pozharsky, the national heroes who led the battle to oust the Polish forces from Moscow during the Time of Troubles in the early 17th century. Later you will see their statue on Red Square.

Hall V is filled with foreign gold and silver objects, mostly ambassadorial presents to the czars. History buffs will be interested in the "Olympic Service" of china presented to Alexander I by Napoleon after the signing of the Treaty of Tilsit in 1807.

Hall VI has vestments of silk, velvet, and brocade, embroidered with gold and encrusted with jewels and pearls. They were once worn by the czars, patriarchs, and metropolitans.

Hall VII contains the regalia and the imperial thrones. The oldest throne, veneered with carved ivory, belonged to Ivan the Terrible. The throne of the first years of Peter the Great's reign, when he shared power with his older brother Ivan, has two seats in front and one hidden in the back. The boys' older sister Sophia, who ruled as regent from 1682 to 1689, sat in the back, prompting the young boys to give the right answers to the queries of ambassadors and others. Another throne, covered with thin plates of gold and studded with more than 2,000 precious stones and pearls, was presented to Czar Boris Godunov by Shah Abbas of Persia. The throne of Czar Alexei, also from Persia, is decorated with 876 diamonds and 1,223 other stones. Among the crowns, the oldest is the sable-trimmed Cap of Monomakh, which dates to the 13th century. Ukraine is now asking for it back, since it originally belonged to the Kievan prince Vladimir Monomakh. It was a gift to the prince from his grandfather, the Byzantine emperor, and is revered as a symbol of the transfer of religious power from Byzantium to Russia. Also on display in this section are several coronation dresses, including the one Catherine the Great wore at her coronation in 1762.

Hall VIII contains dress harnesses of the 16th through 18th centuries. On display are Russian saddles, including one used by Ivan the Terrible, and other items once belonging to the Moscow Kremlin Equestrian Department.

Hall IX has a marvelous collection of court carriages. The oldest one came from England and is believed to have been presented to Czar Boris Godunov by King James I. Here you will find the Winter Coach that carried Elizabeth Petrovna (daughter of Peter the Great and someone who clearly liked her carriages) from St. Petersburg to Moscow for her coronation. Catherine the Great's French carriage, painted by François Boucher, is arguably the most attractive of the collection.

★ The **Almazny Fond** (Diamond Fund) is located in the same building as the Armory. Admission is by its own separate ticket the highest priced of all of them, available at the entrance to the vaulted chambers. Again, joining a tour is recommended, if only because there are no signs, in any language, explaining the displays. This amazing collection of diamonds, jewelry, and precious minerals was established in 1922 by the young Soviet government. The items on display date from the 18th century to the present. Highlights of the collection are the Orlov Diamond, a present from Count Orlov to his mistress, Catherine the Great; and the Shah Diamond, which was given to Czar Nicholas I by the Shah of Persia as a sign of condolence after the assassination in 1829 of Alexander Griboyedov, the Russian ambassador to Persia and a well-known poet.

As you exit the Armory, you will see a courtyard to your left, closed off by a wrought-iron railing. The building on the right-hand side of the courtyard, adjoining the armory, is the **Bolshoi Kremlyovsky Dvorets** (Great Kremlin Palace). It actually consists of a group of buildings. The main section is the newest, built between 1838 and 1849. Its 375-foot-long facade faces south, overlooking the Moskva River. This was for centuries the site of the palace of the grand dukes and czars, but the immediate predecessor of the present building was badly damaged in the 1812 conflagration. For a few years it was the seat of the Russian parliament, which has now changed locations. It is not currently open to the general public.

The other buildings of the Great Kremlin Palace include the **Terem,** one of the oldest parts of the Kremlin, where the czarina received visitors, and the 15th-century **Granovitaya Palata** (Palace of Facets). Both buildings are also closed to the public, but a portion of the Granovitaya Palata's facade, whose diamond-shaped stone facings lend it its name, is visible from the Square of Cathedrals, our next stop in the Kremlin.

Continue up the path past the Great Kremlin Palace. A few steps bring you to the ancient center of the Kremlin, **Cathedral Square.** The paved square is framed by three large cathedrals in the old Russian style, the imposing Ivan Bell Tower, and the Granovitaya Palata. All of the cathedrals here are open to the public as museums.

To your immediate left as you enter the square is the **Blagoveshchensky Sobor** (Annunciation Cathedral), which was the private chapel of the royal family. This remarkable monument of Russian architecture links three centuries of art and religion. Its foundations were laid in the 14th century, and in the 15th century a triangular brick church in the early Moscow style was erected on this site. Partially destroyed by fire, it was rebuilt during the reign of Ivan the Terrible, when six new gilded cupolas were added. Czar Ivan would enter the church by the porch entrance on the southeast side, which was built especially for him. He was married three times too many (for a total of six wives) under the bylaws of the Orthodox religion and was therefore not allowed to enter the church through its main entrance. The interior is decorated by brilliant frescoes painted in 1508 by the Russian artist Feodosy. The polished tiles of agate jasper covering the floor were a gift from the Shah of Persia. Most striking of all is the chapel's iconostasis. The fine icons of the second and third tiers were painted by some of Russia's greatest masters—Andrei Rublyov, Theophanes the Greek, and Prokhor of Gorodets.

Standing opposite the Annunciation Cathedral, to your right as you enter the square, is the **Arkhangelsky Sobor** (Cathedral of the Archangel). This five-domed cathedral was commissioned by Ivan III (also known as Ivan the Great), whose reign witnessed much new construction in Moscow and in the Kremlin in particular. The cathedral was built in 1505–09 to replace an earlier church of the same name. The architect was the Italian Aleviso Novi, who came to Moscow at the invitation of Ivan III. You will notice distinct elements of the Italian Renaissance in the cathedral's ornate decoration, particularly in the scallop-shaped gables on its facade. Until 1712, when the Russian capital was moved to St. Petersburg, the cathedral was the burial place of the Russian princes and czars. Inside you will find 46 tombs, including that of Ivan Kalita (Ivan Moneybags), who was buried in the earlier cathedral in 1340. Ivan Moneybags, who earned his nickname because he was so good at collecting tribute, was the first Russian ruler to claim the title of grand prince. The tomb of Ivan the Terrible is hidden behind the altar; that of his young son Dmitry is under the stone canopy to your right as you enter the cathedral. Dmitry's death at the age of seven is one of the many unsolved mysteries in Russian history. He was the last descendent of Ivan the Terrible, and many believe he was murdered, since he posed a threat to the ill-fated Boris Godunov (who at the time ruled as regent). A government commission set up to investigate Dmitry's death concluded that he was playing with a knife and "accidentally" slit his own throat. The only czar to be buried here after 1712 was Peter II (Peter the Great's grandson), who died of smallpox while visiting Moscow in 1730.

The walls and pillars of the cathedral are covered in frescoes that tell the story of ancient Russian history. The original frescoes, painted right after the church was built, were repainted in the 17th century by a team of more than 50 leading artists from several Russian towns. Restoration work in the 1950s uncovered some of the original medieval frescoes, fragments of which can be seen in the altar area. The pillars are decorated with figures of warriors; Byzantine emperors; the early princes of Kievan Rus, Vladimir, and Novgorod; as well as the princes of Moscow, including Vasily III, the son of Ivan the Great. The frescoes on the walls depict religious scenes, including the deeds of Archangel Michael. The carved Baroque iconostasis is 13 meters (43 feet) high and dates from the 19th century. The icons themselves are mostly 17th-century, although the revered icon of Archangel Michael is believed to date back to the 14th century.

(14) The dominating structure of Cathedral Square is the massive **Uspensky Sobor** (Assumption Cathedral), bordering the north side (to your right as you exit the Cathedral of the Archangel). One of the oldest edifices of the Kremlin, it was designed after the Uspensky Sobor of Vladimir. It was built in 1475–79 by the Italian architect Aristotle Fiorovanti, who had spent many years in Russia studying traditional Russian architecture. Topped by five gilded domes, it is both austere and solemn. The ceremonial entrance faces Cathedral Square; the visitor's entrance is on the west side (to the left). After visiting the Archangel and Annunciation cathedrals, you will be struck by the spacious interior here, unusual for a medieval church. Light pours in through two rows of narrow windows. The cathedral contains rare ancient paintings, including the icon of the Virgin of Vladimir (the work of an 11th-century Byzantine artist), the 12th-century icon of St. George, and the 14th-century Trinity. The carved throne in the right-hand corner belonged to Ivan the Terrible, and the gilded wood throne to the far left was the seat of the czarina. Between the two is the patriarch's throne. Until the 1917 revolution, Uspensky Sobor was Russia's principal church. This is where the crowning ceremonies of the czars took place, a tradition that continued even after the capital was transferred to St. Petersburg. Patriarchs and metropolitans were enthroned and buried here. After the revolution the church was turned into a museum, but in 1989 religious services were resumed here on major church holidays.

(15) To the left of Uspensky Sobor is the smaller, single-domed **Tserkov Rizopolozheniya** (Church of the Deposition of the Virgin's Robe). It was built in 1484–86 by masters from Pskov. Once the private church of the Moscow patriarch, it was rebuilt several times and restored to its 15th-century appearance by Soviet experts in the 1950s. The building boasts brilliant frescoes dating from the mid-17th century covering all of its walls, pillars, and vaults. Its most precious treasure is the iconostasis by Nazary Istomin. On display inside the church is an exhibit of ancient Russian wooden sculpture from the Kremlin collection.

16 Cross the square to the eastern side, which is bordered by the **Kolokolnya Ivan Veliky** (Ivan the Great Bell Tower), the tallest building in the Kremlin. The octagonal main tower is 263 feet high—3 feet higher than the Hotel Rossia (on the opposite side of Red Square), in accordance with the tradition established by Boris Godunov that the bell tower remain the tallest building in Moscow. The first bell tower was erected on this site in 1329. It was replaced in the early 16th century, during the reign of Ivan the Great (hence the bell tower's name). But it was during the reign of Boris Godunov that the tower received its present appearance. In 1600, the main tower was rebuilt, crowned by an onion-shaped dome, and covered with gilded copper. For many years it served as a watchtower; Moscow and its environs could be observed within a radius of 32 kilometers (20 miles). Altogether, the towers have 52 bells, the largest weighing 70 tons. The annex of the bell tower is used for temporary exhibits of items from the Kremlin collection, tickets for which are purchased at the entrance.

Leave Cathedral Square by walking through the open space to the left of the bell tower. You will come out to the road where vehicular traffic passes; across the road are the working buildings of the Russian government. They are off-limits to the public, and uniformed policemen blow whistles at trespassers. To your immediate left is the huge Czar Cannon. It has the largest caliber of any gun in the world, but it has never fired a single shot. Cast in bronze in 1586 by Andrei Chokhov, it weighs 40 tons and is 17½ feet long. Its present carriage was cast in 1835, purely for display purposes.

Not far from the world's largest cannon is the world's largest bell. Like the cannon that was never shot, the Czar Bell was never rung. It is mounted on a stone pedestal at the foot of the Ivan the Great Bell Tower (on the opposite side, to your right). Commissioned in the 1730s, the bell was damaged when it was still in its cast. It weighs more than 200 tons and is 20 feet high. The bas-reliefs on the outside show Czar Alexei Mikhailovich and Czarina Anna Ivanovna.

17 Follow the path along the road leading to your left out of the Kremlin. The last of the buildings open to the public is the **Sobor Dvenadtsati Apostolov** (Cathedral of the Twelve Apostles) and the **Patriarshy Dvorets** (Patriarch's Residence), situated to the north of the Assumption Cathedral. The church was built in 1655–56 by Patriarch Nikon, who used it as his private church. Since 1963 the buildings have housed the Museum of 17th-Century Applied Art. The exhibits were taken from the surplus of the State Armory Museum and include books, tableware, clothing, and household linen.

18 Return to the road, bear left and return to the Kutafya Tower. As you exit, you will notice a rectangular structure of glass and aluminum on your left looking horribly out of place. This is the **Dvorets Syezdov** (State Kremlin Palace), built in 1962 to accommodate meetings of Communist Party delegates from across the Soviet Union. Today it is affiliated with the Bolshoi Theater and is used exclusively for concerts and ballets.

Turn right after passing through the Kutafya Tower and walk back down to the Alexander Garden. Retrace your steps through the garden past the Tomb of the Unknown Soldier. Turn right once again, following the wall of the Kremlin. World-famous for grand military parades during the Soviet era, **Krasnaya Ploshchad** (Red Square) was originally called the Torg, the Slavonic word for marketplace. You may think that the name "Red Square" has something to do with communism or the Bolshevik Revolution. In fact, however, the name dates back to the 17th century. The adjective *krasny* originally meant "beautiful," but over the centuries the meaning of the word changed to "red," hence the square's present name. The square is most beautiful at night. If you can, come back in the evening. It is both romantic and impressive when entirely illuminated by floodlights, its ruby-red stars atop the Kremlin towers glowing against the dark sky. There are five stars in all, one for each of the tallest towers. They made their appearance in 1937 to replace the double-headed eagle, a tsarist symbol that is again finding favor as an emblem of Russia. The glass stars, which are lighted from inside and designed to turn with the wind, are far from fragile: The smallest weighs 1 ton.

As you climb the slight incline leading up to Red Square, the multi-colored onion domes of **St. Basil's Cathedral** slowly come into view. Although it is popularly known as St. Basil's Cathedral, its proper name is the **Pokrovsky Sobor** (Church of the Intercession). It was commissioned by Ivan the Terrible to celebrate his conquest of the Tatar city of Kazan on October 1, 1552, the day of the feast of the Intercession. The central chapel, which rises 33 meters (107 feet), is surrounded by eight towerlike chapels linked by an elevated gallery. Each chapel is topped by an onion dome carved with its own distinct pattern and dedicated to a saint on whose day the Russian army won battles against the Tatars. The cathedral was built between 1555 and 1560 on the site of an earlier Trinity Church where the Holy Fool Vasily (Basil) had been buried in 1552. Basil was an adversary of the czar, publicly reprimanding Ivan the Terrible for his cruel and bloodthirsty ways. He was protected from the czar by his status as a Holy Fool, for he was considered by the Church to be an emissary of God. Ironically, Ivan the Terrible's greatest creation came to be known by the name of his greatest adversary. In 1558 an additional chapel was built in the northeast corner over Basil's remains, and from that time on the cathedral has been called St. Basil's.

Very little is known about the architect who built the cathedral. It may have been the work of two men—Barma and Postnik—but now it seems more likely that there was just one architect, Postnik Yakovlyev, who went by the nickname Barma. Legend has it that upon completion of the cathedral, the mad czar had the architect blinded to ensure he would never create such a masterpiece again.

After the Bolshevik Revolution, the cathedral was closed and in 1929 turned into a museum dedicated to the Russian conquest of Kazan. Although services are occasionally held here on church holidays, the museum is still open. The antechamber contains displays outlining the various stages of the Russian conquest of Kazan as well as examples of 16th-century Russian and Tatar weaponry. Another section details the history of the cathedral's construction, with displays of the building materials used. After viewing the museum exhibits, you are free to wander through the cathedral. Compared to the exotic exterior, the dark and simple interiors are a disappointment. The brick walls are decorated with faded flower frescoes. The most interesting chapel is the main chapel, which contains a 19th-century Baroque iconostasis. *Red Sq.,* ☎ *095/298–3304.* ⊙ *Wed.–Mon. 11–3:30. Closed 1st Mon. of month.*

The statue just outside St. Basil's originally stood in the center of the square. It depicts Kuzma Minin, a Nizhni-Novgorod butcher, and Prince Dmitry Pozharsky, who liberated Moscow in October 1612 from Polish-Lithuanian occupation. The work of Ivan Martos, it was erected in 1818, paid for by public subscription.

The strange, round, white-stone platform in front of the cathedral is the so-called **Lobnoye Mesto.** Its literal translation is "place of the forehead," but it has come to mean "execution site," for it was right next to the platform that public executions were carried out. The platform was built in 1534 and was used by the czars as a podium for public speeches. Imperial *ukazy* (decrees) were proclaimed from here, and when the heir apparent reached the age of 16, he was presented to the people from this platform.

To the left as you exit St. Basil's is the **Spassky Tower** (Tower of the Savior), which served as the main entrance to the Kremlin until Boris Yeltsin's presidency. Indeed, in the centuries before communist power, all who passed through it were required to doff their hat and bow before the icon of the Savior that hung on the front of the tower. The icon was removed, but you can see the outlines of where it was. The tower clock, installed in the last century, chimes a melody every 15 minutes that will become extremely familiar if you listen to Russian radio.

Opposite St. Basil's, at the north end of Red Square, stands the red-brick **Istorichesky Muzey** (Historical Museum), built in 1874–83 in the pseudo-Russian style, which combined a variety of architectural styles. You may remember the building's twin towers from watching Soviet military parades on television. Against the backdrop of the towers' pointed spires, the tanks and missiles rolling through Red Square seemed to acquire even more potency. The museum was closed in 1986 for restoration, and no date has been set for its reopening. Before it closed, its extensive archaeological and historical materials outlined the development of Russia as well as that of the peoples of the former Soviet Union. In typical Soviet fashion, the exhibits focused on the growing political unrest in prerevolutionary Russia, which culminated (naturally, according to Marx) in the Bolshevik Revolution. Much has changed since 1986, and when it finally opens again, the museum's exhibits may be altered to reflect the new Russian political order. The museum also contains a rich collection of Russian arms and weaponry. *1/2 Red Sq.,* ☎ *095/228–8452. Closed for restoration.*

On the west side of the square, running along the Kremlin wall, is the **Mavzolei Lenina** (Lenin Mausoleum). Inside, Lenin's embalmed body lies in state. Except for a brief interval during World War II, when his body was evacuated to the Urals, Lenin has been on view here since his death in 1924. Whether it is really Lenin or a wax look-alike is probably one of those Russian mysteries that will go down in history unanswered. From 1924 to 1930 there was a temporary wooden mausoleum, replaced by the pyramid-shaped mausoleum you will see now. It is made of red, black, and gray granite, with a strip of black granite near the top level symbolizing a belt of mourning. It was from the balcony of the mausoleum that Soviet leaders watched parades.

The Mausoleum is open on Tuesday, Wednesday, Thursday, and Saturday from 10 to 1, and on Sunday from 10 to 2. In the past, there were notoriously endless lines of people waiting to go in, but this is no longer the case. A visit to the mausoleum, however, is still treated as a serious affair. The surrounding area is cordoned off during visiting hours, and all those entering are observed by uniformed policemen. It is forbidden to carry a camera or any large bag. Inside it is cold and dark. It's considered disrespectful to put your hands inside your pockets (the same applies when you visit an Orthodox church), and the guards have been known to reprimand people for unbuttoned collars or sweaters. If you are inclined to linger at all, they will gently but firmly move you along. Before you know it you are ushered out of the mausoleum to the special burial grounds outside the mausoleum. When Stalin died in 1953, he was placed inside the mausoleum alongside Lenin, but in the early 1960s, during Khrushchev's tenure, the body was removed and buried here, some say encased in heavy concrete. Also here are such communist leaders as Zhdanov, Dzerzhinsky, Brezhnev, Chernenko, and Andropov, now mostly discredited. The American journalist John Reed is buried alongside the Kremlin wall. Urns set inside the wall contain ashes of the Soviet writer Maxim Gorky; Lenin's wife and collaborator, Nadezhda Krupskaya; Sergei Kirov, the Leningrad Party leader whose assassination in 1934 (believed to have been arranged for Stalin), was followed by enormous purges; the first Soviet cosmonaut, Yuri Gagarin; and other Soviet eminences.

The hourly changing of the guard outside Lenin's tomb, once a staggeringly formal event, has been eliminated. Local policemen, much more jocular in demeanor, have replaced the ramrod-stiff soldiers who once guarded the way into the tomb.

㉒ Red Square is bordered on the east side by the long facade of **GUM** (pronounced "goom"), short for *Gosudarstvenny Universalny Magazin* or State Department Store. Formerly called the Upper Trading Rows, it was built in 1889–93 on the site where rows of trading stalls once stood. Three long passages with three stories of shops run the length of the building. Each passage is covered with a glass roof, and there are balconies and bridges on the second and third tiers. Another series of passages runs perpendicular to the three main lines, creating a mazelike mall. In feel, it resembles a cavernous turn-of-the-century European train station. There are shops aplenty here now, Western and Russian, and you may enjoy a saunter down at least one of its halls. *3 Red Sq.* ☉ *Mon.–Sat. 8–8, Sun. 10–6.*

Tour 2: Kitai Gorod

★ This tour explores the twisting and winding streets of **Kitai Gorod,** the oldest section of Moscow outside the Kremlin. The literal translation of Kitai Gorod is Chinatown, but there has never been a Chinese settlement here. The origin of the word *kitai* is disputed; it may come from the Tatar word for fortress, but most likely it derives from the Russian word *kita,* in reference to the bundles of twigs that were used to reinforce the earthen wall that once surrounded the area.

Kitai Gorod begins where Red Square ends. Settlement of this area began in the 12th century, around the time that the fortified city of Moscow was founded on Borovitsky Hill (the site of the present-day Kremlin). By the 14th century Kitai Gorod was a thriving trade district, full of shops and markets. At that time it was surrounded by earthen ramparts, which were replaced in the 16th century by a fortified wall. Remnants of that wall remain, and we will pass them later. As Moscow grew, so did Kitai Gorod. At the time of the Bolshevik Revolution it was the city's most important financial and commercial district, with major banks, warehouses, and trading companies concentrated here. These days, with the multitude of shops and new banks springing up throughout it, the area seems intent on inventing itself all over again.

A good starting point for your tour is Nikolskaya ulitsa, which begins at the corner opposite the Historical Museum and runs along the north side of GUM. If you are coming from St. Basil's, walk down to the opposite side of Red Square. If you are coming from outside of Red Square, enter through the passageway to the right of the Teatralnaya subway station (as you are facing it). It is crowded, easily spotted, and is lined with the now ubiquitous *babushki* selling their wares. You can haggle over anything from lingerie to perfume to loaves of bread; unfortunately, their numbers testify to the ugly side of today's new freedom to trade, which in their case is not a matter of freedom but of survival. Taking a right out of the passageway, you will find yourself on Nikolskaya ulitsa. Go a short way farther, to the cobblestone edge of Red Square, to begin your walk.

TIME OUT Before you begin your tour of Kitai Gorod, you may want to take a break at the **Ogni Moskvy** (Lights of Moscow) café on the top floor of the Moskva Hotel (the concrete structure dominating Manezhnaya Square). It can be a trick to find. Enter the hotel by the side entrance across from the Lenin Museum, and take the elevator to the 15th floor. To reach the café, you will need to walk the length of the balcony overlooking Manezhnaya Square. From here you get a bird's-eye view of the Kremlin to the south. To the north, a panoramic view of the entire city opens up. On a clear day you can see all the way to Sparrow Hills, topped by the wedding-cake skyscraper of Moscow University. The food is only average, but with views like these, you won't care. *7 Okhotny Ryad.* ☺ *Daily for lunch 11–4.*

Named after the Kremlin's Nikolskaya Gate Tower, Nikolskaya ulitsa is one of the oldest streets in Moscow. For three centuries the corner with Red Square, between the Historical Museum and GUM, has been marked by the **Kazansky Sobor** (known in Russian as the Cathedral of Our Lady of Kazan). It was built in 1633–36 to commemorate Russia's liberation from Polish occupation during the Time of Troubles. The cathedral was purposely blown up in 1936 and was not rebuilt and fully restored until 1993. With its salmon-and-cream painted brick and gleaming gold cupolas, it forms a freshly pretty corner on the ever-imposing Red Square. Inside and outside hang icons of Our Lady of Kazan, and the small chapel affords an excellent look at the traditional iconostasis and inner design of Russian churches. In the front vestibule, you may buy candles to light a prayer, and you will find other religious articles for sale. Although it is not required, women may feel more comfortable if they are wearing skirts or dresses and have a head covering; many faithful visit throughout the day, and the women are invariably dressed this way. ☺ *Daily 8–7, except Mon., when closing is at service.*

Leaving the church, take a left to make your way through the teeming crowds of shoppers on Nikolskaya ulitsa to No. 7 (on the left-hand side as you walk away from Red Square), the former Slavonic-Greco-Latin Academy. It was opened in the **Zaikonospassky (Behind-the-Icons) Monastery** in 1687 and was Russia's first institution of higher learning. The monastery itself was founded at the beginning of the 17th century by Boris Godunov. Hidden inside the courtyard between buildings No. 7 and No. 8 is the monastery's surviving cathedral, built in 1717–42 in the style of Moscow Baroque. It is currently under *"remont."* (Most visitors to Russia will find this word swiftly becoming indispensable. It means "repair" and identifies reconstruction that is likely to take a very long time.) However, a Sunday service is still held here, and on other days—if you are inclined to cough up a bit of a "contribution"—you may be allowed a quick peek inside.

Farther down the street, also on the left-hand side, is a once brightly painted white-and-aqua building with an elaborate facade (No. 15). The building was erected in 1810–14 on the site of the 16th-century Pechatny Dvor (Printing Yard), where Russia's first printed book was assembled in 1553. The white-stone facade is covered with intricate carvings. Look for the lion and unicorn, the coat-of-arms of the Royal Printing Yard. Today the building is home to the Moscow Institute of Historical Records.

Back just past No. 13 is a local "Byterbrodnaya" (sandwich shop). If you've started your tour near lunchtime or want a quick snack, get in line and order some stuffed blini, sausage rolls, or a plate of steaming *pelmeni* (Siberian ravioli). You eat standing up at the well-worn tables.

Cross the street from the snack shop to go down Kuibyshevsky Pereulok. Halfway down the block, opposite the entrance to the Ploshchad Revolutsii subway, is the **Bogoyavlensky Sobor** (Cathedral of the Epiphany Monastery), founded by Prince Danil of Moscow in the 13th century. The church is much newer than the monastery it was built to serve, erected only in the late 17th century. It is missing its steeple, which gives it the sad look of a tree stub. It, too, is under *remont.*

Continue down the street to where it intersects with Ilinka ulitsa. Before the 1917 revolution, this was Moscow's Wall Street. It is lined with the impressive facades of former banks. On the left-hand corner is the former Ryabushinsky Bank. This art-nouveau masterpiece was designed by Fyodor Shekhtel at the turn of the century for the rich merchant Ryabushinsky. The pale-orange building on the opposite side of the street is the former Birzha (Stock Exchange). Built in the classical style at the end of the 19th century, it now houses Russia's Chamber of Commerce and Industry. As you cross the street, look to your right; Ilinka ulitsa leads directly to the Kremlin's Savior Gate Tower. As you cross the street, watch out for black Volgas and limousines whizzing by—this is the favored route to the office of the president and his colleagues.

Continuing straight, you enter Rybny Pereulok (Fish Lane). Most of the block of Fish Lane is taken up by the twin buildings of the **Gostinny Dvor** (Merchants' Arcade). To your right is the Old Merchant Arcade, originally designed by the Italian architect Quarenghi in 1791–1805; to your left is the New Merchant Arcade, built in 1838–40 on the site of the old fish market.

Walk the length of the buildings, and you come out onto Razina ulitsa, now known again as **Varvarka ulitsa** (Barbara Street), one of Moscow's oldest. The opposite side of the street is lined with quaint old churches and buildings, but the first thing you notice is the gray bulk of the massive Rossia Hotel, dominating the area. With accommodation for 6,000, the Rossia is one of Europe's largest hotels. Russians often joke that the Soviets chose this site for the hotel because foreign tourists wouldn't ever have to leave their room: Varvarka, with its rich mixture of architecture, was all they would ever need to see.

The street takes its name from the **Tserkov Velikomuchenitsy Varvary** (St. Barbara's Church), which is located at the farthest corner, to your right. If you want a close-up of the entire row of buildings, walk all the way down to it and cross the street (carefully! limos whiz by here, too). Next to pink-and-white St. Barbara's stands the **Old English Court,** a white-stone building with a steep shingled roof and narrow windows. Built in the mid-16th century, it became known as the English House because Ivan the Terrible—wanting to encourage foreign trade—presented it to English merchants trading in Moscow. It was reopened as a museum in late 1995, after serious restoration, and its displays about the centuries of Russian-British trade relations may be particularly interesting to U.K. visitors. ⊙ *Tues., Thurs., and week-ends 10–6; Wed. and Fri. 11–7.*

Next comes the white-stone **Tserkov Maksima Blazhennovo** (Church of St. Maxim the Blessed), built in 1698 on the site where the Holy Fool Maxim was buried. Today it contains a folk-art exhibit of wood carvings, embroidery, and other handicrafts. All the art work is for sale. ☎ *095/298–1312.* ⊙ *Daily 11–6.*

The pointed bell tower situated just before the semicircle sidewalk leading to the upper-level entrance to the Rossia Hotel was once attached
➋ to the redbrick **Znamensky Sobor** (Cathedral of the Sign) on the other side of the sidewalk; with its foundation on the slope below, it is set back from the street. The **Znamensky Sobor** was part of the monastery of the same name, built on the estate of the Romanovs in the 16th century, right after the establishment of the Romanov dynasty. After the death of the last heir to Ivan the Terrible, a dark period set in, marked by internal strife and foreign intervention. That period, commonly known as the Time of Troubles, ended in 1613, when the Boyar Council elected the young Mikhail Romanov czar. It is believed that Mikhail Romanov was born in the house at No. 10. Today the mansion houses
➋ a lovely museum called the **Palace of the 16th and 17th centuries in Zaryadye.** The museum, which reopened in 1991 after extensive renovations, is devoted to the *boyar* (nobleman) lifestyle of the 16th and 17th centuries. The rooms are furnished to show how the boyars lived, with period clothing, furniture, and household items on display. During the week, the museum is generally open only to groups with advance reservations, but if you ask, you may be allowed to join a group. On Sunday the museum is open to the general public. Once again, tourists can visit only in groups, but after a short wait, enough people will gather to form a tour. You'll find the entrance downstairs, opposite the lower doorway of the hotel. *10 ul. Varvarka,* ☎ *095/298–3706.* ⊙ *Mon., Thurs.–Sun. 10–6; Wed. 11–5.*

Before leaving this street of museums and churches, take note of the
➋ last one, the blue **Tserkov Georgiya na Pskovskoy Gorke** (Church of St. George on Pskov Hill) at No. 12. The five-domed church, built in 1657, stands right next to the Romanov Mansion. If you stand to the left of the church (on the walkway leading to the Rossia Hotel) you can glimpse a remnant of the 16th-century brick fortification wall mentioned earlier. It is to your left, opposite the hotel's eastern facade. Return now to Varvarka ulitsa and cross to the other side, going a short hop past the final church. With your back to the Kremlin, take a left and climb the narrow Ipatevsky Pereulok, which will lead up to a number of governmental and administrative buildings. At the top of the incline to the right, you will find one of Moscow's best-preserved
➌ 17th-century churches, the **Tserkov Troitsy v Nikitnikach** (Church of the Trinity in Nikitniki). It is a lovely redbrick creation that mixes Baroque decoration with the principles of ancient Russian church architecture. Painted with white trim and topped by five green cupolas, the church was built in 1635–53 for the merchant Grigory Nikitnikov. The private chapel on the south side was the family vault. The

murals and iconostasis were the work of Simon Ushakov, a famous icon
painter whose workshop was located nearby, in the brick building across
the courtyard. The church is open as a museum of 17th-century architecture. *3 Staraya Nikitnikov Ploshchad Pereulok,* ☎ *095/298–5018.*
⊘ *Fri.–Mon. 10–5; Wed., Thurs. noon–7.*

As you exit the church, turn left and walk down to the end of the lane
to come out onto **Novaya Ploshchad** (New Square), which is more like
a boulevard than a square. To your right, at the far bottom of the hill,
Slavyanskaya Ploshchad (Slavic Square) opens up. Until only recently
known as Ploshchad Nogina, the area was almost completely rebuilt
during the Soviet era. A survivor of the reconstruction was the redbrick church at the bottom of the hill, the Church of All-Saints in Kulishki. This is also an example of 17th-century church architecture, but
it has not been as well maintained as the Trinity Church. It was recently returned to the Orthodox Church and is now open for services
(10 AM and 5 PM).

From Novaya Ploshchad, stroll for a long block or two past the governmental buildings, where the Central Committee of the Communist
Party once sat. Now they house the Duma of the Moscow Region. Soon
you will come to the beginning of a busy intersection.

To your right, in the median strip that divides Novaya Ploshchad, is a
park that holds the Plevna Memorial, an octagonal, towerlike monument commemorating the Russian soldiers who fell in the Battle of Plevna
in the Russo-Turkish War (1878). The monument was erected in 1887.

❸① Keep walking up the street on the left side to go to the **Museum of the
History of Moscow,** housed in the former **Church of St. John the Baptist**
(1825). The museum was founded in 1896 and outlines Moscow's architectural history using paintings and artifacts to show the various stages
of development. It is a small museum, and it is worth stopping in for a
view of the Moscow you have been trying to imagine as you explore
the city's oldest parts. *12 Novaya Ploshchad,* ☎ *095/924–8490.* ⊘ *Tues.,
Thurs., weekends 10–6; Wed., Fri. 11–7. Closed last day of month.*

Before you reach it, you will notice a building on the opposite side of
the street that takes up the entire block. This is the **Polytechnical Museum.** The museum was opened in 1872 (it was originally called the
Museum of Applied Knowledge) and today houses exhibits devoted
to achievements in science and technology. *3/4 Novaya Ploshchad,* ☎
095/923–0756. ⊘ *Tues.–Sun. 10–6. Closed last Thurs. of month.*

❸② A short distance from the Polytechnical Museum, Novaya Ploshchad
intersects with the circular **Lubyanskaya Ploshchad,** which was recently
returned to its prerevolutionary name. In 1926 it had been renamed
Dzerzhinsky Square, in honor of Felix Dzerzhinsky, a Soviet revolutionary and founder of the infamous CHEKA, the KGB's forerunner.
His statue once stood in the center of the square, but was toppled in
the aftermath of the failed August 1991 coup. A huge, round flower
bed, planted in spring, has replaced it. The large yellow building facing the square, with bars on the ground-floor windows, is the notorious Lubyanka Prison and KGB headquarters.

The department store on the west side of the square is **Detsky Mir** (Children's World), which used to specialize exclusively in toys and clothing for children. With the new economic reform legislation, the strict
rules governing merchandise and trade have been broken. As a result
you can find just about anything in Detsky Mir today—anything but
children's merchandise, that is!

Still bearing left, walk past Lubyanka Square to the west side, down to where it converges with the broad street of **Teatralny Proyezd** (Theater Passage). In a side street to your right stands the recently refurbished Savoy Hotel (3 ul. Rozhdestvenka), built in connection with the celebrations honoring 300 years of the Romanov Dynasty. On the left-hand side of the street you will pass a statue of Ivan Fyodorov, the printer who produced Russia's first book at the Old Printing House we passed earlier on Nikolskaya Street. The arched gateway just beyond the statue links Teatralny Proyezd with Nikolskaya Street in Kitai Gorod, the street on which you started the tour. Staying on Theater Passage leads into Theater Square, where three of Moscow's most important theaters are located.

㉝ The first building you will encounter, taking up the block on the south-east corner, to your left as you enter Theater Square, is the **Metropol Hotel.** It was reconstructed in the late 1980s, and its brilliant art-nouveau facade has been restored to its original appearance. Like the Savoy, it was built in the early 20th century in preparation for the anniversary celebrations commemorating 300 years of the Romanov dynasty. It has been the venue of many a historical speech, including many by Lenin. The hotel was the focus of heavy fighting during the revolution, and for some time the Central Committee of the Russian Soviet Federal Republic met here under its first chairman, Yakov Sverdlov. Until 1990, Theater Square was named Sverdlov Square, in his honor.

Reaching the square, you will see at the center a large monument to Karl Marx, carved on the spot from a 200-ton block of granite and unveiled in 1961. Slabs around it carry various inscriptions, including the ever-famous "Workers of the world, unite!" Across the boulevard ★ ㉞ opposite, stands the **Bolshoi (Big) Theater,** the oldest in Moscow. Formerly known as the Great Imperial Theater, it was completely rebuilt after a fire in 1854 and now seats 2,155 people. Its opera and ballet companies are world-famous. The building is remarkable architecturally, with its monumental colonnade topped by a quadriga of bronze horses pulling the chariot of Apollo, patron god of music. Its crimson-and-gold interior is similarly grand. If you have the pleasure of seeing a performance at the Bolshoi, don't miss the stage curtain when it is lowered. It falls resplendent, in a thick weave of hammers and sickles. It was also at the Bolshoi that Lenin made his last public speech, in 1922. *Teatralnaya Ploshchad,* ☎ *095/292–9986.*

The Bolshoi Theater is flanked by two more theaters. To the left, on the corner farthest away from you, is the **Central Children's Theater.** ㉟ To the right is the **Maly (Little) Theater,** with the statue of the Russian satirist Alexander Ostrovsky in front of it. The Maly, formerly known as the Little Imperial Theater, is famous for its staging of Russian classics, especially those of Ostrovsky. Opened in 1824, it was once called by Gorky "the Russian people's university." *1/6 Teatralnaya Ploshchad,* ☎ *095/923–2621.*

TIME OUT The small lobby bar at the Savoy Hotel (3 ul. Rozhdestvenka) is a favorite spot with Moscow's foreign community. Join them in its gilded interiors for a spicy-hot bowl of French onion soup or a club sandwich. The hotel also has a famous—and very expensive—restaurant. The bar menu, while by no means cheap, is more reasonably priced. The service is professional, and it's a great place to take a break after fighting the crowds of downtown Moscow.

Having turned left at the corner, walk by the park and the hotel's main entrance. The fragmented brick wall ahead is the other surviving remnant of the 16th-century fortification wall that once surrounded Kitai Gorod. When you reach the Teatralnaya subway station, you may want to make one last stop. The redbrick building on the corner was the Lenin Museum.

36 The **Tsentralny Muzey V. I. Lenina** (Central Lenin Museum) is now closed. After 1991, it ceased receiving funding, and the future of its holdings is undecided. Also unclear is who will take over residence. Quite possibly it will again house a branch of the government of the city of Moscow, whose property it was before the revolution. When open, the museum's 22 halls contained several thousand exhibits, covering virtually every moment in the revolutionary leader's political career. Among them were Lenin's personal belongings—his desk (with secret drawers), a coat with bullet holes (the one he was wearing during an attempted assassination), and his car. *Ploshchad Revolyutsii 2, closed.*

Tour 3: Up Tverskaya Ulitsa

Tverskaya Street is a Russian rendition of New York's Fifth Avenue. As the main shopping artery, it attracts out-of-towners searching hungrily for a good buy, as well as the foreign investor looking for a lucrative place to set up shop. The street is lined with massive apartment buildings whose ground floors house some of the city's best and biggest stores. In recent years, many of the old state-run enterprises have been ousted and replaced with neon-lit private and foreign ventures dealing in credit cards and pricey goods. A stroll up Tverskaya these days promises window-shopping of a very fancy order and a look at some of Moscow's attractive buildings, several graced by a fine Art Nouveau style. It is a lovely, wide boulevard lined with perfumeries, banks and exchanges, eateries, and bookshops. On a sunny day, it is an especially pleasant walk. Keep an eye out for plaques etched in stone on building walls. These will tell you about the famous people, usually artists, politicians, or academicians, who lived or worked there.

There are several metro stops along Tverskaya ulitsa; we will start at the bottom of the street, at the Okhotny Ryad (Hunter's Row) station. If you exit so that you emerge on Ulitsa Pushkinskaya, go right one block. Hotel Moskva and, a bit farther, the edge of Red Square will be on your left. On your right, you'll pass the building that currently houses the Russian Federation's Duma (Parliament). Reaching Tverskaya, which is the next street (running parallel), you'll see the National Hotel on the corner. In final renovations for years, it was, in its day, considered the height of elegance. Just reopened in 1995, it appears to have been restored to its former glory—and perhaps beyond. Next up the street, once joined to the National, stands the fading skyscraper of the Intourist Hotel. In front, it now sports a glass-enclosed section that is a branch of Patio Pizza (the original is across from the Pushkin Fine Arts Museum). Here you can relax for lunch of pizza, sandwiches, salad bar, soft drinks, and beer, while you watch the tourists go by.

Tverskaya Street was given its present form in the mid '30s, during the first plan of reconstruction, though it had been an important route for centuries—the line of the road that led from the Kremlin to the ancient town of Tver. Later that road was extended all the way to the new capital on the Baltic Sea, St. Petersburg. From 1932 to 1990 Tverskaya was known as Gorky Street, in honor of the writer Maxim Gorky, the father of Soviet socialist realism. In 1990, the first section of the street, leading from the heart of town to Triumfalnaya Square, was given back its prerevolutionary name. The renaming was completed a year later, when the second section, ending at the Belorussian Railway Station, was also returned to its old name—Tverskaya Yamskaya. Until the rebuilding in the 1930s, Tverskaya Street was narrow and twisting, lined in places with wooden houses. Today it is a broad, busy avenue, a tribute to the grandiose reconstruction projects of the Stalinist era.

Walking up the left-hand side of the street, you pass, at No. 5, a short building with an arched entrance. This is the **Yermolova Theater,** founded in 1937 and named after a famous Russian actress. One short block
37 farther, on the same side of the street, you come to the **Central Telegraph Office,** whose striking semicircular entrance is adorned with a large, il-luminated, and constantly revolving globe. Inside, you can buy stamps, send a fax home, or even make a phone call abroad. You will find cur-rency-exchange counters in the lobby and the main post office as well.

On the opposite side of the avenue, **Kamergersky Pereulok** leads off to the right. The small green building on the left-hand side of this street
38 houses the **Moscow Art Theater** (MKhAT), famous for its productions of the Russian classics, especially those of Chekhov. Founded in 1898 by the celebrated actor and director Konstantin Stanislavsky (1863–1938) and Vladimir Nemirovich-Danchenko (1858–1943), the theater staged the first productions of Chekhov's and Gorky's plays. It was here that Stanislavsky developed his theories into the "Stanislavsky Method," based on the realistic traditions of the Russian theater. After the successful production of Chekhov's *Seagull* (the first rendition bombed in St. Petersburg), this bird was chosen as their emblem. (An affiliated, modern Moscow Art Theater with a seating capacity of 2,000 was opened in 1972 on Tverskoy Boulevard, near Stanislavsky's home). *Kamergrersky Pereulok 3,* ☎ *095/299–8760 or 095/290–5128.* Take a short walk up this block to have a look at the theater. If you're interested in antiquarian bookshops, you'll find some here.

Returning to Tverskaya, continue up on the left-hand side of the street. The next block is taken up by two large apartment buildings whose lower facade is lined with granite. They were built right after the war, in 1947–50. There is a great story of revenge here. The granite was supposed to have been used to build a Nazi victory monument—it had been brought to Moscow by Nazi troops at the height of the Siege of Moscow, when a German victory seemed imminent.

If you want to take a break from the hustle and bustle of Tverskaya, wander down ulitsa Nezhdanovoi, a side street to the left. You enter the street through the arched passageway of building No. 11, which is the Russian Federation of Science and Technology. This street has long been home to many of Moscow's successful artists. At the end of
39 the block, you come upon the pretty **Tserkov Voskreseniya** (Church of the Resurrection), one of the few lucky churches to have stayed open throughout the years of Soviet rule. As a survivor, the church was the recipient of many priceless icons from less fortunate churches de-stroyed or closed by the Soviets. Services are still held here daily. *Yeliseyevsky Pereulok,* ☎ *095/229–6616.*

Go back to Tverskaya ulitsa. The handsome red building just ahead with its impressive iron gates to its adjacent side street, is the Moscow City Council (Mossoviet). It was built at the end of the 18th century by Matvey Kazakov for the Moscow governor-general. During the re-construction of Tverskaya Street in the 1930s, the building was moved back 14 meters in order to widen the street. The top two stories—a mirror image of the mansion's original two stories—were added at that time. Across the street, another short stretch brings you to the small
40 **Tverskaya Ploshchad** (Square). In the small park to your right stands

a statue of Prince Yuri Dolgoruky, the founder of Moscow in 1147. The equestrian statue was erected in 1954, shortly after the celebrations marking Moscow's 800th anniversary.

TIME OUT Of all the foreign-run joint ventures in Moscow, **Pizza Hut** takes the prize for having most successfully re-created the atmosphere of a Western franchise. Step inside and in an instant you are back on the other side of the ocean. The decor is amazing, if only because it is just like that of any other Pizza Hut. The pizza is good, but the salad bar is a disappointment—lots of coleslaw but no lettuce. Service is swift and pleasant. This is the perfect place for a quick snack and a well-earned break from Russian reality. *Ul. Tverskaya 12, ☎ 095/229-2013. Cash or credit cards.*

Farther up the street, again on the left-hand side, you pass ulitsa Stanislavskovo, named for the theater director Konstantin Stanislavsky, whose Moscow Art Theater we passed earlier. Stanislavsky lived for a
④ time in the building at No. 6. Close by, at No. 7, is the **Russian Folk Art Museum,** founded by a wealthy merchant and patron of the arts, Savva Morozov. It displays a rich collection of Russian folk art dating from the 17th century to the present, including antique and modern pottery, ceramics, glassware, metalwork, wood, bone, embroideries, lace, and popular prints. *ul. Stanislavskovo 7, ☎ 095/291–8718, ◎ Mon., Wed., Fri.–Sun. 11–5:30; Tues., Thurs. noon–7:30.*

Of all the stores and boutiques on Tverskaya Street, you'll find the most dazzling interior in the grocery store at No. 14, just beyond Stanislavskovo but on the right-hand side of the street. Under communist administration, the store had the official, generic title Gastronome No. 1, but it once again carries what most people continued to call it even
④ then—**Yeliseyevsky's,** after the rich merchant from St. Petersburg who owned the store before the revolution. The interior sparkles with chandeliers, stained glass, and gilded wall decorations. Products abound. It's here that you'll find loads of good cognac and Georgian wine (including Stalin's favorite Khvanchkava—still much touted even with its unsavory stamp of approval). They also have coffee beans, and in the back room are Russian chocolate and candy of all sorts.

Back outside you're likely to encounter lots of construction (destined, it would seem, to go on for years), as you head further up the street, toward the plaza named after the revered poet and writer Alexander Pushkin.

④ **Pushkinskaya Ploshchad** (Pushkin Square), where Moscow's first outer ring, the Bulvar (Boulevard), crosses Tverskaya ulitsa, is the site of the city's first McDonald's (opened in 1990). If you're longing for that familiar burger, stop for lunch. There are rarely lines anymore (branches have opened throughout the city), but you'll quickly see how popular it remains. The counters are always crowded, with disorganized but swiftly moving lines. The menu hews to the original, and prices are cheaper than in the States. Russians come by the score but don't dawdle—they take the term "fast food" literally! The park on the right-hand side of the street is a popular meeting place for Muscovites. A fountain stands in the center of a terraced park, which is lined with benches. A bronze statue of Pushkin stands at the top of the park. It is the work of Alexander Opekushin and was erected by public subscription in 1880. Summer and winter, fresh flowers on the pedestal prove that the poet's admirers are still ardent and numerous.

The **Rossia Movie Theater,** bordering the west side of Pushkin Square, was built in 1961. It stands on the site of the former Strastnoi Monastery (Convent of the Lord's Passion), whose history dated back to the mid-17th century; it was destroyed in 1937. All that remains of the ancient monastery is the white-stone Church of the Nativity near the corner with ulitsa Chekhova (to the far left as you face the theater).

Bordering the square to the right and left of the park are the offices of some of Russia's largest and most influential newspapers. Easily spotted is *Izvestia* (*News*), once the mouthpiece of the Soviet government and now considered a liberal newspaper. Between 18 and 20 Tverskaya, if you look down the alley, you'll see the striking facade of *Trud* (*Labor*), the official newspaper of the trade unions and of late a conservative voice. Looking back to the far corner that you came from, you'll see the building of *Moscow News,* the newspaper that helped give *glasnost* true meaning back in the early years of *perestroika.* Its brave editor allowed articles on topics then considered extremely controversial, from Stalinist collectivization to the ethnic strife in Armenia and Azerbaijan.

Continuing along Tverskaya ulitsa, you reach the attractive railings of
44 the former **English Club,** once the social center of the Moscow aristocracy. It stands on the left-hand side of the street, and its entrance is flanked by two smirking lions. Built by Giliardi in 1787, the mansion was rebuilt in the classical style after the Moscow Fire of 1812. Since 1926, it has housed the Museum of the Revolution. Although it retains many of its former exhibits—heavily imbued with Soviet propaganda—the museum has been updated to reflect the changing political situation in Russia. The permanent exhibit, located on the second floor, begins with a review of the first workers' organizations in the 19th century. The exhibits outlining the 1905 and 1917 revolutions include the horse-drawn machine-gun cart of the First Cavalry Army, the texts of the first decrees of the Soviet government on peace and land, dioramas and paintings portraying revolutionary battles, and thousands of other relics. The next rooms outline the history of Soviet rule, with extensive material devoted to Stalin's rise to power. The final exhibit is dedicated to the August 1991 coup. It features a reconstructed version of the barricades set up outside the Russian Parliamentary Building, where Yeltsin made his famous appeals to the Russian people. Explanations of the exhibits are only in Russian, but you can arrange for a guided tour in English by calling ahead. The entrance fee is low, even though foreigners pay more than Russians. You will also find interesting temporary exhibits on the first floor of the museum. Snoop through their gift shop which, features standard Russian souvenirs (including some beautiful amber) and great vintage items like flags and political-rally posters. *Ul. Tverskaya 21,* ☎ *095/299–6724.* ☉ *Tues., Thurs.–Sat. 10–6; Wed. 11–7; Sun. 10–5. Closed last Fri. of month.*

As you continue in the same direction, you'll pass the Moscow Drama Theatre, another bearing the name of Stanislavsky. The next major
45 intersection is **Triumfalnaya Ploshchad,** where the grand boulevard of Moscow, the Sadovaya (Garden) Ring, crosses Tverskaya Street. Traffic here also passes through a tunnel running below Tverskaya Street, and there is an underpass for pedestrians. A statue of the revolutionary poet Vladimir Mayakovsky stands in the center of the square. It is generally believed that Mayakovsky committed suicide in 1930 out of disillusionment with the revolution he had so passionately supported.

Triumfalnaya Ploshchad is a center of Moscow's cultural life. The Tchaikovsky Concert Hall stands on the corner nearest you. It was opened in 1940 and seats 1,600. The Satire Theater is right next door, on the Sadovaya Ring. On the far side of the square stands the Moskva Cinema; the popular Mossoviet Theater is also located nearby, at 16 Bolshaya Sadovaya. To your far left you see the multitiered tower of the imposing Peking Hotel. Opened in 1956 as a mark of Sino-Soviet friendship, it houses one of the city's best Chinese restaurants. Looking to your right, you'll see the American Bar and Grill, popular with Russians as well as the foreign community.

While you're here, it's worth riding the escalator down for a peek at the spectacular interior of the Mayakovskaya subway station. Its ceiling is decorated with colorful, fluorescent mosaics depicting Soviet achievements in outer space. Like many of the early subway stations, it is deep underground and doubled as a bomb shelter during World War II. Stalin made a famous speech here on the 24th anniversary of the Bolshevik Revolution, at the height of the Siege of Moscow.

On the north side of Triumfalnaya Ploshchad, Tverskaya ulitsa becomes **Tverskaya-Yamskaya Street.** This last section of the street has been the object of serious reconstruction in the past few years, and there is little of historical interest along this stretch. The street ends at the Belorussky Vokzal (Belorussian Railway Station), which has two interconnecting subway stations. A statue of Maxim Gorky, erected in the 1950s, stands in a small park outside the station. It is located near the site of the former Triumphal Gates, built in the 19th century by the architect Osip Bove to commemorate the Russian victory in the war with Napoleon. The gates were demolished in a typical fit of destruction in the 1930s. Fragments can be found on the grounds of the Donskoy Monastery (*see* Off the Beaten Track, *below*). A replica of the original gates was erected in 1968 near Poklonnaya Hill, at the end of Kutuzovsky Prospect.

Tour 4: The Old Moscow of Herzen Street

Ulitsa Gertsena (Herzen Street) is one of the many old streets radiating from the Kremlin, running more or less parallel with Tverskaya Street to the northeast and New Arbat to the southwest. The street was laid out along the former road to Novgorod, an ancient town northwest of Moscow, and is divided into two sections. The first part is lined with 18th- and 19th-century mansions and begins at Manezhnaya Square, across from the fortification walls of the Kremlin. The second section, notable for its enchanting art-nouveau mansions, starts at Nikitskyie Vorota (Nikolai Gates) Square, where Gertsena Street intersects with the Boulevard Ring. Before the 1917 revolution, Gertsena Street was named Bolshaya Nikitskaya (the name most of the street signs still carry), after the Nikolai Gates of the former white-stone fortification wall. It was renamed in 1920 in honor of the 19th-century philosopher Alexander Herzen. Although Herzen spent much of his life in self-imposed exile in London and Paris, he exerted a tremendous influence on Russian sociopolitical thought in the mid-19th century as a progressive writer and fierce advocate of liberal reform.

46 The tour begins at **Manezhnaya Ploshchad** (Manege Square). The closest subway station is Okhotny Ryad (Hunter's Row), so named because the square was first occupied by a huge meat (and fish and game) market. Take the exit that leads to the National Hotel, at the corner of Manezhnaya Square and Tverskaya Street.

Bordering the far side of the square, diagonal from the National Hotel, is the Moskva Hotel. Opened in 1935, it was one of the first buildings erected as part of Stalin's reconstruction plan for Moscow. If you look carefully at the facade, you'll notice that the design on the west side doesn't match the design on the east side. Legend has it that Stalin was given a preliminary draft that showed two possible versions for the hotel. He was supposed to sign under the one he liked best, but instead he signed his name right across the middle. The story goes that the architects, too timid to go back to Stalin a second time, went ahead and built the hotel with its asymmetrical facade.

The building next to the National Hotel houses the offices of VAO Intourist, the travel agency that as plain Intourist held a monopoly over the entire tourist industry of the former Soviet Union. Until 1950 the building housed the U.S. Embassy. Older city residents still fondly recall how the Americans posted here joined in the spontaneous celebrations that erupted all over the city when the end of World War II was announced. They'll tell you how the Americans kept the party going, rolling beer kegs out these doors and onto Red Square across the way.

In the 1930s, Manezhnaya Square was renamed "50th Anniversary of the October Revolution Square." Now, with construction of an indoor shopping mall underway on its site, that cumbersome mouthful has been abandoned. The present (and prerevolutionary) name comes from the imperial riding school (Manege) situated on the opposite side of the square from the Moskva Hotel. Built in 1817, it has an interesting design: there are no internal columns supporting its huge roof—just the four walls. After the revolution the building was used as the Kremlin garage and then, in the late '50s, was revamped into the Central Exhibition Hall, which is used primarily for temporary art and photography exhibits. *1 Manezhnaya Ploshchad,* ☎ *095/202–9304.*

㊹ Continuing along the north side of the square, you come to the old campus of **Moscow State University.** It is Russia's oldest university, founded in 1755 by the father of Russian science, Mikhail Lomonosov. The classical buildings here were originally designed by Matvei Kazakov, in 1786–93. They were rebuilt and embellished in the mid-19th century, after the 1812 fire. The university's new campus is situated on Sparrow Hills (formerly Lenin Hills) in the largest of the so-called Stalin Gothic skyscrapers, though some of the law and journalism schools are still housed in the old halls.

㊺ Passing the university, you come to Herzen Street. Turn right, and one block up, at the corner of ulitsa Belinskovo, you reach the city's **Zoological Museum.** It is always swarming with schoolchildren, who take a special delight in its huge collection of mammals, birds, amphibians, and reptiles. The museum also has a collection of more than 1 million insects, and a collection of more than 100,000 butterflies was recently donated by a Moscow resident. *Ul. Gertsena 6.,* ☎ *095/203–3569.* ⊙ *Sun., Tues., Sat. 10–5; Wed., Fri. noon–5. Closed last Tues. of month.*

㊻ Farther up, on the left-hand side of the street at No. 13, is the **Tchaikovsky Conservatory.** You may have seen its magnificent concert hall on television; this is where the famous Tchaikovsky Piano Competition takes place. The conservatory was founded in 1866 and moved to its present location in 1870. Rachmaninoff, Scriabin, and Tchaikovsky are among the famous composers who have worked here. There is a statue of Tchaikovsky in the semicircular park outside the main entrance. It was designed by Vera Mukhina, a famous Soviet sculptor. You can buy tickets (at very reasonable prices) for excellent concerts of classical music in the lobby ticket office in the main building. *Ul. Gertsena 13, ☎ 095/ 229–2183.*

Take a quick diversion off Herzen Street now, turning right onto ulitsa Stankevicha, which begins just past the conservatory. The attractive red sandstone church at No. 8 was Moscow's **Episcopalian Church.** After the revolution it was closed and turned into a recording studio, but recently the English have taken it back.

Continuing now up Herzen Street, you pass, on the left-hand side, a three-story brick house. The word TEATP (theater) is printed in black on a sign hanging down the side. For a time known as the Theater of Revolutionary Satire, today it is famous as the **Mayakovsky Drama Theater.** *Ul. Gertsena 19, ☎ 095/290–6241.*

One more block brings you to the square named **Nikitskyie Vorota,** after the gates of the white-stone fortification walls that once stood here. To your right is a modern building with square windows; this is home to TASS, once the official news agency of the Soviet Union and the mouthpiece of the Kremlin. In the park in the center of the square stands a monument to Kliment Timiryazev, a famous botanist.

The busy road in front of you, intersecting Herzen Street, is the Boulevard Ring, which forms a semicircle around the city center. It begins at the banks of the Moskva River, just south of the Kremlin, running in a northeastern direction. It curves eastward, and then south, finally reaching the river bank again after several miles, near the mouth of the Yauza River, northeast of the Kremlin. Its path follows the lines of the 16th-century white-stone fortification wall that gave Moscow the name "White City." The privilege of living within its walls was reserved for the court nobility and craftsmen serving the czar. The wall was torn down in 1775, on orders from Catherine the Great, and was replaced by the present Boulevard Ring. It is divided into 10 sections, each with a different name. Running along its center is a broad strip of trees and flowers, dotted with playgrounds and benches. You may want to take a break and rest on its benches.

On the other side of the boulevard, facing the square, is the classical **Tserkov Bolshovo Vozneseniya** (Church of the Great Ascension). Like Moscow University, it was designed by Matvei Kazakov and built in the 1820s. For years it stood empty and abandoned, but it has been under major repair, and though the work is not yet complete, religious services have already been resumed here. The church is most famous as the site where the Russian poet Alexander Pushkin married the younger and far less intelligent Natalya Goncharova. History has judged Natalya harshly. She was probably not guilty of adultery, although she did enjoy flirting. Pushkin died outside St. Petersburg six years after their wedding, in a duel defending her honor.

Herzen Street veers sharply to the left here, so that if you continue straight ahead, keeping to the right of the square, you'll end up on ulitsa Kachalova. About half a block down, near the corner, is a marvelous example of Moscow Art Nouveau, the **Ryabushinsky Mansion,** built in 1901 for a wealthy banker and designed by the architect Fyodor Shektel. (If you arrived in Moscow by train, you probably noticed the fanciful Yaroslavl Railway Station, another of his masterpieces, located opposite the Leningrad Railway Station.) Sadly, the mansion has been closed with its museum for *remont,* and it has fallen into a bit of disrepair, after having been wonderfully preserved. This was thanks in part to the fact that Maxim Gorky, the father of Soviet socialist realism, lived here from 1931 until his death in 1936. Considering that Gorky was a champion of the proletariat, his home was rather lavish. But in a typical twist of Soviet reality, Gorky hated the *style moderne.* Those who don't, however, will be charmed by this building of ecru brick and stone painted pink and mauve atop gray foundations. Step back and look up at the beautiful mosaic of irises that runs a border around the top of most of the house, and see how the strangely fanciful yet utilitarian iron fence matches the unusual design of the window frames. The spectacular interior is replete with a twisting marble staircase and stained-glass roof. *Ul. Kachalova 1/6,* ☎ *095/290–5130 (when reopened). Closed indefinitely as the Gorky House Museum.*

Follow the road behind the Church of the Ascension and continue straight onto Paliashvili Street (which leads to the left off Herzen Street). The statue in the park behind the church is of Alexey Tolstoy, a relative of Leo and a well-known Soviet writer of historical novels. As you walk down Paliashvili you pass several side streets with names like Stolovy (Dining Room), Skatertny (Tablecloth), and Khlebny (Bread). The streets are named after the servants of the czar (the waiters, the linen makers, the baker) who lived in this area. Today the district houses many foreign embassies. Walk down Paliashvili Street until you reach the busy intersection with ulitsa Povarskaya, where you should turn right.

Ulitsa Povarskaya (Cook Street) is where the czar's cooks lived. After the revolution the street was renamed Vorovskovo, in honor of a Soviet diplomat who was assassinated by a Russian, but has returned to its prerevolutionary name. Povarskaya Street is an important center of the Moscow artistic community, with the film actors' studio, the Russian Academy of Music (the Gnesin Institute), and the Central House of Writers all located here. Many of the old mansions have been preserved, and the street retains its prerevolutionary tranquility and charm. In the first flush days of summer, your walk is likely to be accompanied by a rousing drum set or tinkling piano sonata issuing from the open windows of the music school.

The mansion at No. 25 (on the left-hand side of the street) houses the
❺❸ Gorky Literary Museum. For Gorky buffs only, the museum is packed with the letters, manuscripts, and pictures of the great proletarian writer. There are also, rather remarkably, portraits of him by Nesterov and Serov. Americans may be particularly riveted to read the first page (in English) of *City of the Yellow Devil,* his book about visiting New York in 1906; its opening chapter is entitled "City of Mammon." There is even a red wooden replica of his childhood home, complete with village yard and outbuildings. You won't get to leave without signing the book of the kindly but fierce matrons who protect this place. *Ul. Povarskaya 25,* ☎ *095/290–5130.* ☉ *Mon., Tues., Thurs. 10–5; Wed., Fri. noon–7. Closed 1st Thurs. of month.*

Near the end of Povarskaya Street, you pass the **Central House for Writers,** which functions as an exclusive club (with one of the city's very best restaurants) for members of the Writers' Union. Next door (No. 52) is a large mansion, enclosed by a courtyard, that houses the administrative offices of the Writers' Union. It is commonly believed that Leo Tolstoy used this mansion as a model for his description of the Rostov home in *War and Peace.* A statue of Tolstoy stands in the courtyard.

Povarskaya Street comes out onto Novinsky Bulvar; to the right is
❺❹ Ploshchad Kudrinskaya (Kudrinsky Square). Down to the far left, you

can see the U.S. Embassy. Cars race in front of you along the busy Sadovaye Koltso (Garden Ring), the major one of the circular roads encompassing Moscow. The first thing to catch your eye will be the 22-story skyscraper directly across the street, one of the seven Stalin Gothics. This one is 160 meters (525 feet) high. The ground floor is taken up by shops and a movie theater, and the rest of the building contains residential apartments. This area saw heavy fighting during the uprisings of 1905 and 1917 (until recently the plaza was named Ploshchad Vosstaniya, or Insurrection Square). The Barrikadnaya (Barricade) subway station is very close by. Cross the street and bear right, through the park and down the hill; you'll see people streaming into the station to your right.

Tour 5: The Arbat, Old and New

Two of downtown Moscow's most interesting and important avenues are **Arbat** and **Novy Arbat** (New Arbat), which run parallel to each other. Arbat Street is revered among Muscovites, who usually refer to it simply as "the Arbat." One of the oldest sections of Moscow, it dates to the 16th century, when it was the beginning of the road that led from the Kremlin to the city of Smolensk. At that time it was also the quarter where court artisans lived, and several of the surrounding streets still recall this in their names—from Plotnikov (Carpenter) to Serebryany (Silversmith) to Kalashny (Pastry Cook). Early in the 19th century it became a district of the aristocracy, while a century later it became a favorite shopping street, a role that has recently been revived. The whole area is now under a preservation order and has become an attractive, cobbled pedestrian precinct with many gift shops and cafés in the restored buildings. Closed to all traffic, the Arbat attracts artists, poets, and musicians as well as enthusiastic buyers of their wares.

Novy Arbat has both a different history and spirit. For almost 30 years it was named Kalinin Prospect, in honor of Mikhail Kalinin, an old Bolshevik whose prestige plummeted after 1991. The first stretch of the former Kalinin Prospect—from the Kremlin to Arbat Square—has been given back its prerevolutionary name of Vozdvizhenka Street. The second section—which begins where Vozdvizhenka ends and runs west for about a mile to the Moscow River—is now called **Novy Arbat.** In contrast to Vozdvizhenka, which has retained some of its prerevolutionary charm, and the Arbat, which is actively re-creating the look of its past, New Arbat is a modern thoroughfare. Once a maze of narrow streets and alleys, the avenue was widened and modernized in the 1960s, with the goal of making it the showcase of the Soviet capital. It is lined with high-rise apartments, department stores, and other public establishments, all built since the 1960s.

We will start at the bottom of Vozdvizhenka and work our way up to Arbat Square. Take the subway to either the Arbatskaya station on the dark blue line or to Biblioteka imeni Lenina (Lenin Library) on the red line. To confuse matters, there is also an Arbatskaya station on the light blue line, but that will leave you at the wrong end of Arbat Square.

When you emerge from the subway, bear left, walking away from the Kremlin. Vozdvizhenka, like many other Moscow streets, continues to undergo massive reconstruction, and some of its prerevolutionary facades are hidden behind scaffolding. The drawings and photographs at the **Shchusev Architecture Museum,** however, can give you an idea what the area used to look like. The museum's permanent home, an 18th-century classical mansion at ul. Vozdvizhenka 5, is closed for reconstruction. The exhibits have been moved to a building right behind it, which can be reached via Marx and Engels Street, the first side street to your left. When you enter this narrow street, the first building on the right is an old, white-brick, two-story one that was the court apothecary in the 17th century. Turn right into its courtyard; the entrance to the museum is to your immediate left. The permanent and temporary exhibits here trace the history of Russian architecture from the 11th century to the present. *Ul. Vozdvizhenka 5,* ☎ *095/290–4855.* ✆ *Tues.–Fri. 10–6, weekends 10–4.*

Returning to Vozdvizhenka, on the right-hand side of the street you will pass Voyentorg (Military Department Store), which is also closed for reconstruction. It became popular at the height of *perestroika,* when military uniforms would fetch a high price on the black market, popular as they were with foreign tourists. Just beyond Voyentorg, you pass a small square that is strangely empty. The statue of Mikhail Kalinin that once stood here has been removed.

Using the underpass just before the square, cross to the right-hand side of the street. You are bound to be curious about the building a bit farther up that looks like a Moorish castle. It was built in the late 19th century by the architect V. A. Mazyrin for the wealthy (and eccentric) industrialist Morozov. (If you have read Tolstoy's novel *Resurrection,* you will find it mentioned there.) The interior is a veritable anthology of decorative styles, ranging from imitation Tudor to classical Greek and Baroque. The building is now the **Friendship House,** its name a holdover from the Soviet days when Russians and foreigners were supposed to meet only in officially sanctioned places. Today it is the site of business functions and public forums, including international events.

The busy intersection just beyond the Friendship House is **Arbatskaya Ploshchad** (Arbat Square), where Vozdvizhenka crosses the Boulevard Ring. To reach the other side of the square, take the pedestrian underpass, which has become a bustling marketplace. The stairs are lined with women selling tiny kittens and puppies; their furry heads stick out from a bag or from underneath a coat, and they are nearly irresistible, so it's best not to stop and look. In the underpass itself, artists set up their easels, trying to entice passersby into getting their portraits painted, and in spring and summer you'll find lots of impromptu flower vendors with the season's latest blooms (usually homegrown) for sale. When you emerge from the dizzying minimarket of the underpass, you will be in front of the Praga restaurant, a three-story classical building whose history dates back to before the revolution. To your left is the Arbat; to your right, Novy Arbat. In the distance to your far left stands a statue erected in the 1950s of the 19th-century Russian writer Nikolai Gogol, at the start of its eponymous section of the boulevard.

Go left to start your stroll down the Arbat, where you could easily spend a whole day browsing through the stores and stopping for a break in its numerous cafés. You may want to allow yourself a couple of hours during this tour to do so—or allot the time at the end to return. The Arbat ends where it intersects the Garden Ring and is marked by another of the Gothic-style "Seven Sisters" skyscrapers that Stalin ordered built; this one is the Ministry of Foreign Affairs. Should you walk all the way to the end, just before you reach it, you will find Alexander **Pushkin's apartment.** The poet lived here with his bride, Natalya Goncharova, for several months in 1831, right after they were married. Experts have re-created the original layout of the rooms and interior decoration, and the apartment is now open as a museum. *53 Arbat,* ☎ *095/241–3010.* ✆ *Wed.–Sun. 10–6.*

This tour takes a right about two-thirds of the way down the Arbat, onto the narrow ulitsa Vakhtangova, which begins at the impressive building at 26 Arbat, the **Vakhtangov Theater.** Named after Stanislavsky's pupil Evgeny Vakhtangov (1883–1922), it is an excellent traditional theater. Turn right to go up ulitsa Vakhtangova.

Walking up the left-hand side of the street, you will reach the building at No. 7. Walk through the archway and head straight back. There are two gems hidden here. The yellow mansion behind the iron gate to your right is **Spasso House,** the residence of the American ambassador. This neoclassical mansion was built in the early 20th century for a wealthy merchant. What you first see is actually the backside of the building; it is much more impressive from the front. To get there, bear right at the small playground, usually filled with children from the nearby school. After you have seen Spasso House, go back and, to the playground's left, and you will have discovered the lovely **Church of the Transfiguration on the Sands.** Built in the 17th century, it was closed after the 1917 revolution and turned into a cartoon-production studio. Like churches throughout Russia, it has been returned to its original purpose and is being restored. The church is famous for having featured in Vasily Polenov's well-known canvas *Moskovsky Dvornik* (*Moscow Courtyard*), which now hangs in the Tretyakov Gallery (*see* Tour 6).

Retrace your path back to Vakhtangov Street and turn left to continue. A few doors up, on the left-hand side of the street, you come to the Alexander Scriabin Museum. It is housed in the composer's last apartment, where he died of blood poisoning in 1915. There are many such dusty house-museums in Moscow, but this one is particularly charming. Visitors here are rare, as Muscovites long ago apparently tired of their own museums, and foreign tourist groups are not usually brought here. The rooms are arranged and furnished just as they were when Scriabin lived here. Downstairs there is a concert hall where accomplished young musicians perform his music. If you want to hear a concert, you should call ahead to find out the current schedule; they are usually held on Wednesday and Friday evenings. *Ul. Vakhtangova 11,* ☎ *095/241–1901.* ⊙ *Thurs., weekends 10–3; Wed., Fri. noon–7. Closed last Fri. of month.*

Leaving the museum, go left and follow the narrow street for approximately one block to come out onto the busy New Arbat Street. Since the entire area was rebuilt in the 1960s, there is little of historical interest here, except for the shops, which abound. Although their names, products, and owners may have changed, often dramatically, since the 1990s, this been a boulevard of storefronts since its construction. How things have changed, however, is perhaps best summed up in the transformation of "Metelitsa," once described as an "ice-cream parlor *cum* wine bar," into a flashy casino and exotic nightclub. To have a look at the street's full offerings, turn right as you come out onto New Arbat, and make your way back toward Arbat Square, where the tour began. As you elbow your way through the crowds of shoppers and vendors, you may want to keep your eye out in particular for the country's largest bookstore, **Dom Knigi** (Book House), which will be at No. 26, on the left-hand side near the street's end. It has an English-language section, but you'll probably find a bigger selection among the individual vendors outside the store.

TIME OUT The **New Arbat Irish Store** (which is, in fact, mainly Russian-run), located near the end of the block of buildings on the right-hand side of the street, has one of Moscow's biggest and best-stocked grocery stores.

The hard-currency section is on the second floor, where the selection (and the prices) match what you might find in New York City. Also upstairs is the small **Shamrock Pub,** where you can get a reasonably priced sandwich or bowl of soup in a lively and friendly atmosphere.

59 Past Dom Knigi, at the corner of ulitsa Povarskaya, the 17th-century **Tserkov Simeona Stolpnika** (Church of St. Simon the Stylite) stands out above in stark contrast to the modern architecture dominating the area. During the reconstruction of New Arbat in the 1960s many old churches and buildings were destroyed, but this one was purposely left standing, as a "souvenir" of the past. For years it housed a conservation museum, but now it has been returned to the Orthodox Church and is active. Nothing remains, however, of the original interiors.

60 The last stop on this tour is a visit to a second **Gogol statue,** the one that originally stood at the start of Gogol Boulevard but was later moved and replaced by a more "upbeat" Gogol. When you reach Arbat Square, turn left up Nikitsky Boulevard. The statue stands inside the first courtyard to your left, near the apartment building where the writer spent the last months of his life. This statue actually captures Gogol's sad disposition perfectly. He gazes downward, with his long, flowing cape draped over his shoulder, protecting him from the world. Gogol is probably best known in the West for his satirical drama *Revizor* (*The Inspector General*), about the unannounced visit of a government official to a provincial town. Characters from this and other Gogol works are engraved on the pedestal.

Tour 6: From the Russian State Library to the Kropotkinskaya District

This tour takes you through an old section of Moscow known as Kropotkinskaya. It takes its name from its main street, which was called Kropotkinskaya under the Soviets but has now been returned to its 16th-century name of Prechistenka. This is yet another ancient section of Moscow whose history dates back nearly to the foundation of the city itself. Almost none of its earliest architecture has survived, but this time the Soviets are not entirely to blame. The area suffered badly during the 1812 conflagration of Moscow, and most of its buildings date to the postwar period of reconstruction, when neoclassicism and the so-called Moscow Empire style were in vogue. Before the revolution, the Kropotkinskaya district was the favored residence of Moscow's old nobility, and it is along its thoroughfares that you'll find many of their mansions and homes, often called "nests of the gentry." It was also the heart of the literary and artistic community, and there were several famous literary salons here. Prince Kropotkin, for whom the street was named, compared it with the Saint-Germain quarter of Paris.

The tour starts at the **Russian State Library,** better known as the Lenin Library. It's located at the bottom of ulitsa Vodvizhenka, at the corner of ulitsa Mokhovaya (Moss Street, where moss used for wall caulking was once sold). To reach it, take the subway to the station directly beneath the library (still called Biblioteka imeni Lenina). The library is Russia's largest, with more than 30 million books and manuscripts. The main facade is adorned with bronze busts of famous writers and scientists. The portico, supported by square black pillars, is approached by a wide ceremonial staircase. Although it's a modern building, built between 1928 and 1940, portions of the building are under reconstruction. When the subway beneath it was being expanded in the 1980s, the library suffered structural damage and a large crack appeared in its foundation.

A former mansion across the street from the library houses the Mokho-
61 vaya Branch of the **Central Revolution Museum.** The museum used to
be devoted to Mikhail Kalinin, the first president of the Presidium of
the Supreme Soviet and long a venerated hero of the Bolshevik Revolution. Many a square received his name during the Soviet era (the ancient town of Tver was also renamed in his honor), but after the 1991
coup Kalinin became a hated symbol of the old regime. The museum
was completely revamped and now houses two small historical exhibits.
The first (on the second floor) is an exhibit of political portrait art, including such interesting historical figures as Rasputin and Sergei Kirov
(the Leningrad Party leader who was assassinated—probably on Stalin's
orders—in 1934). A highlight of the collection is Ilya Repin's portrait
of Alexander Kerensky, head of the transitional government established
after the February 1917 revolution. The exhibit on the first floor,
called "70 Years of Soviet Life," covers the development of Soviet propaganda. On display is a conglomeration of seemingly unconnected
materials, from presents given to Stalin (such as a Chinese vase with
his portrait on it and a huge *palekh* box with "40 Years of October"
painted on the cover) to wire from the Salevetsky Island concentration
camp. Posters glorifying the farm worker, dating from the period of
forced collectivization, are hung near an old voting booth, emphasiz-
ing the scam behind communist elections. The objective of this strange
collection of political materials is to show how Soviet reality differed
from Soviet propaganda. The exhibit ends with a display on the 1991
coup, which includes sections of the barricades set up outside the Russian Parliament Building (the "White House"). *Ul. Mokhovaya 21,* ☎
095/202–0367. ☉ *Tues.–Sun. 10–5:30. Tours in Russian may be arranged in advance,* ☎ *095/202–7126.*

Just beyond the Lenin Library you come to Borovitsky Square, where
several old streets converge. To your left, ulitsa Znamenka descends
toward the Borovitsky Gate of the Kremlin and then continues across
the Great Stone Bridge of the Moskva River. To your right Bolshaya
Polyanka leads up a steep incline. Ulitsa Volkhonka lies straight ahead,
leading into the Kropotkinskaya district. On the hillock to your right,
facing the Kremlin gates, is one of Moscow's most beautiful old mansions, the Pashkov House. The central building is topped by a round
belvedere and flanked by two service wings. Designed by Vasily
Bazhenov, one of Russia's greatest architects, the mansion was erected
in 1784–86 for the wealthy Pashkov family. In the 19th century it housed
the Rumyantsev collection of art and rare manuscripts. Following the
1917 revolution, this museum was closed; the art collection was transferred to the Hermitage and Pushkin museums of fine art, and the
manuscripts were donated to the Lenin Library. The building now belongs to the Russian State Library.

Cross the square and continue straight onto ulitsa Volkhonka, which
was first laid out sometime in the late 12th or early 13th century. It
received its present name in the mid-18th century, in honor of Prince
Volkhonksy, who lived in the mansion at No. 8. After one block you
★ **62** reach Moscow's museum of foreign paintings, the **Pushkin Museum of
Fine Arts,** in the middle of a small park to your right. Founded by Ivan
Vladimirovich Tsvetayev (1847–1913) of Moscow University, the museum was originally established as a teaching aid for art students,
which explains why many of the works are copies. The present building dates from 1895 to 1912 and was first known as the Alexander III
Museum. It was renamed the Pushkin Museum in 1937, on the cen-
tennial of the Russian poet's death. *Ul. Volkhonka 12,* ☎ *095/203–
7412.* ☉ *Tues.–Sun. 10–7.*

The first-floor exhibit halls contain a fine collection of ancient Egyptian art (Hall 1); Greece and Rome are well represented, though mostly by copies (Room 7). The Italian school from the 15th century (Room 5) is represented by Botticelli's *The Annunciation,* Tomaso's *The Assassination of Caesar,* Guardi's *Alexander the Great at the Body of the Persian King Darius,* and *The Beheading of John the Baptist* by Sano Di Pietro, among others. When you reach the Dutch School of the 17th Century (Hall 10), look for Rembrandt's *Portrait of an Old Woman,* who may have been the artist's sister-in-law. Flemish and Spanish art from the 17th century is also well represented, with paintings by Murillo, Rubens, and Van Dyck (Hall 11).

On the museum's second floor you are treated to a stunning collection of Impressionist art. There are many fine canvasses by Picasso (Hall 17), including several from his "blue" period. The same hall contains fascinating works by Henri Rousseau, including *Jaguar Attacking a Horse.* French Impressionism is represented by Cézanne, Gauguin, and Matisse. There is a total of 10 works by Gauguin, mainly in Hall 18, where you also find Cézanne's *Pierrot* and *Harlequin.* The museum owns several works by Matisse (Hall 21), although often they are not all on display. In the same hall you find the poignant *Landscape at Auvers After the Rain* by Vincent van Gogh. The collection ends at Hall 23, where you find works by Degas, Renoir, and Monet, including Monet's *Rouen Cathedral at Sunset.*

Just past the Pushkin Museum lies an entire block between Volkhonka and the quay of the Moskva River that carries an amazing tale of destruction and reconstruction. Since the 1950s the site held the **Moscow Pool,** one of the world's largest outdoor swimming pools. Divided into several sections, for training, competition, diving, and public swimming, it was heated and kept open all year long, even in the coldest days of winter. The pool was connected to the locker rooms by covered tunnels, and you could reach it by swimming through them.

The pool was dismantled in 1994, ironically enough, a victim of the same fate engendered by it, more or less. For 35 years, it occupied the site where the gigantic **Cathedral of Christ Our Savior** once stood. Built between 1839 and 1883 as a memorial to the Russian troops who fell in the 1812 war with Napoleon, the cathedral was the largest single structure in Moscow and dominated the city's skyline. It had taken almost 50 years to build what only a few hours would destroy. On December 5, 1931, the cathedral was blown up. Under Stalin, the site had been designated for a mammoth new "Palace of Soviets," intended to replace the Kremlin as the seat of the Soviet government. Plans called for topping the 420-meter (1,378-foot) structure with a 100-meter (300-foot) statue of Lenin, who—had the plans ever materialized—would have spent more time above the clouds than in plain view. World War II delayed construction, and the entire project was scrapped when it was discovered that the land along the embankment was too damp to support such a heavy structure. The site lay empty and abandoned until 1958, when the Moskva Pool was constructed to fill the space where the church once stood.

In perhaps one of architectural history's stranger twists, therefore, everything has come full circle in the post-perestroika and -glasnost years. The area is currently humming with activity, as workmen swarm over the entire site. What are they doing? Swiftly building anew, a second and equally gigantic Cathedral of Christ Our Savior.

TIME OUT The restaurant at the corner of ulitsa Ostozhenka and Soymonovsky
Proyezd is the second restaurant opened in Moscow by an American
businessman from Trenton, New Jersey. It's hard to miss the shiny neon
lights on its facade—**Tren-Mos Bistro.** They call attention to themselves
in this old district dominated by the elegant mansions of Moscow's bygone aristocracy. The menu features such American favorites as cheese-
burgers and pizza. The prices, however, are rather un-American. *1/9
ul. Ostozhenka,* ☎ *095/202–5722.*

Just beyond the pool, Volkhonka Street intersects with the Boulevard
Ring. To your right, across the street, is the entrance to the Kropotkinskaya subway station. At this point Volkhonka Street ends, splitting
into ulitsa Prechistenka (to the right) and ulitsa Ostozhenka (to the left).
A small park between the two streets holds a statue of Friedrich Engels and, behind it, a restored 17th-century boyars' chamber. Cross the
square and walk up Prechistenka. At the corner with Khrushchevsky
Perevlok stands a fine yellow mansion built in the 19th century by the
64 architect Afansey Grigoriev. Since 1961 it has housed the **Pushkin
Memorial Museum.** Pushkin never lived here and probably never even
visited, so it is a rather dry museum, full of manuscripts and letters.
The museum is especially interesting to students of Russian poetry. The
entrance is around the corner. *12 ul. Prechistenka,* ☎ *095/202–7998.*
✆ *Tues. (groups tours only), Fri.–Sun. 10–6; Wed., Thurs. 11–7.
Closed last Fri. of month.*

Not far from the Pushkin Museum, on the opposite side of the street,
is yet another Grigoriev creation housing yet another literary museum.
65 The Leo **Tolstoy Memorial Museum** is similar to the Pushkin Museum.
It was opened at another location in 1911 and moved here in 1920.
The mansion, a fine example of the Moscow Empire style, belonged
to the minor poet Lopukhin, a distant relative of Tolstoy. The exhibit
halls contain a rich collection of manuscripts and photographs of Tolstoy and his family, as well as pictures and paintings of Tolstoy's
Moscow. Even if you don't speak Russian, you can read the writer's
life story through the photographs, and in each room there is a typed
handout in English to help explain its holdings. If you decide to visit,
look for the picture of 19th-century Moscow in the second hall (on
the left-hand wall). The huge cathedral taking up more than half the
photograph is the Cathedral of Christ Our Savior—the one replaced
by the Moskva swimming pool. *11 ul. Prechistenka,* ☎ *095/202–
3091.* ✆ *Tues.–Sun. 11–5:30. Closed last Fri. of month.*

If you are feeling energetic and want to see more of the area's mansions, you can continue walking straight along Prechistenka ulitsa. No.
17, on the left-hand side, belonged to the poet Denis Davidov; and a
bit farther, at No. 19, you find the former mansion of Prince Dolgoruky. No. 21 now houses the Russian Academy of Arts. The mansion
originally belonged to Count Potemkin and then later to the wealthy
merchant Savva Morozov, whose private art collection was one of the
largest in Moscow (you can see it in the Pushkin Fine Arts Museum
we passed earlier).

We will now begin making our way back toward the Kropotkinskaya
subway. After you exit the Tolstoy museum, turn left onto Lopukhin-
sky Pereulok, and walk one block to Ostozhenka, which runs parallel to Prechistenka. In the distance to your right, you can see the
remnants of the **Zachatievsky Monastery** (Convent of the Conception).
Founded in the 16th century, this is the oldest structure in the district,
although nothing remains of the original buildings. Only the 17th-cen-

tury redbrick Gate Church survives, and even that is in catastrophic condition. It was built by the last surviving son of Ivan the Terrible, in what amounted to a plea to God for an heir (hence the monastery's name). He and his wife failed to have a son, however, and Boris Godunov became the next Russian leader.

Turn left now onto Ostozhenka, walk two blocks, and then turn right onto Vtoroi (2nd) Obydensky Pereulok. Soon you come to the pretty St. Prophet Eliah Church, built in one day in 1702. Turn left and at the end of this short street you come out onto Soymonovsky Proyezd. At the bottom of the street, facing the Moskva River, is one of the finest examples of Moscow Art Nouveau. The facade of the steep-roofed and angled building is covered in colorful mosaics. Known as the **Pertsov House,** it was built in 1905–07 by the architects Schnaubert and Zhukov. Walk all the way to its end, coming out at the river, and straight across you'll see a large, redbrick compound. This is the Red October candy factory. Look to your left, where the buildings of the Kremlin line the distance, the golden cupolas of its churches all agleam. To reach the subway again, walk back up Soymonovsky Proyezd, away from the Moskva River.

Should you wish to linger in the area and see more of its interesting houses, there are several along Ostozhenka Street (the one that split to the left from Volkhonka). The anarchist Bakunin was raised at No. 49. No. 38, was a governor's home in the 1700s; later it became a school, where one of its students was Ivan Goncharov, author of *Oblomov;* today it is the Institute of Foreign Languages. Next, at No. 37 is a small rustic house where one of Russia's greatest writers, Ivan Turgenev, lived and worked. He set his famous story *Mu Mu* at this location. The private home of the Art Nouveau architect Kekushev, who was a contemporary of Shekhtel, stands at No. 21.

Leaving from the upper end of Ostozhenka, you come out at the Park Kultury subway station. At the other end (from Soymonovsky Proyezd), you can take Metro Kropotkinskaya.

Tour 7: Gorky Park Area

This tour takes you to sites around Gorky Park and then, via subway, to Moscow's famous Russian art museum, the Tretyakov Gallery. Gorky Park, popularized by Martin Cruz Smith's cold war novel of the same name, is situated along the right bank of the Moskva River, just beyond **Krymsky Most** (Crimea Bridge). It is between two major subway stops—the Oktyabrskaya station on the orange and circle lines and the Park Kultury station on the red and circle lines. The tour begins at the Park Kultury stop, but if your only destination is Gorky Park, the Oktyabrskaya station is closer.

Leaving the Park Kultury subway station, turn right (as you face the bridge ahead) and walk along Komsomolsky Prospect one long block. When you reach the corner with ulitsa Lva Tolstovo (Leo Tolstoy Street) you will see the striking **Tserkov Nikoly v Khamovnikakh** (Church of St. Nicholas of the Weavers). Turn right here to go around to the church's entrance, which is on the side.

The church, which remained open throughout the years of Communist government, is wonderfully preserved. Its elegant bell tower is particularly impressive. Built in 1679–82 and topped by five gilded domes, the saucy colorfulness of its orange and green trim against its perfectly white facade makes it look like a frosted gingerbread house. In fact, the design was actually meant to suggest a festive piece of woven cloth, for it was the weavers who settled in considerable numbers in this quarter in the 17th century who commissioned the building of this church. Morning and evening services are held daily, and the church, with its wealth of icons, is as handsome inside as out.

67 The next stop is the Leo **Tolstoy House Estate Museum,** winter home of Russia's great novelist. As you start your walk up the street named in his honor, look for an old white-stone building with a wood-shingled roof, on your right. This 17th-century building once housed the Weaver's Guild, members of which were involved in founding the church you have just visited. Tolstoy's estate is a bit farther up the street, on the left-hand side, behind a long, red-wood fence. Tickets to the museum are sold in the administrative building to the far back left. Inside the museum, each room has signs in English explaining its significance and contents, but you might want to consider a guided excursion (which must be booked in advance).

Tolstoy bought the house in 1882, at the age of 54, and spent nine winters here with his family, until 1901. In summer he preferred his country estate in Yasnaya Polyana. The years here were not particularly happy ones. By this time Tolstoy had already reached his "religious conversion," which prompted him to disown his earlier great novels, including *War and Peace* and *Anna Karenina*. His conversion sparked a feud among his own family members, which manifested itself even at the dining table: Tolstoy's wife, Sofia Andreevna, would sit at one end with the sons, while the writer would sit with his daughters at the opposite end.

The ground floor has several of the children's bedrooms and the nursery where Tolstoy's seven-year-old son died of scarlet fever in 1895, a tragedy that haunted the writer for the rest of his life. Also here are the dining rooms and kitchen as well as the Tolstoys' bedroom, in which you can see the small desk used by his wife to meticulously copy all of her husband's manuscripts by hand.

Upstairs, you will find the Tolstoys' receiving room, where they held small parties and entertained guests, who included most of the leading figures of their day. The grand piano in the corner was played by such greats as Rachmaninoff and Rimsky-Korsakov. When in this room, you should ask the attendant to play the enchanting recording of Tolstoy greeting a group of schoolchildren, followed by a piano composition written and played by him. Also on this floor is an oriental den and the writer's study, where he wrote his last novel, *Resurrection*.

Although electric lighting and running water were available at the time to the lesser nobility, Tolstoy chose to forgo both, believing it better to live simply. The museum honors his desire and shows the house as it was when he lived there. *10 ul. Lva Tolstovo,* ☎ *095/246–9444.* ⏲ *Summer, Tues.–Sun. 10–6; winter, 10–4. Closed last Fri. of month.*

Retracing your steps to the Park Kultury subway stop, go right when you reach the corner with busy Zubovsky Bulvar, over the Krymsky Most. The bridge spans the Moskva River, and in nice weather it offers a fine vantage point. Visitors no doubt will feel a surge of excitement looking at the flashing signs of Gorky Park and its attractions beckoning from below. If you want to save on walking, you can take either Trolley Bus 10 or B (both stop on Zubovsky Bulvar, right in front of the subway entrance); they will drop you off directly in front of the main entrance to Gorky Park.

68 Muscovites usually refer to **Gorky Park** as Park Kultury (Park of Culture); its official title is actually the Central Park of Culture and Leisure named for Maxim Gorky. The park was founded in 1928 and covers an area of 110 hectares (275 acres). It is definitely the city's most popular all-around recreation center, and in the summer, especially on weekends, it is crowded with children and adults alike enjoying its many attractions. The park's green expanse is dominated by a giant Ferris wheel; if you're brave enough to ride it, you'll be rewarded with great views of the city; for the even braver, there is also a roller-coaster. Stretching along the riverside, the park includes the Neskuchny Sad (Happy Garden) and the Zelyony Theater (Green Theater), an open-air theater with seating for 10,000. The park has a boating pond, a fair-ground, sports grounds, a rock club, and numerous stand-up cafés. In summer boats leave from the pier for excursions along the Moskva River, and in winter the ponds transform into skating rinks. *9 Krymsky Val.* ☉ *Summer, daily 9–noon; winter, daily 10–10.*

69 Directly across the street from the entrance to Gorky Park is the **House of Artists,** a huge, modern building that also houses a branch of the Tretyakov Gallery. The entrance facing the street leads to the exhibit halls of the Artists' Union, where union members display their work, so this is a spot where you can browse for a sketch or watercolor to take home with you. The extensive exhibit halls are spread out among three floors. *10 Krymsky Val,* ☎ *095/238–9843.* ☉ *Tues.–Sun. 11–9.*

TIME OUT Juice, coffee, and light snacks are available in the café on the ground floor of the House of Artists. It's stand-up only, but you can mingle and hear talk on the latest trends in contemporary Russian art.

If you're looking for the branch of the Tretyakov Art Gallery familiarly known as the "New Tretyakov Gallery," or "New Branch," go around to the side entrance. This annex came into being when the original Tretyakov Gallery had to be closed for restoration work (from 1986 to 1995). From this time on, it has also been the location where the museum will display its collection of art created since the 1920s, encompassing pieces, some previously outlawed, from the socialist realist, modern, and post-modern periods. *11 Krymsky Val (side entrance, on the right),* ☎ *095/230–1116 or 095/230–7788.* ☉ *Tues.–Sun. 10–7.*

★ **70** The final destination on this tour is the main **Tretyakov Art Gallery,** often called the "Old Tretyakov," a museum which many proudly consider the country's most important depository of Russian art. To get there, you will take the subway one stop. Walk up the incline to the left of Gorky Park (as you face its entrance) to find the station. Take the orange line (not the circle line) to the Tretyakovskaya stop. Bear left at every turn as you exit the subway, and when you emerge, look for Ordynsky Pereulok. Going a short distance down this street, you will quickly sight the attractive grounds of the museum opening up on your right. *Lavrushinsky Pereulok 10,* ☎ *095/233–1416 or 095/238–1378.* ☉ *Tues.–Sun. 10–7.*

The Tretyakov Gallery, which holds some of the world's masterpieces of Russian art, had a remarkable philanthropic and altruistic beginning. Officially opened in 1892 as a public state museum, its origins predate that by more than 35 years. In the mid-1800s, a successful young Moscow industrialist, Pavel Mikhailovich Tretyakov, was determined to amass a collection of national art that would be worthy of a museum of fine arts for the entire country. In pursuit of this high-minded goal, he began to purchase paintings, drawings, and sculpture, adjudged both on high artistic merit and on their place within the various important canons of their time. For the most part undeterred by critics' disapproval and arbiters of popular taste, he became one of the—if not *the*—era's most valued patrons of the arts, with honor and gratitude conferred upon him yet to this day.

Up until 6 years before his death, Tretyakov maintained his soon-enormous collection as a private one, but allowed virtually unlimited free access to the public. In 1892, he donated it all to the Moscow city government, along with a small inheritance of other fine works collected by his brother Sergei. The holdings to his collection have been continuously increased by subsequent state acquisitions, including the nationalization of privately owned pieces after the Communist revolution.

A visitor to the museum today will find works spanning the 11th to the 20th century, from sacred icons to stunning portrait and landscape art to the famous Russian Realists' paintings that culminated in the Wanderers' Group to the splendid creations of Russian Symbolism, Impressionism, and Art Nouveau, virtually all of it known far less intimately outside of Russia than should be the case for a collection of such critical importance.

Among the many delights to be found are icons painted by the master Andrei Rublyev, including his celebrated *The Trinity;* also featured are icons of his disciples, Daniel Chorny among them, as well as some of the earliest icons to reach ancient Kievan Rus, such as *The Virgin of Vladimir,* brought from Byzantium. The first floor, which houses the icon collection, is also where drawings and watercolors from the 18th to the 20th centuries are located.

The second floor holds 18th, 19th, and 20th century painting and sculpture and is where indefatigable Russian art lovers will find their longings satisfied several times over. A series of halls of 18th-century portraits, including particularly fine works by Dmitri Levitsky, act as a time machine into the country's noble past, followed by rooms filled with the historical painting of the next century, embodying the burgeoning movements of romanticism and naturalism in such gems of landscape painting as Silvester Shchedrin's *Aqueduct at Tivoli* and Mikhail Lebedev's *Path in Albano* and *In the Park*. Other favorite pieces to look for are Bryullov's *The Last Day of Pompeii,* Ivanov's *Appearance of Christ to the People,* and Orest Kiprensky's well-known *Portrait of the Poet Alexander Pushkin.*

It may be the rich array of works completed after 1850, however, that will please museum-goers the most, for it comprises a selection of pieces from each of the Russian masters, sometimes of their best works. Hanging in the gallery are paintings by Nikolai Ge (*Peter the Great Interrogating the Tsarevich Alexei*), Vasily Perov (*Portrait of Fyodor Dostoevsky*), Vasily Polenov (*Grandmother's Garden*), Viktor Vasnetsov (*After Prince Igor's Battle with the Polovtsy*), and many others. Several canvases of the beloved Ivan Shishkin, with their depictions of Russian fields and forests, including *Morning in the Pine Forest,* of three bear cubs cavorting, fill one room, and of course a number by the equally popular Ilya Repin (*The Volga Boatmen, Easter Procession in Kursk*) also bedeck the walls. Later works, done near the century's end, range from an entire room devoted to the Symbolist Mikhail Vrubel (*The Princess Bride, Demon Seated*) to Nestorov's glowing *Vision of the Youth Bartholomew,* the boy who would become St. Sergius, founder of the monastery Sergeyev-Posad, to the magical pieces by Valentin Serov (*Girl with Peaches, Girl in Sunlight*). In drawing to a close, look for the compositions, of which there are a handful, done just before the revolution by Chagall, Kandinsky, and Malevich, and the stunning *Red Horse Swimming 1912* by Kuzma Petrov-Vodkin.

When you leave the galley, pause a moment to look back on the building itself, which is quite compelling. Tretyakov's original home, where the first collection was kept, still forms a part of the gallery. As the demands of a growing collection required additional space, the house was continuously enlarged and expanded upon, with finally an entire annex built to function as the gallery. In 1900, when no family any longer dwelled in the house, the artist Viktor Vasnetsov undertook to create the wonderful facade the gallery now carries, and more space was later added. Closed entirely in the years 1986 to 1995 for badly needed restoration (mostly inside), new wings and full reconstruction of the main one have given the museum a fresh loveliness meant to carry it well into the next century.

Tour 8: Novodevichy Convent and Cemetery

★ **Novodevichy Monastyr** (New Maiden's Convent) is one of Moscow's finest and best-preserved ensembles of 16th- and 17th-century Russian architecture. There is much to see here. The monastery is interesting not only for its impressive cathedral and charming churches but also for the dramatic chapters of Russian history that have been played out within its walls. It stands in a wooded section bordering a small pond, making this a particularly pleasant place for an afternoon stroll. Although it is no longer a functioning convent, one of its churches is open for services. After the Bolshevik Revolution, the convent was made part of the History Museum. Its exhibits boast rare and ancient Russian paintings, both ecclesiastical and secular, woodwork and ceramics, and fabrics and embroidery. There is also a large collection of illuminated and illustrated books, decorated with gold, silver, and jewels. Attached to the monastery is a fascinating cemetery where some of Russia's greatest literary, military, and political figures are buried. *1 Novodevichy Proyezd,* ☎ *095/246–8526.* ⊘ *Wed.–Mon. 10–5. Closed last Mon. of month.*

To reach the monastery, take the subway to the Sportivnaya station. Leave the subway via the stadium exit, and then follow ulitsa Frunzensky Val to your right. It will lead you through a small park and eventually to the southeast corner of the monastery. When you come out onto Luzhnetsky Proyezd, you will see the monastery's whitewashed walls to your right. Turning right, walk up the street; the main entrance is at the other end, off Bolshaya Pirogovskaya Street. The green-colored gates directly across from you as you enter the street mark the entrance to the cemetery, where we will return later.

Enclosed by a crenelated wall with 12 colorful battle towers, the monastery comprises several groups of buildings. Until the middle of the 20th century, when Moscow's population expanded rapidly, it effectively marked the city's southern edge. It was founded in 1524 by Czar Vasily III to commemorate Moscow's capture of Smolensk from Lithuania and was intended to serve not only as a religious institution but also as a defense fortification. Its location was strategically significant, as it stands on the road to Smolensk and Lithuania. Having been founded by the czar, it enjoyed an elevated position among the many monasteries and convents of Moscow and became a convent primarily for ladies of noble birth. Little remains of the original structure. The monastery suffered severely during the Time of Troubles, a period of internal strife and foreign intervention that began in approximately 1598 and lasted until 1613, when the first Romanov was elected to the throne. Its present appearance dates largely from the 17th century, when the monastery was significantly rebuilt and enhanced.

Among the first of the famous women to take the veil here was Irina, wife of the feebleminded Czar Fyodor and the sister of Boris Godunov. Opera fans may remember the story of Boris Godunov, the subject of a well-known work by Mussorgsky. Godunov was a powerful nobleman who exerted much influence over the czar. When Fyodor died, Godunov was the logical successor to the throne, but rather than proclaim himself czar, he followed his sister to Novodevichy. Biding his time, Godunov waited until the clergy and townspeople begged him to become czar. His election took place at the convent, inside the Cathedral of Smolensk. But his rule was ill-fated, touching off the Time of Troubles.

In the next century, Novodevichy became the residence of yet another royal: Sophia, the half-sister of Peter the Great, who ruled as his regent from 1682 through 1689 while he was still a boy. During this time there was much new construction at the monastery. The power-hungry Sophia, who did not wish to give up her position when the time came for Peter's rule, had to be deposed by him. He then kept her prisoner inside Novodevichy. Even that was not enough to restrain the ambitious Sophia, and from her cell at the convent she organized a revolt of the *streltsy* (Russian militia). The revolt was summarily put down, and to punish Sophia, Peter had the bodies of the dead *streltsy* hung up along the walls of the convent and outside Sophia's window. Despite his greatness, Peter had a weakness for the grotesque, especially when it came to punishing his enemies. He left the decaying bodies hanging for more than a year. Yet another of the convent's later "inmates" was Yevdokiya, Peter's first wife. Peter considered her a pest and rid himself of her by sending Yevdokiya to a convent in faraway Suzdal. She outlived him, though, and eventually returned to Moscow. She spent her final years at Novodevichy, where she is buried.

You enter the convent through the arched passageway topped by the **Preobrazhensky Tserkov** (Gate Church of the Transfiguration), widely considered one of the best examples of Moscow Baroque. To your left as you enter is the ticket booth, where tickets are sold to the various exhibits housed in the monastery. The building to your right is the Lophukin House, where Yevdokiya lived from 1727 to 1731. Sophia's prison, now a guardhouse, is situated to your far right, in a corner of the northern wall.

The predominant structure inside the monastery is the huge five-domed **Sobor Smolenskoy Bogomateri** (Cathedral of the Virgin of Smolensk), dedicated in 1525 and built by Alexei Fryazin. It may remind you of the Kremlin's Assumption Cathedral, after which it was closely modeled. Inside, there is a spectacular iconostasis with 84 wooden columns and icons dating from the 16th and 17th centuries. Also here are the tombs of Sofia and Yevdokiya. Simon Ushakov, a leader in 17th-century icon art, was among the outstanding Moscow artists who participated in the creation of the icons. Yet another historical tale connected to the monastery tells how the cathedral was slated for destruction during the War of 1812. Napoleon had ordered the cathedral dynamited, but a brave nun managed to extinguish the fuse just in time, and the cathedral was spared.

To the right of the cathedral is the **Uspensky Tserkov** (Church of the Assumption) and **Refectory,** originally built in 1687 and then rebuilt after a fire in 1796. It was here that the blue-blooded nuns had their meals.

If a monastery can have a symbol other than an icon, then Novodevichy's would be the ornate belfry towering above its eastern wall. It rises 71 meters (236 feet) and consists of six ornately decorated tiers.

The structure is topped by a gilded dome that can be seen from miles away.

TIME OUT   **U Pirosmani,** a well-known restaurant specializing in the spicy cuisine of Georgia, is situated across the pond from the monastery. On weekdays, it is almost always possible to get a table without a reservation. If you are visiting on a weekend, you may want to book ahead. *4 Novodevichy Proyezd, ☎ 095/247–1926 or 095/246–1638. Food bill paid in rubles, alcohol in dollars. AE.*

Leaving the monastery, retrace your steps, walking back down Luzhnetsky Proyezd to the right. The entrance to the **Novodevichy Kladbishche** (cemetery) is marked by a pair of green gates. Unless you have relatives buried here, you have to buy tickets to enter; tickets are sold in the small wooden kiosk directly across the street. You can also order an excursion in English from the cemetery's excursion bureau, which we highly recommend doing. The Novodevichy contains a fascinating collection of memorial art, but it is difficult for non-Russian speakers to identify the graves. You may wonder how a cemetery could be controversial, but this one was. For more than a generation, the Novodevichy Cemetery was closed to the general public, in large part because the controversial Nikita Khrushchev is buried here, rather than on Red Square, like other Soviet leaders. Thanks to glasnost, the cemetery was reopened in 1987, and now anyone is welcome to visit its grounds, which are not unlike those of Père Lachaise in Paris in the scope of national luminaries from all walks of life for whom it is a final resting place. *Luzhnetsky Proyezd, ☎ 095/246–6614. ☉ Daily 10–5.*

Khrushchev's grave is near the back of the cemetery, at the end of a long tree-lined walkway. If you can't find it, any of the *babushki* will point out the way. They will usually reflect their opinion of him in the way they gesture, for they almost certainly will not speak English. The memorial consists of a stark black-and-white slab, with a curvilinear border marking the separation. The contrast of black and white symbolizes the contradictions of his reign. It caused a great furor of objection among the Soviet hierarchy when it was unveiled. The memorial was designed by the artist Ernest Neizvestny, himself a controversial figure. In the 1960s Khrushchev visited an exhibit of contemporary art that included some of Neizvestny's works. Khrushchev dismissed Neizvestny's contributions as "filth," and asked the name of their artist. When Neizvestny (which means "Unknown") answered, Khrushchev scornfully said that the USSR had no need for artists with such names. To this the artist replied, "In front of my work, I am the Premier." Considering the times, it was a brave thing to say to the leader of the Soviet Union. Neizvestny eventually joined the ranks of the great emigré artists; he is now a world-famous sculptor living in the United States.

Many of those buried in the cemetery were war casualties in 1941 and 1942. The memorials often include a lifelike portrait or a photograph of the person being remembered or convey a scene in that person's life. Flowers and photographs of the dead are at almost all the graves. Among the memorials you might want to look for are those to the composers Prokofiev and Scriabin and the writers Chekhov, Gogol, Bulgakov, and Mayakovsky. Chekhov's grave is decorated with the trademark seagull of the Moscow Art Theater, the first to successfully produce his plays. Along the right-hand wall (the southwest wall of the monastery) you will find a memorial of a crash of a huge Soviet aircraft where all the crew members are interred. The grave of Stalin's wife, Nadezhda Aliluyeva, is marked by a simple tombstone with a bust of this poor woman. She supposedly committed suicide, and many hold Stalin responsible for her death. Theodore Chaliapin, the opera singer who was stripped of his Soviet citizenship while on tour in France in the 1920s, is also buried here. His remains were transferred here in 1984. His grave is marked by a marvelous lifelike representation of him that conveys the fervor and passion that characterized his singing.

Tour 9: The Monasteries of Southeast Moscow

This tour will take you to three ancient monasteries located along the banks of the Yauza River, in the southeast section of Moscow. Their history dates back to Moscow's earliest days, when it was the center of a fledgling principality and constantly under threat of enemy attack. A series of monasteries was built across the river from the Kremlin to form a ring of defense fortifications. Two of the monasteries on this tour were once part of that fortification ring. This former suburban area did not fare well as the city grew. Beginning in the 19th century, factories were built along the banks of the river, including the famous Hammer and Sickle metallurgical plant. Today this is one of Moscow's bleaker sections, marked by busy highways, monolithic residential high-rises, and factories. But in their midst you find the quaint monasteries of Moscow's past, not always in the best condition but nevertheless lasting reminders of Moscow's origins.

A note before setting off: This is a fairly strenuous tour, with lots of walking, so be sure to have stored up your energy and put on your athletic shoes. (You should also wear appropriate dress for visiting churches.) It's not recommended to bring younger-than-teenage children, since the street crossings are complicated and, to westerners unskilled in Muscovite ways, slightly treacherous. Always look for the pedestrian underpasses and crossing signs as you decide your best route to get to the other side.

The tour begins at **Novospassky** (New Savior) **Monastery,** which you can reach by taking the subway to the Proletarskaya station. Take only lefts to get out of the subway, and you will emerge on Sarinsky Proyezd. Standing with your back to the metro, the busy street a short distance ahead is Trety (3rd) Krutitsky Pereulok. This is also in the direction of the Yauza River, and as you head to where the streets intersect, the yellow belfry of the monastery gate church will appear above the construction, in the distance to your right (southwest). When you reach the intersection, use the underground passageways to cross to the other side. It is just a short walk from here up a slight incline to the monastery's entrance.

The monastery was built in 1462, but its history dates back to the 13th century. It was originally located inside the Kremlin, and it is called the "New" Monastery because its new site on the banks of the Yauza River was a transfer ordered by Ivan III, who wanted to free up space in the Kremlin for other construction. Often called Ivan the Great, Ivan III was the first Russian leader to categorically (and successfully) renounce Russia's allegiance to the khan of the Golden Horde. It was during his reign that a unified Russian state was formed under Moscow's rule. The Novospassky Monastery was just one of the numerous churches and monasteries built during the prosperous time of Ivan's reign. In uglier modern history, a site just outside the monastery's walls was one of the mass graves for those executed during Stalin's purges.

You enter the monastery at the near entrance to the left of the Bell Tower Gate, which was erected in 1786. It is now closed from the outside, though once inside the complex you can walk beneath its archway. The entire monastery is, sadly, in a state of semidisrepair. Reconstruction *is* being done, but slowly, already taking more than 30 years. Since the early 1990s, however, when it was returned to the Orthodox Church, the pace has picked up. Still, except on Sunday and church holidays, the monastery grounds often are virtually deserted. A stroll among its decaying buildings will therefore feel like a very private, if not rather eerie, experience.

The first thing you see as you enter the monastery grounds is the massive white **Sobor Spasa Preobrazheniya** (Transfiguration Cathedral). You may notice a resemblance, particularly in its domes, to the Kremlin's Assumption Cathedral, which served as its model. The Transfiguration Cathedral was built in 1642–49 by the Romanov family, commissioned by the czar as the Romanov family crypt. The gallery leading to the central nave is decorated with beautiful frescoes depicting the history of Christianity in Rus. It is worth timing your visit with a church service (daily at 5 PM) to see the interior. Even if the church is closed, the doors may be unlocked. No one will stop you from taking a quick look at the gallery walls.

In front of the cathedral, on the right-hand side, is the small red **Nadmogilnaya Chasovnya** (Memorial Chapel), marking the grave of Princess Alekseyevna Tarankova, the illegitimate daughter of Empress Elizabeth and Count Razumovsky. She led most of her life as a nun in Moscow's St. John's Convent, forced to take the veil by Catherine the Great. During her lifetime her identity was concealed, and she was known only as Sister Dofiya. The chapel over her grave was added in 1900, almost a century after her death. Sister Dofiya's imposter played a more prominent role in Russian history than the real Princess Tarankova. A mysterious character of European origin, the imposter never revealed her true identity. She was imprisoned by Catherine the Great in St. Petersburg's Peter and Paul Fortress, where she died of consumption in 1775. Her death in her flooded, rat-infested cell was depicted in a famous painting by Konstantin Flavitsky in 1864.

None of the monastery's original 15th-century structures has survived. The present fortification wall and most of the churches and residential buildings on the grounds date from the 17th century. To the right as you face the cathedral stands the tiny **Pokrovsky Tserkov** (Church of the Intercession). Directly behind the cathedral is the **Tserkov Znamenia** (Church of the Sign). Painted in the dark yellow popular in its time, with a four-column facade, it was built in 1791–1808 by the wealthy Sheremetyev family and contains the Sheremetyev crypt. In the back right-hand corner, running along the fortification walls, are the former monks' residences.

Leaving the monastery, turn right to go back to the busy Sarinsky Proyezd. To do this, you will have to pick your way across the tram and trolley lines. Once on the other side, before again reaching the Trety Krutitsky Pereulok, you will see on your right an older, tree-lined street leading up an incline. This is the Chetvyorty (4th) Krutitsky Pereulok. Climbing to the top of the hill, where you take a quick right, you will find the Krutitskoye Podvorye (Krutitskoye Ecclesiastical Residence), a historical architectural complex. It is even older than the Novospassky Monastery; the first cathedral on this site was erected sometime in the 13th century. Its name comes from the word *kruta*, meaning "hill." This was originally a small monastery, a site of defense in the 14th century against the Tartar-Mongol invaders, whose prestige grew further at the end of the 16th century, when it became the suburban residence of the Moscow metropolitan. The church and grounds were completely rebuilt, and the present structures date from this period. As monasteries go, its period of revival was short-lived; it was closed in 1788 on orders from Catherine the Great, who secularized many church buildings. In the 19th century it was used as an army barracks, and it is said that the Russians accused of setting the Moscow fire of 1812 were tortured here by Napoleon's forces. In the 20th century, the Soviets turned the barracks into a military prison. Although the buildings have now been returned to the Orthodox Church, the prison remains on the monastery grounds. There is also a police station right outside the main gate, so do not be alarmed if you are greeted by a small band of uniformed policemen as you enter.

To your left as you enter the monastery grounds is the five-domed, red-brick **Uspensky Sobor** (Assumption Cathedral), erected at the end of the 16th century on the site of several previous churches. Stylistically medieval, more than anything else, it is a working church, undergoing restoration like many of its counterparts throughout the city. Still very attractive inside, it has an assemblage of icons, lovely frescoes that have been half-restored, and an impressive all-white altar and iconstasis. The cathedral is attached to a gallery leading to the **Teremok** (Gate Tower), a splendid example of Moscow Baroque. It was built in 1688–94, and its exterior decoration is the work of Osip Startsev. Except for the carved, once-white columns, the walls are completely covered with colorful mosaics. The red, green, and white tiles—all of different sizes and shapes—framed in the red brick of the adjoining buildings give, despite the verging frenzy of the decoration, an overall effect of a compositional whole. The gallery and Teremok served as the passageway for the metropolitan as he walked from his residence (to the right of the Teremok) to the cathedral. Passing through the gate tower, you will see the military prison, replete with lookout towers, located on the opposite side of the Teremok gates.

You should go through, in order to have a full walk around the tranquil grounds. From this side, you can enter the bell tower, which dates from 1680. Taking the stairs inside, through the door off its first level, you'll have access to the gallery itself and can walk along the walls. As you go around the complex, you will encounter young artists who seem to have chosen this quiet place to sketch for their school assignments. ☉ *Wed.–Mon. 9–6, except first Mon. of month. For information about excursions, ☎ 095/276–9256.*

The next monastery on the tour is best reached by subway. Return to the Proletarskaya station and take the subway one stop to the Taganskaya station. Before exiting, transfer to the connecting station on the circle line; you will come out onto Taganskaya Square.

TIME OUT Taganskaya Square is home to Moscow's most renowned drama theater, the Taganka, and the area is rich in restaurants catering to theater crowds. One of the best is the **Skazka** restaurant (1 Tovarishchevsky pereulok, ☎ 095/271–0998), specializing in Russian cuisine. As with most other restaurants in Moscow, you are best off making reservations.

Several streets intersect at this busy square. Go left as you come out of the station and cross the short street to be on the same corner as the Taganka Drama and Comedy Theatre, one of Moscow's most famous theaters and quite slyly subversive when founded in 1964. From here, you should cross the whole left flank of the square in order to reach ulitsa Bolshaya Kommunisticheskaya (Big Communist Street), which is the third street radiating out from your left as you exit the subway. This is an old residential area; the shady street is lined with tall birch trees and two-story apartment buildings. Of late, various commercial enterprises (including Moscow's exclusive Commercial Club, for its business elite) have moved into its renovated residences. It's left to wonder when the street may be renamed, given the contradictions to it that it now displays. One block down, at No. 15, is the lovely **Church of St. Martin the Confessor.** It dates from the late 18th century and is in need of full restoration; its cupola is rusted and little trees are growing on its roof, but it is a working church. Farther down the street, at No. 29, you will find another building of historical importance, the apartment house where the theater director Stanislavsky was born in 1863.

Continue down this long street until you reach the bulging **Andronevskaya Ploshchad.** Carefully make your way to the opposite side of the square and turn left onto Andronevsky Pereulok. On the left-hand side of the street there is a small park; you will pass through the middle of it to reach the entrance to the **Andronikov Monastery.** The whitewashed walls of the monastery's fortification will be visible through the trees.

The Andronikov Monastery is home to the **Andrey Rublyov Museum of Ancient Russian Culture and Art.** The museum is named after the monastery's most celebrated monk, the icon painter Andrey Rublyov, who is believed to be buried here. Rublyov lived in the early 15th century, a time of much bloodshed and violence. Russia was slowly loosening the Mongol-Tatar yoke, and people lived in constant fear as the divided Russian principalities fought among themselves and against the Mongol-Tatar invaders. Rublyov's icons seem even more remarkable when viewed against the backdrop of his turbulent era. His works are amazing creations of flowing pastels conveying peace and tranquility. His most famous work, *The Holy Trinity,* is now housed in the Tretyakov Gallery (*see* Tour 7). The museum in the Andronikov Monastery, strangely enough, does not contain a single Rublyov work. Its collection of ancient religious art is nevertheless a fine one and well worth a visit. Tickets to the exhibits are sold in the office located around the corner to the right as you enter the monastery grounds. The museum is divided into three sections, and you must purchase a ticket for each part that you want to see. *Andronevskaya Ploshchad 10,* ☎ *095/278–1429.* ☉ *Thurs.–Tues. 11–6. Closed last Fri. of month.*

The Andronikov Monastery underwent extensive reconstruction in the 1950s and was refurbished again in the late 1980s. It is in much better condition than the Novospassky Monastery or Krutitskoye Podvorye. A stroll inside its heavy stone fortification is an excursion into Moscow's past. The rumble of the city is drowned out by the loud crowing of birds overhead. Even the air seems more pure here, perhaps because of the old birch trees growing on the monastery grounds and just outside its walls. The Andronikov Monastery was founded in 1360 by the metropolitan Alexei and named in honor of its first abbot, St. Andronik. The site was chosen not only for its strategic importance—on the steep banks of the Yauza River—but also because, according to legend, it was from this hill that the metropolitan Alexei got his first glimpse of the Kremlin.

The dominating structure on the monastery grounds is the **Spassky Sobor** (Cathedral of the Savior), Moscow's oldest stone structure. Erected in 1420–27 on the site of an earlier, wooden church, it rests on the mass grave of Russian soldiers who fought in the Battle of Kulikovo (1380), the decisive Russian victory that eventually led to the end of Mongol rule in Russia. Unfortunately, the original interiors, which were painted by Andrey Rublyov and another famous icon painter, Danil Chorny, were lost to a fire in 1812. Fragments of their frescoes have been restored, however. The cathedral is open for services at 5:30 PM on Saturday and 9 AM on Sunday.

The building to your immediate left as you enter the monastery is the former abbot's residence. It now houses a permanent exhibit entitled "Masterpieces of Ancient Russian Art" from the 13th through 16th centuries. The exhibit includes icons from the Novgorod, Tver, Rostov, and Moscow schools. A highlight of the collection is the early-16th-century *St. George Smiting the Dragon,* from the Novgorod School.

The next building, to the left and across the pathway from the Cathedral of the Savior, is the **Refectory.** Like the Novospassky Monastery, it was built during the reign of Ivan the Great, in 1504–06. Today it houses the museum's exhibit of new acquisitions, which consists primarily of icons from the 19th and 20th centuries. Attached to the Refectory is the Church of St. Michael the Archangel, another example of the style known as Moscow Baroque. It was commissioned by the Lopukhin family—relatives of Yevdokiya Lopukhina, the first, unloved wife of Peter the Great—as the family crypt in 1694. But there are no Lophukins buried here as Peter had Yevdokiya banished to a monastery in faraway Suzdal before the church was even finished, and her family was exiled to Siberia.

The museum's last exhibit is located in the former monks' residence, the redbrick building just beyond the Church of St. Michael. The exhibit is devoted to Nikolai the Miracle Worker and contains icons depicting his life and work.

Leave the monastery through the main gate and return to Andronevskaya Ploshchad. The nearest subway station is Ploshchad Ilyicha. To reach it, turn left from the square onto ulitsa Sergiya Radonezhskovo; the subway is just one long block away. If you want to return to the Taganskaya subway station, you can take bus 53, which stops at the corner of Tukhinskaya and will let you off where you began on ulitsa Bolshaya Kommunisticheskaya.

Excursion 1: Arkhangelskoye Estate Museum

This manor-estate museum is located in the village of Arkhangelskoye, some 26 kilometers (15 miles) from Moscow, on the banks of the Moscow River. The palace, but not the grounds, have been closed for several years for restoration work, and no date has been set for its official reopening, but excursions can still be made out there. Check first with your hotel's service bureau or the tour agency you have chosen for updated information.

The estate, which includes the former palace of Prince Yusupov, comprises a striking group of 18th- and 19th-century buildings whose architecture artfully blends into the landscape. The main complex was built at the end of the 18th century for Prince Golitsyn by the French architect Chevalier de Huerne. In 1810, the family fell upon harder times and sold it to the rich landlord Yusupov, onetime director of the imperial theaters and of the Hermitage Museum. The estate became home to his extraordinary art collection.

The classical palace's holdings included paintings by Boucher, Vigée-Lebrun, Hubert Robert, Roslin, Tiepolo, Van Dyck, and many others, as well as antique statues, furniture, mirrors, chandeliers, glassware, and china. The collection also includes samples of fabrics, china, and glassware, all of which were produced on the estate.

In the French Park are alleys and strolling lanes; many still hold statues and monuments commemorating royal visits; there is also a monument to Pushkin, whose favorite retreat was Arkhangelskoye. In the western part is an interesting small pavilion, known as the Temple to the Memory of Catherine the Great, which depicts the empress as Themis, goddess of justice. It seems that Yusupov, reportedly a Casanova, had turned the head of Russia's empress, renowned herself for having legions of lovers. This "temple" was built as a compliment for a painting she had previously commissioned—one in which she was depicted as Venus, with Yusupov as Apollo. Overall, a definite sense of disrepair—with the exception of the closed palace with its ongoing reconstruction—pervades. Back outside the estate grounds, the Estate (Serf) Theater, on the right side of the main road, was built in 1817 by the serf architect Ivanov; it seated 400 and was the home of the biggest and best-known company of serf-actors. The well-preserved stage decorations are by the Venetian artist Pietrodi Gonzaga.

Excursion 2: Zagorsk (Sergyev Posad)

★ **Zagorsk** is located some 75 kilometers (46 miles) northeast of Moscow, making it a comfortable, and popular, day trip. The city's chief attraction is the **Troitsa-Sergyeva Lavra** (Trinity Monastery of St. Sergius), which for 500 years has been the most important center of pilgrimage in Russia. Before the revolution, the town was known as Sergyev Posad, after the monastery's founder, and in 1991 it was officially returned to its proper name. But the Soviet name of Zagorsk—in honor of a Bolshevik who was assassinated in 1919—has stuck, and you are as likely to hear the town and the monastery itself called one as the other.

The city also claims fame as a center of toy making. The world's first *matryoshka* (the familiar colorful, wooden nesting doll) was designed here at the beginning of the century, and most of the matroshkas you see for sale in Moscow and St. Petersburg are made in Zagorsk. The city even has a toy museum. It is rarely included on organized tours, but it is located within walking distance of the monastery, at 136 Prospect Krasnoi Armii. The museum contains a collection of toys that amused, educated, and illuminated the lives of Russian children for generations. It is well worth an hour of your time, even if your interest is only casual.

The best way to visit Zagorsk is to join an organized tour, since it is a full-day affair, out of the city. All tour services offer day trips to Zagorsk. The cost usually includes lunch in addition to a guided tour and transportation. It is also possible to visit on your own by taking the commuter train from Moscow's Yaroslavsky Vokzal (Yaroslav Railroad Station). The ride takes about two hours; tickets are purchased at the train station for rubles. This is obviously much less expensive than an organized tour, but far from hassle-free. If you choose this alternative, be sure to pack your own lunch, since Zagorsk's only full-fledged restaurant fills up fast with prebooked tourist groups, especially in the summer. You must also take care to dress appropriately for your visit to the functioning monastery, to make certain you won't go all the way there only to be turned back at the entrance. (Russia is far stricter about enforcing dress codes at religious sites than are most similar places in Europe.) Men are expected to remove their hats, and women are required to wear below knee-length skirts (*never* shorts, even walking shorts) and bring something to cover their heads. The grounds are open Tues.–Fri., 10–5.

The monastery was founded in 1340 by Sergius of Radonezh, who would later become Russia's patron saint. The site rapidly became the nucleus of the small medieval settlement, and in 1550 the imposing white walls were built to enclose the complex of buildings. The monastery was a Russian stronghold during the Time of Troubles and the Polish assault on Moscow in the early 17th century, and Peter the Great took refuge here during a bloody revolt of the *streltsy* that took the lives of some of his closest relatives and advisors. After the Bolshevik Revolution, the monastery was closed and turned into a museum. During World War II, however, in an attempt to mobilize the country and stir up patriotism, the Soviet government got the support of the Church by returning to religious purposes some of the church property that had been confiscated earlier, including the Monastery of St. Sergius. Today the churches are again open for worship, and there is a flourishing theological college here. Until the reopening in 1988 of the Danilovsky Monastery in Moscow, this monastery was the residence of the patriarch and administrative center of the Russian Orthodox Church.

The ride to Zagorsk takes you through a lovely stretch of Russian countryside, dotted with colorful wooden cottages. As you approach the town, you see the sad and monolithic apartment buildings of the modern era. Then, peeking out above the sloping hills, the monastery's golden cupolas and soft-blue bell tower come into view.

You enter the monastery through the archway of the **Gate Church of St. John the Baptist.** It was erected in the late 17th century and is decorated with frescoes telling the life story of St. Sergius.

One of the most important historical events in his life occurred prior to 1380, when the decisive Russian victory in the Battle of Kulikovo led to the end of Mongol rule in Russia. Before leading his troops off to battle, Prince Dmitry Donskoy sought the blessing of the peace-loving monk Sergius, a move that is generally thought to have greatly aided the Russian victory.

Although all of the monastery's cathedrals vie for your attention (and each visitor will have a different favorite), the dominating structure is the massive, blue-domed and gold-starred **Uspensky Sobor** (Assumption Cathedral) located in the center. Built in 1554–85 with money donated by Czar Ivan the Terrible—purportedly in an attempt to atone for murdering his own son—it was modeled after the Kremlin's Uspensky Sobor. Its interior boasts frescoes and a 18th-century iconostasis. Among the artists to work on it was Simon Ushakov, a well-known icon painter from Moscow. The cathedral is open for morning services.

The small building just outside the Uspensky Cathedral (near the northwest corner) is the tomb of Boris Godunov and his family. Boris Godunov died suddenly in 1605, during the Polish attack on Moscow led by the False Dmitry, the first of many impostors to claim he was the son of Czar Ivan the Terrible. The death of Boris facilitated the invaders' victory, after which his family was promptly murdered. This explains why Boris was not bestowed the honor of burial in the Kremlin normally granted to czars.

Opposite Boris Godunov's tomb is a tiny and colorful chapel built above a miracle-working fountain. It is called Chapel-at-the-Well. According to legend, the spring here appeared during the Polish Siege (1608–10), when the monastery bravely held out for 16 months against the foreign invaders (this time led by the second False Dmitry). You can make a wish by washing your face and hands in its charmed waters. Towering above the monastery grounds is the five-tiered Baroque Bel-

Zagorsk (Sergyev Posad)

fry, which rises 285 feet. It was built in the 18th century to a design by the master of St. Petersburg Baroque, Bartolomeo Rastrelli.

Along the southern wall of the monastery, to your far left as you entered, is the 17th-century **Refectory and Church of St. Sergei.** The church is at the eastern end, topped by a single gilded dome. The long building of the Refectory, whose colorful facade adds to the vivid richness of the monastery's architecture, is where, in times past, pilgrims from near and far gathered to eat on feast days. The pink building just beyond the Refectory is the Metropolitan's Residence.

A continual service in memorium to St. Sergei is held all day, every day, in the white-stone **Troitsky Sobor** (Cathedral of the Holy Trinity), situated across the path from the Metropolitan's Residence. The church, which is very beautiful inside, was built in the 15th century over the tomb of St. Sergei; over the centuries it has received many precious gifts from the powerful and wealthy rulers who have made the pilgrimage to the church of Russia's patron saint. The icons inside were created by famous master Andrey Rublyov and one of his disciples, Danil Chorny. Ryublov's celebrated *Holy Trinity,* now on display at the Tretyakov Gallery, originally hung here; the work you see is a copy.

The vestry, the building behind the Church of the Holy Trinity, houses the monastery's **Museum of Ancient Russian Art.** It is often closed for no apparent reason or open only to groups, which is yet another reason to visit Zagorsk on a guided tour. The museum contains a spectacular collection of gifts presented to the monastery over the centuries. On display are precious jewels, jewel-encrusted embroideries, chalices, and censers. Next door to the vestry are two more museums, which are open to individual tourists. The first museum contains icons and icon covers, portrait art, and furniture. The other museum (on the second floor) is devoted to Russian folk art, with wooden crafted items and toys, as well as porcelain and jewelry. There is also a gift shop where you can pick up a souvenir of your visit to ancient Zagorsk.

Excursion 3: New Jerusalem Monastery

Novoierusalimsky Monastyr (New Jerusalem Monastery) is located near the town of Istra, some 55 kilometers (34 miles) northwest of Moscow. This is not the most visited place in Russia, and it is included in the standard offerings of tourist agencies only in the summer. In nice weather, it is a marvelous way to spend a day; its location in the picturesque Russian countryside—far from tourist crowds—only adds to its attraction. If you can't book a tour and are feeling adventurous, you could try an excursion on the commuter train. Trains leave from Rizhsky Vokzal (Riga Railroad Station) and take about an hour and a half. The best option of all would be to ask a Russian friend to guide your way and make a day of it in the countryside. Be sure to pack your lunch; the best you'll find in Istra is an occasional cafeteria or outdoor café. The monastery's museums are open 10–5 and are closed Monday and the last Friday of the month.

The monastery was founded in 1652 by Nikon, patriarch of the Russian Orthodox Church. It lies on exactly the same longitude as Jerusalem; and its main cathedral, Voskresensky Sobor (Resurrection Cathedral) is modeled after the Church of the Holy Sepulcher in Jerusalem. Nikon's objective in re-creating the original Jerusalem in Russia was to glorify the power of the Russian Orthodox Church and at the same time elevate his own position as its head. It was Nikon who initiated the great church reforms in the 17th century that eventually led to the *raskol* (schism) resulting in the Old Believer sects of the Russian Orthodox faith. As a reformer, he was progressive and enlightened, but he lusted for power, which eventually was his undoing. In 1658, before the monastery was even finished, the patriarch quarreled with the czar over Nikon's claim that the Church was ultimately superior to the State. Eventually Nikon was defrocked and banished to the faraway Ferapontov Monastery. He died in virtual exile in 1681 and then was buried in the monastery that was supposed to have glorified his power. You can find his crypt in the Church of St. John the Baptist, which is actually inside the Resurrection Cathedral. Ironically, the same church commission that defrocked Patriarch Nikon later voted to institute his reforms.

The monastery also comprises the Moscow Regional Museum, which contains a modest collection of prerevolutionary paintings, portrait art, porcelain, and armory. One section is devoted to the history of the monastery and its reconstruction. There is also a hall for temporary exhibits of contemporary art on the monastery grounds. Besides the Resurrection Cathedral, the ensemble of buildings inside the monastery includes the Moscow Baroque Nativity Church, the Czar's Chambers, and the modest Three-Saints Church. Nikon's three-story Hermitage, where he observed his private prayer alone, is located just outside the monastery's stone walls.

If you follow the path behind the monastery leading to the river, you will reach the Architectural and Ethnographic Museum of the Moscow Region. This open-air museum of restored Russian wooden architecture is set among the coppices on the high banks of the River Istra. Here you will find a 19th-century peasant log cabin, which is particularly interesting since dwelling houses like this are still in use. A huge stove takes up much of the living space, above which the peasants slept.

Also brought to the museum grounds are a wooden inn, a 17th-century wooden church, and a windmill. Examine them closely and you will discover that they were all constructed without a single nail, screw, or bolt and are built entirely of wood.

What to See and Do with Children

The **Moscow Circus** is always a hit with children. There are two big tops: the intimate "Old" Circus at 13 Tsvetnoy Bulvar (☎ 095/200–0668), and the modern "New" Circus at 7 Vernandskovo Prospect (☎ 095/930–2815). Tickets can be bought through the EPS Theater Box Office service (☎ 095/927–6982 or 095/927–6983).

There are performing dolphins at the **Sea Circus,** with acts twice daily weekdays and four times on weekends. Closed Mon.–Tues. (27 ul. Mironovskaya, ☎ 095/369–7966).

Even children who don't know Russian will delight in the performances of the **Obraztsov Puppet Theater** (3 ul. Sadovaya Samotechnaya, ☎ 095/299–6313). Puppetry is a particularly popular and well-honed art form in Russia, and this troupe is world-famous. The theater also boasts a "puppet cuckoo clock," which comes to life every hour on the hour.

Children may be similarly transfixed by the productions at the **Natalya Sats Children's Musical Theatre,** which puts on various fairy-tale shows. Sats was a determined proponent of her own idea of a theater for children, and in defiance of all expectations, it is still resoundingly popular. (5 Prospect Vernadskovo, ☎ 095/930–5177).

A fast elevator ride up the 364-meter (1,200-foot) **Ostankino Television Tower** (15 ul. Akademika Korolyeva, ☎ 095/282–2038) is bound to thrill any child. On a clear day, the view is tremendous. The tower is open for viewing 9–7, closed Monday. Visitors are allowed in at set times (approximately every 30 minutes) in groups. Bring your passport; you'll be asked to fill out a form with all your background information, a holdover from the Soviet days. If you want, you can have lunch at the tower's rotating restaurant, Sedmoye Nebo (Seventh Heaven). The food is bland but cheap. The set meal includes appetizer, main course, ice cream, and coffee. The restaurant is open from 10 to 6:30.

Animal lovers will get a kick out of the **Durova Animal Theater** (ul. Durova 4, ☎ 095/281–2914). The acting troupe at this theater (named for its founder, the famous animal trainer Vladimir Durov) is made up of cats, dogs, goats, and bears. The two stages (Big and Small) each have daily shows on weekdays, and two shows a day on weekends.

At the **Arlecchino Children's Club** (not to be confused with the Arlecchino restaurant, which is primarily for adults and located elsewhere), children between the ages of 3 and 12 can make merry in the many playrooms and have a snack at the café. For today's child: computer games! The entrance fee includes a slice of cake, beverage, and clown show. *19/3 ul. Verkhnyaya Radishchevskaya, ☎ 095/915–1107. ☺ Daily 11–7.*

Winter or summer, **Gorky Park** has something for children of all ages. The Ferris wheel offers spectacular views of downtown Moscow, and the amusement park has plenty of other rides that will thrill youngsters. In summer, excursion boats leave from the park's pier for trips around Moscow. In winter, you can join Muscovites on the crowded skating rinks or take a ride on a horse-drawn troika.

Off the Beaten Path

Donskoy Monastery

The 16th-century Donskoy Monastery is a fascinating memorial to Russian architecture and art. From 1934 through 1992 a branch of the Shchusev Architecture Museum, keeping architectural details of churches, monasteries, and public buildings destroyed under the Soviets, was located—more or less secretly—inside its walls. Today the monastery is once again functioning as a religious institution, and the museum is slowly removing its exhibits from inside the churches. But the bits and pieces of demolished churches and monuments remain, forming a graveyard of destroyed architecture from Russia's past.

The monastery is situated in a secluded, wooded area in the southwest section of Moscow. It is open to the public Tuesday–Friday and Sunday 11–6 and is closed the last Thursday of the month. You can reach it by taking the subway to the Shabolovskaya station. When you exit the subway, turn right and walk one block to Donskaya ulitsa. Turn right again and follow the street until you see the copper-topped domes of the monastery's churches above the trees to your left. Follow the path along the redbrick fortification wall until you reach the main entrance on the other side.

The monastery grounds are surrounded by a high defensive wall with 12 towers. Founded in the late 16th century, it was the last of the defense fortifications to be built around Moscow. It is situated on the site where, in 1591, the Russian army stood waiting for an impending attack from Tatar troops grouped on the opposite side of the river. According to legend, the Russians awoke one morning to find the Tatars gone. Their sudden retreat was considered a miracle, and Regent Boris Godunov ordered a monastery built to commemorate the miraculous victory. Of course, it didn't happen quite like that, but historians confirm that the Tatars did retreat after only minor skirmishes, which is difficult to explain. Never again would they come so close to Moscow.

The victory was attributed to the icon of the Virgin of the Don that Prince Dmitry Donskoy had supposedly carried previously, during his campaign in 1380 (in which the Russians won their first decisive victory against the Tatars). The monastery was named in honor of the wonder-working icon.

When you enter through the western gates, an icon of the Mother of the Don looks down on you from above the entrance to the imposing New Cathedral. The brick cathedral was built in the late 17th century by Peter the Great's sister, Sophia. It has been under restoration for decades; services are held in the gallery surrounding the church, where the architectural exhibits were once housed. The smaller, Old Cathedral stands to the right of the New Cathedral. The attractive red church with white trim was built in 1591–93, during the reign of Boris Godunov. It is open for services.

One of the most fascinating sections of the monastery is its graveyard, where you will find many fine examples of memorial art. After the plague swept through Moscow in 1771, Catherine the Great forbade any more burials in the city center. The Donskoy Monastery, at that time located on the city's outskirts, became a fashionable burial place for the well-to-do. The small **Church of the Archangel** built against the fortification wall to your far right was the private chapel and crypt of the prominent Golitsyn family (original owners of the Arkhangelskoye estate). Many leading intellectuals, politicians, and aristocrats were buried here in the 18th, 19th, and 20th centuries. Among them are the dramatist Alexander Sumarokov, the architect Osip Bove, and the 19th-century philosopher Pyotr Chaadayev, whose modern-day followers still leave flowers at his grave.

If you walk down to the eastern wall of the monastery, you will find remnants of the decorative stone facade of the original **Cathedral of Christ Our Savior** (*see* Tour 6) which the Soviets blew up in 1931 and which is now being rebuilt. One of the facades shows Monk Sergei of Radonezh (*see* Excursion 2) giving his blessing to Dmitry Donskoy before he left for the decisive battle that led to the end of Tatar rule in Russia. The northern wall is lined with portals from ancient churches destroyed or flooded along the Volga to make way for a huge reservoir. As you make your way back to the main entrance, you will notice a cast-iron pedestal in the courtyard outside the New Cathedral. This is what remains of the Triumphal Arch, which once stood at the end of Tverskaya ulitsa. That arch was destroyed in the 1930s. In the 1960s, the original was replicated and erected at the city center's end of Kutuzovsky Prospect.

Kolomenskoye

★ If you want to spend an afternoon in the great Russian outdoors without actually leaving the city, a visit to Kolomenskoye is a must. Situated on a high bluff overlooking the Moskva River, this estate was once a favorite summer residence of Moscow's grand dukes and czars. Today it is a popular public park with museums, a functioning church, old Russian cottages, and other attractions. Take the subway to the Kolomenskaya station on the green line; a walk of about 10 minutes up a slight hill will bring you to the park's entrance. *39 Prospect Andropova,* ☎ *095/115–2384.* ☉ *Wed.–Sun. 11–5.*

As you walk up the hill to Kolomenskoye, the first sight to greet you is the striking blue domes of the **Church of Our Lady of Kazan.** The church is open for worship. A wooden palace once stood in the park opposite the church. It was built by Czar Alexei, Peter the Great's Father, and Peter spent much time here when he was growing up. Nothing remains of this huge wooden palace (Catherine the Great ordered it destroyed in 1767), but there is a scale model at the museum. The exhibits of the museum, devoted to Russian timber architecture and folk crafts, are found in the old servants' quarters, at the end of the tree-lined path leading from the main entrance.

Most remarkable is the **Church of the Ascension,** situated on the bluff overlooking the river. The church dates from the 1530s and was restored in the late 1800s. Its skyscraping tower is an example of the tent or pyramid-type structure that was popular in Russian architecture in the 16th century. The view from the bluff is impressive in its contrasts, and there is always something happening. From your 16th-century backdrop, you can look across the river to the north, to the 20th-century concrete apartment houses that dominate the contemporary Moscow skyline. In summer you'll see Muscovites bathing in the river below the church, and in winter the area abounds in cross-country skiers.

Examples of wooden architecture from other parts of Russia have been transferred to Kolomenskoye, turning the estate into an open-air museum. In the wooded area near the site of the former wooden palace, you will find a 17th-century prison tower from Siberia, a defense tower from the White Sea, and a 17th-century mead brewery from the village of Preobrazhenskaya. One of the most attractive buildings to be seen in its original form is the wooden cottage where Peter the

Great lived while supervising the building of the Russian fleet in Arkhangelsk. It was moved here from that northern city in 1934.

Kuskovo and Ceramics Palace Museum

In the 18th and 19th centuries, this country estate was the Moscow aristocracy's favorite summer playground. It belonged to the noble Sheremetyevs, one of Russia's wealthiest and most distinguished families. Moscow's international airport, built on land once belonging to one of their many estates, takes their name. Kuskovo is located just outside the ring road marking the city borders, but you can reach it by public transportation. Take the subway to Ryazansky Prospect and then Bus 208 or 133 six stops to Kuskovo Park. This is obviously not as accessible as Kolomenskoye, and you may find it more convenient to book a tour that would include transportation. Whatever you do, be sure to phone ahead before making the trek out here, because the estate often closes in humid weather and when it is very cold. *Ul. Yunosti 2, ☎ 095/370–0160. ☉ Nov.–Apr., Wed.–Sun. 10–4; May–Oct., Wed.–Fri. 11–7, weekends 10–6. Closed last Wed. of month.*

The land of Kuskovo belonged to the Sheremetyevs as far back as the early 17th century, but the estate acquired its present appearance in the late 18th century. Often called a Russian Versailles, most work on it was commissioned by Prince Peter Sheremetyev, who sought a suitable place for entertaining guests in the summer. The park was created by Russian landscape artists who had spent much time in Europe studying their art. The French-style gardens are dotted with buildings representing the major architectural trends of Europe: the Dutch cottage, the Italian villa, the grotto, and the hermitage, where, in the fashion of the day, dinner tables were raised mechanically from the ground floor to the second-floor dining room.

The centerpiece of the estate is the wooden palace, built in the early Russian classical style by the serf architects Alexei Mironov and Fedor Argunov. Peter Sheremetyev owned more than 150,000 serfs, many of whom received architectural training and participated in the building of his estate. (Serfs also constituted a theater troupe that gave weekly performances, another common practice on nobles' estates.)

The palace, which is made of timber on a white-stone foundation, overlooks an artificial lake. It has been a museum since 1918, and its interior decorations, including fine parquet floors and silk wall-coverings, have been well preserved. The bedroom, with its fine canopy bed, was merely for show; the Sheremetyevs used the palace exclusively for entertainment and did not live here. The marvelous White Hall, with its parquet floors, gilded wall decorations, and crystal chandeliers, served as the ballroom.

On display in the inner rooms are paintings by French, Italian, and Flemish artists, Chinese porcelain, furniture, ornaments, and other articles of everyday life from the 18th and 19th centuries. The palace also houses a collection of 18th-century Russian art and a rather celebrated ceramics museum with a rich collection of Russian, Soviet, and foreign ceramics.

Ostankino Palace (and Museum of Serf Art)

Like the Kuskovo Palace (*see above*), this museum, which is within the city, is set on grounds that belonged to the wealthy Sheremetyev family. It was commissioned by Count Nikolai Sheremetyev in the late 18th century and was also built by a team of serf architects. They were led by Pavel Argunov, a serf who had contributed much to the Sheremetyev estate in Kuskovo. There is a sad tale of love behind this magnificent estate. In 1801 Count Nikolai married Praskovia Kovalyova, a member of his serf acting troupe. The daughter of a blacksmith, Praskovia had captured the count's heart with her wit and beauty. Their marriage "between unequals" caused quite a scandal, and the couple withdrew from society to their newly built estate in Ostankino. But just two years after their marriage, Praskovia died in childbirth, and the heartbroken count abandoned the estate forever. You can reach it by taking the subway to VDNKh (All-Russian Exhibition Center, opposite the Kosmos Hotel); from there take Tram 11 or 17 to the last stop on the line. *Pervaya Ostankinskaya ul., 5, ☎ 095/286–6288. ⊙ Oct.–Apr., Thurs.–Mon. 10–4; May–Sept., Thurs.–Mon. 11–5.*

This Sheremetyev estate encompassed more than 2 million acres, with 150,000 serfs and an annual income of 1.5 million rubles. The palace's fine decorations include delicate, lacelike gilt carvings on the portals and doors, cornices, columns, and walls. Ornate crystal chandeliers hang from the painted ceilings, and the fine parquet floors are true masterpieces of art. The stoves and fireplaces have lacquered-tile, marble, malachite, and bronze faces. There is also a fine collection of 17th- and 18th-century carvings, crystal, porcelain, and fans.

The highlight of the palace is its theater, which had its heyday in the 18th century. The company included some 200 actors, singers, dancers, and musicians, all of them serfs belonging to the Sheremetyev family. The chairs in the theater were movable so that the auditorium could be transformed into a ballroom within minutes. The devices for scenic, lighting, and sound effects were also invented by the serfs.

Just outside the main entrance to the palace is the attractive redbrick Church of the Trinity, built in 1683 by the serf architect Pavel Potekhin. The church is open for services.

Sightseeing Checklist

This list includes attractions covered in the preceding tours as well as additional ones described for the first time.

Art and Architecture Museums
Andrey Rublyov Museum of Ancient Culture and Art (in the **Andronikov Monastery,** *see* Tour 9)

House of Artists (*see* Tour 7)

Manege Central Exhibit Hall (*see* Tour 4)

Museum of Decorative, Applied and Folk Art. This museum is similar to the Russian Folk Art Museum (*see* Tour 3), only bigger. The highlight here is the Palekh collection. *Delegatskaya ul. 3, ☎ 095/921–0139; tours, 095/923–1741. ⊙ Wed., Sat.–Mon. 10–6; Tues., Thurs. 12:30–8. Closed last Thurs. of month.*

Museum of Horse Breeding. This special curiosity grew out of a collection of paintings belonging to a stud-farm owner who was in charge of Russia's stud farms in the 1920s. On display are canvases and sculptures depicting thoroughbreds, Russian trotters, and troikas in decorative and everyday harness. The collection also includes carriages, dress harnesses, various bells, and toy horses made of china, clay, and glass. *Timiryazevskaya ul. 44, ☎ 095/976–1003. ⊙ Tues.–Sat. 10–6.*

Museum of 17th-Century Applied Art (*see* Tour 1)

Museum of 17th-Century Architecture and Art (*see* Tour 2)

Oriental Art Museum. The museum has a large collection of art from the Central Asian republics, China, India, Japan, and Africa. *12A Nikitsky Bulvar, ☎ 095/202–4555. ⊙ Tues.–Sun. 11–8.*

Ostankino Museum of Serf Art (*see* Off the Beaten Track)

Palace of the 16th and 17th Centuries (in the Romanov House, *see* Tour 2)

Puppet Museum. This museum, located in the Obraztsov Puppet Theater, has a collection of old and modern theatrical puppets from more than 30 countries. It is open 45 minutes prior to performances. *3 ul. Sadovaya-Samotechnaya,* ☎ *095/299–0904. Closed summer.*

Pushkin Museum of Fine Arts (*see* Tour 6)

Russian Folk Art Museum (*see* Tour 3)

Shchusev Architecture Museum (*see* Tour 5)

Tretyakov Art Gallery (*see* Tour 7)

Cathedrals, Churches, Places of Worship, and Monasteries

Andronikov Monastery (*see* Tour 9)

Annunciation Cathedral (Blagoveshchensky Sobor, *see* Tour 1)

Assumption Cathedral (Uspensky Sobor, *see* Tour 1)

Cathedral of the Archangel (Arkhangelsky Sobor, *see* Tour 1)

Cathedral of Christ Our Savior (*see* Tour 6)

Cathedral of the Ephiphany Monastery (Bogoyavlensky Sobor, *see* Tour 2)

Cathedral of Twelve Apostles (*see* Tour 1)

Church of All-Saints in Kulishki (*see* Tour 2)

Church of the Deposition of the Robe (Tserkov Rispolozheniya, *see* Tour 1)

Church of the Great Ascension (*see* Tour 4)

Church of the Intercession in Fili. This 17th-century church is a charming example of Moscow Baroque. It is open as a museum and used as a display hall for temporary art exhibits. It is located near the Fili subway station on the light blue line; follow the subway line (which runs above ground) when you exit the station, and it will lead you directly to the church. *Ul. Novozavodskaya 6,* ☎ *095/148–4552.* ☉ *Thurs.–Mon. 11–5. Closed last Fri. of month.*

Church of the Nativity (*see* Tour 3)

Church of the Resurrection (*see* Tour 3)

Church of St. Barbara (*see* Tour 2)

Church of St. George on Pskov Hill (*see* Tour 2)

Church of St. Martin the Confessor (*see* Tour 9)

Church of St. Martyr George the Victorious. This small, single-domed church in Victory Park near Poklonnaya Gora was built in time for the 50th anniversary celebrations of victory in World War II, along with the War Memorial Obelisk and the Central Museum of the Great Patriotic War (*see* Historical Museums and *see* Monuments). It is one of the few churches completed entirely after the demise of communism, when religion was officially banned by the state. Airy, bright, and hung with icons, it provides a peaceful third side to the triangle of park encomiums, as well as a small bridge between Moscow's religious past and future. *Daily services at 9 AM; 10 AM Sun. and high holy days.*

Church of St. Maxim the Blessed (*see* Tour 2)

Church of St. Nicholas in Khamovniki (*see* Tour 7)

Church of St. Simon the Stylite (*see* Tour 5)

Church of the Transfiguration on the Sands (*see* Tour 5)

Danilovsky Monastery. Originally founded in the 13th century and used as an orphanage by the Soviets, this monastery was returned to the Orthodox Church in the 1980s and restored for the celebrations of 1,000 years of Christianity in Rus in 1988. It is now the seat of the Patriarch of Moscow and All Russia; the Orthodox Church moved its administrative center here from the St. Sergius monastery in Zagorsk. The monastery is open on Sunday, when services are held in its Church of the Intercession. The closest subway stop is the Tulskaya station on the gray line. *22 ul. Danilovsky Val.*

Donskoy Monastery (*see* Off the Beaten Track)

Dormition Cathedral (Uspensky Sobor, *see* Tour 1)

Ivanovsky Monastery (St. John's Convent, corner of Zabelina ul. and Maly Ivanovsky Pereulok, near the Kitai Gorod subway station). The monastery was built in the 16th century and restored in the 19th. Today it is in shambles, having been used as a prison in the Stalinist era. Among the noble women who were forced to take the veil here were Empress Elizabeth's illegitimate daughter, Princess Tarankova, and the mad serf-owner Dariya Saltykova, who was imprisoned here after she murdered 138 of her serfs, most of them young women.

Kazansky Sobor (*see* Tour 2)

Krutitskoye Ecclesiastical Residence (Krutitskoye Podvorye, *see* Tour 9)

Mosque. The *namaz* is recited here five times everyday. *7 Vypolzov Pereulok,* ☎ *095/281–3866.*

New Jerusalem Monastery (*see* Excursion 3)

New Maiden's Convent and Cemetery (Novodevichy, *see* Tour 8)

New Savior Monastery (Novospassky Monastery, *see* Tour 9)

St. Basil's Cathedral (Pokrovsky Sobor, *see* Tour 1)

Trinity Church in Nikitniki (*see* Tour 2)

Synagogue. Moscow's synagogue, located near the Kitai Gorod subway station, holds services every morning at 8. *Ul. Arkhipova 8,* ☎ *095/924–2424.*

Yelokhovsky Cathedral. This attractive, blue-and-gold cathedral is one of Moscow's most important churches. Until the reopening of the Danilovsky Monastery in 1988, this was the seat of the Moscow patriarch. The remains of St. Alexei, metropolitan of Moscow in the 14th century, are buried here in a shrine in front of the iconostasis. Morning and evening services are held daily. The cathedral is located a block south of the Baumanskaya subway station. *Ul. Spartakovskaya 15,* ☎ *095/261–6913.*

Zachaitievsky Monastery (*see* Tour 6)

Zagorsk (Sergyev Posad, *see* Excursion 2)

Znamensky Cathedral (*see* Tour 2)

Historical Buildings and Sites

Arbat (*see* Tour 5)

Armory Palace (Oruzhenaya Palata, *see* Tour 1)

Bolshoi Theater (*see* Tour 2)

Central Telegraph Office (*see* Tour 3)

Diamond Fund (Almazny Fond, *see* Tour 1)

English House (*see* Tour 2)

Friendship House (*see* Tour 5)

Grand Kremlin Palace (Bolshoi Kremlyovsky Dvorets, *see* Tour 1)

GUM (*see* Tour 2)

Ivan the Great Bell Tower (*see* Tour 1)

Kitai Gorod (*see* Tour 2)

Kremlin (*see* Tour 1)

Lenin Mausoleum (Mavzolei Lenina, *see* Tour 1)

Lubyanka Prison (*see* Tour 2)

Merchant Arcade (Gostinny Dvor, *see* Tour 2)

Metropole Hotel (*see* Tour 2)

Ostankino Television Tower (*see* What to See and Do with Children)

Palace of Congresses (Dvorets Syezdov, *see* Tour 1)

Palace of Facets (Granovitaya Palata, *see* Tour 1)

Pashkov House (*see* Tour 6)

Pertsov House (*see* Tour 6)

Printing Yard (Pechatny Dvor, *see* Tour 2)
Pushkin Square (Pushkinskaya Ploshchad, *see* Tour 3)
Red Square (Krasnaya Ploshchad, *see* Tour 2)
Russian State Library (*see* Tour 6)
Slavonic Greco-Latin Academy (*see* Tour 1)
Spasso House (*see* Tour 5)
Tchaikovsky Conservatory (*see* Tour 4)
Terem (*see* Tour 1)
Yeliseyevsky Gastronome (*see* Tour 3)

Historical Museums

Arkhangelskoye Estate Museum (*see* Excursion 1)
Central Museum of the Great Patriotic War. This World War II museum, located in Victory Park, gives tribute to Soviet soldiers who fought against fascism. Finished in 1995 after decades of planning, its opening became a focal point of that year's 50th anniversary celebrations of Allied victory. Monumental in design, in keeping with the lines of social-realist architecture, it is a sight to behold. Stairs lined with bronze sculptures of the war dead lead up to Glory Hall, whose domed ceiling is an enormous laurel wreath, with the Red Army star in its middle.

Exhibits include a gallery of war art and dioramas depicting major battles. Memory Hall, downstairs, is lined with bookcases filled with biographical tomes that give a paragraph of vital statistics for each soldier who was killed. Seeing the number of entries that fill these pages, one understands the sway this war exerts upon people here. *Victory Park, near Poklonnaya Gora,* ☏ *095/449–8069 or 095/449–8044 for excursions.* ☛ *Free.* ☉ *Tues.–Sun. 10–6 (doors close at 5).*
History Museum (*see* Tour 1)
Kolomenskoye Estate Museum (*see* Off the Beaten Track)
Kuskovo Palace Museum (*see* Off the Beaten Track)
Lenin House Museum. This manor house in Leninskiye Gori, about 30 kilometers (18 miles) from Moscow, was Lenin's country retreat and is still open as a museum. The ailing Lenin died here on January 21, 1924. The rooms are furnished as they were when Lenin lived here, and there are documents and manuscripts on display. Built in 1830, the house stands in a park of 175 acres, with 150-year-old oak trees and a number of ponds; before the revolution, it was the home of the mayor of Moscow. Old motor cars stand in the garage, including Lenin's Rolls-Royce, adapted for use in heavy snow. To reach the museum, take the suburban train from the Paveletsky railway station to the Leninskaya station, and from there Bus 27 or 28. *Leninskiye Gori,* ☏ *095/548–9309 or 095/548–9478.* ☉ *Wed.–Mon. 10–6. Closed last day of month.*
Moscow Wax Museum. A Russian Madame Tussaud's, this place has figures of important leaders, all the way up to Yeltsin. *14 ulitsa Tverskaya,* ☏ *095/229–8552.* ☉ *Tues.–Sun. 11–7.*
Museum of the History of Moscow (*see* Tour 2)
Panorama Museum of the Battle of Borodino (1812) and Kutuzov's Hut. The battle panorama, near the Triumphal Arch, is housed in a cylindrical building that was built in 1962 to commemorate the 150th anniversary of the famous Battle of Borodino. Adjacent is a replica of Kutuzov's wooden hut, where the Russian War Council, headed by Field Marshal Mikhail Kutuzov, decided that the army would retreat from Moscow. *38 Kutuzovsky Prospect,* ☏ *095/148–1965; Kutuzov's Hut,* ☏ *095/148–5332. Kutuzov's Hut open Sun., Tues.–Thurs., Sat. 10–5; closed last Thurs. of month. Panorama bldg. open Sat.–Thurs. 11–6.*
Revolution Museum (*see* Tour 3)
Revolution Museum, Mokhovaya Branch (*see* Tour 6)

Train of Mourning (1 Kozhevnicheskaya Ploshchad, ☎ 095/235–2898). This memorial to Lenin is located outside the Paveletsky Railway Station. On display are the engine and carriage that brought the coffin with Lenin's body to Moscow. ☉ *Weekdays 10–6.*

Literary, Musical, and Theatrical Museums

Chaliapin House Museum. Theodore Chaliapin, one of the world's greatest opera singers, lived in this beautifully restored manor house from 1910 to 1922. Chaliapin was stripped of his Soviet citizenship while on tour in France in 1922; he never returned to Russia again. The Soviets turned his home into an apartment building, and until restorations in the 1980s, the building contained 60 communal apartments. With help from Chaliapin's family in France, the rooms have been arranged and furnished as they were when Chaliapin lived here. The walls are covered with works of art given to Chaliapin by talented friends (such as the artists Mikhail Vrubel and Isaac Levitan). Also on display are Chaliapin's colorful costumes, which were donated to the museum by his son. When you reach the piano room, you are treated to original recordings of Chaliapin singing his favorite roles. Entrance is from inside the courtyard. English-language excursions are available. *25–27 Novinsky Bulvar,* ☎ *095/252–2530.* ☉ *Tues., weekends 10–6; Wed., Thurs. 11:30–6:30. Closed last day of month.*

Chekhov Museum. The museum is located in the home where Chekhov lived from 1886 to 1890. The rooms are arranged as they were when he lived here, with his personal effects on display. Also on exhibit are manuscripts, letters, and photographs. *Sadovaya-Kudrinskaya ul. 6,* ☎ *095/291–6154.* ☉ *Thurs., weekends 11–5; Wed., Fri. 2–7. Closed last day of month.*

Dostoevsky Museum. This museum devoted to the great Russian novelist is located on the grounds of the hospital where he was born and where his father worked as a doctor. *2 ul. Dostoevskovo,* ☎ *095/281–1085.* ☉ *Thurs., weekends 11–6; Wed., Fri. 2–7. Closed last day of month.*

Glinka Museum. This museum is devoted to the history of music, with a special emphasis on Russian composers of the 19th century. There is a fine collection of musical instruments. *4 ul. Fadeyeva,* ☎ *095/972–3237.* ☉ *Wed., Fri., weekends 11–6:30; Tues., Thurs. 1–7:30. Closed last Fri. of month.*

Lermontov Museum. The museum is devoted to the poet Mikhail Lermontov and is located in the house where he lived from 1830 to 1832. *Malaya Molchanovka ul. 2,* ☎ *095/291–5298.* ☉ *Thurs., weekends 11–6; Wed., Fri. 2–8:30.*

Mayakovsky Library and Museum. This museum to Russia's great revolutionary poet is located in his former home. *3/6 Proeyzd Serova,* ☎ *095/255–0186.* ☉ *Tues., Fri.–Sun. 10–6; Mon. noon–6; Thurs. 1–9.*

Alexander Pushkin Apartment Museum (*see* Tour 5)

Pushkin Memorial Museum (*see* Tour 6)

Alexander Scriabin Museum (*see* Tour 5)

Leo Tolstoy House Museum (*see* Tour 7)

Leo Tolstoy Memorial Museum (*see* Tour 6)

Tretyakov Art Gallery (*see* Tour 7)

Victor Vasnetsov Museum. This house-museum was the home of the Russian artist Victor Vasnetsov from 1894 to 1926. Built by the artist himself, it is a charming example of the Russian "fairy-tale" architectural style popular at the end of the 19th century. Inside the house, Vasnetsov's paintings of Russian fairy tales are on display. *Pereulok Vasnetsova 13,* ☎ *095/281–1329.* ☉ *Wed.–Sun. 10–4:30. Closed last Thurs. of month.*

Monuments and Statues
Czar Cannon (*see* Tour 1)
Gogol Statue (*see* Tour 5)
Karl Marx's Statue (*see* Tour 2)
Monument to Minin and Pozharsky (*see* Tour 1)
Monument to WWII Missing Soldiers. This statue of a felled fighter is located in the war memorial park of Poklonnaya Gora. It was a gift to the city of Moscow from the Ukraine.
Monument to Revolutionary Thinkers (*see* Tour 1)
Monument to Yuri Dolgoruky (*see* Tour 3)
Monument to Yuri Gagarin. If you are on Leninsky Prospect, you can't miss this soaring statue dedicated to the world's first man in space. A genuinely enduring hero, the Soviet cosmonaut is largely responsible for the popularity of the name Yuri among the 30-something set.
Plevna Memorial (*see* Tour 2)
Space Obelisk. Another honorific to astronautics, this steel monument with its glittering titanium surfaces is near the VDNKh subway station.
Statue of Alexander Pushkin (*see* Tour 3)
Statue of Ivan Fyodorov (*see* Tour 2)
Statue of Vladimir Mayakovsky (*see* Tour 3)
Statue of Worker and Collective Farmer. Striding forward together, arms upraised in the spirit of joint work, this stainless-steel couple is one of communism's most instantly recognizable images. If only the reality of the hammer-and-sickle had proved as magnificent as the symbol. Also located near the VDNKh subway station, it marks the right side of the entrance to the All-Russia Exhibition Center.
Tomb of the Unknown Soldier (*see* Tour 1)
Triumphal Arch (*see* Tour 5)
War Memorial Obelisk. In front of the Central Museum of the Great Patriotic War (*see* Historical Museums) is an obelisk that dominates the sky as you drive down Kutuzovsky Prospect beyond the Triumphal Arch. The goddess Nike, with a golden wreath, and two cherubs blowing golden trumpets at her side, is atop. At the foot is a statue of St. Yuri (George)—long considered a patron saint of Moscow—slaying the dragon of nazism.

Parks and Gardens
Alexander Garden (Alexandrovsky Sad, *see* Tour 1)
All-Russia Exhibition Center. Better known by its old name, VDNKh (USSR Economic Achievements Exhibit), this sprawling 221-hectare (553-acre) park was designed in the late 1930s as a national showcase for the Soviet economy. A perfect example of Soviet propaganda's wishful thinking, the park's displays were meant to show how well the centralized planning system was working, and how each of the former Soviet republics was prospering under communist rule. The park has many pavilions, each built in the architectural style of the different Soviet republics, and devoted to different branches of agriculture, industry, and science. Because the culminating achievement of the Soviet economy was the collapse of the Soviet Union itself, few of the pavilions house any such displays now and, instead, have been rented out to private and joint-venture enterprises. Business fairs are also held here on a rotating basis. Not all attractions here are outdated or interim, however. In summer 1995, a new amusement park opened near the "Cosmos" pavilion. Already working is the giant Ferris wheel—the 3rd largest in the world; eventually more than 30 rides, including roller coasters, with be added. The park is open daily 9–9, pavilions 10–6; it is located right outside the VDNKh subway station. *Prospect Mira,* ☎ *095/181–9162.*

Botanic Garden of the Russian Academy of Sciences. The garden covers an area of some 360 hectares (900 acres) and has been planted in and among the original beech, oak, and spruce forests of the Moscow area. One large landscape section has nearly 3,000 species of native plants of Russia, arranged in naturally landscaped areas. More than 1,700 kinds of trees and shrubs are planted in the dendarium. The park is best reached from the VDNKh subway station (Bus 33). Alternatively, you can walk from the Botanichesky Sad (Botanical Gardens) subway station, located about a kilometer (⅔ mile) from the park's entrance.

Gorky Park (*see* Tour 7)

Izmailovsky Park. Covering almost 1,215 hectares (3,000 acres), it includes large stretches of pine forest. The former summer residence of the czars is located on its grounds, which were once a royal hunting preserve. The park has a fair-ground and an open-air theater. On weekends it is the site of a sprawling flea market, where you can pick up some great souvenirs. *17 Narodny Prospect at Izmailovsky Park subway station.*

Kolomenskoye (*see* Off the Beaten Track)

Patriarch's Pond. On ulitsa Malaya Bronnaya, off the Garden Ring, is a small, quiet park that encircles a pond. A year-round favorite of Muscovites, it is where the devil makes his entrance into Moscow in the opening scene of Mikhail Bulgakov's *The Master and the Margarita.*

Sokolniki Park. This 619-hectare (1,530-acre) park is named after the czar's *sokolniki* (falconers) who dwelled here. The park, which includes an ancient forest, has an open-air theater, a fairground, and in winter, a skating rink. You can rent skates and cross-country skis here in the winter. *Rusakovskaya ul. 62, at Sokolniki subway station.*

Victory Park. Opening up from the edge of Ploshchad Pobedy and Poklonnaya Gora (Hill), where Moscow children sled all winter long, is Victory Park, home to World War II memorials. A stone and marble expanse, lined by groves of young linden and pine trees and filled with fountains, it is a popular visiting spot day and night, when colored lights illuminate the water. The park rises in a series of shallowly elevated pavilions, each marked by a simple stone slab. Although busy Kutuzovsky Prospect runs alongside, its tranquility is almost odd. An abundance of benches makes it a good rendezvous and resting point. *1 Ploshchad Pobedy, off Kutuzovsky Prospect.*

Zoo. Moscow's small zoo is located near the Barrikadnaya or the Krasnopresnenskaya subway station. *1 Bolshaya Gruzinskaya ul.* ☉ *Summer, daily 9–8; winter, daily 9–5.*

Scientific and Technological Museums

Central Armed Forces Museum. The exhibits of Soviet Army tanks and fighter planes date back to 1917. Of particular interest to American tourists are the pieces of the U.S. spy plane shot down over Siberia. *2 ul. Sovietskoi Armii,* ☎ *095/281–1880.* ☉ *Tues.–Sun. 11–6. Closed last Tues. of month.*

Cosmonaut's Museum. The museum is devoted to exploration of outer space. On display are satellites, rockets, space suits, and an audiovisual documentary. The museum is located right next to the All-Russia Exhibition Center, at the subway station VDNKh. *Alleya Kosmonavtov,* ☎ *095/283–7914.* ☉ *Tues.–Sun. 10–7. Closed last Fri. of month.*

Polytechnical Museum (*see* Tour 2)

Zoological Museum (*see* Tour 4)

SHOPPING

It is, at long last, time to cast away cold war images of long lines and empty shelves—it's simply no longer the case. Although the distribution of products can be uneven and unpredictable, there are nonetheless plenty of them. You should be able to locate most items you need, if in a more piecemeal way than at home. You will not go hungry or unclothed should you lose your shirt at one of Moscow's casinos. In fact, you'll find opportunities to buy something any way you turn.

The proliferation of new stores is matched only by the upward bounds in prices.

Food and goods' stores can be roughly divided into two categories: Western-style ("hard currency") shops and Russian stores, though this is likely not to last once more Russian stores take on characteristics of more modern standard. There is also an ever-changing array of kiosks, tabletops, and wooden stalls. Western-style stores carry familiar brands from America and Europe, often Finland, at imported-goods prices, though they are beginning to need to be more competitive, as more stores open. Russian establishments stock a mix of local and imported product—the latter without any fixed schedule of purchase, so you can't count on finding specific items in these stores, though you will find a great deal of whatever stock was bought that week.

In the past, special shops called Beriozka (Birch Tree) operated exclusively for foreigners. Stock was imported, payment was in hard currency only, and it was illegal for Soviet citizens to enter—let alone shop—in one. The Beriozka effectively no longer exists, having mutated into the "hard currency" shop. Technically, this has become an inaccurate denomination, since it is illegal in Russia to accept payment in currency other than rubles. These stores, unlike their Russian counterparts, however, take credit-card payment, calculated at a ruble exchange. (Stores set their own exchange rate and, like hotels, are unlikely to offer the favorable exchange rate you'll get at banks.) You should also be able to pay in cash, in rubles. (No store takes traveler's checks.) At such shops, nationality is no longer relevant; wallet size is—anyone who can afford the higher prices is welcome.

Russian stores have had varying responses to, and degrees of success with, the new economic times. In Old World fashion, they tend to be denoted by their products ("Milk," "Bread," "Lights," "Women's Shoes") but often carry more than their name implies. For food, a "Produkti" ("Products") carries a narrow range of goods; basically, it's a small grocery, as is a "Dieta." The less-frequently encountered but larger Gastronomes might be considered the equivalent of a supermarket.

For foreigners, the main stumbling block is the arduous method of purchase; it is time-consuming and often very trying. If you do not speak Russian, you should stick to Western stores or to street purchases, where you can use the universal language of finger-pointing. If you shop in a Russian store, you choose what you want at one counter, pay a cashier at another counter (more than one cashier if you are buying different types of items), and return with a receipt to collect your goods.

Service may be testier than you are used to, also. A few words in Russian and a composed countenance may ameliorate this, but if they don't, you should not take it personally. Russians seem to have grown so inured to shoving and elbowing for position that they will display an indifference to rudeness that foreign visitors often find appalling. On the bright side, when you encounter good manners, they are impeccable.

The following listings are intended to give a thumbnail sketch of the places you may need as a tourist; they are by no means comprehensive. On the assumption that, despite the improvements, you still don't come to Moscow to shop but may need something in a hurry, most of the stores listed are Western-style. If your schedule permits, it's always interesting to browse the shops frequented by residents and a great way to take the pulse of a place, especially one in flux.

One reminder: Before you spend a lot of money on a souvenir, think about how you will feel if you can't take it home with you. Unfortunately, customs regulations are still vague and seem to change constantly and arbitrarily, depending on who is checking your bag. Art objects, particularly if they appear old or are large, can be deemed as "of value to the Russian nation." Goods in this category can be confiscated at the border. If you are buying paintings or such art objects, it's important to consult with the seller regarding the proper documentation of sale to take with you. Keep receipts of your purchases, wherever possible.

Please also exercise caution when out shopping. You will stand out no matter what you do, and there are pickpocket and mugging rings operating, often in small bands. *Don't* be an easy target.

Shopping Districts

Historically, the main shopping districts of Moscow have been concentrated in the city center, along Tverskaya Street and New Arbat. Extend New Arbat through Kutuzovsky Prospect and, on the other end, add the old Arbat, which has been particularly spruced up for the tourist trade, and these are your best bets.

The closest thing in Moscow to a mall is GUM (pronounced "goom"), a series of shops and boutiques inside a 19th-century shopping arcade, which was once closed to foreigners. GUM, which stands for State Department Store, is located on Red Square, right across from the Kremlin. More change is coming, however, with mall fever due to hit soon enough; a major site outside the Kremlin is already under construction.

Department Stores

The big Russian department stores are TsUM (Central Department Store), at 2 ulitsa Petrovka, and the Moskva Department Store at 54 Leninsky Prospect. Both are open Mon.–Sat., 8–9. You can also visit Petrovsky Passage, at 10 ulitsa Petrovka, home to a series of shops. Detsky Mir (Children's World), the famous children's department store, is at 2 Teatralny Proyezd, and you'll see its sign near Lubyanka Square.

Street Markets

For green markets Moscow, alas, cannot compete with its European neighbors or even nearer rivals, Kiev and St. Petersburg. The best-known was the Tsentralny Rynok (Central Market), on Tsvetnoy Bulvar, but it's been closed for *remont*. It is supposed to reopen, but it's hard to tell.

As an alternative, you might try the Dorogomilovsky Market off Mozhaiska ulitsa, near the Kievsky train station. Beyond its outdoor "Veshch Rynok" (literally, "market of things" which you'll see is certainly apt) is a large covered hall. Inside are rows of vendors hawking homemade cheese and milk products, honey, flowers, and produce of all kinds. Against one wall are sellers of pickled goods, an understandably popular form of food preparation in this part of the world; you may want to sample some of their cabbage and carrot slaws, salted cucumbers, or spiced eggplant or garlic. Tasting is free, but it's unlikely that you'll be allowed to leave without buying something. Remember to bargain. In another corner, you will also find tables of freshly cut meat, plucked chickens, and fish. The squeamish may want to avert their eyes from the whole suckling pigs and the occasional hare or goat, beheaded and proudly strung up for inspection.

You can spend a whole day at Moscow's flea market in Izmailovsky Park. Here you'll find hosts of reasonably priced souvenirs and handicrafts as well as Soviet memorabilia, such as army belts, gas masks, and *matryoshky* (nesting dolls), both classic and nouveau, with some bearing likenesses of recent Soviet leaders, while others depict American basketball stars. Nearby is the former royal residence of Izmailovo, located in an old hunting preserve. The flea market is open weekends 9–6, but it's best to get there early. Many vendors close down their booths by midday. Be sure to wrangle over prices. What began as a place with reasonable prices can be a full-grown tourist trap if you're not careful. *Transportation: subway to Izmailovsky Park station on blue line (not to be confused with next stop, Izmailovskaya station), and follow crowds as you exit.*

Ptichi Rynok (Bird Market) is on Kalitnovskaya ulitsa. Open on Sunday only, this market offers a fascinating glimpse of Russians and their pets. The softhearted should be forewarned that it is very difficult to leave this place without acquiring something. The market is bustling with individuals selling adorable, furry animals—cats, dogs, and hamsters—as well as exotic birds and fish and, occasionally, a monkey. *Transportation: subway to Taganskaya station. Exit from circle-line station, and from there take any bus or trolley from Marksistskaya ulitsa stop (across square from subway, near purple Tagansky department store). Bus line ends at pet market.*

Specialty Stores

For good souvenir-hunting, you can certainly head straight to the Arbat (*see* Tour 5). Stores here cater to tourists and Moscow's expatriate community, so you can expect good selection and service, but prices are on the high end. Its individual outdoor vendors invariably charge much more than they should, so stick to the stores.

Arts and Crafts (Souvenirs)

The **Art Salon of the Arts Industry Institute** has an excellent selection of artwork handcrafted by the institute's students and teachers, including hand-painted trays, quilts, ceramics, and leather goods. *31 ul. Povarskaya, 2nd floor,* ☎ *095/290–6822. Rubles only.*

Central Art Salon. This big salon sells just about everything you might be looking for—from handcrafted nesting dolls to ceramics, *khokhloma* (lacquered wood), and jewelry, all made by members of the Russian Union of Artists. Also on sale are beautiful Dagestani rugs. *6 Ukrainsky Bulvar,* ☎ *095/243–9458.* ☺ *Sun.–Fri. 10–2, 3–7; Sat. 11–6. Rubles only.*

The **art boutiques** inside two **Varvarka Street** churches—St. Maxim the Blessed (open daily 11–6) and St. George on Pskov Hill (open daily 11–7)—offer a fine selection of handicrafts, jewelry, ceramics, and other types of Russian native art. (*See* Tour 2.) *Transportation: subway to Kitai Gorod station.*

If you are enamored of blue-and-white Gzhel ceramicware, try their own shop, **Gzhel,** to find all manner of pieces. *22 ul. Petrovka,* ☎ *095/200–6137.*

Russkyie Souveniry. This state-run souvenir shop is easy to find and filled with handcrafted and mass-produced folk art, *palekh* boxes, and jewelry, but its prices are very inflated. *9 Kutuzovsky Prospect.* ☉ *Mon.–Sat. 11–2, 3–8. Rubles only.*

Anyone intrigued by the beauty and variety in Russian patterns can find the full catalog at **Russkye Uzory** (Russian Patterns). *16 ul. Petrovka,* ☎ *095/923–1883.*

The **Museum Shop** at the **Museum of the Revolution** is good for amber, nesting dolls, and other Soviet memorabilia such as pins, postcards, and T-shirts. *21 Tverskaya ul.,* ☎ *095/299–1695.* ☉ *Tues.–Sun. 10–5. Rubles only.*

Salon Iskusstva has a big section of Russian items, such as samovars, dolls, and boxes. *52 ul. Bolshaya Yakimanka.* ☉ *Mon.–Sat. 10–7.*

You'll see occasional kiosks or counters in churches selling Russian Orthodox religious items, but for an excellent full array, try **Sofrino** at 11 ulitsa Nikolskaya (☎ *095/925–4480*).

Food
Arbat Irish Store offers an extremely well-stocked grocery store and small department store selling electronics, household goods, car accessories, and clothing (primarily jeans). The relatively reasonable prices here make for long lines, especially on the weekend. *21 Novy Arbat,* ☎ *095/291–7641.* ☉ *Daily 10–9. Rubles downstairs; credit cards only upstairs.*

Danone is a sleek shop on Tverskaya dishing out only Dannon yogurt products. Able to buy by the six-pack here, health nuts should take heart. *4 ul. Tverskaya,* ☎ *095/292–0512.*

Garden Ring Irish Supermarket. There are three of these small and expensive groceries. Each, despite the prices, is quite popular among expatriates, who seem to relish in particular the roast chickens. *2 ul. Bolshaya Sadovaya,* ☎ *095/209–1572; 113 Leninsky Prospect,* ☎ *095/956–5458; 2 ul. Serafimovicha,* ☎ *095/231–8187.* ☉ *Daily 9–noon. Rubles, credit cards.*

Global USA. Huge (billed as an American supershop), it's where you'll find almost every brand of every product you may be looking for. *35 ul. Usacheva,* ☎ *095/245–5657; 78 Leningradsky Prospect,* ☎ *095/151–3354.* ☉ *Daily 10–8. Rubles, credit cards.*

Kalinka-Stockmann is a major chain, with five stores offering office supplies, electronics, and clothing; its grocery shop has a broad assortment, including fresh fruits and vegetables. Like Sadko, it is not cheap. *4/8 ul. Zatsepsky Val,* ☎ *095/233–2602.* ☉ *Daily 10–9. Rubles, credit cards.*

Sadko's Foodland has been on the scene forever. It has a large selection of imported grocery items, including cheese and other dairy products, alcohol, office supplies, and health and beauty products. *16 ul. Bolshaya Dorogomilovskaya,* ☎ *095/243–7502.* ☉ *Mon.–Sat. 10–8, Sun. 10–6. Credit cards.*

Men's and Women's Clothing
The two **Benetton** shops, one on the first floor of GUM and the other on the Arbat, carry their trademark line of sweaters, skirts, pants, and jeans. ☎ *095/921–5065. Credit cards only.*

Galeries Lafayette, the chic emporium from France, has clothing that runs the gamut from wool leggings to cloche hats to silk suits. *Ground level of GUM.*

Levis, with its classic stock, is certain to become the fixture in Moscow that it already is most everywhere else in the world. *3 Stoleshnikov Pereulok; 15 ul. Profsoyuznaya; 3 ul. Sadova-Spasskaya.*

Rifle Jeans sells Italian jeans, denim jackets and skirts, corduroys, and sweatshirts. *10 Kuznetsky Most,* ☎ *095/923–2458.* ☉ *Mon.–Sat. 10– 7. Credit cards, rubles.*

Reebok's big airy shop sells sports outfits, shoes, and equipment. *23 ul. Krasnaya Presnya,* ☎ *095/252–6591.*

Fans of rival company **Nike** can find their store at 1 Kundrinsky Pereulok, across from Barrikadnaya subway station.

Those looking for high-fashion items might check the **Stockmann Boutique** (73 Leninsky Prospect, ☎ 095/134–3546). They can also try **Les Boutiques Renoir** (15 Bolshoi Cherkassky Pereulok, ☎ 095/924–6229).

Women interested in seeing the latest Russian haute couture may satisfy their curiosity at the designer houses the **Gallery of Fashion,** where 18 different collections can be found (11123 Pyatnitskaya ul., ☎ 095/ 233–2508) or at the **Yelena Pelyevina Salon** (42 Komsomolsky Prospect, ☎ 095/242–3726), where Russian folk-inspired patterns and garments are the focus.

SPORTS AND FITNESS

Participant Sports

Access to Moscow's municipal athletic facilities is usually restricted to those holding a season pass or to club members. In addition most facilities—particularly when it comes to pools—require a special "doctor's certificate" attesting to one's good health. In principle, it is possible to obtain such a certificate by visiting a Russian clinic, but this is a time-consuming process. The listings here are therefore limited to those places that are open to short-term visitors and where it is not necessary to produce a doctor's certificate.

The two largest sport complexes, each with a range of facilities, are the **Luzhniki Sports Palace** (with Lenin Stadium) and the **Olympisky Sports** compound. The first is located at Luzhniki on the banks of the Moscow River at the foot of Lenin Hills (☎ 095/246–5515); the latter is at 16 Olympisky Pereulok (☎ 095/288–5663 or 5118). You can check with them (in Russian only) regarding what gyms, courts, pools, and tracks may be available for use during your stay.

Bowling
The bowling alley at the Kosmos Hotel (150 Prospect Mira, near the VDNKh subway station, ☎ 095/215–8680) is open daily 3 PM–midnight. For tickets, inquire at the service bureau off the first-floor lobby.

Cycling
There is a cycle racetrack in the Krylatskoye Sports complex (2 Krylatskaya ul., ☎ 095/140–0347 or 095/141–2224). They also have a rowing canal.

Fitness Centers
Unfortunately, virtually all of Moscow's gyms are for members only. Some offer short-term memberships, so if you are in town for a while,

you can explore that option. Most good hotels have their own fitness centers, but use is restricted to guests. Those without these options can pay a fee for single visits to the gym at the Metropole Hotel (1/4 Teatralny Proyezd, ☎ 095/927–6000). The pool here is small but still large enough to satisfy lap swimmers. Also available is the Laetitia-Fizkulture gym at the Metallurg Hotel (12 Oktyabrsky Prospect, ☎ 095/971–2108), open weekdays 10–8. The Scorpio Health Club (1 ul. Zaporozhskaya, ☎ 095/448–0135) has everything and a pool and is open Monday–Saturday 11–11. The Palace Hotel (*see* Lodging, *below*) has a weight-machine room, Jacuzzi, and sauna but no pool. The Presnya Hotel has a tiny gym, massage, and sauna. Fees depend on what you want to use, and pool charges are always considerably higher.

Running
The best spots for jogging are along Luzhniki's riverside or through the parks at Izmailovsky or Sokolniki. You will definitely want to avoid Moscow's heavy traffic and accompanying noxious fumes. Because it is difficult to find a comfortable place and you will be in a conspicuous minority, all but utter diehards may want to give themselves a few days' break.

Skating
If you've packed your skates, head straight for Gorky Park (9 ul. Krymsky Val), where in winter months the park's lanes are flooded to create impromptu skating rinks. The park also has two large rinks where you can skate to piped-in Russian pop music. Be prepared for some cultural differences, however. Russians do not skate in orderly circles or clean snow off the ice regularly. The park is open 10–10; the closest subway station is the Oktyabrskaya on the orange and circle lines. You can rent skates at Sokolniki Park (16 ul. Sokolnichesky Val, ☎ 095/268–8277), near the subway station of the same name. To use the facilities, you must lease the rink, so this is not the place to come unless you're with a group. ☉ 10–7. Luzhniki's popular Northern Lights rink is open to all skaters over the age of 7. Entry fee and skate rental, open evenings 5–9 (Luzhnetskaya Naberezhnaya, ☎ 095/201–1655).

Swimming
Opt for the Metropol or Scorpio Health Center pools, or on Sundays from 4 to 8, try the Chaika Pool (3 Turchaninov Pereulok, ☎ 095/246–0263), the only time this pool is open for a fee to nonmembers. There are 8 pools at the Olympic Nautical Sports Center (30 ul. Ibragimova, ☎ 095/369–0649), on a fee basis.

If you have Moscow friends and/or a car, you can join in a summer tradition by heading to Serebryanny Bor (Silver Pine Beach) for a dip in the Moscow River, where you'll encounter lots of interestingly clad, overheated city dwellers. You can also rent rowboats there.

Tennis
Courts are in scant supply and are usually reserved in advance by residents. Olympisky rents courts at expensive rates, and the Olympic Nautical Complex also has courts.

Spectator Sports

Tickets for sporting events can be purchased at the sports arena immediately prior to the game or at any of the numerous theater box offices (*teatralnaya kassa*) located throughout the city. You can also ask your hotel's service bureau for assistance in obtaining tickets to sporting events, but the fee will probably far exceed the value of the ticket itself.

Horse-Racing

The race course (Hippodrome) is at 22 Begovaya ul., (☎ 095/945–4516). Races are held on Wednesday and Friday at 6 PM and on Sunday at 1 PM. Betting is in rubles. In winter troikas are sometimes raced.

Ice Hockey

Ice hockey matches are held at the Dynamo Stadium (36 Leningradsky Prospect, ☎ 095/212–7092), which is Moscow's second-largest stadium, accommodating 60,000. Matches are also held at Luzhniki's Lenin Stadium (☎ 095/246–5515), its largest, seating 100,000.

Soccer

The Russian national sport is soccer (in Russian, *futbal*), and it can ignite feverish passions. The city has several first-rate soccer teams, foremost among them Spartak and Dinamo. A game between them would be considered the team event of the year. Soccer matches are also frequently played at the Central Lenin Stadium and at the stadiums belonging to individual teams.

DINING

The dining scene in the Russian capital continues to change, almost convulsively. From the state-run restaurants, once the only kind available, to the collectively owned cooperatives that followed perestroika, to the private-enterprise restaurants proliferating now, the changes are nothing short of astonishing. Whereas only two years ago, one was hard-pressed to find anything decent—let alone outstanding—there is no such shortage now: You may pick and choose among all three types of establishments. The contrasts, however, may leave you a bit wobbly. At a small restaurant or *stolovaya* you can experience the discomforts of Soviet management techniques. But right up the street you may find an establishment so elegant it could compete in Paris or New York.

The latter, of course, comes at a price, and cost is the issue. If you have the cash, there are restaurants aplenty. Tourists whose wallets are fat compared with the average Russian's may even think most spots are good bargains. Those Russians with an increased discretionary income enjoy going out, but most of them are young. As a result, the boom is in restaurants that resemble those back home, as companies build similar tastes here. Travelers searching for "real" Russian food are probably not very interested in this kind of dining and may have to rough it at the low end or fork over a considerable amount of cash at the high end. Still, either way you won't go hungry.

Although impromptu appearances are increasingly acceptable in Moscow, it is usually expected that you will devote some old-fashioned planning to dining out. Even if a restaurant is half-empty, you may be refused a table if you don't have a reservation. This is especially true in the evening, and sometimes it happens even during the day.

Reserve plenty of time for your meal. In Russia dining out is an occasion, and Russians often make an evening (or an afternoon) out of going out to eat. Often the meal is accompanied by a floor show or musical entertainment. Almost all the expensive hotel restaurants offer a New Orleans Jazz Brunch on Sunday, when you can enjoy their haute cuisine and decor at greatly reduced prices.

CATEGORY	COST*
$$$$	over $45
$$$	$30–$45
$$	$20–$30
$	under $20

per person, excluding drinks and service

What to Wear

Dress at the restaurants reviewed below is casual, unless noted otherwise.

$$$$ **Exchange.** This American steak house is located in the midwestern mall of the Radisson Slavyanskaya Hotel. The homesick American will enjoy the leafy salads and thick, juicy sirloins flown in from New York. The black-and-white interior decor makes for an elegant yet relaxed atmosphere, the perfect re-creation of America in Moscow. If you're not a meat lover, try the poached cod fillet or the chicken breast broiled to perfection in a tangy ginger sauce. The French onion soup or caesar salad makes a good starter. Order a bottle of imported wine from the extensive wine list, and top off your meal with a piece of apple pie. True to the American way, the restaurant offers a nonsmoking section. This is the ideal place to come for a well-earned break from Russian reality. ✕ *Radisson Slavyanskaya Hotel, 2 Berezhkovskaya Naberezhnaya,* ☎ *095/941–8020. Reservations advised. Hard currency only. AE, DC, MC, V.* ☻ *Daily noon–3, 6–10:30.*

$$$$ **Glazur.** This Danish-Russian joint venture is one of the most upscale
★ establishments catering to the city's foreign community. It stands out from the pack for its subdued atmosphere and exquisite cuisine. Located in a renovated 19th-century mansion on the Garden Ring, the restaurant has an elegant interior, tastefully decorated in brown and gold. The Russian and European dishes are beautifully prepared; the food, much of it imported from Belgium and Denmark, is a gourmet's heaven. The *russkaya zakuska,* a beef-gelatin aspic with colorful layers of finely diced ham, chicken and tongue, makes a good starter. A specialty of the house is *baklazhany zarevshan,* a spicy Armenian mixture of eggplant, carrots, onion, and garlic. For your main course, try the *svinina à la gousar,* a pork dish served with a creamy mushroom sauce. The wine list is excellent. Top off your meal with a flaming ice cream surprise, the chef's special rendition of baked Alaska. Service is swift, friendly, and professional. The musical entertainment in the evenings varies, ranging from jazz to classical to Russian folk. ✕ *Smolensky Bulvar 12,* ☎ *095/248–4438. Jacket and tie. Reservations accepted. Credit cards only. AE, MC, V.* ☻ *Daily noon–5, 6–midnight.*

$$$$ **Grand Imperial.** This truly old-style restaurant serves superbly prepared and often rich dishes, such as veal Romanoff. The succulent food is well matched by the sumptuous surroundings. Every detail is fine—from the original art, to the crystal chandeliers, to the flowers, to the antique silver service personally collected by the owners. ✕ *9/5 Gagarinsky per.,* ☎ *095/291–6063,* 🖷 *095/290–0249. Reservations advised. Jacket and tie. AE, DC, MC, V, rubles.* ☻ *Daily 7–noon.*

$$$$ **Le Romanoff.** This also ranks among Moscow's finest gourmet experiences. Located on the second floor of the Baltschug Hotel, it is exquisitely managed and offers a Russian/Continental cuisine that pleases both the eye and the palate. The menu is unique, the atmosphere is elegant, and the wine list is superb—the perfect spot for an important dinner. ✕ *Ul. Balchug 1,* ☎ *095/230–6500. Jacket and tie. Reservations required. AE, DC, MC, V.*

$$$$ **Metropol.** The renovated interiors of the Metropol Hotel's grand dining hall are a stunning memorial to Russian Art Nouveau. The nearly three-story-high dining room, replete with stained-glass windows, marble pillars, and leaded-glass roof, recalls the splendor of prerevolutionary Russia. The beautifully laid tables and formally dressed waiters add to the elegance. In terms of its opulent atmosphere, visitors will be pleased, but they can find themselves disappointed when it comes to the food and service. The pricey menu features such Russian delicacies as smoked salmon and beef Stroganoff, but the preparation is uninspired. The highlight of the week is Sunday brunch, when the restaurant puts out an impressive spread, including an array of meat and fish dishes, home-baked French pastries, and exotic fresh fruits. ✕ *Teatralny Proyezd 1/4,* ☏ *095/927–6040. Reservations advised. Jacket and tie. AE, DC, MC, V.* ☻ *Daily 7–2, 6:30–midnight.*

$$$$ **Panda.** This American-style Chinese restaurant, virtually Moscow's first, was an overnight hit. All seafood and other hard-to-find ingredients are flown in from abroad to guarantee quality and freshness, and an award-winning Chinese cook oversees the careful preparation of each dish. The Hunan and Szechuan selections are especially good, though somehow all still retain some hint of Russian flavoring. Prices are high. Takeout orders are accepted throughout the day and evening. ✕ *Tverskoy Bulvar 3/5,* ☏ *095/298–6565. Reservations advised. AE, DC, MC, V.*

$$$$ **Praga.** Centrally located on Arbat Square, in a handsome prerevolutionary building, this restaurant was once one of Moscow's finest state-run dining establishments. Radical changes in the capital's restaurant scene have left the staff here nostalgic for the days when lines formed outside its doors and it took a good connection or a bribe to land a table. Although it's named for the Czech capital, the restaurant has never offered anything but standard Russian cuisine, the quality of which has fallen to new lows in recent years. If you are with a Russian who does the ordering, things might improve. The menu is huge but the actual availability of dishes listed on it is limited. Standard offerings include beef Stroganoff and chicken Tabaka (roasted spring chicken). What keeps the place in business is its striking interiors. A grand marble staircase with heavy brass railings leads you to the elegant second-floor dining halls, where gilded ceilings, parquet floors, and brass chandeliers create an Old World atmosphere. A Russian band often will play later in the evening, and things can get very boisterous as diners kick up their heels. Double-check your bill carefully. Prices are steep to begin with, and virtually every slice of bread seems to be tallied singly. The waiters here were spoiled by years of corruption and have been known to add extra items to the check. ✕ *Ul. Arbat 2,* ☏ *095/290–6191. Reservations advised. Jacket and tie. Rubles only.* ☻ *Daily noon–11:30.*

$$$$ **Savoy.** Located in the Savoy Hotel, this restaurant's fancy interior and
★ elegant menu are likely to please Russophiles and gourmands alike. The food—a mixture of Russian, Scandinavian, and French cuisine—is excellent. Ingredients are trucked in from Finland, and the Russian chef has won several international awards for his imperial creations. The restaurant features a special Czar's Menu, a re-creation of one of the 12 menus served at the coronation of Czar Nicholas II in 1896. But food aside, the real reason to come here is to see the inside. With its delicate, gilded wall coverings, long mirrors, and gilded ceiling paintings, it echoes the opulence of St. Petersburg's imperial palaces. Dinner can easily run into five-digit figures; you may prefer the more reasonable prix-fixe lunch. ✕ *Ul. Rozhdestvenka 3,* ☏ *095/929–8600. Reservations advised. Jacket and tie. Traveler's checks accepted. AE, DC, MC, V.* ☻ *Daily 7:30 AM—11 PM.*

80

Dining

Moscow Dining and Lodging

Sadovaya-Samotech.
Sadovaya-Sukharevskaya
Kazan' Station
31
32
33
34
Yermolovoy
Sadovaya-Spasskaya
Novokirovsky
Novaya Basmannaya
Chekhova
Uspensky
Bol. Sukharevsky
Sretenka
Kostyansky
Khmeleva
Zemlyanoy Val
30
Strastnoy bulvar
Petrovka
Rozhdestvensky bulvar
Sret. bul.
Novokirovsky per.
Bolshoy Haritonevsky
Chaplyhina
Mashkova
Rozhdestvenka
Bolshaya Lubyanka
Markhlevskovo
Myasnitskaya
Christoprudny bulvar
Potapovsky
Pokrovka
Lyalin p.
35
P. Stoleshnikov
Kamergersky P.
Pushechnaya
KGB
Stankevicha
Nezhdanovoy
Tverskaya
36
37
Polytech Museum
Obukha
Semashko
40
38
39
Maroseyka
41
43
44
KREMLIN
42
Ilyinsky
Podkolokolny
Arsenal
Yanysheva
Palace of Congresses
Presidium and Kremlin Theater
Varvarka
Foreign Literature Center
Great Kremlin Palace
45
Ul'yanovskaya
Russian State Library
Kremlyovskaya
Moskvoretskaya nab.
Volkhonka
Labaznaya
46
Raushskaya nab.
Osipenko
Nabere zhnaya Maksima Gorkovo
Kotelnicheskaya Nab.
Teterinsky P.
Kanal
Ozerovskaya Nab.
Sadovnicheskaya Nab.
Internatsionalnaya
Zemlyanoy Val
Vodootvodny
Staromonetny per.
polyanka B.
Bolshaya Ordynka
Zemlyachki
47
Taganskaya
48
Vorontsovskaya
Babyegorodsky
Khvostov 1p.
A.N.Ostrovskovo
Pyatnitskaya
Novokuznetskaya
Narodnaya
river
Spasonalivkovsky 1p.
49
Tatarsk. B.
Bakhrushina
Krasnokholmskaya nab.
Novospassky P.
Zhitnaya
Valovaya
Zatsepsky Val
Kozhevnicheskaya
y Val
Dobryninskaya
Zatsepa
Letnikovskaya
Shabolovka
Mytnaya
Lyusinovskaya
Dubininskaya
N
51
Leninsky prospekt
50

0   1 mile
0   1   2 km

$$$$ Strastnoy Bulvar 7. This is the name and address of a small but excellent restaurant located near Pushkin Square. It is a bit on the pricey side, but if tony atmosphere and intimate conversation are in order, this is the place. The suckling pig stuffed with mushrooms and the perch with crabmeat stand out as house specialties. Russian musicians play discreetly throughout the evening. ✕ *Strastnoy Bulvar 7,* ☎ *095/299–0498. Jacket and tie. Reservations required. AE, MC, V, or rubles according to restaurant exchange rate.*

$$$ Arlecchino. Diners may think they've left Russia when they enter this art deco dining room and taste the imported Italian food prepared by Italian and Italian-trained Russian chefs. A quiet, sophisticated establishment, it's a popular rendezvous for businesspeople. The restaurant's one banquet room seats 20. The best entrées are usually the daily veal or seafood specials, but it would be a shame to pass up the pasta. The extensive menu is complemented by an excellent wine list and dessert tray. At night, the club attracts a flashier crowd. ✕ *Ul. Druzhinnikovskaya 15 (in Kino Center),* ☎ *095/205–9056. Jacket and tie. Reservations required. AE, DC, MC, V, or rubles according to restaurant exchange rate.*

$$$ Baku. When you're tired of caviar and herring, try this rowdy joint venture named for the capital of Azerbaijan. Once a dull state enterprise, the restaurant is now under the management of a Lebanese-Azerbaijani partnership. The revised menu features exotic dishes from both countries. For a taste of Azerbaijan, try the *mutton shashlik* (shish kebab) served with a pomegranate sauce. The Beirut humus and tabuleh are also excellent. The drab interior, with its imitation marble walls, is still industrial, but the place turns lively after 9 PM, when the "variety" show featuring exotic Arab dancers begins. If you'd rather avoid the raucous late-night crowd, stop by during the day, when the menu is the same and the atmosphere as dull as the interior. ✕ *Ul. Tverskaya 24,* ☎ *095/299–8506. Reservations advised. AE, DC, MC, V.* ☺ *Daily 11–11.*

$$$ Kropotkinskaya 36. This was Moscow's first cooperative, and when it opened in 1987, it was known simply by its address. Since then the street has been given back its prerevolutionary name, and the restaurant has turned private. If you're looking for a good spot to dine *à la russe,* try this. Their blinis with caviar are delicious, and you can always rely on the hearty meat-filled Siberian pelmeni. The more adventurous can order roast suckling pig, but only if they're truly hungry, for it comes on a platter. Service is decent, though not what it once was. You'll enjoy the interior, which is elegant and intimate, with mirrored walls, yellow tablecloths, and plush auburn drapes. Background music is by a tenor soloist, who does a repertoire of Russian classics and beyond ("Strangers in the Night"). A romantic setting. ✕ *Ul. Prechistenka 36,* ☎ *095/201–7500. Reservations advised. Jacket and tie. AE, D, MC, V.* ☺ *Daily noon–11.*

$$$ Skazka. The name, which means fairy tale, says it all. If you're tired of the industrial cuisine of state-run enterprises and the stuffy atmosphere of Moscow's private establishments, this cozy restaurant just off Taganka Square features dark-wood carvings and long narrow windows filled with pyramid-shaped frosted glass. A soft, red light filters through the heavy glass, creating a romantic yet casual atmosphere. The service is friendly and professional, and the food is excellent. The restaurant offers traditional Russian cuisine, such as Siberian pelmeni—tender, meat-filled dumplings—and mushroom noodle soup, appropriately called "Like at Home with Mama." For dessert, try the house specialty, *rizhok,* a delectable layered pastry baked on the premises. The musical entertainment runs the gamut and changes every 20 minutes, from jazz to Russian folk to classical piano and violin. Do be careful near here at night, though; traditionally, residents will tell you, it's an area favored by "bandits." ✗ *Tovarishchevsky Pereulok 1,* ☎ *095/271–0998. AE, MC, V.* ☉ *Daily noon–5, 7–11.*

$$$ Tren-Mos. Once you get past the quintessentially stern Russian doorman, the atmosphere at this American-Russian joint venture is straight out of New Jersey. Opened in 1989 by an enterprising businessman from Trenton, the restaurant takes its name from the sister-city relationship between Trenton and the Lenin District of Moscow (Trenton-Moscow). The red, white, and blue interior is a showcase of American regalia. A portrait of George Washington peers down at dining guests, and the walls are draped in various state flags. Although the chef is French, the menu is as American as the decor. If you've been longing for a cheeseburger with fries or a sirloin steak, this is just the place for you. ✗ *119 Ostozhenka ul.,* ☎ *095/202–5722. Reservations advised. Jacket and tie. AE, DC, MC, V.* ☉ *Daily noon–5 and 7–11.*

$$ Ampir. Situated above the Garden Ring, across the street from the lively American Bar and Grill, Ampir is perfectly Russian (or at least new Russian) in atmosphere and a fine spot for an authentic dining experience in Moscow at a reasonable cost. Ignore such dishes as Turkey Arkansas and Boar à la Texas (fried boar with cranberry sauce), which are strictly for show, and head for the serious Russian cooking. The array of hot and cold *zakuski* (appetizers) is excellent, and you should join in the tradition of partaking of these heartily by ordering more than one. Baked pike-perch, roasted cheese, and crab salad are tasty choices. Soups, particularly mushroom, are well done here. For an entrée, try the *shashlik,* which fish lovers can get made of sturgeon, which is delicious. The staff is respectfully friendly and speaks English adequately, if haltingly. In further keeping with Russian ways, orders may take a while to appear, though champagne and vodka glasses always seem to be swiftly refilled. ✗ *4/1 ul. Sadovaya-Triumfalnaya,* ☎ *095/299–7974. AE, DC, MC, V.*

$$ Atrium. Hidden away in one of the numerous and monolithic apartment buildings lining Leninsky Prospect, this popular cooperative can be tricky to find. It's a journey to get here by public transportation (three stops up the hill on a crowded trolley bus from the Leninsky Prospect subway station); the restaurant is best reached by car. Once inside, you'll wonder where you have landed. Its candlelit interiors, decorated with growling lions, armored knights, and velvet-wrapped pillars, provide a soothing change from Moscow's harried pace. Although this isn't a gourmet's paradise, the standard Russian dishes are pleasantly prepared. The appetizers and soups are excellent. Ask for *syr v testu* (garlic cheese sticks) and Staromoskovsky (Old Moscow) soup, made with a mushroom bouillon and chock-full of tender pieces of veal, chicken, and pork. For your main course, try the *zharkoye,* a veal stew served in an earthenware pot. ✗ *Leninsky Prospect 44,* ☎ *095/137–3008. Reservations required. AE, MC, DC, V.* ☉ *Daily noon–4, 6–11.*

$$ Azteca. One of Moscow's most popular places, this noisy watering hole offers a satisfying Mexican menu of traditional favorites for southwestern palates. Among the nachos, guacamole, and fajitas are several chicken dishes and a few exotic ones, such as roasted duck tacos. A children's menu is also available. Pretty much any drink is served from the well-stocked bar, which makes a potent, if lemony, margarita. For a final flourish, flag down the roving *compadre* whose holster packs tequila bottles instead of six-shooters. The walls are covered in a bright Aztec motif, and the staff's mood matches the festive costumes. They have been known to break out in spontaneous dance while taking your order, inspired no doubt by the ensemble of guitar, drum, and pipe players who cheerfully rally the dinner crowd with Latin melodies all night long.

✕ *11 ul. Novoslobodskaya,* ☎ *095/957–8467. AE, MC, V.* ☉ *Daily noon–3, 7–11. Parking fee at night if you use their lot.*

$$ Delhi. This Indian restaurant was born out of the once great friendship between India and the USSR. Established as a political gesture, it opened during the 1987 Festival of India held in Moscow and continues to satisfy the cravings for authentic Indian cuisine of foreigners and local residents alike. With an Indian chef and management, the kitchen prepares excellent chicken and lamb tandoori dishes. Accompany your meal with *Nan and Tandoori roti,* crisp Indian bread baked in a tandoor. For starters, try the *subzi chaat,* diced potatoes and seasonal vegetables tossed with mint chutney and fragrant spices. Two dining rooms are available. One is ornately decorated with silver Indian elephants and chandeliers. Classical Indian dancers provide the evening entertainment here. The livelier other room has "family entertainment." The floor show, which changes every 15 days, features magicians, jugglers, contortionists, and fire-eaters. ✕ *ul. Krasnaya Presnya 23B,* ☎ *095/255–0492 or 095/252–1766. Reservations advised. Traveler's checks accepted. AE, DC, MC, V.* ☉ *Daily noon–3, 6–11.*

$$ El Rincón Español. This Spanish restaurant and bar's central location, reasonable prices, and lively atmosphere make this a popular watering hole with European expatriates. Wash down your Galician chicken pie or chorizo (spicy fried sausage) with a refreshing glass of San Miguel beer. The nominally Spanish menu includes several European dishes, such as French onion soup and chicken cordon bleu. Although these can be tempting, you should stick to the Spanish fare, as the European dishes tend to be bland and unimaginative. Service is polite and swift. This is one of the few restaurants in Moscow where it's possible to get a table without an advance reservation, making this a good choice for a meal on the go. ✕ *1318 ul. Pushkinskaya,* ☎ *095/229–7023. Reservations accepted. AE, DC, MC, V.* ☉ *Daily noon–5 AM.*

$$ Lasagna. This small and unpretentious bistro is situated in a historic residential district not far from the Tretyakov Art Gallery. The kitchen is mildly unpredictable, but it tries very hard to reinvent Italian cuisine using exclusively Russian ingredients. The extensive menu features such Italian specialties as ravioli, tortellini and, of course, lasagna. The pastas and breads are all homemade, and as long as you're not a connoisseur of Italian cuisine, you won't be disappointed; the quality of the food increases exponentially the longer you've been in Russia. The atmosphere is quiet and subdued. Crystal chandeliers and old-fashioned, green plush chairs help create a feeling of elegance. In the dim, candlelit setting, you'll barely notice the industrial carpeting or the seemingly incongruous modern art on the walls. Popular with local business people, this is a great place for a quiet evening of dining and conversation, a rare find in Moscow. ✕ *Ul. Pyatnitskaya 40,* ☎ *095/231–1085 or 095/233–1459. Reservations advised. AE, DC, MC, V.* ☉ *Mon.–Sat. noon–1, 7–11; Sun. 3–11.*

$$ U Pirosmani. Named for the Georgian artist Niko Pirosmani, this pop-
★ ular cooperative is located near the Novodevichy Monastery. Its rustic interior, with white-washed walls and wood-paneled ceilings, re-creates the atmosphere of an artist's studio. Ask for a table in the main hall, which affords picturesque views of the 16th-century monastery across the pond from the restaurant. The blackboard menu reads like a Georgian cookbook. Instead of wrestling with the decision of which of its tasty main courses to try, ask for a sampling of appetizers. The spread, which includes lobio, satsivi, and *gruzinskaya kapusta* (a spicy, marinated red cabbage), will be enough to feed the hungriest tourist. The kitchen also serves delightful *khinkali,* Georgian meat dumplings.

Order a bottle of Georgian wine to accompany your meal, and top it all off with a sweet Georgian pastry, baked on the premises. Although the restaurant is very popular and often crowded, service is astonishingly good by local standards. ✕ *Novodevichy Prospect 4,* ☎ *095/247–1926. Rubles accepted for food, dollars accepted for alcohol. AE.* ☉ *Daily noon–4, 6–10:30. Moderate–Inexpensive.*

$$ **U Uzefa.** Moscow's only Jewish restaurant is strong on traditional dishes using ingredients such as herring, cream cheeses, and matzo; they also have gefilte fish. A jolly family atmosphere pervades, and it tends to get crowded by the later hours. Service is no-nonsense. Yiddish folk songs are performed throughout the evening. ✕ *11/17 Dubininskaya Ploshchad,* ☎ *095/238–4646. Rubles only.* ☉ *Daily 6:30–11:30.*

$ **American Bar and Grill.** A real success story here, befitting its name, this restaurant delivers exactly what it promises—and probably a little bit more once you throw in the atmosphere. The original is located just off Tverskaya and is a haunt well-traveled by young expatriates and locals alike, who pore over the menu of burgers, salads, appetizers, and steaks amid animated conversation and a fair amount of smoking. A second, near Taganskaya, has improved on the first. It's more than three times as big, with a terrific upstairs bar and a glass-enclosed atrium dining room downstairs. In warm weather, a café patio is open. The menu here also expands on the first's, adding lots of barbeque dishes (from the "Smoke Pit"), more grill items, chicken-fried steak, and pizza. In both cases, a real attraction is the continued low costs. With the exception of one or two of the dinner plates, everything here costs less than $12. ✕ *32/1 ul. Tverskaya-Yamskaya,* ☎ *095/251–2847; 59 Zamlyanoi Val. AE, MC, V.* ☉ *Daily 6–2 or later.*

$ **Aragvi.** This state-run restaurant specializing in the spicy cuisine of former Soviet Georgia has been a tourist trap for years. The kitchen is a bit unpredictable, but the gorgeous interiors, with elaborately painted walls and colorful mosaics, make up for the hit-or-miss food. A safe bet is the chicken *satsivi,* served in a walnut and coriander sauce, or the *lobio,* butter beans in a spicy sauce. The so-called Marble Hall, with its high ceilings and wall paintings depicting ancient Georgia in the spirit of socialist realism, features loud and lively Georgian musical entertainment. For solitude and relatively smoke-free dining, reserve one of the private rooms on the second floor, a favorite haunt of Lavrenti Beria, Stalin's henchman. Cognac, champagne, and a limited selection of Georgian wines are available. ✕ *Ul. Tverskaya 6,* ☎ *095/229–2906. Reservations advised. No credit cards.* ☉ *Daily noon–1.*

$ **Margarita.** This café, named after the heroine of Mikhail Bulgakov's famous novel *Master and Margarita,* is in one of Moscow's quainter neighborhoods. Always patronized by a mixed crowd of Russians and foreigners, Margarita combines a slightly offbeat, rustic atmosphere with a simple, inexpensive menu. The service is uncommonly fast, making it an excellent bet for a quick lunch. Try the stuffed-tomato appetizer, the soup of the day, and the Russian pot pie for a can't-miss meal. ✕ *Malaya Bronnaya ul. 28,* ☎ *095/299–6534. Reservations advised. Rubles only.*

$ **Moosehead Canadian Bar.** If you're looking for a comfortable, lively pub, try this loose-spirited restaurant, a 1995 newcomer to the list of places that pander to young Russian and expatriate movers and shakers. It has a warm, welcoming atmosphere, with wood paneling and local art on the walls. The lights are low; the music, at least on weekends, is not. Rove among the dining rooms—one intimate, one wide—and two barrooms, where you can grab a table, a seat at the bar, or simply stand to chat and people-watch. The menu is hearty. Breakfast caters to healthy appetites, and you'll find a hearty portion of corned beef hash here, and certainly nowhere else. Chili, burgers, soups, salads, steak, and pasta are also available. The good-natured staff, almost all of which comprises native English speakers, works hard to look after you. Alas, no Moosehead on tap—but there is Guinness, Harp, and Tuborg plus plenty of imports by the bottle. ✕ *54 ul. Bolshaya Polyanka,* ☎ FAX *095/230–7333. AE, DC, MC, V.* ☺ *Daily noon–5 AM.*

$ Moskovskye Zory. This log-cabin restaurant between Pushkin Square and Mayakovsky Square is a great place for a quick, delicious lunch. It's a tiny eatery and has just a few tables, which are decked with red tablecloths. The owner is especially friendly to Americans. The dependably tasty offerings are usually limited to two types of traditional Russian soup, salad, and a few main courses. German beer and Georgian wines are usually available. Avoid the coffee at dessert time. ✕ *Maly Kozikhinsky Pereulok 11,* ☎ *095/299–5725. Reservations required. Rubles only.*

$ Patio Pizza. An airy place to find pizza bliss, this cheerful restaurant has a huge back room with glass ceiling and walls, so the sun pours in all day. The original is a stone's throw from the Pushkin Fine Arts Museum; a newer branch is located in the front section of the Intourist Hotel at the tip of Tverskaya ulitsa. The menu runs the gamut of pizzas, with a real salad bar and Italian entrées. The pizza has a thin and dusty crust; daily specials include such dishes as lasagna al forno and baked cannelloni. The sole near-Russian entry, Trota alla Romana, is trout with potatoes, turnips, and buttered carrots. Kids can have pint-size pizzas and kiddie cocktails. Tables are comfortably spaced, topped with checkerboard tablecloths. Pop music plays softly, and the rooms are always filled with a pleasantly bustling crowd. ✕ *30 ul. Volkhonka,* ☎ *095/201–0050. Reservations not required. AE, DC, MC, V. Free parking and an exchange office outside.*

$ Ukraina. The main restaurant in the Ukraina Hotel has traditionally catered to tourist groups. In recent years it has become a popular night spot with young and restless Russians, who come here in the evenings for the positively tasteless erotic floor show. During the day, however, the only entertainment is an occasional Russian folk ensemble. The Stalinesque decor takes you back to the 1950s, with orange taffeta curtains, heavy chandeliers, massive marble pillars and, for good measure, Ukrainian embroidered tapestries draping the walls. The menu, like the decor, is a reflection of the former Soviet Union. Traditional Ukrainian dishes such as chicken Kiev and borscht are featured side by side with Russian and other national cuisines of the former Soviet republics. Bow-tied waiters offer polite and friendly service. Although the food is heavy and bland, the restaurant remains popular with foreigners and Russians alike thanks to its extremely reasonable prices. This is a good place to spend a rainy afternoon over a bottle of wine and a long lunch. ✕ *Kutuzovsky Prospect 2/1,* ☎ *095/243–4732. Reservations advised. Rubles only.* ☺ *Daily noon–4:30, 6–midnight.*

$ Uzbekistan. As its name indicates, this restaurant specializes in the spicy cuisine of the Central Asian republic of Uzbekistan. It's long been popular with tourists, but its reputation is much better than it deserves. Opened in 1949, the restaurant is a relic of the Stalinist era, when the great "friendship" of the numerous ethnic groups caught inside the borders of the Soviet Union was celebrated by opening restaurants specializing in the national cuisine of the various republics (the Aragvi and Ukraina restaurants opened under similar circumstances). The decor—high ceilings, massive pillars, ornate wood carvings, and fancy chandeliers—is a uniquely Soviet mix of Stalinism and traditional Central Asian decoration. The house specialty—*manty* (rubber dumplings filled with mystery meat and served with a thick glob of sour cream)—

are just barely edible. The kitchen does a better job with the *plof* (pilaf) and *lagman* (meat and noodle soup). The restaurant makes up for the bland cuisine with its colorful atmosphere and lively entertainment. If you're looking to mingle with the locals, you can join them here for a shot or two (or three) of vodka. ✕ *Ul. Neglinnaya 29,* ☎ *095/924–6053. Reservations advised. Rubles only.*

$ **Yakimanka.** A band sings Western music in heavy Russian accents as diners lounge on sunken couches before low, candlelighted tables in the back room or sit at conventional tables—also lighted by candles— in the front room. This exotic bit of central Asia in Moscow is a good spot for a relaxing evening meal. Sample Yakimanka's grape leaves stuffed with meats, rice, and garlic, or try the pilaf with beef and vegetables. Don't miss the pickled-garlic appetizer. ✕ *Ul. Bolshaya Polyanka 2/10,* ☎ *095/238–8888. Reservations required. Rubles only.*

LODGING

You might think that a world capital with a population of more than 9 million would have a large number of hotels, but this is not the case in Moscow—at least not yet. Significant improvements have occurred, but they are not comprehensive. Since 1990 a welcome entity—the luxury hotel—has appeared in large numbers, but the city suffers from a deficit of decent mid-range hotels, and hangovers are still evident at the old Intourist standbys. In fairness to the latter, some of them have upgraded their service (a bit), and sales and management teams are making an effort to keep afloat in a more competitive environment. However, they will probably remain in a class by themselves in terms of service, furnishings, and atmosphere—a class, unfortunately, that foreign tourists will not be entirely comfortable with. If you're not staying at one of the top hotels, be patient and ready to roll with the punches. Russia is for the intrepid traveler.

All prices are quoted in U.S. dollars.

CATEGORY	COST*
$$$$	over $350
$$$	$250–$350
$$	$125–$250
$	under $125
¢	under $60

All prices are for a standard double room for two, excluding service charge.

$$$$ **Baltschug Kempinski.** Situated on the banks of the Moskva River, opposite the Kremlin and Red Square, this five-star hotel boasts extraordinary views—and prices, too. Long in a state of disrepair, its 19th-century building, once an aristocratic apartment house, has been completely reconstructed. The modern interiors sparkle, but they lack the distinct character of prerevolutionary Russia found in hotels such as the Metropole or the Savoy. The spacious rooms are done in stately red and cream and are equipped with all amenities. The Swiss management has thought of such niceties as bathroom slippers, perhaps to encourage guests to stay home and enjoy the picture-postcard views across the river. The location is central but not particularly convenient: the hotel is not accessible by public transportation, and the city's main attractions are on the other side of the river. You're best off having a car and driver if you stay here. Make sure you specify that you want a room with a view; otherwise you could end up staring at the factory bordering the hotel's eastern side. 🛏 *Ul. Balchug 1,* ☎ *095/230–*

6500, FAX 095/230–6502. *From outside Russia,* ☎ 007–501–230–9500, FAX 007–501–230–9502. *202 room with bath, 32 suites. 3 restaurants, café, nighttime bar, 24-hr room service, cable TV with CNN and BBC, complimentary minibar, fitness center with sauna and 20-meter pool, business center, hard-currency shops. Traveler's checks accepted. AE, DC, MC, V.*

$$$$ **Metropol.** Originally built in 1899–1903 by William Walcott, this lav-
★   ish, first-class hotel reopened in 1991 after five years of extensive renovations. Now operating as a British-Russian joint venture, the Metropol
is a member of the Inter-Continental Hotel groups. Its posh interiors
have been the site of many historic events. Lenin spoke frequently in
the assembly hall of the building, and in 1918–19 the Central Committee of the Russian Republic met here under its first chairman, Yakov
Sverdlov (for whom the square outside the hotel was named until 1991).
Today this hotel is one of Moscow's most elegant, with outstanding service and amenities. The nicely appointed rooms feature hardwood
floors, Oriental rugs, large closets, and modern furnishings. Antiques
grace all the suites and the two presidential ones come with private saunas.
The lobby, restaurants, and other common areas will transport you back
a century. The location, opposite the Bolshoi Theater and a five-minute
walk from the Kremlin, can't be beat. 🏠 *Teatralny Proezd 1/4,* ☎ *095/
927–6000,* FAX *095/975–2355. From outside Russia,* ☎ *7501–927–
1000,* FAX *7501–927–1010. 328 rooms with bath, 75 suites. 4 restaurants, 2 bars, 24-hr room service, in-room movies and cable TV television
with CNN and MTV, satellite telephone, fitness center with sauna and
swimming pool, travel agent, theater-ticket agency, casino, conference
facilities. Traveler's checks accepted. AE, DC, MC, V.*

$$$$ **National.** When first built in 1903, the National was one of Moscow's
★   premier hotels. Reopened in 1995 after years of renovation, it is again
bidding to be the city's most luxurious accommodation, a contest it
probably wins. Like the Metropole, its location in the heart of Moscow
is superb for travelers who want to feel at the vortex of the tornado.
Located across the street from Red Square, at the foot of ulitsa Tverskaya, this heavily trafficked corner would be noisy were it not for the
hotel's soundproofing. Inside, you'll find the serenity of a bygone era.
All renovations in the stunning landmark building have retained the
grandeur of the original Art Nouveau style. A great marble staircase
spirals upward in a winding railing of pewter vine; the elevators,
topped by silvered twists of ivy, echo the design. Behind the stairs, through
lavender and light green stained glass, you can glimpse the atrium and
tearoom below. There are four styles of suites (including ultra-deluxe
corner ones), two styles of doubles, and two of singles. All rooms, except for a few doubles done in a more modern style, are elegantly plush
with polished oak furniture upholstered in silk. The white-tiled Ital-
ianate bathrooms are sparkling and modern. If price is no object—but
luxury, quiet, and elite service are—this is the place to stay. Literally
topping all of it is the pool in the fitness center, on the hotel's top floor,
where swimmers look out, eye level, at the crenelated top of the Kremlin and the cupolas and domes of its cathedrals—a magnificent sight,
particularly at night. 🏠 *14/1 Okhotny Ryad,* ☎ *095/258–7000; fax
095/258–7100. 231 rooms, including 36 suites. 4 restaurants, 4 bars,
tearoom, business center, 12 conference and banquet facilities, room
service, fitness center, solarium, service bureau, exchange office, car
service. Traveler's checks for $US (only). AE, DC, MC, V.*

$$$$ **Olympic Penta.** Opened in 1991 under German management, this was
one of Moscow's first joint-venture hotels. It was built by a Finnish
contruction team, and everything here is imported, down to the last

doorknob. The rooms are large and fully equipped with every conceivable amenity. The fitness center is one of the best in town. Service is good, although the European-trained Russian staff has been known to let its Soviet upbringing rear its ugly head. The location—near the Olympic Sports Stadium—is rather far from the city's tourist attractions, but it's convenient to all major arterial roads or the subway stop a 10-minute walk away. ☎ *Olympysky Prospect 18/1,* ☎ *095/931–9000 or 095/931–9833,* 𝔽𝔸𝕏 *095/931–9020. 490 rooms with bath, 10 suites. Restaurant, café, beer hall, bar, 24-hour room service, minibar, cable TV, satellite telephone, fitness center with sauna and 22-meter pool, gift shops, car service, conference facilities. Traveler's checks accepted. AE, DC, MC, V.*

$$$$ Palace. With the exception of the National, the Palace is Moscow's most recently opened top-class hotel, but somehow its late 1970s decor—lots of brass, hanging plants, muted rose and evergreen textile carpets—conspires to make it look just a touch dated, at least among its rivals. Still, it is particularly popular with the European business community (Americans seem to prefer the Slavyanskaya), to which it caters with a full range of traveler's amenities. With that purpose in mind, it's heavy on double rooms for the single traveler; you'll find these offer all you need, though they are a bit crowded with furniture. The real winners are those who can afford the duplexes (double suites), which have a stunning bilevel arrangement of two upstairs bedrooms (each with full, separate bath), a dining room, and a living room below, decorated in rose-and-mint furnishings trimmed in varnished golden pine with tasteful paintings and sculpture throughout. The hotel's location, at the far upper end of Tverskaya, is excellent, but this main road isn't always easy to navigate by car. Service is pleasant, despite a hovering air of distraction. A Marco Polo Hotel. ☎ *19 Pervaya Tverskaya-Yamskaya,* ☎ *095/956–3152,* 𝔽𝔸𝕏 *095/956–3151; from overseas, same number plus 7 503 satellite prefix. 221 rooms, including 22 suites. 3 restaurants, café, guest bar, lobby bar, room service, minibar, satellite tv, fitness center, Jacuzzi and sauna (no pool), car and limousine service, conference and banquet facilities, 48 no-smoking rooms, 5 rooms for the disabled. Traveler's checks accepted. AE, DC, MC, V.*

$$$$ Pullman Iris. Under French management, this new hotel is located in a bleak residential district on the northwest outskirts of town, adjacent to the world-famous Fyodorov Eye Institute. The hotel hoped to attract foreign patients, but their numbers are smaller than anticipated, and the hotel is operating far below capacity. Its distant location is unfortunate, because this is one of the finest of the new foreign-run hotels in Moscow. The spacious rooms are cheery and bright, with lots of closet space and large bathrooms. The views are quite dismal, though, since the hotel is surrounded by monotonous high-rises. There are few shops or restaurants of any interest to the tourist in the area. The hotel's own French restaurant, however, has earned an excellent reputation among the city's foreign community. Complimentary shuttle service is provided to guests, making it easier to enjoy the city's attractions. Buses run hourly to Red Square, and five times daily to the Sovincenter. ☎ *Korovinskoye Shosse 10,* ☎ *095/488–8000,* 𝔽𝔸𝕏 *095/ 488–8888; from outside Russia, 502/220–8844, 195 rooms with bath. 2 restaurants, bar, 24-hour room service, minibar, satellite telephone, cable TV, fitness center with swimming pool, car service, complimentary shuttle service to city center, excursion bureau, gift shop. Traveler's checks accepted. AE, DC, MC, V.*

$$$ Aerostar. The Aerostar, not to be confused with the rundown Aeroflot
★   Hotel next door, is a Russian-Canadian joint venture with Aeroflot and IMP Group Limited. Opened in 1992, the hotel was originally com-

missioned for the 1980 Olympics but never completed for that purpose. The Canadian team has worked wonders with the austere Soviet design, transforming it into a first-rate, Western-style hotel. The lobby areas are bright and cheery, and the rooms are nicely appointed, with European furnishings and redwood paneling. Unusual for Russia, the hotel has no-smoking rooms available. The rooms on the northeast side look out onto the Petrovsky Palace, a striking, crenelated redbrick palace where the czars broke their journey between St. Petersburg and Moscow. Service is excellent, and business travelers find the location—halfway between the city center and Sheremetyevo International Airport—very convenient. Tourists, though, may find the city's major attractions are too far away. Many of the city's expatriates are making the trek out here to eat at the hotel's Taiga Restaurant. The house specialty is fresh lobster flown in from Nova Scotia, and on Sunday the restaurant features a lavish champagne brunch. ☒ *Leningradsky Prospect 37,* ☎ *095/213–9000 or 9001, satellite* FAX *7 502/213–9001. 386 rooms with bath, 31 suites. 2 restaurants, 2 bars, 24-hour room service, international TV programming including CNN and BBC, satellite telephone, gift shop, fitness center, business center, exchange bureau, excursion bureau, car rental, conference facilities. Traveler's checks accepted. AE, DC, MC, V.*

$$$ Mezhdunarodnaya. Its name means "International," but foreign residents have dubbed it "the Mezh." Built by the American financier Armand Hammer in 1980, until the opening of the Radisson Slavyanskaya Hotel, this huge complex was the hub of international business in Moscow, when such business was first being done. Its atrium lobby and indoor mall, therefore, were once an oasis for foreign shoppers who came for the restaurants and well-stocked hard-currency stores. But when times changed for the better in Russia, they seemed to change for the worse here, and the best enterprises moved out to more exciting premises. Newly revamped management is vowing a return to its previous high standards but admits it may take two or three years. The rooms are bigger than at the Radisson, but the views are no better and the Italian furnishings have seen better days. The hotel is located within sighting distance of the city center but far from the subway, and only one city bus stops anywhere near the hotel. You're better off elsewhere, at least until standards improve again. ☒ *Krasnopresnenskaya Naberezhnaya 12,* ☎ *095/253–1391 or 095/253–1392,* FAX *095/253–2051. 530 rooms with bath. 5 restaurants, 6 bars, hard-currency shops and grocery store, service bureau, fitness center with pool and sauna, minibar. Traveler's checks accepted with commission. AE, DC, MC, V.*

$$$ Presnya. Once an exclusive domain of the Communist Party, management of this modest hotel was taken over by an Austrian firm, which undertook to transform it into a Western-style hotel. So far, however, it has not entirely followed through on this. It's located in a quaint residential neighborhood in the city center not far from Patriarch's Pond, and that is its best recommendation right now. A few years ago, a handful of rooms were renovated, and they are quite attractive, but the remainder are still outfitted with the same overscale, slightly shabby communist-era fixtures. All rooms are very clean and more than functional but do not befit a hotel in the expensive range. Service is friendly and efficient, the atmosphere quiet and composed. In the absence of full renovations, if management lowered prices this could be the midrange hotel that Moscow currently lacks. A Marco Polo hotel. ☒ *Spiridonevsky Pereulok 9,* ☎ *095/244–3631,* FAX *095/956–6306; satellite fax, use 7 503 prefix. 68 rooms with bath. Restaurant, lobby bar, summer terrace café, room service, minibar, cable TV, fitness center* *with sauna, business center, gift shop, car service, conference facilities. Traveler's checks accepted. AE, DC, MC, V.*

$$$ **Radisson Slavyanskaya.** Designed with the frustrated business traveler
★ in mind, the hotel offers every modern amenity American-style: no-nonsense comfort in an efficient atmosphere. Its huge, two-story lobby is lined with first-class restaurants, shops, a fully equipped fitness center with Olympic pool, an independent press center, an English-language movie theater, and much more. Among the offices opened here are a full-fledged travel agency and a full-service bank. With everything you might want or need located inside the hotel, if the rest of Moscow closed down, you might never know it if you were holed up here. The location is central, but alongside Kiev Railway Station, notorious for its pickpockets, so a walk outside the hotel will place you in a different reality altogether. Still, you needn't feel endangered. There are always lots of people around, and a protective wall and the guards posted at the hotel's main entrance keep the uninvited from wandering onto the hotel grounds. The rooms are nicely appointed but small; the views are nothing to write home about. This is a good choice for visitors who favor comfort and service over character and who don't want or need intensive contact with the real Moscow. ⚐ *Berezhkovskaya Naberezhnaya 2,* ☎ *095/941–8020,* FAX *095/941–8000; fax from outside Russia, 7502–224–1225. Reservations may be made through Radisson Hotels in U.S.,* ☎ *800/333–3333. 407 rooms with bath, 24 suites. 2 restaurants, café, lobby bar, fitness center with 25-meter lap pool, 24-hr room service, satellite telephone, minibar, cable TV with CNN, hard-currency shops, exchange bureau, car rental, excursion bureau, conference facilities. Traveler's checks accepted. AE, DC, MC, V.*

$$$ **Savoy.** This luxury hotel aims to recapture the opulent tone of the early 20th century. The Savoy was built in 1912 in connection with celebrations commemorating the 300th anniversary of the Romanov dynasty. Most of its working life, however, it served as an Intourist hotel (under the name Berlin). After the demise of the Soviets, it was Moscow's first joint-venture hotel (Finnish-Russian) to be completely renovated. Its somewhat frayed interiors, replete with gilded chandeliers, ceiling paintings, and polished redwood paneling, invoke the spirit of pre-revolutionary Russia. The rooms are somewhat small and dark (a legacy of Soviet remodeling), but they are nicely appointed with pretty, rose-colored wallpaper and matching upholstery. The views are mostly negligible, owing to the hotel's side-street location, but this does give the advantage of quiet. One of the gilded suites contains a piano purchased especially for Luciano Pavarotti when he stayed here while performing at the Bolshoi Theater. Popular with businesspeople who eschew busy hotel lobbies, the Savoy is centrally located, just off Theater Square and within walking distance of the Kremlin. The staff is cheerful and helpful. ⚐ *Ul. Rozhdestvenka 3,* ☎ *095/929–8500,* FAX *095/230–2186. 86 rooms with bath, 29 suites. Restaurant, 2 bars, 24-hr room service, satellite telephone, cable TV with CNN, minibar, business center, casino, excursion and travel bureau. Traveler's checks accepted. AE, DC, MC, V.*

$$ **Belgrade II.** Built in 1975 as one of two twin towers (the other is now the Zolotoye Koltso), this former Intourist-run hotel is a typical Brezhnev-era high-rise. Often, groups booked through Russian agencies get placed here. The hotel's main advantage is its central location, near the subway and the Arbat. The interior decor is unimaginative, and the hotel has the same institutional feeling as the Intourist (*see below*). The rooms could use some sprucing up, and renovations are underway to replace the cheap, plywood furnishings and worn industrial carpeting. You can get similar accommodations at half the price at the Zolotoye Koltso across the street. ☎ *Smolenskaya Ploshchad 8,* ☎ *095/248–2841,* FAX *095/230–2129. 487 rooms with bath. 2 restaurants, 2 snack bars, 2 bars, exchange bureau, excursion bureau. AE, DC, MC, V.*

$$ **Intourist.** Centrally located at the bottom of Tverskaya ulitsa, at the back flank of the National Hotel, to which it once was joined, this aging skyscraper is a popular holding spot for tourist groups. Unfortunately, its super location also attracts a seedy-looking presence outside the hotel's main entrance which makes coming and going, particularly at night, a rather unpleasant experience. Its smoke-filled lobby features the usual oversize and drab decor, although the gift and souvenir shops are better stocked than most. The hotel staff, when not busy taking personal phone calls, is receptive and relatively helpful. The interior has remained basically unchanged since the hotel opened in 1970 and the rooms are in poor condition. Although they all come with telephone and television, you also get stained furnishings, worn carpeting, and monotone polyester curtains. Despite the drawbacks, the rates here remain relatively high. This is mostly due to the hotel's prime location, which is the only reason to stay here. ☎ *Ul. Tverskaya 3. 443 rooms with bath. 3 restaurants, 7 snack bars, casino, excursion bureau. DC, MC, V.*

$$ **Novotel.** If you need a room near the Airport, this is the place to stay. Professional European soccer teams patronize Novotel because of its few distractions. The rooms and beds are comfortable, the hallways are quiet, and at the moment, the price is still right. They are a hair's breadth from the Expensive category, though, so you may want to double-check with your travel agent before you book. In addition, the staff is eager to please, and the modern facilities are well maintained. ☎ *Sheremetyevo II Airport,* ☎ *095/578–9401 or 095/578–9110,* FAX *095/578–2797, from outside Russia: 7 502 220–6604. 155 rooms, 40 suites. AE, DC, MC, V.*

$$ **Ukraina.** This imposing skyscraper on the banks of the Moskva River ★ is one of the seven Stalin Gothics. The red carpeting, high ceilings, and colorful socialist-realist ceiling paintings are trademarks of the Stalinist era. The rooms are worn but relatively clean in a city where standards of cleanliness are low. Redwood and oak furnishings and fancy chandeliers create an atmosphere of faded elegance. Doors have locks and dead bolts, and supposedly soon to come are electronic strip locks. The old tradition of floor attendants has been retained here, so you'll also find a hotel staff member on every floor. The hotel is situated across the Moscow River from the Russian "White House" (where the president works). Rooms on the higher floors on this side have great views and cost 15% more. This is an almost central location, right off Kutuzovsky Prospect at the foot of Novy Arbat. Subway travelers, however, will find their station is a good 10-minute trek away. Plusses here are the well-stocked hard-currency store and the German-run joint-venture restaurant, tucked away on the third floor. A minus is the sometimes scary-looking crowd of men who seem to permanently lounge on the steps of the entryway. ☎ *Kutuzovsky Prospect 2/2,* ☎ *095/243–2596; reservations, 095/243–3030; fax 095/243–3092. 1,010 rooms with bath. 2 restaurants, 6 snack bars, 3 bars, hard-currency shop, clothes boutique, casino, sauna. AE, DC, MC, V.*

$ **Kosmos.** This huge, 26-story hotel was built by the French for the 1980 ★ Olympics. It is French-equipped and furnished, but years of heavy tourist traffic have dulled its shine. Service varies wildly, with large groups getting preference over individual tourists. The slot machines and late-night bars attract unsavory types, including plenty of prostitutes, but the rooms themselves are adequate and clean. Overall, service and accommodations here are far superior to those at the Intourist Hotel, another popular destination with tourist groups. Its spacious, two-story lobby is reminiscent of a mall, full of well-stocked, hard-currency stores and shops. The hotel is across the street from the All-Russia Exhibition Center, a part of town that has interesting sites, but is far from downtown, though convenient to the subway (right across the street). ☎ *Prospect Mira 150,* ☎ *095/217–1086 or 095/217–1649,* FAX *095/ 215–8880. 1,777 rooms with bath. 4 restaurants, 8 bars, swimming pool, sauna, bowling alley, hard-currency grocery store. AE, MC, V.*

$ **Leningradskaya.** This Soviet fortress is another of Moscow's seven Stalin Gothic skyscrapers. Its awe-inspiring, monumental interior features high ceilings, red carpets, and heavy bronze chandeliers. A faded gem of the Stalinist era, the hotel is often used to house Russian parliament members. The rooms are modestly furnished but surprisingly clean and well maintained. Ask for a room high up—the views from the lower floors are strictly industrial. The location is relatively central but not exactly convenient or calm. The hotel stands at a busy intersection, right across from the Leningrad, Kazan, and Yaroslav railway stations. To reach the subway you have to dash across the highway and then make your way through the rather unsavory crowds that live at the train station. There is also a major casino on the ground floor. Nevertheless, the reasonable rates here make this is an okay choice for budget-minded travelers, though it's not recommended as comfortable for women traveling alone. Just be sure to pack plenty of patience; the hotel staff long ago wearied of their jobs. ☎ *Ul. Kalanchevskaya 21/40,* ☎ *095/975–3032,* FAX *975–8002. 346 rooms with bath. Restaurant, 2 snack bars, casino, hard-currency shop, exchange bureau. AE, DC, MC, V.*

$ **Rossiya.** Pack your compass and map if you're staying here, because negotiating the seemingly endless corridors from of this huge hotel is a cartographer's nightmare. The mammoth building is one of Europe's largest hotels, able to accommodate up to 6,000 guests. Opened in 1967, it once numbered among the Soviet Union's finest hotels, but it suffered two fires and service and accommodations have rapidly sped downhill in recent years. All the rooms come with television and telephone, but there's no guarantee they'll work. Cockroaches (and worse) are also not unheard of. As with the Intourist, the main reason to stay here is the location: just off the edge of Red Square, with stupendous views of it and the Kremlin, if you have a room on the west side. Deteriorating conditions have forced the hotel to reduce its rates, making this one of the cheaper choices in downtown Moscow. ☎ *Ul. Varvarka 6,* ☎ *095/298–1567. 2,800 rooms with bath. 8 restaurants, 20 snack bars, 2 bars, pool and sauna, exchange bureau. Traveler's checks accepted. AE, MC, V.*

$ **Soyuz.** Yugoslav-built in 1980, this hotel on the northwest outskirts of town has an interesting avant-garde design. Its distant location keeps its rates in the inexpensive category, though the service and atmosphere here are good. The rooms come with modern furnishings and cheery, flowery wallpaper. Some of them have views of the Moskva River, where in summer Muscovites come in droves to swim and sunbathe. The lobby area, too, is bright and cheery, with lots of windows and plants. The public areas and rooms are quite clean by local standards, but the location is a serious drawback. The surrounding area is likely to have a dispiriting effect on first-time visitors, and the hotel is convenient only to the Sheremetyevo Airport (15 minutes away). The closest subway stop—Rechnoy Vokzal, the last stop on the green line—is a 20-minute bus ride away, and it can take more than an hour to reach the city center by car. ☎ *Ul. Levoberezhnaya 12,* ☎ *095/457– 2088,* FAX *095/457–2096. 154 rooms with bath. Restaurant, bar, snack bar, exchange bureau. AE, DC, V.*

$ Zolotoye Koltso. Formerly named the Belgrade I, this hotel offers a good deal for your money in a convenient downtown location. It's situated at the tip of Smolenskaya Square, right before you reach the imposing Ministry of Foreign Affairs, close to the subway and the Arbat. The rooms are very basic, with narrow twin beds, mismatched upholstery, and worn industrial carpeting. All the singles and suites come with telephone and television, which you'll find only sporadically in the doubles. Standards of cleanliness are higher here for some reason than at the Belgrade, the hotel's twin across the street. Some of the rooms come with pleasant views of the Moskva River. Service is friendly, and there's an attendant on every floor. Considering its location, the rates are reasonable, and you can get an entire suite here for less than the price of a single at the nearly identical Belgrade. ⊠ *Smolenskaya Ploshchad 5,* ☎ *095/248–6843; reservations, 095/248–7395,* ℻ *095/248–7395. 460 rooms with bath. 2 restaurants, café, 2 bars, casino, business center, excursion bureau. AE, DC, MC, V.*

¢ Molodyozhnaya. Its name means "youth," and the hotel traditionally catered to groups of young people traveling under the auspices of Sputnik (the former Soviet youth tourist agency). It was built for the 1980 Olympics and features the typical drab decor of a Brezhnev-era high-rise. Basically, it's for those seeking hostel accommodations. The rock-bottom prices may make you indifferent to its cement-and-steel lobby decorated with a mosaic depicting happy proletariat youth. The rooms are standard size and adequate, provided you are not a stickler for cleanliness. The decor is standard Soviet fare—heavy on the plywood and polyester. Its location on the outskirts of town is far from the city's tourist attractions, but there's a subway stop within walking distance. The three- and five-person "suites" are good for friends traveling together. ⊠ *Dmitrovskoye Shosse 27,* ☎ *095/210–4565,* ℻ *095/210–4311. 600 rooms with bath. Restaurant, 4 bars. No credit cards; cash only.*

¢ Sevastopol. This is a huge complex comprising four 16-story high-rises. Although the hotel is far from the city's tourist attractions, the subway is close by. The green stucco walls give the place an institutional feeling more appropriate to a dormitory than a hotel, and you can't expect to get more than the basic plywood furnishings. But for tourists on a shoestring budget who don't mind roughing it a bit, like the Molodyozhnaya this is a bearable if far from luxurious option. During summer months be certain beforehand that they will have hot water. Citywide, section by section, it is turned off for three to four weeks for pipe *remont.* At this hotel this usually occurs in June. ⊠ *Pervaya Bolshaya Yushunskaya ul., reservations* ☎ *095/318–0918; Bldg. 1,* ☎ *095/119–8182; Bldg. 2,* ☎ *095/318–4972; Bldg. 3, 095/318–6483; Bldg. 4, 095/318–8371. 2,588 rooms with bath. 9 restaurants, 8 snack bars, bar, casino, sauna, excursion bureau. DC, MC, V.*

THE ARTS AND NIGHTLIFE

The Arts

Moscow is famed for its rich cultural life. The city boasts more than 60 officially registered theaters, with new ones opening all the time. Except at the most renowned theaters, such as the Bolshoi, tickets can be obtained for rubles at the theaters themselves or at theater box offices (*teatralnaya kassa*) scattered throughout the city. If you're intimidated by the language barrier, avail yourself of the EPS Theater Box Office in the main lobby of the Metropol Hotel (☎ 095/927–6982 or 6983) or the service bureau in your hotel. The prices are inflated, but they can often get tickets to sold-out performances. Another alternative is to purchase a ticket from a scalper immediately prior to the performance there is no guarantee that you'll get a good seat.

Every Friday the English-language newspaper *Moscow Times* publishes a schedule of cultural events for the coming week.

Art Galleries

Numerous private galleries have opened in the past few years, and you certainly will enjoy seeing, and probably purchasing, some of the excellent work done by Russian artists. The Friday edition of the *Moscow Times* carries a review of the current exhibits. For opening hours, check with the galleries themselves; some are open only by appointment, and most are closed on Sunday and Monday. A partial listing of galleries includes: Art Moderne, 39 ul. Bolshaya Ordynka, ☎ 095/233–1551; Central House of Artists, 10 ul. Krymsky Val, ☎ 095/238–1245; Contemporary Art Center, 2/6 ul. Bolshaya Yakimanka, ☎ 095/238–2454; Elite Gallery, 2/11 Leontevsky Pereulok, ☎ 095/929–7056; Fine Arts Gallery, 38 Arbat, 4th floor, ☎ 095/241–1267; International University Gallery, 17 Leningradsky Prospect, ☎ 095/250–3481; M'ARS Gallery, 32 ul. Malaya Filyovskaya, ☎ 095/146–2029; Moscow Gallery Hall, 20 Kuznetsky Most, ☎ 095/925–4264; Moscow Palette Gallery, 35/28 ul. Povarskaya, ☎ 095/291–1124; NB Gallery, 6/2 ul. Sivtsev Vrazhek (apt. 2), ☎ 095/203–4006; Ridzhina Gallery, 36 ul. Myasnitskaya, ☎ 095/921–1613; Today Gallery, 35 Arbat, ☎ 095/248–4976; Vostochnaya Gallery, 10 ul. Khmelyova, ☎ 095/208–1167.

Drama

Even if you do not speak Russian, you might want to explore the intense world of Russian dramatic theater. The partial listings below cover Moscow's major drama theaters. Take heed that evening performances here begin at 7 PM *sharp*.

Chekhov Moscow Art Theater, or MKhAT (Kamergrersky Pereulok 3, ☎ 095/229–8760). Founded in 1898 by the celebrated actors and directors Konstantin Stanislavsky and Vladimir Nemirovich-Danchenko, this theater is famous for its productions of the Russian classics, especially those of Chekhov. An affiliated, modern Moscow Art Theater with a seating capacity of 2,000 is located at 22 Tverskoy Bulvar.

LenKom Theater (Ul. Chekhova 6, ☎ 095/299–9668). This very popular theater presents new plays by young authors.

Maly Theater (Teatralnaya Ploshchad 1/6, ☎ 095/923–2621). Moscow's first dramatic theater is famous for its staging of Russian classics, especially those Ostrovsky.

Mayakovsky Theater (19 ul. Bolshaya Nikitskaya, ☎ 095/290–4232). Named after the great writer, this stages serious dramas, both classic and contemporary.

Mossoviet Theater (ul. Bolshaya Sadovaya 16, ☎ 095/200–5943). This spot is good for contemporary drama.

Taganka Theater (Taganskaya Ploshchad, ☎ 095/951–1217). The best-known of Moscow's avant-garde and experimental companies. Performances sell out far in advance.

Satire Theater (Triumfalnaya Ploshchad 2, ☎ 095/299–6305). This theater specializes in satirical comedies, such as Mayakovsky's *The Bathhouse* and *The Bedbug*.

Sovremmenik Theater (Chistoprudny Bulvar 19A, ☎ 095/921–6473). This is one of Moscow's youngest theaters, with an experimental repertoire and company of young actors.

Vakhtangov Theater (Arbat 26, ☎ 095/241–0728). Named after Stanislavksy's pupil Evgeny Vakhtangov, this is an excellent traditional theater, good for contemporary dramas.

Yermolova International Theater Center (Tverskaya ul. 5, ☎ 095/203–7952). The repertoire here varies from the Russian classics to modern, Western plays.

Music

Moscow's musical life has always been particularly rich; the city has a number of symphony orchestras as well as song-and-dance ensembles. Moiseyev's Folk Dance Ensemble is well known in Europe and America, but the troupe is on tour so much of the year that when it performs in Moscow, tickets are very difficult to obtain. Other renowned companies include the State Symphony Orchestra and the Armed Forces Song and Dance Ensemble. Except for tickets for special performances, tickets usually are easily available and inexpensive.

Glinka Music Museum Hall (Ul. Fadeyeva 4, ☎ 095/972–3237). This is one of many small concert halls scattered throughout the city.

Kolonny Zal (Pushkinskaya ul. 1, ☎ 095/292–4864) This is also called the Hall of Columns and holds chamber-music and symphony concerts.

National Academy of Music (Ul. Paliashvili 1, ☎ 095/290–6737). The academy is highly recommended for student productions of chamber music, symphony concerts, and operas.

Tchaikovsky Concert Hall (4/31 Triumfalnaya Ploshchad, ☎ 095/299–0378). This huge concert hall with seating for more than 1,600 is home to the State Symphony Orchestra.

Tchaikovsky Conservatory (Ul. Bolshaya Nikitskaya 13, ☎ 095/229–8183; 095/299–0658). The acoustics of the magnificent Great Hall are superb, and portraits of the world's great composers hang above the high balcony. Rachmaninoff, Scriabin, and Tchaikovsky are among the famous composers who have worked here. The adjacent Small Hall is usually reserved for chamber-music concerts.

Scriabin Museum Hall (Ul. Vakhtangova 11, ☎ 095/299–1192). Performances are held in a small concert hall located in the apartment building where the composer Alexander Scriabin lived. Concerts are usually held on Wednesday and Friday evenings.

Russian Army House (12 Suvorovskaya Ploshchad, ☎ 095/281–5550). This theater is home to the Armed Forces Song and Dance Ensemble.

Opera and Ballet

Bolshoi Opera and Ballet Theater (1 Teatralnaya Ploshchad, ☎ 095/292–9986). Visitors always get a thrill out of a visit to this world-renowned theater. The current quality of its productions is erratic, however, due to management changes and the loss of many of its best performers. The gilded, 19th-century auditorium is itself a sight to behold, as is the Russian flair for set and costume design, which alone is enough to keep an audience enthralled.

Kremlin Palace (in the Kremlin, ☎ 095/926–6934, 095/925–0422, or 095/924–5676). This modern concert hall, where Soviet Communist Party congresses were held, now has regular performances by opera and ballet troupes, including those from the Bolshoi. Of late it also has become the place for international megastars acts, including Elton John, Diana Ross, and Julio Iglesias. Entrance is through the white-washed Kutafya Gate, near the Manege.

Operetta Theater (6 Pushkinskaya ul., ☎ 095/292–0405). Come here for classical and modern dance and music.

Pokrovsky Chamber Musical Theater (Leningradsky Prospect 71, ☎ 095/198–7204). This experimental theater stages interesting productions of Russian classics.

Stanislavsky and Nemirovich-Danchenko Musical Theater (Ul. Pushkin-skaya 17, ☎ 095/229–8388). This offers classical and modern operas, ballets, and operettas.

Nightlife

Moscow's after-hours scene has virtually created itself in the past few years. It may still have a long way to go, but there are already a fair number of choices despite predictable lapses of taste (many clubs and bars feature erotic floor shows that rival those of Times Square). Casi-nos, with their special brand of flashy tackiness, abound, but those interested in less overdone entertainment may take heart. As incomes rise and exposure to new types of leisure activity spreads, a wider range of night spots is opening.

Before you go out, remember that as a foreigner, you should take special precautions at night. Press reports have a way of exaggerating the situation, but, as everywhere, foreign tourists are easy crime targets, and Moscow is one of the world's biggest cities; more lawlessness than before is beseiging its streets, though this is more between national groups than individual tourists. Use common sense and make arrangements for the trip home before you leave. Keep in mind that the more you drink (and it's easy to drink a lot here), the more vulnerable you become. Do not drive under any circumstances if you drink; laws here are harsher than at home, and traffic police are entitled to stop cars at will—and they do.

Bars and Lounges

All the major hotels have their own bars and nightclubs. The lobby bars in the National, Savoy, and Metropole hotels feature glitzy, pre-revolutionary decor and a soothing atmosphere. The Palace and the Slavyanskaya have more energized lobby bars, filled with businesspeople and *novy russky* types, Russian yuppies down to their beepers and cel-lular phones. The top-floor bar of the Baltschug Hotel offers magical views of the Kremlin. At the other end of the spectrum are the bars of the old Intourist hotels (Belgrade, Kosmos, Intourist), where the at-mosphere ranges from sleazy to scary. Be forewarned that hard-cur-rency prostitution is a thriving business in most hotels.

Some favorite bars to just relax and have fun and drinks in are the Ar-madillo Tex-Mex Bar (1 Khrustalny Pereulok, ☎ 095/298–5091); the 24-hour Piano Bar Old Square (8 Bolshoi Cherkassky Pereulok, ☎ 095/298–4688); Rosie O'Grady's (9 ul. Znamenka, ☎ 095/203–9087); the Shamrock Bar, upstairs at the Arbat Irish House (19 Novy Arbat, ☎ 095/291–7641); the Sports Bar and Grill (10 Novy Arbat, ☎ 095/290–4311); and the TrenMos Bistro (1/9 ul. Ostozhenka, ☎ 095/202–5722).

Casinos

Moscow has a serious case of casino fever. The number of casinos, both upscale and back-alley, that have opened in the past few years, at last unofficial count equaled the number in Las Vegas. It all makes perfect sense: people spend money in an inflationary environment, and Russia has experienced one of the world's highest inflation rates. If you feel like trying your luck, here are some of the better-known places. Don't feel so lucky that you forget where you are, though; flashing your cash is a *bad* idea. Most casinos will provide complimentary car service to and from big hotels; check with your hotel bureau. Casinos usually open late (11 or 12) and stay open until the morning.

The gem of the bunch is **Casino Royal** (Begovaya ul. 22, ☎ 095/945–1963), in the elegant Hippodrome, built for Nicholas I in 1834. The **Savoy, Metropole, Mezhdunarodnaya, Leningradskaya,** and **Ukraina** hotels all have their own casinos. The **Alexander Blok** (☎ 095/255–9323) is a floating casino, a ship moored permanently near the Mezhdunarodnaya Hotel. There are also the Horseshoe Casino (71 ul. Profsoyuznaya, ☎ 095/333–6210); the Karo (2 Pushkinskaya Ploshchad, ☎ 095/229–0003); and the Metelitsa Cherry Casino (21 Novy Arbat, ☎ 095/291–1113).

Dance Clubs and Discos
A dance scene is definitely on the up-and-up here. A few places are the expected noisy dens; others are quite mod and trendy. They open late and stay open even later. The omnipresent cover charges are frequently steep.

NightFlight (Tverskaya ul. 17, ☎ 095/229–4165). This Swedish-Russian joint venture was Moscow's first authentic disco, and it seems to attract a lusty crowd, hungry for hunting. **Hermitage Club** (3 ul. Karetny Ryad, ☎ 095/299–1160) transforms its hip self from a bar on Tuesdays and Wednesdays to an energetic dance spot the rest of the time. **Manhattan Express** (corner of Rossiya Hotel) is a big, flashy dance space often with performers and live bands (☎ 095/298–5355). **Master Disco** (6 ul. Pavlovskaya, ☎ 095/237–1742) is for house parties and more. The trendy **Pilot Art Night Club** is loud, cavernous, and filled with large screens and hanging airplane parts (6 ul. Tryokhgorny Val, ☎ 095/252–2764). For all-night dancing and carousing, check out the brazen **Red Zone** (39 Leningradsky Prospect, ☎ 095/212–1676), located in the skating arena of the Army Central Sports Club (TsSKA). If bared flesh makes you blush, better to go elsewhere. **Titanic** (Young Pioneer's Stadium, 31 Leningradsky Prospect, ☎ 095/213–4581) is for the college age; experimental music plays.

Jazz, Rock, Blues, and Beyond
Those who like to just listen to their music can choose among the following. Rock concerts are usually held in the city's sports stadiums; or, for big acts, the Kremlin Palace; for listings of upcoming concerts, check the Friday edition of the *Moscow Times.* Local rock can also be found at the **Moskovsky Club** (6 ul. Tverskaya, ☎ 095/292–1282) or at the **Stanislavsky Club** (23 ul. Tverskaya, ☎ 095/564–8004). For jazz, there's the **Arbat Blues Club** (11 Filippovsky Pereulok, ☎ 095/291–1546); **Chyortova Dyuzhina** (Baker's Dozen; 19 ul. Bolshaya Nikitskaya, ☎ 095/290–2254); or **Metro Express** (32 ul. Baumanskaya). Funky blues is played at the **BB King Blues Club** (4/2 ul. Sadovaya-Samotyochnaya, ☎ 095/299–8206), a club whose opening featured the man himself. For Karaoke fun, try **Karaoke President** (4 ul. Stroitely, ☎ 095/230–2337), where you can sing along in Russian, English, Korean, and presumably, Japanese. As its name implies, the **Nostalgie Art Club** (12a Chistoprudny Bulvar, ☎ 095/916–9978) has a mix of swing, dixieland, and blues. You'll find a different mix—punk and grunge—at the **Jerry Rubin**

Commune (62 Leninsky Prospect, ☏ 095/246–9639). Finally, reggae lovers should head to 17B ul. Lapina for the **Island Reggae Club.**

MOSCOW ESSENTIALS

Arriving and Departing

By Boat

Moscow has two river ports: the Northern River Terminal (Severny Rechnoy Vokzal, 51 Leningradskoye Shosse, ☏ 095/457–4050) and the Southern River Terminal (Yuzhny Rechnoy Vokzal, Andropov Prospect, ☏ 095/118–7955). International cruise lines offering tours to Russia usually disembark in St. Petersburg and continue from there by land. It is possible, however, to book a two-way cruise from Moscow along the Moscow-Volga canal, which makes for a pleasant way to see the ancient cities of the Golden Ring. Some 129 kilometers (80 miles) long, the canal links the Russian capital with the Caspian Sea, the Black Sea, the White Sea, and the Azov Sea. The Moscow port for long-distance passengers is the **Rechnoy Vokzal** (northern port) on the Khimki reservoir.

By Car

You can reach Moscow from Finland and St. Petersburg by taking the Helsinki–St. Petersburg Highway (*shosse*) through Vyborg and St. Petersburg and continuing from there on the Moscow–St. Petersburg Highway. Be warned that driving in Russia is invariably more of a hassle than a pleasure. Gas shortages are frequent, repair shops are rare, and roads are very poorly maintained. In addition, you face the risk of car theft, a crime that is on the rise.

By Plane

AIRPORTS AND AIRLINES

As the single most important transportation hub in the CIS, Moscow has several airports. Most international flights arrive at **Sheremetyevo II** (☏ 095/578–9101), which currently handles an estimated 15,000 passengers daily. One of the most modern in Russia, Sheremetyevo II was built in 1979, when there was much less international traffic; these days it is just barely coping. Expect to stand an hour or two at passport control. Disembarked passengers descend a long staircase, then collect en masse in a large, dimly lit chamber to vie for the three or four lines to the passport officials' booths. Their legendary slowness is fact, not myth. The baggage area is located directly beyond. There may or may not be luggage carts, for which, officially, you pay in rubles. Since you probably will not be able to bring any with you, make sure you have a few singles in your pocket and start getting creative. After you have collected your bags, you'll go through customs. This is frequently in a single line, so you may have another hour or so on your feet. Leaving customs, usually also in single file, you will be greeted by mobs of Russians awaiting arriving passengers and eager gypsy cab drivers shouting "*Taksi! Taksi!*" Take a deep breath and plow straight through until you find your host or group. Welcome to the capital city.

In addition to its international airport, the city has four domestic terminals. **Sheremetyevo I** (☏ 095/578–5973 or 095/507–5614), some 30 kilometers (19 miles) northwest of the city center, services domestic flights to St. Petersburg and the former Baltic republics (Estonia, Latvia, and Lithuania). It has also been handling international flights of some new Russian airlines, so if you fly Transaero you may go here. **Domodedovo** (☏ 095/234–8656 or 095/234–8655), one of the largest airports in the world, is located some 48 kilometers (30 miles) southeast of Moscow; flights depart from here to the republics of Central Asia. **Vnukovo** (☎ 095/436–2967), 29 kilometers (18 miles) southwest of the city center, services flights to Georgia, the southern republics, and Ukraine. **Bykovo,** the smallest of the domestic terminals, generally handles flights within Russia and some flights to Ukraine. Be sure to find out from your travel agent which airport your flight is supposed to leave from.

If you are departing from Domodedovo or Vnukovo airport, look for the special lounges set aside for foreign tourists; they are much more comfortable than the general waiting area.

For general information on arriving international flights, call 095/578–7518 or 095/578–7816. These lines are often busy; if possible, call the airline. For information on domestic Aeroflot flights, call 095/155–0922. Calling the airports directly is usually a complete waste of time; the line is almost always busy, and even if it's not, no one answers.

Aeroflot (☎ 095/156–8019) operates flights from Moscow to just about every capital of Europe, as well as to Canada and the United States. **Transaero** is another Russian carrier that has several routes internationally as well as within the CIS (☎ 095/578–0537 or 095/578–0538). Among the international airlines with offices in Moscow are **Air France** (☎ 095/237–2325 or 095/237–3344), **Alitalia** (☎ 095/923–9840), **Austrian Air** (☎ 095/253–8268 or 095/253–1670), **British Airways** (☎ 095/253–2492), **Delta** (☎ 095/253–2658 or 095/253–9871), **Finnair** (☎ 095/292–8788 or 095/292–3337), **Japan Airlines** (☎ 095/921–6441), **KLM** (☎ 095/253–2150 or 095/253–2151), **Lufthansa** (☎ 095/975–2501), **SAS** (☎ 095/925–4747) and **Turkish Airlines** (☎ 095/292–1667).

BETWEEN THE AIRPORT AND DOWNTOWN

You would be wise to make advance arrangements for your transfer from the airport. There are plenty of gypsy cabs available, but you should *not* take them; they are notorious for swindles and much, much worse. In a pinch, use the services offered on the airport's ground floor. These private firms are somewhat costly but less risky. Most hotels will provide airport transfers (for an additional fee) upon request by previous fax (which you should make sure is confirmed). All of the airports are serviced by municipal buses operating out of the **City Airport Terminal** (*Aerovokzal*) at 37 Leningradsky Prospect, near the Aeroport subway station. Service is somewhat unreliable and inconvenient, especially if you have any luggage, but very inexpensive. The schedule is slightly erratic, but theoretically a bus departs from Sheremetyevo II (International) Airport every two hours or so; service to Domodedovo and Vnukovo domestic airports is more frequent. The Sheremetyevo II bus stop is 100 meters to the right as you leave, at a small shelter that has a yellow bus-route sign on it for bus 551, which is the one you take into Moscow. It *will,* inexorably, creep into the city.

By Train

Moscow is also the hub of the Russian railway system, and the city's nine railway stations handle some 400 million passengers annually. There are several trains daily to St. Petersburg, and overnight service is available to Helsinki. All the major train stations have a connecting subway stop, so they are easily reached by public transportation. The most important stations are: **Belorussky Vokzal** (Belorussian Station), for trains to Belorussia, Lithuania, Poland, Germany, and France; **Kazansky Vokzal** (Kazan Station), for points south, Central Asia, and Siberia; **Kievsky Vokzal** (Kiev Station), for Kiev and western Ukraine, Moldova,

Slovakia, the Czech Republic, and Hungary; **Kursky Vokzal** (Kursk Station), for eastern Ukraine, the Crimea, and southern Russia; **Leningradsky Vokzal** (Leningrad Station), for St. Petersburg, northern Russia, Estonia, and Finland; **Paveletsky Vokzal** (Pavelets Station), for eastern Ukraine and points south; **Rizhksy Vokzal** (Riga Station), for Latvia; **Yaroslavsky Vokzal** (Yaroslav Station) for points east, including Mongolia and China; the Trans-Siberian Express departs every day at 2.

The past few years have witnessed increased crime on the most heavily traveled routes, and as a result many travelers to St. Petersburg now prefer the high-speed, day-train *Avrora,* which makes the trip in just under six hours. Of the numerous overnight trains, the most popular is the *Krasnaya Strelka* (*Red Arrow*), which leaves Moscow at 11:55 PM and arrives the next day in St. Petersburg at 8:25 AM. Overnight trains are considered more dangerous than day trains, and if you are traveling alone, you should take added precautions. Experienced travelers in Russia bring their own lock and buy out the entire compartment so as not to risk their luck with unknown compartment mates.

For information on train arrival and departure schedules, call 095/266–9333. For booking and ticket delivery, call 095/266–8333. Tourists must travel on a special, higher-priced ticket for foreigners. You can purchase it at the railway station on the day of departure (up to 24 hours in advance) or at the special ticket office for foreigners at 6 ulitsa Griboyedova (subway station: Chistye Prudy). Tickets may be purchased up to 10 days in advance; bring your passport.

Getting Around

If you look at a map of Moscow, you will see that the city consists of a series of distinct circles with the Kremlin and Red Square at its center. The most famous and important sites are clustered within the first circle, which was once enclosed by the fortification walls of Kitai Gorod, the city's oldest settlement outside the Kremlin. This area can be easily covered on foot. Beyond that, the sights are more spread out and are best reached by subway. To get a sense of the city's geographic layout, you might consider hiring a car for a few hours and traveling around the main roads encircling the city—the Boulevard and Garden Rings. The walking tours below begin at the city center and follow the historic routes that radiate out from the Kremlin.

By Bus, Tram, and Trolley

Buses, trams, and trolleys operate on the honor system. Upon boarding, you validate your ticket by punching it in one of the machines attached to a wall of the vehicle. The buses and trolleys are almost always overcrowded, and chances are good that you won't be able to reach the canceling machine. Ask the person next to you to pass your ticket along; the canceled ticket will make its way back to you, and you should hold on to it until you get off.

You can purchase strips of tickets at subway stops and at kiosks throughout the city, or from the bus driver after you have boarded (although the driver will often be out of tickets, so it's best to buy it beforehand). The ticket is valid for one ride only; if you change buses you must pay another fare. Buses, trams, and trolleys operate from 5:30 AM to 1 AM, although service in the late-evening hours and on Sunday tends to be unreliable.

By Car

Your hotel may make arrangements for you. Otherwise, several international car rental agencies have offices in Moscow. **Avis** (Berezhkovskaya

Naberezhnaya 15, ☎ 095/240–9974) rents Opels or Opel Astras. **Europcar** (Krasnopresnenskaya Naberezhnaya 12, Mezh. 1, 1st floor, ☎ 095/253–1369) rents Ford Sierras, Mercedes-Benzes, Volvos, and the tiny Ukrainian Zaporozhets. **Hertz** (Sheremetyevo II airport, ☎ 095/578–7532) rents Toyota Corollas; for a $15 fee they will deliver the car to your location. All of these agencies require advance reservations (2–3 days is a good idea), and you will have to show your driver's license, an international license, and a credit card.

Each of them also rents cars with drivers. **Budget** (57 Bolshaya Gruzinskaya ul., ☎ 095/250–3093 or 095/254–4125) offers this service exclusively and uses only Lincoln Town Cars. Other companies that provide cars with drivers are **InTourService** (☎ 095/203–1497) and **InNis** (☎ 095/927–1187). Ask which cars they are using.

By Subway

The Moscow subway (in Russian, *metro*) ranks among the world's finest public transportation systems. Opened in 1935, the system's earliest stations—in the city center and along the circle line—were built as public palaces and are decorated with chandeliers, sculptures, stained-glass windows, and beautiful mosaics. With more than 200 kilometers (124 miles) of track, the Moscow subway carries an estimated 8 million passengers daily. Even in today's hard economic times, the system continues to run efficiently, with trains every 50 seconds during rush hour. It leaves New Yorkers green with envy.

The subway is easy to use and amazingly inexpensive. Stations are marked with a large illuminated "M" sign and are open daily 5:30 AM–1 AM. The fare is the same regardless of distance traveled, and there are several stations where lines connect and you may transfer for free. You purchase a subway token (available at all stations) and insert it into the slot at the turnstile upon entering. Stations are built deep underground (they were built to double as bomb shelters); the escalators are steep and run fast, so watch your step. If you use the subway during rush hour (4–6 PM), be prepared for a lot of pushing and shoving.

Pocket maps of the system are available at newspaper kiosks or from individual vendors at subway stations. Plan your route beforehand and have your destination written down in Russian and its English transliteration to help you spot the station. Each station is announced over the train's public address system as you approach it, and the name of the next one is given before the train moves off. Reminders of interchanges and transfers are also given.

If you want to avoid the lines for subway tokens, you can purchase a pass (*yediny bilyet*) that is valid for all modes of public transportation. Metro passes are on sale at the same counters as the subway tokens. They are inexpensive and well worth the added convenience. When you have a pass, you must use a far turnstile. Before entering, you show it to the watchful matron standing guard; look for the crush of other passengers doing this. You can't go through the token turnstile with a pass, and if you try, two steel bars will slam closed on you.

By Taxi

Foreign tourists should exercise caution when using taxicabs. This industry was hard hit in recent times, and most public cabs disappeared overnight. A comeback is underway, with a revamped fleet of cars ordered from Korea. For now you will sight most cabs—light-colored Russian Volgas with taxi lights on top—on major roadways. It is advised not to get into a car with more than one person in it, and you

Moscow Metro

Rechnoi Vokzal
Vodny Stadion
Voikovskaya
Sokol
Aeroport
Dynamo

Planernaya
Skhodnenskaya
Tushinskaya
Shchukinskaya
Oktyabrskoye Polye
Polezhayevskaya

Begovaya
Ulitsa 1905 Goda
Molodyozhnaya
Kuntsevskaya
Pionerskaya
Filiovsky Park
Bagrationovskaya
Fili
Kutuzovskaya
Studencheskaya

Kievskaya

Smolenskaya
Arbatskaya
Smolenskaya

Aleksandrovsky Sad

Biblioteka
Imeni Lenina
Arbatskaya
Kropotkinskaya

Park Kultury

Frunzenskaya
Sportivnaya
Leninskiye Gori
Universitet
Prospekt Vernadskogo
Yugo-Zapadnaya

Shabolovskaya
Leninsky Prospekt
Akademicheskaya
Profsoyuznaya
Noviye Cheryomushki
Kaluzhskaya
Belyayevo
Konkovo
Tyoply Stan

Otradnoye
Vladkino
Petrovsko-
Razumovskaya
Timiryazevskaya
Dmitrovskaya

Savyolovskaya

Mendeleyevskaya
Belorusskaya
Novoslobodskaya
Tsvetnoi
Bulvar
Barrikadnaya
Krasnopresnenskaya
Mayakovskaya

Pushkin-
skaya
Tverskaya
Chekovskaya

Okhotny Ryad
Teatralnaya
Ploshchad
Revolyutsii
Vorovitskaya

Tretyakovskaya
Novokuznetskaya
Polyanka

Oktyabrskaya
Serpukhovskaya

Tuzhnaya
Nagatinskaya
Nagornaya
Nakhimovksy Prospekt
Kakhovskaya
Sevastopolskaya
Chertanovskaya
Yuzhnaya
Prazhskaya

Medvedkovo
Babushkinskaya
Sviblovo
Botanichesky Sad
VDNKh
Alekseevskaya
Rizhskaya

Prospekt
Mira

Sukharevskaya

Turgenevskaya
Chistye Prudy
Krasniye
Vorota

Liubyanka

Komsomolskaya

Kuznetsky Most

Kitai Gorod

Ploshchad
Ilyicha

Marksistskaya
Taganskaya

Paveletskaya
Proletarskaya
Dobryninskaya
Avtozavodskaya
Kolomenskaya

Kashirskaya

Kantemirovskaya
Lenino
Orekhovo
Domodedovskaya
Krasnogvardeiskaya

Varshavskaya

Ulitsa
Podbelskovo
Cherkizovskaya
Preobrazhenskaya
Ploshchad
Sokolniki
Krasnoselskaya

Shcholkovskaya
Pervomaiskaya
Izmailovskaya
Izmailovsky
Park
Semyonovskaya
Elektrozavodskaya
Baumanskaya

Novogireyevo
Perovo
Shosseh
Entuziastov
Aviamotornaya

Kurskaya

Volgogradsky
Prospekt
Tekstilshchiki
Kuzminki
Ryazansky
Prospekt
Vykhino

(Under
Construction)

are best off ordering a cab by phone or through your hotel's service bureau. In today's strained economy, foreign tourists are crime targets. Gypsy cabs are common and often cruise the larger hotels and hard-currency restaurants in search of innocent foreigners. If you speak Russian, you can order a cab by telephone. For municipal services, call 095/927–0000. There is sometimes a delay, but the cab usually arrives within the hour. If you order a cab in this way, you pay the official state fare in rubles (which is very reasonable when calculated in dollars), plus a fee for the reservation. Drivers will appreciate and expect a tip of at least 20%. If you hail a cab on the street, expect to negotiate and probably pay in dollars; fares for foreigners generally begin at $5. **Belmi Taxi Service** (☎ 095/318–8800) provides city cabs as well as airport service in vans or buses, picking up from hotels or privately. Their prices are higher than city cabs'.

Guided Tours

Every major hotel maintains a tourist bureau through which individual and group tours to Moscow's main tourist sights can be booked. In addition, there are numerous private agencies that can help with your sightseeing plans. It would be a good idea to start by checking the daily offerings from **Patriarchi Dom,** a Russian-American venture that has an ongoing roster of tours. They have something for everyone, from the requisite trip to the Kremlin to neighborhood walking tours to day trips outside the city, including one to a McDonald's factory. They offer cooking classes and shopping excursions, too. Their monthly listing is available at most hotels and Western stores. Since you join a group of other people who have also opted for that day's excursion, the fees are reasonable; you'll pay the normal entrance charges wherever you visit as well. They will arrange special tours for you, if some place you want to go to is not already on their schedule. ☎ /FAX 095/255–4470. ☺ 9–6, Mon.–Fri., and they will answer messages left on their machine between 12 and 6 on weekends.

Apex Travel World, located in the Radisson Slavyanskaya Hotel (☎ 095/941–8306 or 095/941–8426), can arrange a wide range of tours, as you wish. They will also make hotel, plane, and train reservations for other CIS destinations. Call at least a day in advance to make arrangements. To book out-of-city excursions, call their office at 095/978–0354 or 095/978–5047.

VAO Intourist's (13 Mokhovaya ul., ☎ 095/292–1278 or 095/292–1362) special travel department will provide you with any tour you want in Moscow; they also set up trips elsewhere in the CIS and help with visa support. They work within the system of Intourist offerings, so you'll be staying at their hotels; but because the network of their services is so extensive, you should be able to have whatever excursion you want.

Sputnik (6 Maly Ivanovsky Pereulok, ☎ 095/925–8741 or 095/924–3494; FAX 095/230–2787) is a company handling group and individual tours in Moscow and some day trips out of town. They can tailor plans to suit your needs.

You should call around to get competitive rates. They can vary widely, depending on the trip you want, the number of people you have, and your transportation needs.

Important Addresses and Numbers

Embassies

United States (19/23 Novinsky Bulvar, ☎ 095/252–2451 or 095/252–2459), **Canada** (23 Starokonyushenny Pereulok, ☎ 095/956–6666), and **United Kingdom** (14 Naberezhnaya Morisa Toreza, ☎ 095/956–7200).

If there is a line of visa applicants at the entrance to the U.S. embassy, be aware that you do not need to stand in it if you are a U.S. citizen. Just walk to the front and show the guard your passport, and he will let you by.

Emergencies

Fire (☎ 01), **Police** (☎ 02), **ambulance** (☎ 03). You will probably want to ask the assistance of a hotel staff member before trying to place an emergency call, since few telephone operators speak English.

HOSPITALS AND CLINICS

With luck, you won't have to experience the medical system. It is plagued by a lack of medicines, low hygiene standards, and shortages of disposable needles and basic medical equipment. If you are simply feeling under the weather and the situation is not urgent, you may be best off not contacting a doctor at all. If you think you are seriously ill, contact one of several Western establishments that have opened over the last two years, creating a base of clinics used by the foreign community as well as Russians who can afford the higher fees. Most of these clinics are membership organizations, but all will provide service to tourists, though perhaps not with 24-hour access; the cost of individual treatment will be higher than for members, too. Be sure to ask what payment method they accept. Usually it will be rubles, dollars, or a credit card, but it varies by clinic and without exception you will need to settle accounts up front.

In an emergency, you can also contact your country's consular section for help with the logistics of serious medical treatment. For U.S. citizens, contact *American Citizens Services* (☎ 095/956–4232 or 095/956–4295, after-hours emergency, 095/252–1898). Canadian citizens should call the embassy number, where they will be connected to a duty officer. British citizens can call 095/956–7269 or 095/956–7273, for their embassy's clinic, 24 hours.

The American Medical Center (Vtoroy Tverskoy-Yamskoy Pereulok 10, ☎ 095/956–3366) is a membership group that offers full-range family practice and emergency services, including evacuation assistance. If treatment is needed outside their clinic, they use various hospitals, but primarily Zil. The office is open 24 hours. There is a pharmacy on the premises. A tourist plan is available.

The Columbia-Presbyterian Moscow Clinic (with U.S. Global Health) (Chetvortoy Dobryninsky Pereulok 4, 4th floor, ☎ 095/974–2332) is a membership facility providing comprehensive outpatient care and emergency referrals to the Kuntsevo Hospital (Kremlin VIP), plus help with evacuation. Pharmacy for their patients. They offer a tourist membership that you can join by calling in the U.S. (☎ 212/479–1950). They will also bill insurance plans directly. ☉ *Weekdays 8–8, Sat. 10–4.*

The European Medical Center has two branches (3 Gruzinsky Pereulok, Korpus 2, ☎ 095/253–0703; Vtoroy Tverskoy-Yamskoy Pereulok 10, ☎ 095/251–6099; night emergency ☎ 095/229–6536). Not a membership group, it has full-range service, including day and night house calls. Hospital referral is usually to the ZKB Presidential Hospital. Both English and French are spoken. Pharmacy stocked with French medicine.

International Medical Clinic (31 Grokholsky Pereulok, 10th floor, ☎ 095/280–8388/7177/8374, pharmacy ☎ 095/280–8765) is a non-member service that gives comprehensive care, hospitalization referral to the Kuntsevo (Kremlin VIP) Hospital, and evacuation via their in-house company (they are part of SOS International). In case overnight observation is necessary, they have on-site accommodations. English, French, and German spoken. Pharmacy.

Mediclub (56 Michurinsky Prospect, ☎ 095/931–5018) is a Canadian clinic that provides full medical and ambulance service, hospital referral to Glavmosstroy Hospital, and assistance with evacuation. English and French are spoken. Pharmacy with Western and Russian medicines. Cash payment only. ☉ *Weekdays 9–6; you may call after hours, but unless you are a member, it is not guaranteed that you will reach a doctor.*

In other cases foreign tourists are usually hospitalized in the **Botkin Hospital** (5 Vtoroy Botkinsky Proyezd, ☎ 095/945–0033).

There is also a **Crisis Center** hotline in English, operating 24 hours. It is free and confidential, for adults and children. The trained counselors are native English speakers. Call 095/244–3449 and ask for the Crisis Center.

DENTISTS
Russian dental facilities are as grim as other medical facilities. Of the above clinics, the **American Medical Center, European Medical Center,** and **Mediclub** also offer dental services; the **International Medical Clinic** also has access to dental facilities. **U.S. Dental Care** (8 Shabolovka ul., Corpus 3, ground floor, ☎ 095/931–9909, FAX 095/931–9910) is an independent clinic offering all types of dental treatment, with the exception of orthodontia. Laboratories and pharmacy are on-site. Optional membership, and all services are available to tourists. ☉ *Weekdays 9–6; after-hours emergency.* The **Pullman-Iris Hotel** (10 Korovinskoye Chaussee, ☎ 095/488–8279, emergency 095/488–8000) also has a Western dental office, where Russian, English, French, and German are spoken. They offer a free shuttle service to and from city center, since they are located outside of it. ☉ *Weekdays 10–5.*

English-Language Bookstores
Zwemmer's is a British oasis tucked into an English-language bookstore; it's handily located at 18 Kuznetsky Most, around the corner from the metro station of the same name, but its prices seem high. ☎ *095/928–2021.* ☉ *Daily 10–7.*

Post International Bookstore is Moscow's newest, and its U.S. (not import) prices and mail-order service are welcome. *½ Putinskye Pereulok (behind the Rossiya Cinema),* ☎ *095/209–9168. Open weekdays 9–6.*

Russia's largest bookstore, **Dom Knigi** (The Book House, 26 Novy Arbat, ☎ 095/290–4507), has a small foreign-literature section (inside the doors, bearing immediately to the right), but be sure also to examine the selection outside the front-door, where individual sellers spread out their wares. The bookstore on the first floor of the **Kosmos Hotel** (150 Prospekt Mira) has a good selection of maps, postcards, and English-language guidebooks to Moscow and the surrounding region, and most hotel newsshops carry a smattering of best-sellers and paperback classics.

The English-language newspapers *The Moscow Times* and *The Moscow Tribune* are published daily and carry world and local news. Pick them up in just about any Western store or major hotel.

Late-Night Pharmacies

Pharmacies are generally open only until 8 or 9 PM, and though they are becoming well stocked, Western-brand medicines may not be recognizable to you in their Russian packaging. For prescription refills, you'll have the best luck contacting one of the foreign clinics' pharmacies. You can also try the conveniently located **Farmakon** (4 ul. Tverskaya, ☎ 095/292–0843), where you can also count on finding toothpaste, Q-tips, shaving cream, and the like, on its second floor.

Travel Agencies

There are many choices. Listed here are some Moscow travel agents, not local tour companies offering excursions. They can provide air (and sometimes train) ticketing for international travel and, as noted, travel to other points within Russia and the CIS.

American Express (21-A Sadovaya-Kudrinskaya, ☎ 095/254–4305 or 095/254–4495; open weekdays 10–1 and 2–5) handles arrangements for domestic and air tickets but not for trains. It will also help with car hire and hotel reservations. It is not necessary to be a member to receive these services. For members, it will replace your lost traveler's checks and credit cards, or issue you a cash advance against your credit card, provided you can write a personal check. The office has an ATM machine for its card holders; there is a 5% commission on its use.

VAO Intourist (13 Mokhovaya ul., ☎ 095/292–2791 or 095/292–2275) runs a special travel department out of what was formerly Intourist. They can help with domestic and international air and train tickets, accommodations throughout the CIS as well as in Moscow, and visa support.

Alpha Omega (5 Proezd Serova, 3rd floor, ☎ 095/928–9459 or 095/921–6853) can book air tickets on international charters and on Transaero and Aeroflot in the CIS. Credit cards are accepted. They deliver tickets, for which service there is a fee.

Apex Travel World (Radisson Slavyanskaya Hotel, ☎ 095/941–8306 or 095/941–8426), though primarily a tour agency, may be able to arrange train ticketing in the CIS to points out of Moscow. American Express refers its customers to them for this service.

SVO Travel (15 Novy Arbat, ☎ 095/202–6409 or 095/202–1328) is a Canadian agency that handles ticketing on international flights. For CIS cities, it can book on Transaero, but it does not handle any Aeroflot ticketing. No trains. Free ticket delivery.

Time Travel (Radisson Slavyanskaya Hotel, ground floor, ☎ 095/941–8665, 095/257–9220 or 095/257–9258) can arrange domestic and international tickets for both air and train travel. They'll also prepare excursion packages and make hotel reservations.

For those wanting to go from Moscow to the Ukraine, **Tour Service International** (☎ 095/493–2330) offers visa support, including courier service (for which there is a fee) for its application, and hotel bookings. This may be your most expeditious route if you decide to visit Kiev only after you have arrived in Moscow.

For international plane tickets, you may also call the airlines directly. Ask them where you can pick up your tickets in Moscow.

Where to Change Money

All the major hotels have exchange bureaus where you can change your dollars for rubles. You can also use the Russian banks. In addition, you will find exchange bureaus all over the city, bearing the "Obmen Valuty/Exchange" sign. They should have their daily rates posted in easy view. Exercise reasonable caution when using them, and don't be surprised to find a security guard, who may let only one or two people inside at a time. By law it's required that you be issued a receipt, but you may find this erratic in practice. It is difficult to exchange traveler's checks for rubles, and almost impossible to cash them for dollars, but you can do so at the **Dialog Bank** in the Slavyanskaya Hotel (2 Berezhkovskaya Naberezhnaya, first floor, ☎ 095/941–8434). The **American Express Office** (*see* Travel Agencies, *below*) will cash American Express traveler's checks for rubles and, if it has cash available, for dollars. You can also obtain dollars by writing the office a personal check and having the exchange charged to your American Express card. Some Russian banks have begun to accept traveler's checks, so you can try them, too.

Visitor Information

Moscow does not have a tourist information center *per se,* but the service bureaus of all the major hotels offer their guests (and anyone else willing to pay their fees) a wide variety of tourist services, including help in booking group or individual excursions, making a restaurant reservation, or purchasing theater or ballet tickets. You may also find help (as the hotels themselves often do) from the VAO Intourist Service, today's incarnation of the old Intourist. There are several tour agencies you can use, too. For listings, see Guided Tours, *above.* For the latest on what's happening in Moscow, there are two English-language newspapers—*The Moscow Times* and *The Moscow Tribune.* On Thursdays, the Russian newpaper *Moscow News* publishes an English-language translation of its paper. If you have a radio, FM station 104.7 has English-language programming between 6 and 10 AM and 6 and 9 PM.

3 St. Petersburg

By Lauri del
Commune

ST. PETERSBURG, born in the heart of an emperor, is Russia's adopted child. So unlike the Russian cities that came before it, St. Petersburg—with its strict geometric lines and perfectly planned architecture—is in many ways too European to be Russian. And yet it is too Russian to be European. A powerful combination of both East and West, of things Russian and things European, St. Petersburg is, more than anything, a city born of the passion of its founder, Czar Peter the Great, to bring an unwilling Russian nation into the fold of Europe and into the mainstream of history.

It was less than 300 years ago when the grand, new capital of the budding Russian empire, St. Petersburg, was built to face Europe, with its back to the reactionary Moscow. Unlike some cities, it was not created by a process of gradual, graceful development but was forcibly constructed, stone by stone, under the force and direction of Peter the Great, for whose patron saint the city is named.

But if Peter's exacting plans called for his capital to be the equal of European ones, they always took into account the city's unique attributes. Peter knew that his city's source of life was water, and whether building palace, fortress, or trading post, he never failed to make his creations serve it. With most of the city nearly at sea level (there is a constant threat of flooding), it seems to rise from the sea itself. Half of the River Neva lies within the city's boundaries. When, outward bound, it reaches the Gulf of Finland, it subdivides into the Great and Little Neva and the Great and Little Nevka. Together with numerous affluents, they combine to form an intricate delta.

Water weaves its way through the city's streets as well. Covering more than 100 islands and crisscrossed by more than 60 rivers and canals, St. Petersburg can be compared to that other great maritime city, Venice, but the Russian one has a uniquely northern appeal. Even during economic hardship and political crisis, its imperial palaces sparkling on the embankments maintain the city's regal bearing, especially in the cold light of the Russian winter. In the long days of summer, the colorful facades of its riverside estates glow gently, in harmony with the dark blue of the Neva's waters. Between June and July, when the city falls under the spell of the White Nights, the fleeting twilight imbues the streets and canals with an even more delicate charm.

St. Petersburg is not just about its fairy-tale setting, however, for its history is integrally bound up in Russia's dark side too, its centuries-long procession of wars and revolutions. In the 19th century, the city stood witness to the struggle against czarist oppression. Here the early fires of revolution were kindled, first in 1825 by a small band of starry-eyed aristocratic officers, the so-called Decembrists, and then by organized workers' movements in 1905. The full-scale revolutions of 1917 led to the demise of the Romanov dynasty, the foundation of the Soviet Union, and the end of the city's role as the nation's capital. But the worst ordeal by far came during World War II, when Leningrad withstood a 900-day siege and blockade by Nazi forces. Nearly 650,000 people died of starvation, and more than 17,000 were killed in air raids and by indiscriminate shelling.

St. Petersburg has had its name changed three times during its brief history. With the outbreak of World War I, it became the more Russian-sounding Petrograd. After Lenin's death in 1924, it was renamed

Leningrad in the Soviet leader's honor. Today, with the latest Russian revolution, its original name has been restored. A sign of the changing times is that—for the first time—the city's residents were given a choice in the matter. Many people opposed the change, primarily because memories of the siege of Leningrad and World War II became an indelible part of the city's identity. But for all the controversy surrounding its name, many residents refer to the city simply—and affectionately—as Peter.

EXPLORING

Tour 1: Palace Square, the Winter Palace, and the Hermitage Museum

Numbers in the margin correspond to points of interest on the St. Petersburg map.

★ ❶ The place you must begin your acquaintanceship with St. Petersburg is **Dvortsovaya Ploshchad** (Palace Square). One of the world's most magnificent plazas, it is a stunning ensemble of buildings and open space that manages to combine several seemingly incongruous architectural styles in perfect harmony. It is where the city's imperial past has been preserved in all its glorious splendor, but it is also resonant with the revolutionary history that followed. It was here that on Bloody Sunday in 1905 the last Russian czar's fate was effectively sealed after palace troops opened fire on peaceful demonstrators, killing scores of women and children. It was across Palace Square that the Bolshevik revolutionaries stormed the **Winter Palace** in their successful attempt to overthrow Kerensky's provisional government in October 1917, an event that led to the birth of the Soviet Union. Almost 75 years later, it was also on Palace Square that during tense days, citizens held all-night vigils to demonstrate their support for perestroika and democracy. Beautiful Palace Square today is a bustling hubbub of tourist and marketing activity, lively yet seemingly imperturbable as ever to the many changes to which it has borne witness.

The focal point of Palace Square is the **Zimny Dvorets** (Winter Palace), residence of Russia's rulers from Catherine the Great (1762) to Nicholas II (1917). It is built in the ornate style of Russian Baroque, adorned with rows of columns and outfitted with 2,000 heavily decorated windows. The roof balustrade is lined with statues and vases. Created by the Italian architect Bartolomeo Francesco Rastrelli at the behest of Empress Elizabeth I, the Winter Palace stretches from Palace Square to the Neva River embankment. It was the fourth royal residence on this site, the first having been a wooden palace for Peter the Great. Oddly enough, the all-powerful czar had to observe some bureaucratic fine print himself. Since it was forbidden to grant land from this site to anyone not bearing naval rank, Peter had to obtain a shipbuilder's license before building his palace. The present palace was commissioned in 1754, by Peter's daughter Elizabeth, when Russian Baroque was in vogue, but by the time of its completion in 1762, both the fashion and the empress had changed. After assuming power, Catherine the Great left the exterior unaltered but had the interiors redesigned in the neoclassical style of her day. In 1837 the interiors were revamped once again after the palace was gutted by fire. The Winter Palace contains more than 1,000 rooms and halls, three of the most celebrated of which are the Gallery of the 1812 War, where portraits of Russian commanders who served against Napoleon are on display; the Great Throne Room, richly decorated in marble and bronze; and the Malachite Hall, designed

St. Petersburg

by the architect Alexander Bryullov and decorated with malachite columns and pilasters. Today the only parts of the Winter Palace on view to the public are those that form part of the Hermitage art museum. When enjoying the museum, therefore, do so also with a view to imagining it as the royal residence it once was.

The centerpiece of Palace Square is the **Aleksandrovskaya Kolonna** (Alexander Column), a memorial to Russia's victory over Napoleon. Measuring 25 meters (82 feet) from the pedestal to the top, the Alexander Column was commissioned in 1830 by Nicholas I in memory of his brother, Czar Alexander I, and was designed by August Ricard de Montferrand. The column was cut from a single piece of granite and, together with its pedestal, weighs more than 650 tons. It stands in place by the sheer force of its own weight; there are no attachments affixing it to the pedestal. In 1832 the column was erected by 2,000 soldiers and 400 workmen, using an elaborate system of pulleys and ropes. The column is crowned by an angel (symbolizing peace in Europe) crushing a snake, an allegorical depiction of Russia's defeating Napoleon.

The eastern side of Palace Square is formed by the huge inverted circle of the **Glavny Shtab** (General Staff Building), whose form and size give Palace Square its unusual shape. During czarist rule military headquarters and the ministries of foreign affairs and finance were here. Created by the architect Carlo Giovanni Rossi in the neoclassical style and built between 1819 and 1829, the General Staff Building is actually two structures connected by a monumental archway. Together they form the longest building in Europe. The arch is another commemoration of Russia's victory over Napoleon. Atop it is an impressive 10-meter (33-foot) bronze of Victory driving a six-horse chariot, created by the artists Vasily Demut-Malinovsky and Stepan Pimenov. The passageway created by the arch leads from Palace Square to St. Petersburg's most important boulevard, Nevsky Prospect.

The **Shtab Gvardeiskovo Korpusa** (Headquarters of the Guard Corps), to the left of the General Staff Building, serves as an architectural buffer between the neoclassical General Staff Building and the Baroque Winter Palace. Designed by the architect Alexander Bryullov and built between 1837 and 1843, this modest building is noteworthy for the very fact that it easily goes unnoticed. Instead of drawing attention to itself, it leads the eye to the other architectural masterpieces bordering each side of Palace Square. Bryullov's creation was considered the ultimate architectural tribute. In his restraint he deferred to the masters who came before him; instead of disturbing the beauty they created, Bryullov used his talent to enhance it.

★ ❷ No matter what your plans while in St. Petersburg, make sure you set aside at least half a day for a visit to the **Ermitazh** (Hermitage Museum). The museum extends through the lavish Winter Palace as well as the various buildings later annexed to it in order to house the private art galleries of the czars. The museum gets its name from Catherine the Great who, by naming her private apartments thus, meant them to be a place for retreat and seclusion. Between 1764 and 1775, the empress undertook, in a competitive spirit with rulers whose storehouses of art greatly surpassed Russia's, to acquire some of the world's finest art. In doing so, sometimes acquiring entire private collections outright, she quickly filled her gallery with masterpieces collected from all over the world. This section of the Hermitage Museum is now known as the Little (*maly*) Hermitage. It is attached to the Great (*bolshoi*) Hermitage, which was built in 1783 to house the overflow of art from the Little Hermitage and also contained conference chambers for the czar's ministers. Attached to the Great Hermitage by an arch straddling the Winter Canal is the **Hermitage Theater** (1783–87), created for Catherine the Great by the Italian architect Giacomo Quarenghi. Yet another addition, the New Hermitage, was added between 1839 and 1852; it became Russia's first public museum, although admission was by royal invitation only. Its facade is particularly striking, with ten atlantes supporting the portico. *36 Dvortsovaya Naberezhnaya,* ☎ *812/311–3420.* ⊘ *Tues.–Sun. 10:30–6.*

Today's Hermitage Museum contains one of the world's richest repositories of art, continuously enlarged with czarist treasures and acquisitions, all later confiscated and nationalized by the Soviet government after the 1917 Bolshevik Revolution, along with private collections. With more than 400 exhibit halls, the Hermitage cannot possibly be seen in a single day. It has been estimated that in order to spend one minute on each object on display, a visitor would have to devote an entire year to the endeavor. Official guided tours tend to be rushed, and you will probably want to return on your own.

The entrance to the museum is on the side of the Winter Palace that faces the Neva River, not the one facing Palace Square. It is best to begin your tour around 11:30 AM, when the early morning crowds have dispersed. During peak tourist season, or when there is a special exhibition, you may encounter long lines at the museum entrance. Don't forget your umbrella, no matter what the time of year or the weather forecast. It rains at some point almost every day in St. Petersburg, and you don't need to get off to a wet start.

When you first enter the Hermitage, the *kassa* is ahead of you, slightly to the left. Once you have your tickets, you can check your things and then return to enter the hall that was to your left as you came in. Be forewarned that the ticket takers are strict about oversize bags and about foreigners trying to enter on Russian-rate tickets.

The hall will take you to the second-floor galleries by way of the **Jordan Staircase,** a dazzling creation of marble, granite, and gold. The stair once served as the place of passage for the royal family to go to the Neva River for christening.

Although the museum is divided into eight sections, they are not clearly marked, and the floor plans that are available are not terribly useful, though they are in English as well as Russian. All of this makes it easy to get lost in the mazelike complex of the Hermitage, but do not despair. Enjoy your wander, and don't be shy about asking the special assistants placed throughout the museum to point you in the right direction.

There are three floors in the museum. In brief, the ground floor covers prehistoric times, showing the discoveries made on former Soviet territory, including examples of Scythian relics and artifacts; art from the Asian republics, the Caucasus, and their peoples; and Greek, Roman, and Egyptian art and antiquities.

On the second floor you will find many of the rooms on display as part of the former Winter Palace. One of the first rooms you pass through is the Malachite Room, with its displays of personal items of the royals. In the White Dining Room the Bolsheviks seized power from the Provisional Government in 1917. Balls were held in the small Concert Hall (which now also holds a silver coffin with remains of the hero Alexander Nevsky) and, on grand occasions, in the Great Hall.

A wealth of Russian and European art is also on this floor: Florentine, Venetian, and Italian art through the 18th century, including Leonardo's

Benois Madonna and *Madonna Litta* (Room 214); Michelangelo's *Crouching Boy* (Room 229); two Raphaels; eight Titians; and works by Tintoretto, Lippi, Caravaggio, and Canaletto. The Hermitage also boasts a superb collection of Spanish art, of which works by El Greco, Velázquez, Murillo, and Goya are on display. Spectacular presentations of Flemish and Dutch art include roomfuls of Van Dyck, including portraits done in England when he was court painter to Charles I; the Hermitage has more than 40 canvases by Rubens (Room 247) and 25 Rembrandts, including *Danae, Flora,* and *The Prodigal Son* (Room 254). There is a smattering of excellent British painting, extending also to the next floor, with paintings by Joshua Reynolds, Thomas Gainsborough, and George Morland.

It is in its collection of French art, beginning on the second floor and occupying most of the third, that the Hermitage is truly extraordinary, however. The museum claims second place only to the Louvre for the scope of its French offerings. On this floor you will find early French art and handicrafts, including tapestries, as well as works by Lorrain, Watteau, and Poussin, including his *Tancrède et Herminie* (Room 279).

Going up to the third floor, you can start with the art of the 19th century, where you will find Delacroix, Ingres, Corot, and Courbet. You will then come to a stunning array of Impressionist and Postimpressionists, including Monet's deeply affecting *A Lady in the Garden,* Sisley, Pissarro, Renoir, and *Woman at Her Toilette* and *After the Bath* by Edgar Degas. Sculptures by Auguste Rodin and a host of pictures by Cézanne, Gauguin, and Van Gogh are followed by Picasso and a lovely room of Matisse, including one of the amazing *Joys.* Somewhat later work—paintings by the Fauvist André Derain and by Cubist Fernand Léger, for example—hang here, too. Rounding out this floor, if your senses can absorb any more, is the museum's collection of Oriental and Middle and Near Eastern art; its (small) American collection; and two halls of medals and coins.

TIME OUT The **Literary Café** at 18 Nevsky Prospect (☎ 812/312–6057) is a short walk from the Hermitage Museum. The menu is classic Russian fare, with service to match, alas, but the café stands out for its pleasant atmosphere and 19th-century decor; live chamber music further adds to the Old World atmosphere. There is also a small charge to enter, ostensibly for the musicians, but it probably subsidizes the well-heeled atmosphere. In 1837 the beloved Russian poet Alexander Pushkin was served his last meal here before setting off for his fatal duel. To reach the café, walk across Palace Square, through the arch of the General Staff Building, and then take a left onto Nevsky Prospect. It's at the end of the block, at the corner of the Moika River canal (Naberezhnaya reki Moiki) and Nevsky Prospect. ⊘ *Daily noon–4:30 and 7–11.*

Possibly the most prized section of the Hermitage—and definitely the most difficult to get into—is the **Osobaya Kladovaya** (Special Collection), sometimes referred to as the Zolotaya Kladovaya (Gold Room). This spectacular collection of gold, silver, and royal jewels is well worth the hassle and expense of admission. Entry is restricted to groups of 17, which must book in advance. The easiest way to join one of these groups is through your hotel's tourist bureau, which may be able to attach you to a prebooked tour.

The collection is divided into two sections. The first section, covering prehistoric times, includes gold and silver treasures recovered from the Crimea, Ukraine, and Caucasus. The second section is a dizzying display of precious stones, jewelry, and such extravagances as jewel-encrusted pillboxes, miniature clocks, and cigarette cases, from the 16th through the 20th centuries.

Tour 2: Vasilievsky Island and the Left Bank

This is a long tour, divided into two sections, though there is (literally) a bridge between them. You may choose to do them as two excursions, if you have the time and want to linger in each place. If not, do plan a lunch break midway.

Vasilievsky Ostrov, the largest island in the Neva Delta, is one of the city's oldest developed sections and is where Peter the Great wanted his city's center located. Now it is a popular residential area, with most of its historical sites contained on its eastern edge. The island's western tip, facing the Gulf of Finland, houses the city's main sea terminals. The island is also home to the city's most renowned academic institutions, including the St. Petersburg branch of the Academy of Sciences, St. Petersburg University, the Repin Art Institute (formerly St. Petersburg Academy of Arts), and the city's oldest institution of higher learning, the St. Petersburg Institute of Mining Technology.

Peter the Great's original plans for the island called for a network of canals, intended to transport goods from the main sea terminal to the city's commercial center at the opposite end of the island. These plans to re-create Venice never materialized, although some of the smaller canals were actually dug (and later filled in). These would-be canals are now streets, and are called "lines" (*liniya*). Instead of names, they bear numbers and run parallel to the island's three main thoroughfares: the Great, Middle, and Small Avenues (Prospects).

Begin your tour of Vasilievsky Island at its easternmost tip, which is known colloquially as the **Strelka** (arrow or spit). It is most easily reached by going across the **Dvortsovy Most** (Palace Bridge), the one in front of the Hermitage, or by taking Trolley 1 or 7 from any stop on Nevsky Prospect. The Strelka affords a dazzling view both of the Winter Palace and of the Peter and Paul Fortress, off to its left (*see* Tour 3, *below*), and reveals the city's triumphant rise from a watery outpost to an elegant metropolis. Seen against the backdrop of the Neva, the brightly colored houses lining the embankment seem like children's toys—the building blocks of a bygone aristocracy. They stand at the water's edge, supported not by the land beneath them but almost by the panorama of the city behind them. Gazing at this architectural wonder, you start to understand the scope of Peter the Great's vision for his country. The view is also revealing because it makes clear how careful the city's founders were to build their city not despite the Neva but around and with it. The river's natural ebb and flow accords perfectly with the monumental architecture lining its path.

As you stand in Pushkin Square, as the park on the Strelka is called, you will be between two thick, brick-red columns, known as the **Rostralnyie Kolonny** (Rostral Columns). Erected between 1805 and 1810 in honor of the Russian fleet, their name comes from the Latin *rostrum,* meaning "prow." Modeled on similar memorials in ancient Rome, the columns are decorated with ships' prows, with sculptures at the base depicting Russia's main waterways, the Dnieper, the Volga, the Volkhov, and Neva rivers. Although the columns originally served as lighthouses—until 1855 this was St. Petersburg's commercial harbor—they are now lit only on special occasions. The columns were designed to frame the architectural centerpiece of this side of the embankment—the old **Stock Exchange** (Birzha), now the Voenno-Morskoy Muzey (Naval War Museum).

❹ Erected in 1804–10 and, like the Rostral Columns, designed by the Swiss architect Thomas de Thomon, the neoclassical **Stock Exchange** was modeled on the Greek temple at Paestum. Since Peter the Great's time, it was intended to symbolize St. Petersburg's financial and maritime strength. Since 1940, the building has housed the **Voenno-Morskoy Muzey** (Central Naval Museum), which was itself founded in 1805. Its collection dates from Peter's reign and includes, in accordance with his orders, a model of every ship built in Russian shipyards since 1709. On display are exhibits of Russia's naval history to the present. The collection also contains a 3,000-year-old dugout found on the bottom of the Bug River as well as Peter the Great's personal belongings, including his first boat and the ax he used to build it. *4 Pushkin Sq., Vasilievsky Ostrov,* ☎ *812/218–2501 or 812/218–2502.* ☉ *Wed.–Sun. 10:30–4:30. Closed last Thurs. of month.*

Flanking both sides of the Stock Exchange and lending balance to the architectural ensemble of the spit are two virtually identical buildings in the Greek classical style. Originally warehouses intended to serve the city's busy port, they now house museums: to the north, the ❺ **Dokuchayev Soil Museum** and to the south, the **Zoologichesky Muzey** (Zoological Museum). The prize of this museum's unusual collection, which contains over 40,000 species, is a stuffed mammoth recovered from Siberia in 1901. *1 Universitetskaya Naberezhnaya,* ☎ *812/218–0112.* ☉ *Sat.–Thurs. 11–5. Closed holidays.*

Farther along the embankment, just past the Soil Museum, is the former **Customs House.** Constructed in the 19th century in the same style as the warehouses, it is known as the **Pushkin House** and maintained by the Academy of Sciences' Institute of Russian Literature. It holds a special place in the heart of the Russian people. Here valuable manuscripts and original works by some of Russia's most beloved authors are stored in special archives, including effects of such Russian literary giants as Gogol and Tolstoy. *3 nab. Makarova,* ☎ *812/218–0502.* ☉ *Wed.–Sun. 11–5.*

Returning to the Stock Exchange, continue along the **Universitetskaya Naberezhnaya** (University Embankment), which leads away from the Strelka. The Neva will be to your left. The next building you will encounter is the **Kunstkammer** (Chamber of Art, also called Chamber of Curiosities). Another fine example of Russian Baroque, painted bright azure with white trim, the building stands out from the surrounding classically designed architecture. Its playful character seems to reflect its beginnings; it was originally commissioned in 1718 to house Peter the Great's collection of oddities, gathered during his travels. Completed by 1734, the Kunstkammer (from the German *Kunst,* meaning "art," and *Kammer,* meaning "chamber") was destroyed by fire in 1747 and almost entirely rebuilt. Today it houses the Museum of Anthropology and Ethnography but still includes a room with Peter's original collection, a truly bizarre assortment ranging from rare precious stones to preserved human organs and fetuses. The museum is enormously popular, so purchase entrance tickets early in the day. *3 Universitetskaya Naberezhnaya,* ☎ *812/218–1412.* ☉ *Sun.–Thurs. 11–4. Closed last Thurs. of month.*

Next to the Kunstkammer stands the original building of the Russian Academy of Sciences. Erected on strictly Classical lines in 1783–89, it is considered Giacomo Quarenghi's grandest design, with an eight-column portico, a pediment, and a double staircase. The academy, founded in 1724 by Peter the Great and known as the Russian Academy of Sciences until the 1917 Revolution, had its administrative offices transferred to Moscow in 1934. The building now houses the St. Petersburg branch of the Russian Academy of Sciences and is not open to the public.

Continue along the embankment, crossing Mendeleyevskaya Liniya (Mendelyev Line) and passing an imposing statue of the 18th-century Russian scientist Mikhail Lomonosov. You will come to the main campus of **St. Petersburg University,** whose name has changed as often as the city's. One of Russia's leading institutions of higher learning, with an enrollment of over 20,000, St. Petersburg University was founded by Alexander I in 1819. Its campuses date from the time of Peter the Great. The bright red Baroque building to your immediate right is the **Twelve Colleges Building,** named for the governmental administrative bodies established during Peter's reign. Designed by Domenico Trezzini and completed 16 years after Peter's death, in 1741, the building was transferred to the university at the time of its establishment and today houses the university's library and administrative offices. The building is not open to the public, but no one will stop you from looking around.

The next building in the university complex is the **Rector's Wing,** where the plaque on the outside wall attests that the great Russian poet Alexander Blok was born in 1880. The building was originally commissioned in 1727 as a palace for Peter the Great's grandson, who ruled only briefly. Completed in 1761, the building was later given to the University.

Farther up the embankment, at the corner of Syezdovskaya Liniya stands one of St. Petersburg's grandest buildings—and its oldest—the **Menshikovsky Dvorets** (Menshikov Palace). Alexander Menshikov, St. Petersburg's first governor, was one of Russia's more flamboyant characters. A close friend of Peter the Great (often called his favorite), Menshikov rose from humble beginnings as a street vendor, reportedly getting his start when he sold a cabbage pie to Peter the Great—or so the legend goes. Eventually becoming one of Russia's most powerful statesmen (he was granted the entire island outright for a while), Menshikov was famous for his corruption and political maneuvering. His palace, the first stone building in St. Petersburg, was at the time of its completion in 1720 the city's most luxurious building. Although only a portion of the original palace has survived, it easily conveys a sense of Menshikov's inflated ego and love of luxury. Particularly noteworthy is the tilework in the restored bedrooms, whose walls and ceilings are completely lined with handcrafted ceramic tiles. After Peter's death and Menshikov's subsequent exile to Siberia in 1727, his palace was turned over to a military training school and was significantly altered over the years. In June 1917 it served as the site of the First Congress of Russian Soviets. Neglected until 1967, when badly needed restoration work was launched, the Menshikov Palace is today a branch of the Hermitage Museum. In addition to the restored living quarters of the Menshikov family, there is an exhibit devoted to early 18th-century Russian culture. *15 Universitetskaya Naberezhnaya,* ☎ *812/213–1112.* ☉ *Tues.–Sun. 10:30–4.*

As you leave Menshikov Palace, crossing Syezdovskaya Liniya, you'll come upon a small square to your right. This is **Rumantsev Square,** established in honor of the 18th-century general who led Russia to victory in the Russo-Turkish wars of 1768–74. Its obelisk, designed by Vikenty Brenna, originally stood in the Field of Mars (Marsovo Pole) and was moved to its present site in 1818. The new site was chosen for its proximity to the military school in the former Menshikov Palace, where Rumantsev once studied.

9 Another notable building farther up the embankment is the **Repin Institute of Painting, Sculpture, and Architecture.** Built between 1764 and 1788 and designed by Alexander Kokorinov and Vallin de la Mothe, it is a fine example of early Russian classicism. The sculptures above the main entrance on the embankment portray Hercules and Flora. This was founded as the Russian Academy of Arts in 1757 by Elizabeth I. The institute maintains a public museum of graduation works from the original Academy. The institute's many famous graduates included Dmitri Levitsky, Orest Kiprensky, and, of course, Ilya Repin (1844–1930), for whom it is now named. *17 Universitetskaya Naberezhnaya,* ☎ *812/213–6496.* ☉ *Wed.–Sun. 11–6.*

On the landing in front of the Academy of Arts, leading down to the Neva, stand two of St. Petersburg's more magnificent landmarks, the famous Egyptian Sphinxes. These twin statues date from the 15th century BC and were discovered during an excavation in Thebes in the 1820s. They were apparently created during the era of Pharaoh Amenhotep III, whose face is supposedly depicted on them.

TIME OUT   If you want a rest and a bite to eat at a popular local establishment, try **Lukamore** (19 nab. Leytenanta Shmidta, ☎ 812/218-5900). It's a short walk (four blocks) up the embankment from the Academy of Arts and is located on the corner of the 13th Line and the embankment. If you arrive before the lunch crowds, which begin around 1 PM, you will probably be seated without a wait. The cuisine is far from gourmet, and the café's dark lighting creates a rather dismal atmosphere. This is the real St. Petersburg, though, and despite gloomy appearances, a few items on the menu are worth trying. The *griby v smetane* (mushrooms in cream) is good and filling, as is the borscht. Since this is a state-run restaurant, whose patrons are predominantly Russian, you should expect the slow and inattentive service typical of such enterprises. ☉ *Daily noon–11. Rubles only.*

If you have time, you should visit one last famous building on Vasilievsky Island. If you go to the end of the embankment, at the corner of 21 **10** liniya, you will find the **Gorny Institut** (Mining Institute). It can be reached either by walking or by taking any of the trams that stop at the corner of 11 liniya and the embankment. Founded in 1773 by Catherine the Great, this is St. Petersburg's oldest technical institution of higher learning. The present building in the Neoclassical style was built between 1806 and 1811 by Andrei Voronikhin, architect of the Kazan Cathedral on Nevsky Prospect. The main entrance is supported by 12 Doric columns and is lined with statues designed by Demut-Malinovsky and Pimenov (creators of the sculpture above the General Staff Building). The institute boasts an unusual museum of precious stones and minerals, including a piece of malachite weighing over a ton and an iron meteorite. *2 21-aya Liniya,* ☎ *812/218–8605 or 812/218–8681.* ☉ *Weekdays 9–6.*

At this point you conclude your tour of Vasilievsky Island by crossing the **Most Leytenanta Shmidta** (Lieutenant Schmidt Bridge), which will take you across the Neva and back toward the city center. Built in 1842–50, this was the first stationary bridge to connect Vasilievsky Island with the left bank of the Neva; it was renamed in honor of the naval officer who was a leader of the Black Sea Fleet mutiny during the 1905–07 Revolution.

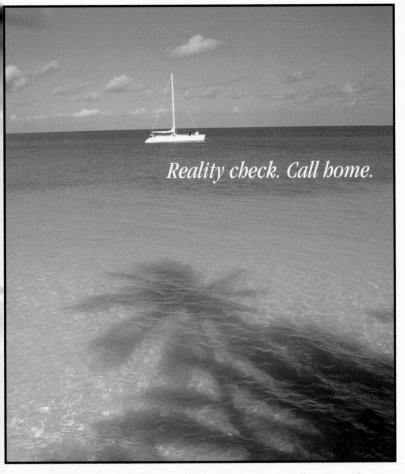

Reality check. Call home.

—— *AT&T USADirect® and World Connect®. The fast, easy way to call most anywhere.* ——

Take out AT&T Calling Card or your local calling card.** Lift phone. Dial AT&T Access Number for country you're calling from. Connect to English-speaking operator or voice prompt. Reach the States or over 200 countries. Talk. Say goodbye. Hang up. Resume vacation.

Austria*†††.....................022-903-011	Luxembourg..........................0-800-0111	Turkey*.............................00-800-12277
Belgium*.....................0-800-100-10	Netherlands*..................06-022-9111	United Kingdom.................0500-89-0011
Czech Republic*.............00-420-00101	Norway.............................800-190-11	
Denmark.............................8001-0010	Poland†◆¹.............0◊010-480-0111	
Finland.............................9800-100-10	Portugal†.........................05017-1-288	
France.................................19-0011	Romania*.....................01-800-4288	
Germany.............................0130-0010	Russia*†(Moscow)..................155-5042	
Greece*..........................00-800-1311	Slovak Rep.*..................00-420-00101	
Hungary*....................00◊-800-01111	Spain●..........................900-99-00-11	
Ireland.........................1-800-550-000	Sweden.........................020-795-611	
Italy*.................................172-1011	Switzerland*.......................155-00-11	

AT&T
Your True Choice

**You can also call collect or use most U.S. local calling cards. Countries in bold face permit country-to-country calling in addition to calls to the U.S. World Connect® prices consist of USADirect® rates plus an additional charge based on the country you are calling. Collect calling available to the U.S. only. *Public phones require deposit of coin or phone card. †May not be available from every phone. †††Public phones require local coin payment during call. ◆Not available from public phones. ◊Await second dial tone. ¹Dial 010-480-0111 from major Warsaw hotels. ●Calling available to most European countries. ©1995 AT&T.

For a free wallet sized card of all AT&T Access Numbers, call: 1-800-241-5555.

All the best trips
start with Fodor's.

Returning across Lieutenant Schmidt Bridge, you may tour the Left Bank of the Neva, which at this stretch is called *Krasnovo Flota naberezhnaya* (Red Fleet Embankment). Before the 1917 Revolution it was called the English Embankment, as this was the center of the city's English community. Here one can find some of St. Petersburg's finest aristocratic estates. For instance, as you take a left off the bridge and follow the embankment, you come to No. 28, formerly the mansion of Grand Duke Andrei Vladimirovich Romanov. Today it is a so-called Wedding Palace, the only place under communism where marriages could be performed; the state-run, secular ceremonies, still the usual type held here, are perfunctorily recited with assembly-line efficiency.

Continue down the embankment with the Neva River on your left. You will pass a long, light-yellow building built along Classical lines. This is the former **Senate and Synod,** Russia's highest judicial and administrative body before the revolution. Designed by Carlo Rossi and erected between 1829 and 1834, it now houses state historical archives and is closed to the public.

Across the street from it, if you continue going straight, is a large open square on your right. First called Senatskaya Ploshchad (Senate Square), ⓫ it was renamed **Dekabristov Ploshchad** (Decembrists' Square) earlier this century. Officially it has returned to its original name, but it's hardly ever used. It holds one of St. Petersburg's best-known landmarks, the *Medny Vsadnik* (*Bronze Horseman*). The square took its new name from the dramatic events that unfolded there on December 14, 1825, when, following Czar Alexander I's death, a group of aristocrats tried to stage a rebellion on the square in an attempt to prevent the crowning of Nicholas I as the new czar, and perhaps do away with the monarchy altogether. Their coup failed miserably, bloodily suppressed by troops already loyal to Nicholas, and those rebels who were not executed were banished to Siberia. Although the Decembrists, as they came to be known, did not bring significant change to Russia in their time, their attempts at liberal reform were often cited by the Soviet regime as proof of deep-rooted revolutionary fervor in Russian society. In 1925 the square was renamed in their honor.

In the center is the grand statue called the *Bronze Horseman,* erected as a memorial from Catherine the Great to her predecessor, Peter the Great. (The simple inscription on the base reads, "To Peter the First from Catherine the Second, 1782.") Created by the French sculptor Etienne Falconet and his student Marie Collot, the statue depicts the powerful Peter, crowned with a laurel wreath, astride a rearing horse that symbolizes Russia, trampling a serpent that represents the forces of evil. The enormous granite rock on which the statue is balanced comes from the Gulf of Finland. Reportedly, Peter would stand on it to survey his city from afar. Moving it was a herculean effort, requiring a special barge and machines, and taking nearly a year. The statue was immortalized in a poem of the same name by Alexander Pushkin, who wrote that the czar "by whose fateful will the city was founded beside the sea, stands here aloft at the very brink of a precipice, having reared up Russia with his iron curb."

The golden yellow building on the other side of Decembrists' Square ⓬ is the **Admiralty.** You should walk around to the front of this lovely building by crossing the square diagonally. The Admiralty is considered the city's architectural center, and its flashing spire—visible at various points throughout the city—is one of St. Petersburg's most renowned emblems.

A series of important constructions, all related to the naval industry, predate the present building. The first was a shipyard of Peter's, followed by an earthen fortress that guarded the port; after these came the first Admiralty, made of stone and topped by the famous spire that has endured to grace each successive Admiralty.

The current building was designed by Andrei Zakharov and was built between 1806 and 1823, after it was decided that the city required a much grander Admiralty to match its more impressive buildings. It is adorned with classical sculptures glorifying Russia's naval prowess, including a frieze of Neptune handing over his trident to Peter. Used as a shipbuilding center through the 1840s, it has belonged to the Higher Naval Academy since 1925 and is not open to the public.

An Admiralty Lawn once adorned its front expanse, but in Alexander's time it was turned into a small park bearing his name (to which it has been returned, after having been named for Maxim Gorky under the communists). As you walk through it, you'll see various statues, mostly of artists such as the composer Mikhail Glinka and the writer Mikhail Lermontov; the one accompanied by the delightful camel is of Nikolai Przhevalsky, a 19th-century explorer of Central Asia.

Proceed through the park and you will come out on Admiraltysky Prospect, the eponymous avenue running lengthwise. Ahead of you is the back of massive **Isaakievsky Sobor** (St. Isaac's Cathedral). Its entrance is on the other side, so go right on the prospect a bit to take a left and go around the cathedral's side. Where the prospect meets Konnogvardysky bulvar is the gracefully designed Manège. Another Quarenghi creation, this former barracks of the imperial horse guards is used as an art exhibition hall.

Entering St. Isaac's in front, you will buy your tickets inside. (Russians purchase lower-rate tickets at the *kassa* outside.) The guard should usher you to the proper counter; you probably will be offered a guided tour, which you can refuse. Tickets are sold both to the church ("the museum") and to its outer colonnade; the latter affords a walk on the upper balustrade, where you will get an excellent view of the city. You can purchase tickets for either or both.

Of the grandest proportions, St. Isaac's is the world's third-largest domed cathedral. Its beauty is a matter of taste: Some consider the massive design and highly ornate interior to be excessive, while others revel in its opulence. Commissioned in 1818 by Alexander I to celebrate his victory over Napoleon, it took more than 40 years to build. The French architect Ricard de Montferrand devoted his life to the project and died the same year the cathedral was finally consecrated, in 1858. The interior is lavishly decorated with malachite, lazulite, marble, and other precious stones and minerals. Gilding the dome required 100 kilos (220 pounds) of gold. The church can hold up to 14,000 worshipers. After the 1917 Revolution it was closed for services and in 1931 was opened as a museum. Since 1990, occasional services have resumed, and talk is mounting of its eventual return to the Orthodox Church. When the city was blockaded during World War II, the gilded dome was painted black to avoid being targeted by enemy fire. Despite efforts to protect it, the cathedral nevertheless suffered heavy damage, as bullet holes on the columns on the south side attest. *1 Isaakievskaya Ploshchad,* ☎ *812/315–9732. Admission for foreigners: $8.* ☉ *Mon., Tues., Thurs.–Sun. 11–7.*

★ **St. Isaac's Square** opens up in front of its **cathedral.** It is the city's most recent square, having been completed only after the cathedral was built.

In its center stands a statue of Czar Nicholas I (1825–55). Unveiled in 1859, the Nicholas Statue was commissioned by the czar's wife and three children, whose faces are engraved (in the allegorical forms of Wisdom, Faith, Power, and Justice) on its base. It was designed, like St. Isaac's Cathedral, by Montferrand. The statue depicts Nicholas I mounted on a rearing horse whose hind legs actually serve as the statue's support. Other engravings on the base describe such events of the czar's reign as the suppression of the Decembrists' uprising and the opening ceremonies of the St. Petersburg–Moscow railroad line.

(14) On the opposite side of the square, directly across from St. Isaac's Cathedral, is **Mariinsky Dvorets** (Maria's Palace). Completed in 1844 for the eldest and favorite daughter of Nicholas I, it was subsequently used as the residence of the Provisional Government (briefly) and the seat of the Leningrad Soviet's Executive Committee; today, it is the home of the St. Petersburg City Council. The roof is still adorned with Soviet regalia, although the banner flying above it is the reclaimed Russian flag. Since this is a working governmental building, access to the public is restricted; group tours, however, can be arranged by special request. *6 Isaakievskaya Ploshchad, ☎ 812/319–9443.*

To the left, past the Nicholas Statue and in front of the Mariinsky Dvorets is the short **Siniy Most** (Blue Bridge), so called because of the paint on its underside. The bridge, which spans the Moika River, is so wide (116 meters, or 328 feet) but so stubby that it seems not to be a bridge at all but, rather, some quaint raised footpath on St. Isaac's Square.

Passing over the Moika via the Blue Bridge, you will spot a stone column. Its marks show the different water levels of the many floods that have plagued the city over the years.

TIME OUT The **Astoria Hotel,** on the east side of the square, is one of St. Petersburg's best. Don't be intimidated by the regal dress of its doormen. Take the lobby elevator to the fourth floor and you will find a self-service café (open daily 7–4 and 5–10) that offers coffee and tea, imported beverages, and a variety of light snacks, from smoked salmon to cream-filled pastries.

You can end your tour here, perhaps choosing to return to the Astoria for coffee or a snack. If you prefer to end up on Nevsky Prospect, follow the Moika embankment a few blocks down to where they intersect.

Going this way, shortly before you reach Nevsky, on the right-hand side, you may notice estate grounds behind a tall fence and then a yellow-stone building with an open courtyard alongside. The grounds belonged to Count Razumovsky, who had his palace here in the late 18th century. The adjacent house, dating from the early 1750s, belonged to the merchant Stegelmann, who was in charge of selling supplies to the royal court. Both houses were later taken over, linked, and made into a foundling hospital and orphanage. Today they house the Pedagogical Institute.

Tour 3: Peter and Paul Fortress and the Petrograd Side

★ (15) This tour takes you to the site where the city began, the **Petropavlovskaya Krepost** (Peter and Paul Fortress). The fortress was erected in just a year's time, from 1703 to 1704, to defend St. Petersburg in the Great Northern War against Sweden. It was never used for its intended purpose, however, since the Russian line of defense quickly moved farther north and then won the war, without ever having to be mobilized as an active fort. Indeed, the Fort St. Petersburg (as it was first called) and the city of St. Petersburg itself (which sprung up later and took its name) have never had to do battle with an outside enemy from here. Instead of being used for its original purpose, the fort has been used mainly as a political prison, primarily under the czars. The fortress is located on Zayachy Ostrov (Hare Island), almost directly across the Neva from the Winter Palace. Cut off from the north by the moatlike Kronverk Canal, Hare Island is connected by a footbridge to **Troitskaya Ploshchad** (Trinity Square, sometimes still referred to by its Soviet name, Kirov Square) on Petrogradsky Ostrov (Petrograd Island). This section of the city, which actually consists of a series of islands, is commonly referred to as the **Petrogradskaya Storona** (Petrograd Side) and is one of its earliest residential areas. Trinity Square, named for the church that once stood here (demolished in 1934), is the city's oldest square. You can reach Hare Island from central St. Petersburg by crossing the **Troitsky Most** (Trinity Bridge) from the Palace Embankment. It is also easy to reach by subway; the closest station is Gorkovskaya. After exiting the station, walk through the small park in front of you, heading in the direction of the Neva. The fortress will emerge through the trees to your right.

Cross the footbridge and enter the fortress through **Ioannovskyie Vorota** (St. John's Gate), the main entrance to the outer fortification. Once inside, you will need to stop at the ticket office, which is inside the outer fortification wall (the ticket booth to your immediate left sells only theater tickets). Although entry to the fortress grounds is free, you must buy tickets here for the exhibits. Without them you will be sent back to the ticket office. *3 Petropavlovskaya Krepost,* ☎ *812/238–4540.* ☉ *Thurs.–Tues. 11–5. Closed last Thurs. of month.*

Entrance to the inner fortress is through the **Petrovskyie Vorota** (St. Peter's Gate). Designed by the Swiss architect Domenico Trezzini, it was built from 1717 to 1718. Its decoration includes the double-headed eagle of the Romanovs and a wooden bas-relief depicting the Apostle Peter casting down Simon Magus. The allegory was meant to inspire confidence in Peter the Great's impending victory over Charles XII of Sweden, which did not come until 1721.

After passing through St. Peter's Gate, the first building to your right is the **Artillery Arsenal,** where weaponry was stored. Just to your left is the **Inzhenerny Dom** (Engineer's House), which was built from 1748 to 1749. It is now a branch of the Museum of the History of St. Petersburg (as are all exhibits in the fortress) and presents displays about the city's prerevolutionary history. The small building right after the Engineer's House is the **Gauptvakhta** (Guardhouse), built in 1743 and later reconstructed. Today it houses administrative offices of the museum and is not open to the public.

As you continue to walk down the main center lane, away from the St. Peter's Gate, you will soon come to the main attraction of the fortress, the **Petropavlovsky Sobor** (Cathedral of Sts. Peter and Paul). Constructed between 1712 and 1733 on the site of an earlier wooden church, it was designed by Domenico Trezzini and later embellished by Bartolomeo Rastrelli. It is highly unusual for a Russian Orthodox church. Instead of the characteristic bulbous domes, it is adorned by a single, slender gilded spire whose height (121 meters, or 400 feet) made it the city's tallest building. The spire is identical to that of the Admiralty across the river, except that it is crowned by an angel bearing a golden cross. The spire remained the city's highest structure—in accordance with Peter the Great's decree—until 1962, when the television tower was erected, greatly marring the harmony of the city's skyline.

The interior of the cathedral is also atypical. The Baroque iconostasis, designed by Ivan Zarodny and built in the 1720s, is adorned by freestanding statues. Another uncommon feature is the pulpit. According to legend, it was used only once: in 1901, to excommunicate Leo Tolstoy from the Russian Orthodox Church.

Starting with Peter the Great, the cathedral served as the imperial burial grounds. You can identify Peter's grave—a place of his own choosing, to the far right as you face the iconostasis—by the czar's bust on the railing. Nearly all of Peter's successors were buried in the cathedral as well, with a few notable exceptions: Peter II, Ivan IV, and the last czar, Nicholas II, who was executed with his family in Ekaterinburg in 1918. It is said, however, that the recently identified remains of the czar will at some point in the future be given a final resting place here. In 1992, in recognition of Russia's imperial past, the most recent Romanov pretender, Grand Duke Vladimir, was bestowed the honor of burial in the Peter and Paul Fortress, although not in the royal crypt.

You may exit the cathedral through the passageway to the left of the iconostasis. This leads to the adjoining **Usypalnitsa** (Grand Ducal Crypt), built between 1896 and 1908. It contains an exhibit on the architectural history of the fortress.

As you leave the cathedral, you will notice a small Classical structure to your right. This is the **Botny Domik** (Boathouse), built in 1762–66 to house Peter the Great's boyhood boat. The boat has since been moved to the Central Naval Museum on Vasilievsky Island (*see* Tour 2, *above*), and the building is not open to the public. The wooden figurine on its roof is meant to symbolize navigation.

The long pink-and-white building to your left as you exit the cathedral is the **Komendantsky Dom** (Commandant's House). Erected between 1743 and 1746, it once housed the fortress's administration and doubled as a courtroom for political prisoners. The Decembrist revolutionaries were tried here in 1826. The room where the trial took place forms part of the ongoing exhibits, which deal with the history of St. Petersburg from its founding in 1703 to 1917.

Across the cobblestone yard, opposite the entrance to the cathedral, stands the **Monetny Dvor** (Mint), which dates from 1716. The present building was erected between 1798 and 1806. The mint is still in operation, producing coins, medals, military decorations, and *znachki,* Russian souvenir pins. The coins that were taken on Soviet space missions were made here.

Take the pathway to the left of the Commandant's House (as you are facing it), and you will be headed right for the **Nevskyie Vorota** (Neva Gate), built in 1730 and reconstructed in 1787. As you walk through its passageway, note the plaques on the inside walls denoting flood levels of the Neva. The most recent, from 1975, shows the river more than 9 feet above normal. The gate leads out to the **Komendantskaya Pristan** (Commandant's Pier). It is this side of the fortress that was meant to be viewed by would-be invaders and convince them to turn back. Up above to the right is the **Signal Cannon,** fired every day at noon. From this side you get a splendid view of St. Petersburg. You may want to step down to the sandy beach, where even in winter hearty swimmers enjoy the Neva's arctic waters. In summer the beach is lined with sunbathers, standing up or leaning against the fortification wall (supposedly this allows for a more even tan).

Returning back inside the fortress, consider that it was also through the Neva Gate that prisoners were led to execution. Several of the fortress's bastions, concentrated at its far western end, were put to use over the years mainly as political prisons. One of them, **Trubetskoi Bastion,** is open to the public as a museum. If you turn left from the gate and walk the length of the fortification wall, you can identify the museum by the diagonal stripes on its door and the iron gate enclosing the entrance. Aside from a few exhibits of prison garb, the only items on display are the cells themselves, restored to their chilling, prerevolutionary appearance.

The first prisoner confined in its dungeons was Peter the Great's own son Alexei, who was tortured to death in 1718, allegedly under the czar's supervision. The prison was enlarged in 1872, when an adjacent one, Alexeivsky Bastion, which held such famous figures as the writers Fyodor Dostoevsky and Nikolai Chernyshevsky, was too small to contain the swelling numbers of dissidents of the czarist regime. A partial chronology of revolutionaries held here includes some of the People's Will terrorists, who killed Alexander II in 1881; Lenin's elder brother Alexander, who attempted to murder Alexander III (and was executed for his role in the plot); and Leon Trotsky and Maxim Gorky, after taking part in the 1905 Revolution. The Bolsheviks themselves imprisoned people here for a short period, starting with members of the Provisional Government who were arrested and "detained for their own safety" for a few days, as well as sailors who mutinied against the communist regime in Kronstadt in 1921. They were apparently the last to be held here, and in 1925 a memorial museum (to the prerevolutionary prisoners) was opened instead.

You may want to visit one more building associated with the fortress but situated outside its walls. Across the Kronverk Canal to the north ⑯ of the fortress is the horseshoe-shaped **Artilereysky Muzey** (Artillery Museum). Leaving the fort by its western end and crossing the footbridge there, bear right; leaving by the way you came in and crossing its footbridge, bear left. The large museum will soon be visible. The building once served as the city's arsenal and was turned over to the Artillery Museum in 1872. The museum itself dates from the days of Peter the Great, who sought to present the entire history of weaponry, with a special emphasis on Russia. Today the Artillery Museum is the main army museum of St. Petersburg. *7 Park Alexandrovsky,* ☎ *812/ 232–0296.* ☼ *Wed.–Sun. 11–8.*

TIME OUT   If you have walked all the way over to the Artillery Museum, you may as well walk a bit farther and try out St. Petersburg's floating café, the **Petrovsky.** It is located on a ship permanently moored in the Kronverk Canal, just south of the Artillery Museum. The upper deck contains a fullfledged restaurant that never seems to have any available tables. Down below, however, is an intimate café where you can enjoy a cup of strong coffee, pastry, or even a shot of cognac. *3 Naberezhnaya Mytninskaya.* ☼ *Daily noon–midnight.*

Return now to Trinity Square. At the northern edge of the square, at the corner of Kuybysheva ulitsa and Kamennostrovsky Prospect, stands the former mansion of Mathilda Kshesinskaya, a famous ballerina and mistress of the last Russian czar, Nicholas II. Built in the Art Nouveau style in 1905, the mansion served as Bolshevik committee headquarters in the months leading up to the October Revolution. In 1957 it was turned into the Museum of the Great October Socialist Revolu- ⑰ tion and was renamed the **Russian Political History Museum** in 1991. It offers temporary exhibits on Russian political movements, both before and after the 1917 Revolution. One hall contains an interesting collection of wax figures, showing victims and perpetrators of violence in Russian history, including Alexander II, who was assassinated by terrorists, and Stalin. The beautiful mansion itself is interesting as well, simply because it gives you a sense of prerevolutionary St. Petersburg and the lifestyle of its upper classes. *214 Kuybysheva ul.* ☎ *812/233–7052.* ☉ *Fri.–Wed. 10–5:30.*

⑱ Not far from the Kshesinskaya Mansion is St. Petersburg's only **Mechet** (Mosque). As you leave the mansion, take a right, and then turn right again onto Kronversky Prospect. It's hard to miss the bright azure domes above the trees. Built in 1910–14 to serve St. Petersburg's Muslim community, the Mosque was designed after the Gur Emir in Samarkand, where Tamerlane is buried. *7 Kronversky Prospect,* ☎ *812/233–9819.* ☉ *Daily 10–7. Services daily at 1:30.*

Now head back (left) in the direction of the Neva River. When you reach the waterfront, turn left again, to walk along Petrovskaya Naberezhnaya (Petrov Embankment). A few minutes away, you'll find
⑲ the **Domik Petra Pervovo** (Peter the Great's Cottage). Built in just three days in May 1703, the cottage was home to Peter the Great during construction of the Peter and Paul Fortress. It is made of wooden logs painted to resemble bricks. Inside, 18th-century furniture is on display, arranged as it might have been in Peter's day, along with a few of Peter's personal effects. The stone structure enclosing the cottage was erected in 1784 by Catherine the Great to protect it from the elements. The cottage consists of just three rooms whose ceilings are surprisingly low—considering that Peter the Great was nearly 7 feet tall. *6 Petrovskaya Naberezhnaya,* ☎ *812/232–4576.* ☉ *Wed.–Mon. 11–6. Closed last Mon. of month and in humid weather.*

In the courtyard in front of the cottage stands a bronze bust of Peter the Great. The large stone sculptures of the Shchi-Tsza (Lion-Frogs) flanking the stairwell leading down the embankment side were brought to Russia from Manchuria in 1907.

Keep walking east along the embankment. When you reach the corner where Petrovskaya and Petrogradskaya embankments meet (and the Great Nevka converges with the Neva River), you'll be in front of a blue-and-white building in the Russian Baroque style. This is the **Nakhimov Academy of Naval Officers.**

⑳ Permanently moored in front of it is the cruiser **Avrora.** Launched in 1903, it fought in the 1904–05 Russo–Japanese War as well as in World War II, but it is best known for its role in the Bolshevik Revolution. At 9:40 PM on November 7, 1917, the cruiser fired the shot signaling the storming of the Winter Palace. A cherished relic in the Soviet era, the *Avrora* was carefully restored in the 1980s and opened as a museum. Although the revolution it launched brought itself under fire in the end, the cruiser is still a favorite place to bring children, and on weekends you may encounter long lines. On display are the crew's quarters and the radio room used to broadcast Lenin's victory address. *4 Petrogradskaya nab.,* ☎ *812/230–5202.* ☉ *Tues., Wed., Sat.–Sun. 10:30–4.*

Across the river from the *Avrora* stands the enormous **St. Petersburg Hotel.** Before 1992 it was named the Leningrad, which was probably a more appropriate name since this Intourist offering clearly belongs to the Soviet era. Built in the monotonous style of a Brezhnev-era high-rise, the concrete-and-steel structure seems horribly out of place among the prerevolutionary architecture lining the embankment.

From here you can return to your starting point by retracing your steps along the embankment. If you want to see more of the Petrograd Side's residential areas, you can take the longer route back via Kuybysheva ulitsa. Walk down to the bridge to your left (as you face the cruiser *Avrora*) and turn left onto Kuybysheva. This will take you back to Trinity Square. From here the Trinity Bridge is to your left and the Gorkovskaya subway stop a short walk to your right.

Tour 4: Nevsky Prospect and the Alexander Nevsky Lavra

★ ㉑ We turn now to the inner city and St. Petersburg's most famous avenue, **Nevsky Prospect.** Laid out in 1710, it is one of the city's first streets. Just short of 5 km (3 mi) long, beginning and ending at different bends of the Neva River, it starts at the foot of the Admiralty building and runs in a perfectly straight line to the Moscow Railway Station, where it curves slightly to end a slight distance farther at the Alexander Nevsky Lavra, or monastery. Because St. Petersburg was once part of the larger lands of Novgorod, the road linking them was known as Great Novgorod Road, and trade and transport traveled over it. By the time Peter the Great built the first Admiralty, however, another major road clearly was needed to connect the Admiralty directly to the shipping hub. It was decided to begin the new avenue at the Admiralty. It was originally called the Great Perspective Road, and after that, the Nevsky Perspektiv, and finally Nevsky Prospect.

"There is nothing finer than Nevsky Prospect, not in St. Petersburg at any rate, for in St. Petersburg it is everything . . ." wrote the great Russian author Nikolai Gogol more than 150 years ago. Today it may not be as resplendent as it was in the 1830s, when noblemen and ladies strolled along the elegant avenue or paraded by in horse-drawn carriages. It still remains, however, the pulse of the city, unquestionably its main thoroughfare. Through the 18th century it was built up with estates and manors of the gentry, most of which still stand as testimony to the city's noble past. The next century saw a boom of mercantile growth that added sections further south as centers for commerce, finance, and trade. Under the Communists, few new sites were planned on the Prospect. Instead, old structures found a new use, and the bulk of the Soviets' building was directed outside the city center.

Nevsky Prospect boasts the city's finest hotels and shops, but it also attracts all the problems of its difficult economy. It is the favorite gathering place of homeless children, whose dirty faces and pitiful looks evoke sympathy but whose tricks may easily catch you off guard and without a wallet. The street is also roamed by bands of colorfully dressed Gypsy women and children, who can smell a tourist miles away. Unfortunately, a stroll down today's Nevsky Prospect requires some caution. As in any large city, you need to use common sense.

★ ㉒ Start at the relatively peaceful **Alexander Nevsky Lavra** (monastery), which is at the southeastern end of Nevsky Prospect. It can be reached by taking the subway to the Ploshchad Alexandra Nevskovo station, which comes out at the foot of the Moskva Hotel, one of Intourist's gargantuan complexes. The entrance to the Lavra is across the square from the subway exit. The monastery complex includes the Church of the Annunciation, converted under the Soviets into the Museum of City Sculpture, the Holy Trinity Church, a theological seminary, and several cemeteries. Entrance to the monastery grounds is free, but you must purchase a ticket for the two most interesting cemeteries and the museum. The ticket office is outside the monastery, to the right of the main gate. *1 Ploshchad Alexandra Nevskovo,* ☎ *812/274–0409 or 812/277–1716.* ☯ *Fri.–Wed. 11–6.*

The word *lavra* in Russian is reserved for a monastery of the highest order, of which there are just four in all of Russia and Ukraine. Named in honor of St. Alexander Nevsky, this monastery was founded in 1710 by Peter the Great and given *lavra* status in 1797. Prince Alexander of Novgorod (1220–1263), the great military commander became a beloved national hero because he halted the relentless eastward drive for Russian territory by the Germans and the Swedes. Peter chose this site for the monastery, thinking that it was the same place where the prince had fought the battle in 1240 that earned him the title Alexander of the Neva (Nevsky), though the famous battle actually took place some 20 kilometers (12 miles) away. Alexander Nevsky had been buried in Vladimir, but in 1724, on Peter's orders, his remains were transferred to the monastery that was founded in his honor.

Entrance to the monastery is through the archway of the elegant **Gate Church,** built by Ivan Starov in 1783–85. The walled pathway is flanked by two cemeteries, whose entrances are located a short walk down the path. To the left lies the older Lazarus Cemetery. The list of famous people buried here reads like a catalogue of St. Petersburg architecture and includes Quarenghi, Rossi, Voronikhin, and Thomas de Thomon. The cemetery also contains the tombstone of the father of Russian science, Mikhail Lomonsov. The **Tikhvin Cemetery,** on the opposite side, was the final resting place of a number of St. Petersburg's great literary and musical figures. The grave of Fyodor Dostoevsky, located in the northwestern corner, is easily identified by the tombstone's sculpture, which portrays the writer with his flowing beard. Continuing along the path you'll soon reach the composers' corner, where Rimsky-Korsakov, Mussorgsky, Borodin, and Tchaikovsky are buried.

Having pondered St. Petersburg's cultural legacy, return to the path and cross the bridge spanning the quaint **Monastyrka Canal.** As you enter the monastery grounds, the **Church of the Annunciation** greets you on your left. The red-and-white rectangular church was designed by Domenico Trezzini and built between 1717 and 1722. The Museum of City Sculpture inside contains models of St. Petersburg's architectural masterpieces as well as gravestones and other fine examples of memorial sculpture. Also in the church are several graves of 18th-century statesmen. The great soldier, Generalissimo Alexander Suvorov, who led the Russian army to numerous victories during the Russo-Turkish War (1768–74), is buried here under a simple marble slab that he purportedly designed himself. It reads simply: "Here lies Suvorov."

Continuing along the same path, you'll reach the monastery's main cathedral, the **Troitsky Sobor** (Trinity Cathedral), which was one of the city's few churches left functioning during the Soviet era. Designed by Ivan Starov and completed at the end of the 18th century, it stands out among the monastery's predominantly Baroque architecture for its monumental Classical design. Services are held here daily, and the church is open to the public, although it closes between 2 and 5 in the afternoon for housekeeping. The magnificent interior, with its stunning gilded iconostasis, is worth a visit. The large central dome, adorned by frescoes designed by the great architect Quarenghi, seems to soar toward the heavens. It is in this church that the main relics of Alexander Nevsky are kept.

Return now to Alexander Nevsky Square. The bridge to your right, also named for Alexander Nevsky, is the city's longest; it leads to some of St. Petersburg's main bedroom communities, where, these days, most of its residents live. You should take the subway one stop north to the Mayakovskaya station, but at that stop, follow the signs for the adjacent Vosstaniya exit, to emerge at a better location for viewing the next sights. It is at this point that the avenue's most interesting architecture

❷❸ begins, starting at **Ploshchad Vosstaniya** (Insurrection Square). Originally called Znamenskaya Ploshchad (Square of the Sign) for a church of the same name that stood on it, the plaza was the site of many revolutionary speeches and armed clashes with military and police forces—hence its second name. Like Decembrists' Square, it's now officially back to its first name, but it's unusual to hear it called that—yet at least. (The subway station of the same name hasn't changed.) The busy Moscow Railroad station is here, and from this point, the street is lined with almost every imaginable shop, from fruit markets to art salons to bookstores. A stroll here is not a casual affair, for Nevsky is almost always teeming with bustling crowds of shoppers and street artists. Budding entrepreneurs, who sell their wares on the sidewalk on folding tables, further obstruct pedestrian traffic. Here you will also see an increasingly rare sight, the old men of the Great Patriotic War (the Russian name for World War II) still proudly wearing their medals.

Head west, away from the monastery and the railway station, and after three blocks you'll reach the **Fontanka (Fountain) River** and one of the

❷❹ city's most beautiful bridges, the **Anichkov Most**, each corner of which bears one from a quartet of exquisite equestrian statues. Designed by Peter Klodt and erected in 1841, the bronze sculptures depict phases of horse-taming. Taken down and buried during World War II, the beautiful monuments were restored to their positions in 1945. The bridge was named for Colonel Mikhail Anichkov, whose regiment had built the first, wooden drawbridge here. At that time, early in the 18th century, the bridge marked the city limits, and the job of its night guards was much the same as that of today's border guards, to carefully screen those entering the city. As you cross the bridge, pause for a moment to look back at No. 41, the colorful Baroque building on the corner of Nevsky and the Fontanka. The highly ornate, deep rose mansion belonged to Prince Beloselsky-Belozersky. Finished in 1848, by Stackenschneider, who wanted to replicate Rastrelli's Stroganov Palace, this lavish building, once opulent inside and out, housed the local Communist Party headquarters during the Soviet era. Today it is the setting for classical music concerts. The interiors have unfortunately been largely destroyed and are no longer nearly as magnificent as the facades.

Over the Fontanka, on the opposite corner, stands the **Anichkov Palace,** named for the colonel whose regiment built the bridge. It was built by Empress Elizabeth for her lover Alexei Razumovsky between 1741 and 1750. As if to continue the tradition, Catherine the Great later gave it to one of her many favorites, Grigory Potemkin. An able statesman and army officer, Potemkin is famous for his attempts to fool Catherine about conditions in the Russian south. He had fake villages put up along the banks of the Volga River for her to view as she passed by during her 1787 tour of the area. The term "Potemkin village" has come to mean any impressive facade that hides an ugly interior—a phrase put to good use during the Soviet era.

The Anichkov Palace was originally designed by Mikhail Zemtsov and completed by Bartolomeo Francesco Rastrelli. The building has undergone a number of changes, and little remains of the elaborate Baroque facade. This was once a suburban area, which explains why its main entrance faces the Fontanka rather than Nevsky, where there is only a side entrance. Today it houses the Youth Palace (once the Pioneer Palace), which offers activities for young people.

The next stop is **Ploshchad Ostrovskovo** (Ostrovsky Square), named for the famous Russian playwright and created by Carlo Rossi. You may also hear it referred to as Ploshchad Alexandrinskaya. The square is dominated by the city's oldest theater **Pushkin Drama Theater,** originally named the Alexandrinsky Theater (for the wife of Nicholas I) and built in Classical style between 1828 and 1832. Six Corinthian columns adorn the Nevsky facade. Apollo's chariot dominates the building, with statues of the muses Terpischore and Melpomene to keep him company. In the small garden in front of the theater stands the **Catherine Monument,** which shows the empress towering above the principal personalities of her famous reign. Depicted on the pedestal are Grigory Potemkin, Generalissimo Suvorov, the poet Gavril Derzhavin, and others. Among the bronze figures is the Princess Dashkova, who conspired against her own sister's lover—who just happened to be Catherine's husband, Peter III—to help the empress assume the throne.

Before moving beyond Ostrovsky Square, step around to the back of the Pushkin Theater, where the amazing **ulitsa Zodchevo Rossi** begins. The proportions of this extraordinary street are perfect. It is bounded by two buildings of exactly the same height, its width (22 meters, or 72 feet) equals the height of the buildings, and its length is exactly 10 times its width. A complete view unfolds only at the end of the street, where it meets Lomonosov Square. The perfect symmetry is reinforced by the identical facades of the two buildings, which are painted the same subdued yellow and decorated with impressive white pillars. One of the buildings is the famous **Vaganova Ballet School** (founded in 1738), whose pupils included Karsavina as well as Pavlova, Nijinsky, and Ulanova.

Back at Ostrovsky Square, take note of the Neoclassical building to your left, on the west side of the square. This is the **Russian National Library,** the nation's largest after the State Library in Moscow. Opened in 1814 as the Imperial Public Library, it was Russia's first built for that purpose and today is known fondly as the "Publichka." It has over 20 million books and claims to have a copy of every book ever printed in Russia. Among its treasures are Voltaire's personal library and the only copy of *Chasovnik* (1565), the second book printed in Russia. The building comprises three sections. The main section, on the corner of Nevsky Prospect and Sadovaya ulitsa, was designed by Yegor Sakolov and built between 1796 and 1801. The wing nearest you, built between 1828 and 1832, was designed by Carlo Rossi as an integral part of Ostrovsky Square. True to the building's purpose, the facade is adorned with statues of philosophers and poets, including Homer, Virgil, and the Roman goddess of wisdom, Minerva.

You may want to cross Nevsky at this point to peek inside the **Yeliseyevsky Food Emporium** (No. 56), a name to which it's been returned, after officially having been called Gastronome No. 1 under the communists. It is located directly across the street from the Catherine Monument. Built at the turn of the century for the immensely successful grocer Yeliseyev, it is decorated in the style of early Art Nouveau, with colorful stained-glass windows, gilded ceilings, and brass chandeliers. Before the revolution it specialized in imported delicacies, and after several lean decades, goods again overflow its shelves. (The Moscow branch is on Tverskaya ulitsa.)

26 As you pass Sadovaya ulitsa, taking up the entire block on the other side of the street is the huge **Gostinny Dvor,** St. Petersburg's answer to the GUM department store in Moscow. Started by Rastrelli in 1757, it was not completed until 1785, by Vallin de la Mothe, who was responsible for the facade with its two tiers of arches. When it was erected, traveling merchants were routinely put up in guest houses (called *gostinny dvor*), which, like this one, doubled as places for doing business. This arcade was completely rebuilt in the last century, by which time it housed some 200 general-purpose shops that were far less elegant than those in other parts of the Nevsky. It remained a functional bazaar until alterations in the 1950s and 1960s connected most of its separate shops into St. Petersburg's largest department store. Many sections of the store are operating, but a large portion of Gostinny Dvor has been gutted, undergoing what Russians call "capital" repairs. Virtually across the street is the city's other major "department store," also an arcade, called Passazh (Passage) and built in 1848.

TIME OUT The **Konditorei** on the other side of Nevsky Prospect, at No. 40, offers a soothing place to take a break. The wood-paneled interior and parquet ceilings have been restored to their original, prerevolutionary appearance. Coffee, ice cream, and scrumptious cakes are available in a no-smoking environment. If you're looking for something more substantial, try the German restaurant and bar next door.

On its side of the street, a bit farther down, at nos. 40–42, is the blue-and-white **Armenian Church,** built by Velten between 1771 and 1780 and set back from the street. A fine example of early Classical style, the church fell into disrepair and is under full restoration, but it is holding some services and is open to the public. At the corner of Mikhailovskaya ulitsa is the **Grand Europe Hotel** (*see* Tour 5).

You will next notice, at No. 34, another recessed church, the Catholic **Church of St. Catherine.** Built between 1762 and 1783 by Vallin de la Mothe and Antonio Rinaldi, it is done in a mixture of Baroque and Classical, styles that were then converging in Russia. The grave of the last king of Poland (and yet another lover of Catherine the Great), Stanislaw Poniatowski, is here.

On the corner across, at No. 33, stands a building with a notable red-and-white tower. This was **Gorodskaya Duma** (City Duma), the city hall under the czars. Its clock tower, meant to resemble those in European cities, was erected by Ferrari between 1799 and 1804. It was equipped with signaling devices that sent messages between the Winter Palace and the royal summer residences.

27 Cross the short Kazan Bridge over the Griboyedov Canal, and you'll come to the city's largest bookstore, which still goes by its generic Soviet name **Dom Knigi** (House of Books). Before the revolution, it was the offices of the Singer Sewing Machine Company, whose distinctive globe trademark still adorns the roof. Here one finds Russians in a favorite pursuit, buying and perusing books. The store contains a wonderful collection of books and maps.

28 Across the street from Dom Knigi is one of the city's more resplendent works of architecture, the **Kazansky Sobor** (Kazan Cathedral). Czar Paul I commissioned it after a visit to Rome, wishing to copy—and perhaps present the Orthodox rival to—St. Peter's. Erected between 1801 and 1811 to a design by Andrei Voronikhin, the huge cathedral is approached through a monumental, semicircular colonnade. Inside and out, the church abounds with sculpture and decoration. On the Nevsky side the frontage holds statues of St. John the Baptist and the apostle Andrew as well as such sanctified Russian heroes as Vladimir and Alexander Nevsky. Take note of the enormous bronze front doors. They are exact copies of Ghiberti's Gates of Heaven at Florence's Baptistery.

In 1932 the cathedral, which was closed right after the revolution, was turned into the Museum of Religion and Atheism, with the emphasis on the latter. The history of religion was presented from the Marxist point of view, essentially as ossified archaeological artifact. The museum still operates here but has dropped the 'Atheism' from its name and reorganized its displays. Simultaneously, it is again open as a place of worship, with services resumed in the cathedral.

Back outside the church, have a look at the square that forms its front lawn. At each end are statues of a military leader, one of Mikhail Barclay de Tolly, the other of Mikhail Kutuzov. Both reflect the importance in the 19th century of the cathedral as a place of military tribute, specifically after Napoléon's invasion in 1812. Kutuzov is buried in the cathedral's northern chapel, where he is supposed to have prayed before taking command of the Russian forces. *2 Kazanskaya Ploshchad,* ☎ *812/312–0495 or 812/312–3586.* ✆ *Mon., Tues., Thurs.–Sat. 11–5; Sun. 2–6. Church services Mon.–Sat. at 9 AM and 6 PM, Sun. and holidays at 10 AM.*

Crossing the street and continuing one block down Nevsky, you'll reach the **Lutheran Church,** another church on a recessed lot. Designed by Alexander Briyullov, its rounded arches and simple towers follow the Romanesque tradition. This church currently cannot be used at all. Its fate echoed that of the giant Cathedral of Christ Our Savior in Moscow: During the years when religion was repressed, this church also was turned into a municipal swimming pool. When you enter, go up the staircase to the third floor. From the upper bleachers, you can look down at the remnants of the pool that is slowly being ripped out, to be turned anew into a church. Farther down, at No. 20, is the **Dutch Church** (now a library), yet another reminder of the religions that once peacefully coexisted in old St. Petersburg.

Return now to the other side of the street. Before you cross the little bridge spanning the Moika Canal, you'll be at the magnificent green building overlooking the embankment. This is the former **Stroganov Palace,** completed in 1754. This palace is an outstanding example of Russian Baroque and one of Rastrelli's finest achievements. Its entrance is unique, in that it faces Nevsky Prospect. Above the archway, you will still find the family coat of arms: two sables holding a shield with a bear's head above. It symbolizes the Stroganovs' source of wealth— vast holdings of land with all its resources, including furs—in Siberia. You can go into the courtyard and even peek inside, for there is a small branch of the applied arts section of the Russian Museum operating here; the renovation is extensive but far from complete. Unfortunately, most of the palace's interior was ravaged by fire at the end of the 18th century, though the outside remained intact. As you leave, it's fun to remember that this was the birthplace of beef Stroganoff.

On the last few blocks of Nevsky Prospect are a few more buildings of historical importance. No. 18, on the right-hand side, is the **Literary Café.** Originally a private dwelling, Kotomin's house, it subsequently held a café called the Wulf and Beranger. Reportedly, it was here that Pushkin ate his last meal before setting off for his fatal duel. Called **Chicherin's House,** No. 15 was one of Empress Elizabeth's palaces before becoming the Nobles' Assembly and, in 1919, the House of Arts. Farther down, at No. 14, is one of the rare buildings on Nevsky Prospect built *after* the Bolshevik Revolution. The blue sign on the facade dates from World War II and the siege of Leningrad. It warns pedestrians that during air raids the other side of street is safer. The city was once covered with similar warnings; this one was left in place as a memorial.

The golden building of the Admiralty marks the end of Nevsky Prospect. To return to the subway, take trolleybus 1, 5, 7, or 14 one stop to Nevsky Prospect Station. Since trolley buses on Nevsky are notoriously over-crowded, you might prefer to walk. Palace Square and the Winter Palace, if you somehow haven't noticed, are nearby, across from the street flank-ing the Admiralty's right side.

Tour 5: From the Square of the Arts to the Field of Mars

This tour takes you to some of St. Petersburg's prettiest inner streets, squares, and gardens, starting at Ploshchad Iskusstv (Square of the Arts). To get there, go down Nevsky Prospect (you can take the subway to the stop of the same name) to ulitsa Mikhailovskaya. Walking up this short street will take you past the handsome Grand Hotel Europe, built in the 1870s. Given its Art Nouveau facade in 1910, it remains one of St. Petersburg's most elegant places of lodging.

Straight up this street is the plaza, originally named Mikhailovsky Ploshchad for Grand Duke Mikhail Pavlovich (1798–1849), the **30** younger brother of Alexander I and Nicholas I. His palace, **Mikhailovsky Dvorets,** stands at the square's far end.

The square's appearance is the work of Carlo Rossi, who designed the facade of each building encircling it as well as the palace. Each structure as well as the plaza itself, with its statue of Alexander Pushkin, was made to complement Mikhail's residence on its north side. Built between 1819 and 1825, it comprises a principal house and two service wings. The cen-tral portico with eight Corinthian columns faces a large courtyard now enclosed by a fine Art Nouveau railing, a late (1903) addition.

The building to the right of the palace appears to be an extension of the right wing but is a different building entirely, the **Ethnography Mu-seum.** It contains a fascinating collection of applied art and many so-ciological displays about peoples of the 19th and 20th centuries, including the various ethnic groups of the former Soviet Union. *4/1 In-zhenernaya ulitsa,* ☎ *812/219–1174 or 812/219–1676.* ☉ *Tues.–Sun. 11–6. Closed last Fri. of month.*

If you stand in front of the palace and turn to survey the entire square, the first building on your right, with old-fashioned lanterns adorning its doorways, is the **Mussorgsky Theater of Opera and Ballet,** better **31** known as the **Maly Theater** (Little Theater), as it was called from 1917 to 1991. Before the revolution it was the Mikhailovsky Theater, but French companies performed here so often that it was more com-monly referred to as the French Theater. Today it is St. Petersburg's second most important theater, after the Mariinsky (Kirov).

The next house, No. 3, was built in the 1820s for the Golenshishchev-Kutuzovs, a high-ranking military family. From 1924 to 1939, the painter Isaac Brodsky lived here, and the house is now a memorial museum to him. On view are some of his works as well as some from his pri-vate collection, which included pieces by Ilya Repin and Valentin Serov. *3 Ploshchad Iskusstv,* ☎ *812/314–3658.* ☉ *Mon.–Sat. 11–8.*

Popularly known as "Jacquot's House," No. 5 had a famous café *cum* art salon in its basement from 1911 to 1915, called the Stray Dog. A diverse range of painters, writers, and musicians including Anna

Akhmatova, Nikolai Gumilev, and Osip Mandelstam used it as a creative meeting point.

Bordering the square's south side, on Mikhailovskaya ulitsa's east corner, is the former **Nobles' Club,** now home to the **St. Petersburg Philharmonic.** Its main concert hall, with its impressive marble columns, has been the site of many famous performances, including Tchaikovsky conducting his own Sixth (*Pathetique*) Symphony, his final masterpiece. (He died 9 days after doing so.) More recently, in 1942, when Leningrad was completely blockaded, Dmitri Shostakovich's Seventh (*Leningrad*) Symphony was premiered here, an event broadcast in the same spirit of defiance against the Germans in which it was written. Later the concert hall was officially named for Shostakovich.

The buildings on the square's remaining side are former residences and school buildings, including a boys' high school at No. 4. They all now belong to the Russian Museum.

★ **The Russian Museum,** one of the country's most important art galleries, has been housed in the Mikhailovsky Palace since 1896, when Nicholas II turned it into a museum. He did so in tribute to his father, Alexander III, who had a special regard for Russian art and regretted, after seeing Moscow's Tretyakov Gallery, that St. Petersburg had nothing like it. The museum's entrance is around the corner. Leave the Square of Arts and go down ulitsa Inzhenernaya toward the Griboyedev (Ekaterinsky) Canal. Take a right and you will find the entrance a few steps away.

Officially named the Gosudarstvenny Muzey Russkovo Isskustvo (State Museum of Russian Art), its collection is now the equal—or more important, the complement—of the Tretyakov's, with scores of masterpieces on display. Outstanding icons include the 14th-century *Boris and Gleb* and the 15th-century *Angel Miracle of St. George.* Seventeenth and 18th-century paintings are also well represented, especially with portraiture. One of the most famous 18th-century works here is Ivan Nikitin's *The Field Hetman.* By far the most important cache, however, comprises 19th-century works—huge canvases by Repin, many fine portraits by Serov (his beautiful *Countess Orlova* and the equally beautiful, utterly different portrait of the dancer Ida Rubinstein), and Mikhail Vrubel's strange, disturbing *Demon Cast Down.* Since so little of this work was well known in the West, it is fascinating to see stylistic parallels and the incorporation of outside influences into a Russian framework. Painters of the World of Art movement—Bakst, Benois, and Somov—are also here. There are several examples of 20th-century art, with works by Kandinsky and Kazimir Malevich. Natan Altman's striking portrait of the poet Anna Akhmatova is in Room 77. The museum usually has at least one excellent special exhibit going on. *4/2 Inzhenernaya ul.,* ☎ *812/219–1615,* ℻ *812/314–4153.* ☉ *Mon. and Wed.–Sun. 10–6.*

Go right when you leave the museum, and facing you straight ahead is the almost outrageously colorful **Khram Spasa na Krovi** (Church of the Saviour on the Spilled Blood). Its highly ornate, old Russian style seems more befitting to Moscow than St. Petersburg, where the architecture is generally more subdued and subtle; and indeed, the architect Alfred Parland was consciously aiming to copy Moscow's St. Basil's. The drama of the church's inception more than matches the frenzy of its design, however. It was commissioned by Alexander III to memorialize the shocking death of his father, Alexander II, who was killed in 1881 on the site by a terrorist's bomb.

The church opened in 1907 but was closed by Stalin in the 1930s. It suffered damage throughout the years, especially during World War II. Under meticulous reconstruction for decades (painstaking attempts have been made to replace all original components with identically matched materials), it is due to reopen by 1996. The interiors reportedly are as extravagant as the exterior, with glittering stretches of mosaic from floor to ceiling. Scenes of martyrdom include one that draws a parallel between the czar's death and the crucifixion of Christ. Stone carvings and gold leaf adorn the walls, the floors are all of pink Italian marble, and the remarkable altar is made entirely of semiprecious gems and supported by four jasper columns.

To the right as you walk past the church is a small park behind a lovely wrought-iron fence. Known as **Mikhailovsky Sad** (Mikhailov Gardens), it forms the back of the Grand Duke's former estate. One the other side of this pleasant park runs Sadovaya ulitsa.

★ ㉞ You should follow the street you're on, however, as it curves around gently to the right. Opposite the gardens' outer edge, across the street, spreads **Marsovo Pole** (Field of Mars). The site was once a marsh, from which both the Mya and the Krikusha rivers began. Peter the Great had it drained (and the rivers linked by a canal), and the space was subsequently used for parades and public occasions. The field acquired its present name around 1800, when it began to be used primarily for military exercises. Shortly after 1917, it was turned into a burial ground for Red Army victims of the revolution and ensuing civil war. The massive granite **Monument to Revolutionary Fighters** was unveiled there on November 7, 1919, with an eternal flame lit 40 years later, also on the revolution's anniversary.

The long line of buildings flanking the left side of Marsovo Pole are the former **Barracks of the Pavlovsky Guards Regiment.** They were completed in 1819, in homage to the regiment's victories in the war against Napoléon. Go down this side of the street, and you will reach **Millionaya ulitsa** (Millionaire's Street), which, as the name implies, was once one of St. Petersburg's swankest.

㉟ On this street, in front of you, is the **Mramorny Dvorets** (Marble Palace), designed by Arnoldo Rinaldi and built between 1768 and 1785 for Grigori Orlov, one of Catherine the Great's favorites, but not completed until after his death. Its name derives from its pale pink-purple marble facing. From 1937 to 1991, it housed the Lenin Museum; in the courtyard was the armored automobile from which he made his revolutionary speech at the Finland Station. The palace now belongs to the Russian Museum.

Take a right and walk down Millionaya Street the length of Mars Field.
㊱ On the left you will pass **Suvorovskaya Ploshchad** (Suvorov Square), where there is a statue of the military commander Alexander Suvorov, cast as Mars, god of war. Appropriately enough, when first unveiled in 1801, the statue stood in Marsovo Pole, but in 1818 it was moved to its present location.

Walk up to the river and continue going east (right). Very soon you will find yourself in front of the marvelous grille railing that marks the entrance to **Letny Sad** (Summer Gardens). The graceful wrought-iron fence, designed in 1779 by Yuri Felten, is supported by pink granite pillars decorated with vases and urns.

★ ㊲ The Summer Garden was another of Peter the Great's passions, inspired by Versailles. When first laid out in 1704, it was given a regular, geometric style and decorated with statues and sculptures as well as imported trees and plants. Grottoes, pavilions, ponds, fountains, and intricate walkways were woven throughout it, and it is bordered on all sides by rivers and canals. In 1777, however, disastrous floods did so much damage (including entirely destroying the system of fountains) that the imperial family stopped using the garden for entertaining. When they decamped for environs farther afield, they left the Summer Garden to the public use of the upper classes. Today it remains a popular park, accessible to everyone, but you will have to imagine the first formal gardens, for they are no longer there.

You enter at the far left end of the railing. Just inside this southeastern corner is Peter's original Summer Palace, **Letny Dvorets.** Designed by Domenico Trezzini and completed in 1714, the two-story building is quite simple in design, as most of Peter's dwellings were. The walls are of stucco-covered brick, painted primrose yellow. Open since 1934 as a museum, it has survived without major alteration. Two other attractive buildings nearby are the **Coffee House** (built by Rossi in 1826) and the **Tea House** (by L. I. Charlemagne in 1827), neither of which, alas, serves the beverages for which they are named.

As you walk through the park, have a look at some of its statues, of which more than 80 still remain. You can see *Peace and Abundance,* sculpted by Pietro Baratta in 1722, an allegorical depiction of Russia's victory in the war with Sweden. Another statue, just off the main alley, is of Ivan Krylov, "Russia's La Fontaine." It is by Peter Klodt (who also did the Anichkov Bridge horse statues) and was unveiled in 1855. Scenes from Krylov's fables, including his version of "The Fox and the Grapes," appear on the pedestal. As in many other parks and public places, the sculptures are protected from the harsh weather with wooden covers from early fall to late spring.

Exiting at the south end of the park will bring you out in front of the former castle of Czar Paul I, across the street. Called the **Inzhenerny Zamok** (Engineer's Castle), this orange-hued building belonged to one of Russia's stranger and more pitiful leaders. Paul I grew up in the shadow of his powerful mother, Catherine the Great, whom he despised; no doubt correctly, he held her responsible for his father's death. By the time Paul became czar, he lived in terror that he, too, would be murdered. He claimed that, shortly after ascending the throne, the Archangel Michael appeared to him in a dream and instructed him to build a church on the site of his birthplace. Paul then proceeded to erect not just a church but a castle, which he tried to make into an impenetrable fortress. Out of spite toward his mother, he took stones and other materials from castles that she had built. The Fontanka and Moika rivers cut off access from the north and east; and for protection everywhere else, he installed secret passages, moats with drawbridges, and earthen ramparts. All of Paul's intricate planning, however, came to naught. On March 24, 1801, a month after he began living there, he was murdered—suffocated with a pillow in his bed. Historians speculate that his own son, Alexander I, knew such a plot was underway and may even have participated.

After Paul's death, the castle stood empty for 20 years, when it was turned over to the Military Engineering Academy. One of the school's pupils was Fyodor Dostoevsky, who as a novelist was absorbed with themes of murder and greed. The building now belongs to the Russian Museum.

The tour ends here. From the castle, you can walk down ulitsa Sadovaya until it intersects with Nevsky Prospect. If you take the first right off of it, you will return to the Square of Arts. If you like, you can stop in the Mikhailovsky Gardens now; there is an entrance on this side, to the right.

TIME OUT The Grand Hotel Europe has a lovely mezzanine café, where you can relax and enjoy a pot of tea or a glass of champagne, served with bowls of strawberries. While there, take a peek at the beautifully renovated Art Nouveau lobby, replete with stained-glass windows and antique furnishings.

Excursion 1: Petrodvorets (Peterhof)

Several extraordinary palaces are located in the suburbs of St. Petersburg. Following the 1917 Revolution, these former summer residences of the czars were nationalized and turned into public museums. They can all be reached by commuter trains (*elektrichka*), but the simplest way to see the palaces is to book an excursion (available through any tour company). The cost is reasonable and covers transportation, guided tour, and admission fee.

During World War II and the siege of Leningrad, most of the suburban palaces were occupied by enemy forces and used as army headquarters, barracks, or stables. At the end of the war, what little remained of the former palaces was burned and looted by the retreating German troops. Museum workers had managed to evacuate much of the art housed in the palaces before the German occupation, but for the most part the original interiors were lost forever. Painstaking restoration using pieces of fabric, photographs, and written descriptions has returned the palaces to their former splendor, although some renovation work is still ongoing.

An organized excursion to any of the suburban palaces will take at least four hours. If you travel on your own, it's likely to take up the entire day. Although you'll find some cafeterias and cafés, they're nothing special, so you may prefer to pack a lunch or bring a snack with you.

Of all the palaces you will see in Russia, one that will make a distinct and lasting impression is **Petrodvorets,** situated on the shore of the Baltic Sea, some 29 kilometers (18 miles) from St. Petersburg. Petrodvorets, originally called Peterhof, is more than just a summer palace: It is an imperial playground replete with lush parks, monumental cascades, and gilded fountains.

Petrodvorets is best visited in summer; a winter visit can be quite disappointing. From late September to early June the fountains and cascades are closed down, acquiring the depressing look of a drained pool. You can reach the palace by commuter train from St. Petersburg, but, minimal fog permitting, the best way to go is by hydrofoil, by which your first view is the panorama of the grand palace overlooking the sea. Be aware that the lines to get into the palace can be excruciatingly long in the summer. Sometimes guided tours get preferential treatment. *Ul. Kominterna, town of Petrodvorets,* ☎ *812/427–9527. Great Palace open Tues.–Sun. 10:30–6. Closed 1st Tues. of month. Transportation: commuter train from Baltisky Vokzal (Baltic Station) to Novy Petergof Station, approximately 40 min from St. Petersburg. From station take Bus 351 to Dvorets. In summer, hydrofoils to Petrodvorets leave from pier outside the Hermitage Museum approximately every 30 min. Ride takes about ½ hr.*

Petrodvorets

TO ST. PETERSBURG

Gulf of Finland

Alexandria Park

Lower Park

Upper Park

Adam Fountain, **12**
Bird Cages, **18**
Bolshoi Dvorets, **8**
Chess Hill, **15**
Cup Fountains, **6**
Eve Fountain, **5**
Golden Hill
Cascade, **2**

Great Cascade, **7**
Hermitage Pavilion, **4**
Hydrofoil Pier, **1**
Little Oak
Fountain, **14**
Marly Palace, **3**
Mezheumny
Fountain, **11**

Monplaisir, **20**
Neptune Fountain, **10**
Oak Fountain, **9**
Pyramid Fountain, **16**
Sun Fountain, **19**
Triton Fountain, **13**
Umbrella Fountain, **17**

The myriad complex of gardens and residences at Petrodvorets was masterminded by Peter the Great, who personally drew up the first plans, starting around 1720. His motivation was twofold. First, he was proud of the capital city that he was building and wanted its newmade imperial grandeur showcased with a proper summer palace. Second, he became attached to this spot while erecting the naval fortress of Kronstadt on a nearby island across the Gulf of Finland; because it lay in easy view, he often stayed here during the fort's construction. When it was finished, at a time when he had had a series of naval victories (including the Northern War against the Swedes), he threw himself into establishing many parts of the grounds that would be called Peterhof (Peter's Court), a German name changed to Petrodvorets after World War II.

If you travel by hydrofoil, you will arrive at the pier of the Lower Park, from where you work your way up to the Grand Palace. If you arrive by land, you'll simply go through the process in reverse. Either way, the perspective always emphasizes the mightiness of water. Half-encircled by the sea, filled with fountains and other water monuments, with the Marine Canal running straight from the foot of the palace into the bay—Peter's place was also his loving tribute to the role of water in the life, and strength, of his city. The Lower Park was a formal Baroque garden in the French style adorned with statues, fountains, and cascades. Peter's playful spirit is still very much in evidence here. The fun-loving czar installed "trick fountains"—hidden water sprays built into trees and tiny plazas and brought to life by stepping on a certain stone or moving a lever, much to the surprise of the unsuspecting visitor and the delight of the squealing children who love to race through the showers on hot summer days.

Located in the eastern half of Lower Park is the oldest building at Petrodvorets, **Monplaisir** (literally "My Pleasure"). This is where Peter the Great lived while overseeing construction of the main imperial residence, and as was often the case with Peter, he greatly preferred this modest Dutch-style villa to his later, more extravagant living quarters. The house is open to the public and makes a pleasant tour. Some of its most interesting rooms are the **Lacquered Study,** decorated with replicas of panels (the originals were destroyed during World War II) painted in Chinese style; Peter's **Naval Study;** and his bedroom, where personal effects, such as his nightcap and a quilt made by his wife, are on display. Attached to Peter's villa is the so-called **Catherine Wing,** built by Rastrelli in the mid-18th century, in an utterly different style. The future Catherine the Great was staying here at the time of the coup that overthrew her husband and placed her on the throne; it was later used mainly for holding balls.

In the western section of the Lower Park, you can find another famous structure, the **Hermitage.** This two-story pavilion gives new meaning to the concept of a movable feast. The building, which was used primarily as a banqueting hall (for special guests), was at one time equipped with a device that would lift the dining table—diners and all—from the ground floor to the private dining room above. A slightly different system was put in place after Czar Paul I's chair broke while doing this. The center part of the table could be lifted out, and guests would write down their dinner preferences and then signal for their notes to be lifted away. Shortly thereafter, the missing piece would be lowered, complete with the meals everyone had ordered. The only way to the Hermitage was over a drawbridge, thus ensuring privacy.

A walk up the path through the center of the Lower Park (along the Marine Canal) leads you to the famous **Great Cascade.** Running down the steep ridge separating the Lower Park and the Grand Palace towering above, the cascade comprises three waterfalls, 64 fountains, and 37 gilded statues. The system of waterworks has remained virtually unchanged since 1721. The ducts and pipes, which convey water over a distance of some 20 kilometers (12 miles), work without pumping stations: The water flows downhill, while the fountains operate on the principle of communicating vessels. The centerpiece of the waterfalls is a gilded Samson rending the jaws of a lion from which a jet of water spurts into the air. The statue represents the Russian victory over the Swedes at Poltava on St. Samson's day. The present figure is a meticulous replica of the original, which was carried away by the Germans.

Crowning the ridge above the cascade is the magnificent **Bolshoi Dvorets** (Great Palace). Little remains of Peter's original two-story house, built between 1714 and 1725 under the architects Leblond, Braunstein, and Machetti. The building was altered considerably and enlarged by Peter's daughter Elizabeth. She entrusted the reconstruction to her favorite architect, the Italian Bartolomeo Rastrelli, who transformed the modest residence into a sumptuous blend of medieval architecture and Russian Baroque. Before you begin your tour of the palace interiors, pause for a moment to enjoy the breathtaking view from the marble terrace. From here a full view of the grounds below unfolds, stretching from the cascades to the Gulf of Finland to the city horizon on the shore beyond.

An integral part of visiting any museum-palace in Russia is encountering the autocratic *babushki* who now control them. In this, Petrodvorets is no exception. No matter how annoying, they deserve respect, for they have survived the 900-day siege of Leningrad, witnessed the palaces' destruction, and seen their nearly miraculous rise from the ashes. As you enter the palace, you will be given tattered shoe covers to protect the highly polished floors as you walk through the splendid halls. One cautionary note: On most occasions flash photography is not allowed, although for a fee, fast film and videotaping are. Sometimes the babushki aren't aware of the difference. So hang on tight to your equipment to avoid having it confiscated by an overzealous custodian of Peter's treasures.

The palace's lavish interiors are primarily the work of Rastrelli, although several of the rooms were redesigned during the reign of Catherine the Great in accordance with the architectural style of her day, Classicism. Of Peter's original design, only his **Dubovy Kabinet** (Oak Cabinet) survived the numerous reconstructions. The fine oak panels (some are originals) lining the walls were designed by the French sculptor Pineau. The entire room and all its furnishings are made of wood, with the exception of the white marble fireplace, above which hangs a long mirror framed in carved oak.

One of the largest rooms in the palace is the **Tronny Zal** (Throne Room), which takes up the entire width of the building. Classically designed, this majestic room—once the scene of great receptions and official ceremonies—features exquisite parquet floors, fine stucco ceiling moldings, and dazzling chandeliers. The pale green and dark red decor is bathed in light, which pours in through the two tiers of windows (28 in all) taking up the long sides of the room. Behind Peter the Great's throne at the eastern end of the room hangs a huge portrait of Catherine the Great. The empress, a picture of confidence after her successful coup, is shown riding a horse, dressed in the uniform of the guards regiment that supported her bid for power.

Next to the Throne Room is the **Chesmensky Zal** (Chesma Hall), whose interior is dedicated entirely to the Russian naval victory over the Turks in 1770. The walls are covered with 12 huge oil canvases depicting the battles, which were created by the German painter P. Hackert at Empress Catherine's behest. According to legend, the artist complained that he could not paint a burning ship since he had never seen one. Catherine arranged to have ships blown up for him to use as models. Such were the days of divine right. Arguably the most dazzling of the palace's rooms is the **Audients Zal** (Audience Hall). Rastrelli created the definitive Baroque interior with this glittering room of white, red, and gold. Gilded Baroque bas-reliefs adorn the stark white walls, along which tall mirrors are hung, further accentuating the richness of the decor.

Other notable rooms include the **Kitaiskye Kabinety** (the Chinese Study Rooms), designed by Vallin de Mothe in the 1760s. As was the fashion in Europe at the time, the rooms are ornately decorated with Chinese motifs. Finely carved black-lacquered panels depict various Chinese scenes. Between the two rooms is the **Kartinny Zal** (Picture Hall), whose walls are paneled with 368 oil paintings by the Italian artist Rotari. The artist used just eight models for these paintings, which depict young women in national dress.

After a tour of the palace interiors, a stroll through the Upper Park is in order. Located on the south side of the palace, this formal garden with its symmetrical design is far less imaginative than the Lower Park, with its playful fountains and cascading waterfalls. Its focal point is the Neptune Fountain, originally made in Germany in the 17th century and bought by Paul I in 1782. During the war the three-tiered group of bronze sculptures was carried away by the Germans. It was eventually recovered and reinstalled in 1956.

Excursion 2: Pushkin (Tsarskoye Selo)

The town of **Pushkin,** located 24 kilometers (15 miles) south of St. Petersburg, was the summer residence of the imperial family from the days of Peter the Great right up to the last years of the Romanov dynasty. Formerly known as **Tsarskoye Selo** (the czar's village), its name was changed after the 1917 Revolution, first to Detskoye (Children's) Selo and then to Pushkin, in honor of the great Russian poet who studied at the lyceum here. During the 18th and 19th centuries, Tsarskoye Selo was a popular summer resort for St. Petersburg's aristocracy and well-to-do. Not only was the royal family close by, but it was here, in 1837, that Russia's first railroad line was opened, running between Tsarskoye Selo and Pavlosk, followed three years later by a line between here and St. Petersburg.

★ Pushkin's main attraction is the dazzling **Yekaterininsky Dvorets** (Catherine Palace), a perfect example of Russian Baroque. The exterior is painted bright turquoise and features row after row of white columns and pilasters with gold Baroque moldings alternating the entire length (985 feet) of the facade. Although much of the palace's history and its inner architectural design bears Catherine the Great's stamp, it is for Catherine I, Peter the Great's second wife, that the palace is named. Under Empress Elizabeth, their daughter, the original modest stone palace was completely rebuilt. The project was initially entrusted to the Russian architects Kvasov and Chevakinsky, but in 1752 Elizabeth brought in the Italian architect Bartolomeo Rastrelli (who went on to build the Winter Palace in St. Petersburg). Although Catherine the Great had the interiors remodeled in the Classical style, she left

Alexander Park

Catherine Park

Great Pond

Aleksandrovsky
Dvorets, **4**
Cameron Gallery, **9**
Cameron's
Pyramid, **10**
Canal, **16**
Chapel, **1**
Chesma Column, **11**

Chinese Theater, **2**
Chinese Village, **3**
Concert Hall, **8**
English Garden, **17**
Great Pond, **14**
Grotto, **15**
Lyceum, **7**

Marble Bridge, **12**
Pushkin
Monument, **6**
Ruined Tower, **13**
Yekaterininsky
Dvorets (Catherine
Palace), **5**

Rastrelli's stunning facade untouched. *7 ul. Komsomolskaya, town of Pushkin,* ☎ *812/465–3429.* ☉ *Wed.–Mon. 10–5. Closed last Mon. of month. Park open daily. Transportation: commuter train from Vitebsky Vokzal (Vitebsk Station) to Pushkin–Detskoe Selo, approximately 30 min from St. Petersburg. From station take Bus 371 or 382 to Dvorets (palace).*

You'll enter the palace grounds through the gilded and black iron gates designed by Rastrelli. The *E* atop is for Catherine (Ekaterina in Russian) the First's initial. To your right, a visual feast unfolds as you walk the length of the long blue-and-gold facade toward the museum entrance. Sparkling above the palace at the northern end are the golden cupolas of the Palace Church. Inside, the palace is just as spectacular; many of the rooms are famous in their own right. While little of Rastrelli's original interior remains, the many additions and alterations made between 1760 and 1790 under Catherine the Great do; these were carried out by top architects, the Scottish Charles Cameron and the Italian Giacomo Quarenghi.

Entering the palace by the main staircase, which was not added until 1861, you will see displays showing the extent of the wartime damage and the subsequent restoration work. Like Peterhof, the palace was almost completely destroyed during World War II. It was used by the occupying Nazi forces as army barracks, and as the Germans retreated, they blew up what remained of the former imperial residence. Today the palace again stands in all its glory, although the interior is still being restored.

The largest and arguably most impressive room is the **Bolshoi Zal** (Great Hall), which was used for receptions and balls. The longer sides are taken up by two tiers of gilt-framed windows. Tall, elaborately carved gilded mirrors have been placed between them. The light pouring in through the windows bounces off the mirrors and sparkles on the gilt, amplifying the impression of spaciousness and light. The huge ceiling painting, depicting Russian military victories and accomplishments in the sciences and arts, makes the room seem even larger. It is easy here to imagine the extravagant lifestyles of St. Petersburg's prerevolutionary elite.

On the north side of the State Staircase is one of the palace's most famous rooms, the **Yantarnaya Komnata** (Amber Room), so named for the engraved amber panels that once lined its walls. A treaty gift to Peter the Great from the king of Prussia in 1716, all the panels were stolen by the Nazis. They have never been found, and while speculation continues to circulate about their eventual rediscovery, in 1979 the Soviet government finally gave up hope of ever retrieving them and began the costly work of restoring the room. The restoration is far from complete, but the few restored panels—and a prewar black-and-white photograph of the room—give you some idea of how marvelous the original interior was.

Leaving the Amber Room, you will come to the large **Kartinny Zal** (Picture Gallery), which runs the full width of the palace. The paintings are all from Western Europe and date from the 17th to the early 18th century.

Highlights among the other splendid rooms on the north side include the Blue Drawing Room, the Blue Chinese Room, and the Choir Anteroom, all of which face the courtyard. Each has pure silk wall-coverings. The Blue Chinese Room, originally designed by Cameron, has been restored on the basis of the architect's drawings. Despite its name, it is a purely Classical interior, and the only thing even remotely Chinese is the Oriental motif on the blue silk covering the wall. The fine golden-yellow silk of the Choir Anteroom is from the same swatch used to decorate the room in the 18th century. When the postwar restoration began, an extra supply of the original silk was discovered tucked away in a storage room of the Hermitage.

Having savored the treasures inside the palace, you can now begin exploring the beautiful **Yekaterininsky Park** outside, with its marble statues, waterfalls, garden alleys, and boating ponds, pavilions, bridges, and quays. The park is split into two sections. The inner, formal section, known as the French Garden, runs down the terraces in front of the palace's eastern facade. The outer section centers around the Great Pond and is in the less rigid style of an English garden. If you follow the main path through the French Garden and down the terrace, you will eventually reach Rastrelli's Hermitage, which he completed just before turning his attention to the palace itself. Other highlights of the French Garden include the Upper and Lower Bath pavilions (1777–79) and Rastrelli's elaborate blue-domed Grotto.

There is much to be seen in the English Garden, too. A good starting point is the **Cameron Gallery,** which actually forms a continuation of the palace's parkside frontage. It is over to the right (with your back to the palace). Open only in the summer, it contains a museum of 18th- and 19th-century costumes. From its portico you get the best views of the park and its lakes—which is exactly what Cameron had in mind when he designed it for Catherine the Great in the 1780s. The double-sided staircase leading majestically down to the Great Pond is flanked by two bronze sculptures of Hercules and Flora.

From here, go down and begin your exploration of the park. Just beyond the island in the middle of the Great Pond, which is actually an artificial lake, stands the **Chesma Column,** marking the Russian naval victory in the Aegean in 1770. At the far end of the pond is **Cameron's Pyramid,** where Catherine the Great reportedly buried her favorite dogs.

If you follow the pond around its right side, you will come to the pretty, blue-and-white **Marble Bridge,** which connects the Great Pond with a series of other ones and small canals. At this end, you can rent rowboats. Further beyond, up to the right, you will find the "**Ruined Tower.**" It's not authentic or old, just built to enhance the romantic ambience of these grounds.

Outside the park, just north of the Catherine Palace, stands yet another palace, the **Alexandrovsky Dvorets,** a present from Catherine to her favorite grandson, the future Czar Alexander I, on the occasion of his marriage. Built by Quarenghi between 1792 and 1796, the serene and restrained Classical structure was the favorite residence of Russia's last czar, Nicholas II. The building is not open to the public.

Attached to the Catherine Palace is the **Lyceum.** Built in 1791 and originally intended for the education of Catherine the Great's grandchildren, it later became a school for the nobility. Its most famous student, who was enrolled the first year it opened, was the adored Alexander Pushkin. The building is now open as a museum; and the classroom, library, and Pushkin's bedroom have been restored to their appearance at the time he studied there. In the school's garden is a statue of the poet as a young man, sitting on a bench, presumably deep in verse.

Excursion 3: Pavlovsk

The imperial estate of Paul I (in Russian Pavel, hence Pavlovsk) is located some 30 kilometers (18 miles) south of St. Petersburg and only 5 kilometers (3 miles) from Pushkin and the Catherine Palace. Because of the proximity of the two towns, it's often suggested that tours to them be combined. If you decide to do this, make sure to give yourself enough time to do justice to both.

The estate grounds of Pavlovsk had always been the royal hunting grounds, but in 1777 Catherine the Great awarded them to her son Paul I, upon the birth of his first son (future czar Alexander I). Construction of the first wooden buildings started immediately, and in 1782 Catherine's Scottish architect Charles Cameron began work on the Great Palace and the landscaped park. In contrast to the dramatically Baroque palaces of Pushkin and Peterhof, Pavlovsk is a tribute to the reserved beauty of Classicism. Paul's intense dislike of his mother apparently manifested itself in determinedly doing exactly what she would *not*— and here, visitors may be grateful, to excellent result. The place is popular with St. Petersburg residents, who come here to stroll through the 600-hectare (1,500-acre) park, with its woods, ponds, alleys, and pavilions. *20 ul. Revolutsia, town of Pavlovsk, ☎ 812/470–6965. ☉ Tues.–Sun. 10–5:00. Closed 1st Tues. of month. Transportation: commuter train from Vitebsky Vokzal (Vitebsk Station) to Pavlovsk, approximately 25–35 min from St. Petersburg. From station walk to palace, or take Bus 370 or 383.*

A tour of Pavlovsk begins with the **Bolshoi Dvorets** (Great Palace), which stands on a high bluff overlooking the river and dominates the surrounding park. The building is painted golden yellow and crowned with a flat, green dome supported by 64 small white columns. Built in 1782–86 to be the summer residence of Paul and his wife, Maria Fyodorovna, the original design of this stone palace was based on a Roman villa. It was enlarged by Vincenzo Brenna in 1796–99, when a second story was added to the galleries and side pavilions. Despite a devastating fire in 1803 and further reconstruction by Voronikhin in the early 19th century, Cameron's basic design survived.

In front of the palace stands a statue of the snub-nosed Paul I, a copy of the statue at Gatchina, Paul's other summer residence. When you enter, you'll find many rooms on view, and you may start either on the ground or the first floor. The splendid interiors, with their parquet floors, marble pillars, and gilded ceilings, were created by some of Russia's most outstanding architects. Besides Cameron, Brenna, and Voronikhin, the roll call includes Quarenghi, who designed the interior of five rooms on the first floor, and Carlo Rossi, who was responsible for the library, built in 1824. The state apartments on the ground floor include the pink-and-blue **Ballroom;** the formal **Dining Hall,** where the full dinner service for special occasions is set out; and the lovely **Corner Room,** with walls of lilac marble and doors of Karelian birch. Among the lavishly decorated state rooms on the second floor is the famous **Greek Hall,** whose layout is that of an ancient temple. Its rich green Corinthian columns stand out starkly against the white of the faux marble walls. The hall, which also served as a small ballroom, linked the state rooms of Paul I to those of his wife, Maria. The last room on his side, leading here, was the **Hall of War.** Her first private suite, called the **Hall of Peace,** was designed to correspond to it. The gilded stucco wall moldings are decorated with flowers, baskets of fruit, musical instruments, and other symbols of peace.

Past all the empress's apartments, you'll come to the light-filled **Picture Gallery,** with its floor-length windows and eclectic array of paintings. From it, via a small, pink marble waiting room, you will reach the palace's largest chamber, **Throne Hall.** Once it held Paul I's throne, but at a victory party after Napoléon's defeat, it was taken out and somehow never returned.

Leave the palace to explore its grounds. Covering over 1,500 acres, Pavlovsk's splendid park boasts numerous pavilions, tree-lined alleys, waterways, and statues. Like the palace, the park was designed by the leading architects of the day—Brenna, Cameron, Voronikhin, and Carlo Rossi. Once again, the Pavlovsk park differs greatly from the blueprint ones of the other imperial palaces. They applied strict rules of geometrical design, whereas at Pavlosk nature was left unfettered, with simple beauty, instead of precisely determined effect, the result.

The combined length of the park's paths and lanes is said to equal the distance between St. Petersburg and Moscow (656 kilometers [410 miles]). Since you can't possibly cover the entire territory in one day anyway, you might just want to follow your whim and see where it leads you. If you walk down the slope just behind the palace to the **Czar's Little Garden** (Sobstvenny Sadik), you can see the Three Graces Pavilion. Created by Cameron, the 16-columned pavilion encloses a statue of Joy, Flowering, and Brilliance. A stone staircase, decorated with lions, is directly behind the palace and will take you to the Slavyanka canal. On the canal's other side, down to the left is the graceful **Apollo Colonnade,** whose air of ruin was not entirely man-made; built in 1783, it was struck by lightning in 1817 and never restored. If you bear right at the end of the stairs, you will come to the **Temple of Friendship,** meant to betoken the friendship between Empress Maria and Catherine the Great, her mother-in-law. Beyond it is a monument from the empress to her own parents; the center urn's medallion bears their likenesses. Of the other noteworthy pavilions and memorials dotting the park, the farthest one up the bank is the **Mausoleum of Paul I.** Set alone on a remote and overgrown hillside toward the center of the park, it was built by Maria for her husband after he was murdered in a palace coup. Paul was never interred here, however, and lest it sound too heartrending for his widow (portrayed as inconsolable in a statue here), evidence indicates that she was well aware of the plot to kill her husband.

Excursion 4: Lomonosov

The town of Lomonosov is located on the Gulf of Finland, some 40 kilometers (25 miles) west of St. Petersburg and about 9 km (5½ miles) northwest of Petrodvorets. Renamed for the 18th-century scientist Mikhail Lomonsov, it was originally named Oranienbaum for the orangery attached to its palace. It was the property of Alexander Menshikov, Peter the Great's favorite, who followed Peter's lead and in 1710 began building his own luxurious summer residence on the shores of the Baltic Sea. Before his plans could be realized, however, Peter died and Menshikov was stripped of his formidable political power and exiled, leaving his summer estate only half finished. The palace reverted to the crown and was given to Peter III, the ill-fated husband of Catherine the Great. Most of the buildings on the grounds were erected during his six-month reign, in 1762, or completed later by Catherine. Overall the estate, as it turned out, is perhaps the least commanding of the suburban imperial palaces. It is, however, the only one to have survived World War II intact. With its seaside location and extensive park, it is a splendid place to spend a warm summer day. *48 ul. Yunovo Lenitsa, town of Lomonosov,* ☎ *812/422–8806.* ⊙ *Wed.–Sun. 11–5. Transportation: commuter train from Baltisky Vokzal (Baltic Station) to Oranienbaum-1 (not II), approximately 1 hr from St. Petersburg. Also, from May to Sept., hydrofoils leave from Tuchkov Bridge on Vasilievsky Island.*

Menshikov's Great Palace, the original one here, is also its biggest. It is situated on a terrace overlooking the sea. Built between 1710 and 1725, it was designed by the same architects who built Menshikov's grand mansion on Vasilievsky Island, Giovanni Fontana and Gottfried Schaedel. The Great Palace has been under reconstruction for some time and is currently not open to the public.

Nearby is **Peterstadt Dvorets,** the modest palace that Peter III used, a two-story stone mansion built between 1762 and 1785 by Arnoldo Rinaldi. Its interior is decorated with handsome lacquered wood paintings. That it seems small, gloomy, and isolated is perhaps appropriate since it was here, in 1762, that the czar was murdered in the wake of the coup that put his wife, Catherine the Great, on the throne.

The building on the estate that most proclaims its imperial beginnings, however, is unquestionably Catherine's **Kitaisky Dvorets** (Chinese Palace), also designed by Rinaldi. Intended as one of her private summer residences, it is quite an affair—Rococo inside, Baroque without. Lavishly decorated, it has ceiling paintings created by Venetian artists, inlaid-wood floors, and elaborate stucco walls. The small house outside served as the kitchen.

Down the slope to the east of the Great Palace is the curious **Katalnaya Gorka** (Sledding Hill). All that remains of the slide, which was several stories high, is the pavilion that served as the starting point of the ride, where guests of the empress could catch their breath before tobogganing down again. Painted soft blue with white trim, the fanciful pavilion looks like a blue-frosted birthday cake. Also on the premises, near the pond, is a small amusement park offering carnival rides.

What to See and Do with Children

The **Avrora Cruiser,** famous for having fired the shot that signaled the 1917 revolution, is docked on the bank of the Neva, across from the St. Petersburg Hotel. *4 nab. Petrogradskaya,* ☎ *812/230–5202.* ⊙ *Tues.–Thurs. and weekends 10:30–4.*

A **boat ride** on the Neva or through the city's twisting canals is always a pleasant way to spend a summer afternoon. For trips through the canals, take one of the boats at the pier near Anichkov Bridge on Nevsky Prospect. Boats cruising the Neva leave from the pier outside the Hermitage Museum. *Mid-May–mid-Sept. Departures early morning–late afternoon.*

The **St. Petersburg Circus** dates from 1867. Though perhaps not as famous as the Moscow Circus, it remains a popular treat for children. *3 Fontanka Naberezhnaya,* ☎ *812/314–8478. Performances daily 7:30 PM; matinees on weekends.*

Avid young circus fans may get a kick out of its adjacent **Circus Art Museum** as well, with displays about the world of the circus. ☎ *812/ 210–4413.* ⊙ *Weekdays noon–6.*

The **Railway Museum,** showing Russia's railroad history complete with moving model trains, makes a hit with kids and parents alike. *50 ul. Sadovaya,* ☎ *812/315–1476.* ☉ *Sun.–Thurs. 11–5:30.*

In summer, children delight in **Petrodvorets** (*see* Excursion 1, *above*), the amusement park of the czars, where Peter the Great's trick fountains come to life in the most surprising ways. Located 29 kilometers (18 miles) south of the city, it can be reached by hydrofoil from the pier outside the Hermitage museum. They may also like the rides at **Lomonsov.**

Within the city, don't overlook the horseback and carriage rides for hire in **Palace Square.**

St. Petersburg's three puppet theaters all perform regularly for children: **Bolshoi Puppet Theater** (10 ul. Nekrasova, ☎ 812/273–6672), **Puppet-Marionette Theater** (52 Nevsky Prospect, ☎ 812/311–1900), and **Sharmanka** (151A Moskovsky Prospect, ☎ 812/294–6311). The last is a new "cinematic" theater whose fascinating and bizarre performances may frighten very young children.

They may also enjoy a show at the **Improvisionational Children's Theater on Ice** (148 Ligovsky Prospect, ☎ 812/112–8625, open weekdays 11–3) or at the **Through the Looking-Glass Children's Theater** (8 ul. Shamsheva, ☎ 812/238–1205, open Tues.–Sun. noon–5).

Although nothing extraordinary, the **Zoo** is always an option. It's near the Peter and Paul Fortress, directly behind the Gorkovskaya subway station. *1 Park Alexandrovsky,* ☎ *812/232–2839.* ☉ *Daily 10–8.*

Off the Beaten Path

Chesmenskaya Tserkov

Surrounded by dreary Soviet high-rises in a remote residential area, this bright red, white-striped church is a delightful surprise. A rare example of pseudo-Gothic Russian architecture, it was built to accompany the Chesma Palace (across the street), which served as a staging post for the imperial court en route to the summer palaces of Tsarskoye Selo (now Pushkin) and Pavlovsk. Commissioned by Catherine the Great, the palace was built to commemorate the Russian naval victory at Chesma in the Aegean in 1770. Both buildings were constructed by Yuri Felten, architect of the famous Summer Garden fence. After the Bolshevik Revolution, the palace became a home for the elderly and is not open to the public. The church, in turn, was made into a branch of the city's Naval Museum, dedicated to the battle at Chesma. In recent years, baptisms and weddings have occasionally been performed here, although regular church services have not yet resumed. Not far from the Pulkhovskaya Hotel, the Chesma Church is within walking distance of the Moskovskaya subway stop. *14–16 ul. Lensoveta,* ☎ *812/293–6114 (palace).* ☉ *Tues.–Sun. 10–5.*

Piskaryevskoye Kladbishche

The vast extent of this city's suffering during the 900-day siege of Leningrad becomes clear after a visit to the sobering Piskaryevskoye Cemetery. Located on the outskirts of town, the field here was used, out of necessity, as a mass burial ground for the hundreds of thousands of World War II victims, some of whom died from the shelling, but mostly from cold and starvation resulting from its blockade between 1941 and 1944. The numbingly endless rows of common graves carry a simple slab indicating the year in which those below it died. In all, nearly 500,000 people are buried here, and individual graves were impossible. The cemetery, with its memorial monuments and an eternal flame, has been made into a moving historical marker. Inscribed on the granite wall at the far end of the cemetery is the famous poem by radio personality Olga Bergholts, which ends with the oft-repeated phrase, "No one is forgotten, nothing is forgotten." The granite pavilions at the entrance house a small museum with photographs and memoirs documenting the siege. On display is Tanya Savicheva's diary, scraps of paper on which the young schoolgirl recorded the death of every member of her family. The last entry reads, "May 13. Mother died. Everyone is dead. Only I am left." (Later, she too died as a result of the war.) *74 Nepokorennykh,* ☎ *812/247–5716.* ⊙ *Daily 10–6. Transportation: Bus 123 from subway stop Ploshchad Muzhestva.*

Pushkin Apartment Museum

This former palace of Prince Volkhonsky is where, on January 27, 1837, the beloved Russian poet Alexander Pushkin died after participating in a duel to defend his wife's honor. Although he lived there less than a year, the apartment/museum has been restored to its appearance at that time. While few of the furnishings are authentic, his personal effects (including the waistcoat he wore at the duel) and those of his wife are on display. The library, where Pushkin died, has been rebuilt according to sketches made in his last hours by his friend and fellow poet, Vasily Zhukovsky, who was holding vigil. A moving account leads you through the apartment and retells the events leading up to the poet's death. The museum is a short walk from the corner of Nevsky Prospect and the Moika Embankment. *12 nab. Reki Moiki,* ☎ *812/311–8001.* ⊙ *Wed.–Mon. 11–5. Closed last Fri. of month.*

Smolny

Confusion abounds when you mention the Smolny, for you can mean either a beautiful Baroque church or a classically designed institute that went down in history as Bolshevik headquarters in the 1917 Revolution. It doesn't help matters much that the two architectural complexes are right next door to each other, on the Neva's left bank. Construction of the Smolny Convent and Cathedral began under Elizabeth I and continued during the reign of Catherine the Great, who established a school for the daughters of the nobility within its walls. The centerpiece of the convent is the magnificent five-domed **Cathedral of Resurrection,** which was designed by Bartolomeo Rastrelli. Some say it is his greatest creation. At first glance, the highly ornate blue-and-white cathedral seems to have leaped off the pages of a fairy tale. Its five white onion domes, crowned with gilded globes supporting crosses of gold, convey a sense of magic and power. Begun by Rastrelli in 1748, the cathedral was not completed until the 1830s, by the architect Vasily Stasov. The cathedral is now open to the public, but few traces of the original interior have survived. *3/1 Ploshchad Rastrelli,* ☎ *812/271–9182.* ⊙ *Mon., Tues., Thurs.–Sun. 11–6; Wed. 11–5. If a concert is being held in evening, museum closes 1 hr earlier. Transportation: Trolleybus 5 from Ploshchad Vostaniya to Rastrelli Sq.*

The **Smolny Institute,** just south of the cathedral, is a far different structure. Designed by Giacomo Quarenghi in 1806–08, the Classical building was done in the style of an imposing country manor. The Smolny Institute will long be remembered by the Russian people as the site where Lenin and his associates planned the overthrow of the Kerensky government in October 1917. The rooms Lenin used during his time at the institute once housed a museum that has now closed. Today the building houses the offices of the mayor of St. Petersburg, and is generally open to the public. *1 Proletarsky Diktatury,* ☎ *812/278–1968.*

Yusupovsky Dvorets

Located on the banks of the Moika River, this elegant yellow palace belonged to one of Russia's wealthiest families, the Yusupovs. It was here on the cold night of December 17, 1916, that Prince Yusupov and others loyal to the czar spent several frustrating and frightening hours trying to kill the invincible Rasputin, the "mad monk" who courted the czarina during the tumultuous years leading up to the Bolshevik Revolution. When the monk did not succumb to the arsenic-laced cake given to him, the conspirators proceeded to shoot him several times (thinking him dead after the first shot, they had left the room, only to return and find he'd staggered outside—whereafter they shot him again). They then dumped him into the icy waters of an isolated section of a nearby canal. The building now serves as a cultural center for teachers but is also open for excursions (by advance booking only). On display are the rooms in which Rasputin was (or began to be) killed as well as a waxworks exhibit of Rasputin and Prince Yusupov, who was forced to flee the country when the monk's murder was uncovered. *94 nab. Reki Moiki,* ☎ *812/311–5353.*

Sightseeing Checklist

This list includes attractions covered in the preceding tours as well as additional attractions described for the first time.

Churches, Monasteries, and Places of Worship

Alexander Nevsky Monastery (*see* Tour 4)

Armenian Church (*see* Tour 4)

Buddhist Temple (91 Primorsky Prospect, ☎ 239–1341)

Chesma Church (Chesmenskaya Tserkov, *see* Off the Beaten Path)

Choral Synagogue and Jewish Religious Center (2 Lermontovsky Prospect, ☎ 812/114–1153) is open daily 10–5; there is another synagogue at 2 Alexandrovsk Fermy Proezd (☎ 812/264–3981).

Church of the Savior on the Spilled Blood (Khram Spasa na Krovi, *see* Tour 5)

Dutch Church (*see* Tour 4)

Kazansky Cathedral (*see* Tour 4)

Mosque (Mechet, *see* Tour 3)

St. Isaac's Cathedral (Isaakievsky Sobor, *see* Tour 2)

St. Nicholas Cathedral (Nikolsky Sobor). This 18th-century Russian Baroque cathedral is surrounded by picturesque canals and green spaces. It's well worth a visit to hear the beautiful choir. *1/3 Nikolskaya Ploshchad,* ☎ *812/114–0862. Morning services at 7 and 10* AM.

St. Peter Lutheran Church (*see* Tour 4)

Sts. Peter and Paul Cathedral (*see* Tour 3)

Smolny Convent and Cathedral (*see* Off the Beaten Path)

Historic Buildings and Sites

Admiralty (*see* Tour 2)

Anichkov Bridge (Anichkov Most, *see* Tour 4)

Avrora Cruiser (*see* Tour 3)

Decembrists' Square (*see* Tour 2)

Engineer's Castle (Inzhenerny Zamok, *see* Tour 5)

Gostinny Dvor (*see* Tour 4)

Kazan Cathedral (Kazansky Sobor, *see* Tour 4)

Lomonsov (Summer Palace of Peter III, *see* Excursions)

Manège (*see* Tour 2)

Marble Palace (Mramorny Dvorets, *see* Tour 5)

Maria's Palace (Mariinsky Dvorets, *see* Tour 2)

Menshikov Palace (Menshikovsky Dvorets, *see* Tour 2)

Nevsky Prospect (*see* Tour 4)

Palace Square (Dvortsovaya Ploshchad, *see* Tour 1)

Pavlosk (Palace of Paul I, *see* Excursions)

Peter and Paul Fortress (Petropavlovskaya Krepost, *see* Tour 3)

Peter I's Summer Palace (Letny Dvorets, *see* Tour 5)

Peter the Great's Cottage (Domik Petra I, *see* Tour 3)

Petrodvorets (Summer Palace of Peter I, *see* Excursions)

Piskaryevskoye Cemetery (Piskaryevskoye Kladbishche, *see* Off the Beaten Path)

Pushkin (Summer Palace of Catherine the Great, *see* Excursions)

Rossi Street (ulitsa Zodchevo Rossi, *see* Tour 4)

Rostral Columns (*see* Tour 2)

Smolny Institute (*see* Off the Beaten Path)

Square of Art (Ploshchad Iskuustv, *see* Tour 5)

Senat and Synod (*see* Tour 2)

St. Isaac's Square (*see* Tour 2)

Strelka (Spit of Vasilievsky Island, *see* Tour 2)

Stroganov Palace (*see* Tour 4)

Winter Palace (Zimny Dvorets, *see* Tour 1)

Yelisevsky Food Emporium (*see* Tour 4)

Yusupov Palace (Yusupovsky Dvorets, *see* Off the Beaten Path)

Museums

Anna Akhmatova Literary Museum. Opened in 1989, the museum is located in the former palace of the Count Sheremetyev, which was home to the famous St. Petersburg poet for many years. *34 nab. Reki Fontanki,* ☎ *812/272–2211 or 812/272–5895.* ☉ *Tues.–Sun. 10:30–6:30. Closed last Wed. of month.*

Artillery Museum (*see* Tour 3)

Dostoevsky Literary Museum. The writer's last residence, where he wrote *The Brothers Karamazov. 5/2 Kuznechny Pereulok,* ☎ *812/311–4031.* ☉ *Tues.–Sun. 10:30–5:30. Closed last Wed. of month.*

Ethnography Museum (*see* Tour 5)

Hermitage Museum (Ermitazh, *see* Tour 1)

House Museum of Alexander Blok. *57 ul. Dekabristov,* ☎ *812/113–8616.* Home of the famous Symbolist poet. ☉ *Mon., Tues., and Thurs.–Sun 11–6.*

House Museum of Chaliapin. Apartment museum of the great opera star. *26 ul. Graftio,* ☎ *812/234–2698.* ☉ *Wed.–Sun. 10–6.*

Kirov Museum. Home of the former head of the city's Communist Party, who, it later became clear, was murdered by Stalin, marking the beginning of the infamous purges. *26/28 Kamennostrovsky Prospect,* ☎ *812/233–3822.* ☉ *Mon., Tues., and Thurs.–Sat. 11–6.*

Mining Institute Museum (*see* Tour 2)

Museum of Anthropology and Ethnography (Kunstkamera, *see* Tour 2)

Museum of the Defense of Leningrad (*see* Monuments, *below*). *9 pereulok Solyanoy,* ☎ *812/275–7208, Mon., Tues., and Thurs.–Sun. 10–5.*

Pushkin Apartment Museum (*see* Off the Beaten Track)

Rimsky-Korsakov Museum. In the composer's apartment; classical concerts are occasionally held in its small concert hall. *28 Zagorodny Prospect, Apt. 39,* ☎ *812/113–3208.* ☉ *Wed.–Sun. 11–6.*

Russian Political History Museum (*see* Tour 3)

State Museum of Russian Art (*see* Tour 5)

Zoological Museum (*see* Tour 2)

Parks and Gardens

Botanical Gardens. Founded as an apothecary garden for Peter the Great, it displays—literally—millions of different forms of plant life. *2 ul. Pro-*

fessora Popova, ☎ *812/234–1764. Hothouses open Mon.–Thurs., weekends 11–4.*

Field of Mars (Marsovoye Pole, *see* Tour 5)

Kirovsky Park on Yelagin Ostrov. Yelagin Ostrov (island) is named after its 18th-century aristocratic owner. The park covers most of the island and has an open-air theater, boating stations, and a beach. To reach the park, take Tram 2 or 31 from the Chernaya Rechka subway station. *4 Yelagin Ostrov*, ☎ *812/239–0911.* ☉ *Daily 10–8.*

Mikhailovsky Gardens (Mikhailovsky Sad, *see* Tour 5)

Moskovsky Park Pobedy (Moscow Victory Park). This lovely park, filled with lakes and offering a small amusement park, boating, and other attractions, is near Ploshchad Pobedy. *25 ul. Kuznetsovskaya*, ☎ *812/298–0881.* ☉ *Weekdays 9–6.*

Primorsky Park Pobedy (Seaside Park of Victory). This beautiful park is situated on an isolated island off the coast of Finland. Biking, boating, and swimming in summer. Kirov Stadium is here. *21 Krestovsky Prospect*, ☎ *812/234–2146. Tram 33, 34, 11, or 21 from Vasilieostrovskaya subway station.*

Summer Gardens (Letny Sad, *see* Tour 5)

Statues and Monuments

Alexander Column (Aleksandrovskaya Kolonna, *see* Tour 1)

Bronze Horseman (Medny Vsadnik, *see* Tour 2)

Catherine Monument (*see* Tour 4)

Egyptian Sphinxes (*see* Tour 2)

Horse Tamers' Statues (*see* Tour 4)

Monument to the Heroes of the Defense of Leningrad During World War II. You are likely to see this on the way from the airport or if you visit the Park Pobedy region. Financed and built by city residents, it faces the southern part of St. Petersburg, which saw the fiercest fighting. The center obelisk inside a broken ring symbolizes the breaking of the enemy blockade. Surrounding it are groups involved in the battles—sailors, partisans, soldiers, and people's volunteers. Underneath is a memorial hall museum.

Statue of Nicholas I (*see* Tour 2)

Statue of Alexander Pushkin (*see* Tour 5)

Suvorov Monument (*see* Tour 5)

SHOPPING

If you have come to St. Petersburg to shop, you will be disappointed. Despite improvements, they consist mostly of at last bringing in a solid array of products that are considered "normal"—whether juice, cosmetics, or socks—elsewhere. In other words, apart from certain arts and crafts, there is nothing to whet your appetite for the unusual or exquisite; you'll have to let your experience of St. Petersburg alone fulfill that. The good news, of course, is that basic items are no longer scarce.

The same sense of a two-tiered system of stores exists in St. Petersburg as in Moscow and Kiev. The "Western style" shops taking credit-card payment have effectively replaced the old Beriozkas, which were stocked only for foreigners. With increased competition, some of their prices have gone down, and they are open to anyone who can afford them.

State-run shops are much better stocked than ever, and you might as well look into some of these groceries and department stores if you don't want anything too fancy. Only rubles will be accepted here, however, and you'll have a tough time maneuvering through the cashiers if you don't speak some Russian.

Kiosks, tables on the street, and impromptu markets offer a colorful jumble of junk most of the time. But this mini-industry of individual entrepreneurs, which mushroomed wildly in the first years of glasnost, is on the wane. Everything's being tidied up and taken back inside.

Shopping Districts

Historically St. Petersburg's main shopping district centers are two: **Nevsky Prospect** and **Gostinny Dvor.** Located smack in the center of town, at 35 Nevsky Prospect, Gostinny Dvor is easily reached by subway; a station right outside its doors is named in its honor. Some sections of Gostinny Dvor are currently closed due to ongoing restoration.

Department Stores

Major department stores in the downtown area include the popular **DLT** (*Dom Leningradskoi Torgovly*), just off Nevsky Prospect, at 21/23 Bolshaya Konyushennaya ulitsa, and **Passage,** at 48 Nevsky Prospect, which cater primarily to the local population. Their souvenir sections, however, are often a shopper's paradise as prices, in rubles, are significantly lower here than in the souvenir shops around hotels and in other areas usually frequented by tourists. The patient shopper may chance upon some tremendous bargains.

Outside the large department stores of Nevsky Prospect, you will find some boutiques and lots of "variety shops," which can be a bit bewildering. Part souvenir-oriented, part practical, look if you have them time; you never know what you may find.

Specialty Stores

Art Galleries

Although they cater primarily to the lucrative tourist market, art shops in St. Petersburg offer items of much higher quality than what you will find on the streets. Nevsky Prospect is lined with such shops, where local artists sell their wares on commission. Before making a major purchase at these stores, be sure to ask if they will take care of the paperwork necessary to allow you to take the item out of the country. It's also a good idea to clarify whether they charge an additional fee for this service. Some of the best art shops include **Lavka Khudozhnikov** (8 Nevsky Prospect, ☎ 812/312–6193); **Arianda** (11 Konnogvardeiski Prospect, apt. 17, ☎ 812/311–6997, appointment necessary); **Gallery 102** (102 Nevsky Prospect, ☎ 812/275–5766); **Golubaya Gostinaya** (38 Bolshaya Morskaya ul., ☎ 812/315–7414); and **Palitra Art Gallery** (166 Nevsky Prospect, ☎ 812/277–1216).

Clothing Stores

You aren't here to find clothes, presumably, but if you are, try the department stores listed above. Chic boutiques in the better hotels have some designer pieces, usually at higher-than-designer prices. If you're looking for handmade traditional Russian garments, check out Aquilon Salon (6 Kamennostrovsky Prospect, ☎ 812/232–6783).

Craft and Souvenir Shops

Besides the counters in hotel-lobby shops, where prices are often wildly inflated, you can look for special gifts in **Art Boutique** (51 Nevsky Prospect, ☎ 812/113–1495); **Guild of Masters** (82 Nevsky Prospect, ☎ 812/279–0979); **Podarki** (Bolshoi Prospect, ☎ 812/232–2092); **Her-**

itage (116 Nevsky Prospect, ☎ 812/279–5067); **Marble Palace** (5/1 ul. Millionaya, ☎ 812/312–1859); **Russian Art Ltd.** (1, ☎ 812/210–9808); **The Russian Arts** (53 ul. Saltykova-Shchedrina, ☎ 812/275–6960); **Russki Dom 1,** 5 ul. Tchaikovskovo, ☎ 812/275–1565); **Stroganov Palace** (17 Nevsky Prospect, ☎ 812/312–1859); **Khudozhestvenny Salon** (31 Nevsky Prospect, ☎ 812/314–8081), and **Nasledie** (116 Nevsky Prospect, ☎ 812/279–5067.

Farmers' Markets

The farmers' markets in St. Petersburg are lively places where a colorful array of goods and foods are sold by individual farmers, often from out of town and sometimes from outside the Russian republic. In recent years the variety of goods available at the market (in Russian, *rynok*) has increased tremendously. Because markets are much cleaner and better-lit than in Moscow, it's also fun to visit and browse. In addition to the fine cuts of fresh and cured meat, dairy products, and homemade jams and jellies, piles of fruits and vegetables can be found, even in winter. Try some homemade pickles or pickled garlic, a tasty local favorite. You can also find may welcome surprises like hand-knitted scarves, hats, and mittens. You are expected to bargain, and—as in any crowded area—watch out for pickpockets. St. Petersburg's most popular markets are the **Kuznechny Rynok,** 3 Kuznechny Pereulok, just outside the Vladimirskaya metro station; the **Sytny Rynok,** 3/5 Sytninskaya Ploshchad, in the Petrograd Side district, not far from the Gorkovskaya subway station; and the huge, sprawling flea market known as **Sennoi Rynok,** Sennaya Ploshchad, at the exit from the subway station of the same name. Farmers' markets are generally open daily from 8 AM to 7 PM and usually close at 5 PM on Sunday.

Grocery Stores

For those looking for a big Western supermarket that takes credit cards, there are two: **Kalinka-Stockmann** (1 Finlandsky Prospect, ☎ 812/542–2297, open daily 10–9) and **SPAR** (30 Slavy Prospect, ☎ 812/260–4121, open daily 10–10). **Babylon Super** (54/56 Maly Prospect, ☎ 812/230–8096, open Mon.–Sat. 10–2, Sun. noon–8) is a superstore like the other two but accepts only rubles. For imported cheese and excellent fruit and vegetables, try **Express Market,** with two shops: at 73 Moskovsky Prospect (☎ 812/252–4144) and at the corner of Nevsky Prospect and Kharkovskaya ulitsa (☎ 812/277–7771), each open daily 10–10. Otherwise, have a go at the local *dietas, gastronoms,* and *produkti.*

SPORTS AND FITNESS

Participant Sports

Unfortunately, athletic facilities available to tourists in St. Petersburg are rather limited. As in Moscow, access to the municipal facilities is restricted and requires a special "doctor's certificate" attesting to the user's health. They are possible to get, but you'd have to spend at least a few hours at a Russian clinic to do so. Most hotels have their own athletic facilities, however, and sometimes they are open to nonguests also; these spots do not require a doctor's certificate.

Cycling

You may enjoy biking through St. Petersburg's parks and along its picturesque canals and river embankments. You can rent bikes from the Burevestnik Cycling Club (81 Prospect Engelsa, ☎ 812/554–1741), which can also arrange tours.

Fitness Centers and Sports Complexes

The **Army Sports Club** (13 ul. Inzhenernaya, ☎ 812/219–2967) has a pool and both volleyball and basketball courts. The **Dinamo Sports Center** (44 Dinamo Prospect, ☎ 812/235–0170) has a range of facilities, including volleyball courts and running tracks. Weightlifters can try the **Olympia Shaping Center** (14 6th ul. Krasnoarmeiskaya, ☎ 812/110–1887); a one-month package here is very reasonable, so you may simply want to purchase one, even if your stay is shorter.

If your own hotel doesn't have a place to work out, the fitness center at the **Astoria Hotel** is open to nonguests. Its pool (10 meters) is by far the largest in the city's hotels. ☎ *812/311–4206. ⊘ Weekdays 7:30 AM–10 PM, weekends 9–9. Fee for use of gym, pool, and sauna for 2 hours, $20.*

The **Hotel Rossiya** (11 Chernyshevskovo Ploshchad, ☎ 812/296–7221) has a gym, pool, and sauna.

Running

Runners, like cyclists, can find some lovely spots to run through or alongside. You might stick to the Neva embankments or head for gardens like Letny Sad or the Field of Mars. It's easier here than in Moscow to avoid huge clumps of traffic and the attendant congestion. And though you'll still be in a minority, you probably won't feel as conspicuous if you just put on those track shoes and go.

Skating Rinks

You can skate at the following rinks: **Moskovskovo Park Pobedy** (25 ul. Kuznetsovskaya, ☎ 812/298–0881; open Mon.–Fri. and Sun. 9–6); **Tavricheskovo Sad** (50 ul. Saltykova-Shchedrina, ☎ 812/272–6044); and **Yubileyny Palace of Sports** (18 ul. Dobrolyubova, ☎ 812/238–4061, daily 11–6.

Swimming

The fitness centers listed above have pools. The **World Class Fitness Center** also offers a 25-meter, 6-lane pool. Onetime use is an option, but at twice the members' price.

Tennis Courts

Tennis players should be able to find an open court. Public indoor courts are located in the **Primorsky Park Pobedy** (Seaside Park of Victory, 9 Krestovsky Prospect, on Krestovsky Island, ☎ 812/235–2077). The park can be reached by Tram 21, 33, or 34 from the Vasileostrovskaya subway station. There are municipal courts at 37 ul. Kazanskaya, ☎ 812/315–6220. Outdoor public courts are across the street from the Field of Mars at 16 Aptekarsky pereulok. The World Class Fitness Center (*see above*) has tennis courts available for rental, if they aren't previously reserved. If these options don't pan out, check with the **Lawn Tennis Sports Center** (116 Metallistov Prospect, ☎ 812/540–1886) or **Kirov Stadium** (1 Morskoi Prospect, ☎ 812/235–4877).

Spectator Sports

Tickets for sporting events can be purchased at the sports arena immediately prior to the game or at one of the many theater box offices (*teatralnaya kassa*) located throughout the city: 22–24 Nevsky Prospect, 33 Nevsky Prospect, 42 Nevsky Prospect, 74 Nevsky Prospect, and 27 Sredny Prospect (Vasilievsky Island).

Basketball and Volleyball

Basketball and volleyball matches are held at **Yubilieny Sports Palace** (19 Prospect Dobroluybova, ☎ 812/238–4122) and **Zimny Stadium** (2 Manezhnaya Ploshchad, ☎ 812/315–5710).

Hockey

The hockey arenas are also at the **Yubilieny Sports Palace** and at the **Sports and Concert Complex** (8 Yuri Gagarin Prospect, ☎ 812/298–2164).

Soccer

International matches are held at the **Petrovsky (formerly Lenin) Stadium** (2-g Petrovsky Ostrov, ☎ 812/238–4129) and at the **Kirov Stadium** (1 Morskoi Prospect, Krestovsky Ostrov, ☎ 812/235–0078).

DINING

In the age-old rivalry between Moscow and St. Petersburg, the capital wins when it comes to the sheer breadth of offerings for the tourist dining out. For such a large city, St. Petersburg's restaurant scene still seems more limited than it should. Of course if you look back into the not-so-distant past, when the best you could do was a large and rowdy state enterprise in one of the city's foreign hotels, you realize how good things really are. There is still plenty of that type of dining, but there's also a fair crop of smaller, more relaxed establishments. Like the city itself, restaurants here seem less "foreign" than in Moscow or Kiev; the accent is on warm atmosphere, friendly service, tasty food, and a decidedly more European ambiance. You won't have that "either/or" feeling—that either you're at a rowdy expatriate establishment and still aware that you're from elsewhere, or that you're adrift in a strange brew of strictly Russian places, where heavy atmosphere, unpredictable food, and tacky decor make you feel equally alien.

Remember that landing a table in a good restaurant is still not done on a whim: You must plan ahead. Reservations are almost always essential, especially in the evening, partly because there just aren't *that* many places. You're likely to have better luck if you ask your hotel or tour guide for help—the best meals are often still had through connections. Keep in mind that at large establishments with live entertainment dining out will be an all-night affair, for at restaurants featuring floor shows, eating out means not only a meal but drinking and dancing the night away as well. Although you may find it in poor taste, the entertainment usually entails exceptionally loud music (with some perennial favorites played over and over again), colored disco light shows, and scantily clad dancers. Few restaurants offer no-smoking sections.

As with the shopping scene, St. Petersburg's restaurants can be divided roughly into categories based on the type of payment they accept and the clientele they seek to serve. Prices, in general, are lower than Moscow's and higher than Kiev's. Private and (the remaining) cooperative restaurants, which often accept both credit cards and rubles, are far more expensive—and usually of much better quality—than the state-run restaurants operating exclusively in rubles.

CATEGORY	COST*
$$$$	over $40
$$$	$25–$40
$$	$10–$25
$	under $10

per person, excluding drinks and service

What to Wear

Dress at the restaurants reviewed below is casual, unless noted otherwise.

$$$$ **Europe.** This elegant restaurant in the Grand Hotel Europe is in a cat-
★ egory all of its own. It offers luxury and fine dining of a kind that St.
Petersburg has not seen since the 1917 Revolution. Like the grand dining room at the Metropole in Moscow, this has a breathtaking interior, complete with stained-glass roof and private balconies, and seems
fit for a czar. But then, so do the prices. The menu, which features European and Russian cuisines, is exotic by local standards. For starters,
try the fresh goose liver, served with a honey-and-wine sauce. The main
dishes vary, but a highlight is the fillet of salmon, filled with cream cheese
and served with a wine-and-herb sauce. If you're not up for an opulent dinner, you may enjoy the popular Sunday morning jazz brunch.
Don't think about it too long, though, because tables book up fast, especially in the summer. ✗ *1/7 Mikhailovskaya ul., in Grand Hotel Europe,* ☎ *812/312-0072; or 812/119-6000, ext. 6330 Reservations
required. Jacket and tie. AE, MC, V. Hard currency only. Breakfast
Mon.–Sat. 7-10, dinner every day except Sun. 6-11, Sun. brunch
noon–3.*

$$$$ **Imperial.** This is the Nevsky Palace Hotel's swank restaurant, and
whereas the Europe emphasizes Old World grandeur, it settles for
sleek comfort. It, too, is a top-class spot, nicely nestled above Nevsky
Prospect, so at some tables you can watch the Russian world go by.
The changing dishes are strong on good Continental fare; in the
evenings there's a buffet, if you can't choose among all of them. There's
usually a jazz trio livening things up in the background. ✗ *57 Nevsky
Prospect,* ☎ *812/113–1518. Reservations advised. Jacket and tie. AE,
MC, V.* ☺ *Daily 7–11, noon–3, 7–11.*

$$$$ **Venice.** Situated among the gloomy high rises of Vasilievsky Island, this
Italian-Russian joint venture is easy to spot: It's the only building in
the area that isn't dominated by the color gray. Its distant location makes
it truly convenient only for those already staying at the Pribaltiskaya
Hotel, for whom the immaculate and snazzy interior is a welcome change
of pace. There's often a singer performing, but it's not the standard
over-the-top floor show by any means, and because the dining room
is spacious, you won't be acoustically overwhelmed. The service, provided by formally dressed waiters, is rather pretentious but not too stiff,
and the food is a delight. With an Italian chef and imported ingredients (right down to the flour and salt), the kitchen produces authentic pasta and Italian meat dishes. The computerized menu changes weekly
depending on shipments, but standard offerings include a tangy pasta
arrabbiata and a succulent lasagna. The wide selection of Italian and
other imported wines is unusual for St. Petersburg. Attached to the restaurant is an inexpensive pizzeria, which operates for rubles and has take-
out, very popular with foreign students staying in the university
dormitory across the street. ✗ *21 ul. Korablestroitelei,* ☎ *812/352–
1432. Reservations advised. Jacket and tie. AE, DC, MC, V.* ☺
Noon–midnight.

$$$ **Angleterre.** This pretty restaurant off the main lobby of the Angleterre
Hotel offers average food at above-average prices. Though it advertises
European cuisine, the unimaginative menu is dominated by standard Rus-
sian dishes, such as borscht, herring, and beefsteak in mushroom–sour
cream sauce. The food, once it actually makes it to your table, is quite
good, if unsurprising. What the restaurant lacks in speed and innova-
tion, however, it does make up for in atmosphere. The lovely all-white
room is lit by crystal chandeliers and through its discreetly curtained

glass walls light from the exquisite lobby outside also filters through. The quiet piano music tinkling in the background brings back the hotel's better days at the turn of the century. The restaurant also offers a popular buffet breakfast, which comes with all the blini you can eat and at a more reasonable prix fixe than the prices found on the lunch and dinner menus. *39 Bolshaya Morskaya ul., through the Hotel Astoria* ☎ *812/210–5906. Reservations advised. AE, MC, V.* ⊙ *Daily 11–11.*

$$$ Aphrodite. This Russian-Finnish restaurant has a decidedly Scandinavian slant, serving lots of fish and seafood among its equally interesting Russian dishes. Its two white rooms, graced with archways and filled with soft, filtered light, provide a soothing place to unwind after a long day of touring. Talk is quiet (it's a good choice for dinner *à deux*), background music is light (Sinatra classics are a favorite), and service is attentive—even deferential. The eccentrically amusing array of appetizers includes smoked reindeer salad, oysters on the half shell, and warm frogs' legs. The excellent selection of fish dishes features salmon, sturgeon, turbot, and perch. You may want to try the red perch in paper with ginger and bacon or the wolffish in spices with vegetables. Other appetites can have a beefsteak but may be more interested by the rabbit stew or elk steak. The wine list is small and decent. ✕ *86 Nevsky Prospect,* ☎ *812/275–7620. Reservations accepted. No credit cards; rubles only.* ⊙ *Daily noon–midnight.*

$$$ Brasserie. This restaurant off a ground-floor wing of the Grand Hotel Europe is the perfect place for a refreshing Caesar salad or a well-prepared steak. The menu has some nice Russian standbys but aims toward bistro exotic—try the garlicky snails with tomato bread. There is always a satisfying plat du jour as well. The relaxed atmosphere is enhanced by the efficient and excellent service: Come to the Brasserie if the outside has been getting you down. ✕ *1/7 Mikhailovskaya ul.,* ☎ *812/119–6000. Reservations accepted. AE, MC, V.* ⊙ *Mon.–Sat. 11–11, Sun. 3–11.*

$$$ Dvoryanskoye Gnezdo (Noblemans' Nest). Tucked away in the garden pavilion of the amazing Yusupov Palace, this very chic spot is particularly attractive to the after-theater crowd (the Mariinsky is not far away). Formal attire matches its service, decor, and food, which is mainly of the European, French-influenced variety. You may be able to close your eyes and imagine the carriages waiting outside the door. ✕ *21 ulitsa Dekabristov,* ☎ *812/312–3205. Jacket and tie. Rubles only.* ⊙ *Daily noon–midnight. Reservations required.*

$$ Bubnovy Valet (Jack of Diamonds). Tucked away on a side street off Bolshoi Prospect in the Petrograd Side district, this modest private restaurant is run by former employees of Intourist. Although the restaurant claims to offer European cuisine, the menu is dominated by standard Russian dishes. The decor is pretentious and cold, but the food is well prepared and served by courteous waiters in formal dress. For appetizers, you can't go wrong with the blini, little pancakes served with black or red caviar. Another recommended Russian appetizer is the *griby v smetane* (mushrooms baked in sour cream sauce). Their excellent soups include *solyanka*, a spicy thick stew made with vegetables and meat or fish, and borscht. The dessert menu features fruit mousse and a rich Russian favorite, *Krem so smetanoi*, which is simply cream with sweetened sour cream (and countless calories). Beverages, alcoholic and nonalcoholic, are available only for hard currency (cash). The closest subway station is Petrogradskaya. ✕ *32 ul. Lenina (Shirokaya),* ☎ *812/ 230–8830. Reservations advised. No credit cards.* ⊙ *Daily noon–midnight. No credit cards. Rubles only (except for beverages).*

$$ CAT. A popular café with the young and trendy, on a side street off Nevsky Prospect, it has Russian food all the same, solid and predictable. You may be better off dropping in for lunch, when it's a convenient place

160

St. Petersburg Dining and Lodging

Morskoy

Krestovsky

Sportivnaya ul.

Novy Krestovsky most

Popova professora ul.

Malaya Nevka

Levashovsky

Zelenina ul. Bolshoy ul.

Chkalovsky

Lenina ul.

Kammenostrovsky prosp.

5

6

PETROGRAD SIDE

Korpusnaya ul.

Krasnogo Kursanta ul.

Petrovsky

Shchorsa

Bolshoy

7

8 9

Maxim Gorki

Kronverk.

Canal

Morskaya nab.

Malaya

Dobrolubova

Neva

Birzhevoy most

Maly

Makarova nab.

Dvortsovy most

Dvorcovaya

1

2

VASILIEVSKY ISLAND

Sredny

8-9 Liniya

4-5 Liniya

Syezdovskaya l.

Mend.

12-13 Liniya

16-17 Liniya

20-21 Liniya

Bolshoy

Universitetskaya

Nevsky

Admiratevsk

Gorokhovaya l.

18

3

24-25 Liniya

Kosaya liniya

nab. Leytenanta Shmidta

most Leytenanta Shmidta

nab. Krasnova Flota

Profsoyuzov bulvar

15

Moika

14

16

4

Bolshoy

Neva

Truda ul.

reka

Dekabristov ul.

Mayarova

ul. Plekhanova

17

12

Piserova ul.

Maklina

13

Korsakova

reka Fontanka

Masnaya ul.

Turgeneva ploshchad

Ogorodnikova

Kurlandskaya

Gaza ul.

Drovanaya

Lermontovsky

Mayorova

Jeggorova ul.

Moskovsky

31

Obvodnyi Canal

Baltijski Station

Varshavski Sta

Bolshoy

Smolachkova ul.

Chugunnaya ul.

Zamshina ul.

Grenadorsky most

Lesnoy

Arsenalnaya ul.

Mineralnaya ul.

Poljustrovski

Zhukova ul.

Vyborgskaya ul.

Karl Marx

Pirogovskaya

Jova ul.

Petrogradskaya nab.

Nevka

Smirnov ul.

Kondratjevski

Sverdlovskaya nab.

27

Svobody most

Lebedeva ul.

11

Komsomola

Finlandski Station

ul.

28

Troitskaya Pl. Petrovskaya nab.

Lenina Ploshchad

Arsenalnaya nab.

Neva

Troitsky most

Liteinyi most

Voinova ul.

Chaykovskogo ul.

Taurien Park

Tavricheskaya ul.

Mochovaya ul.

Saltykova-Shchedrina ul.

Bolseochtinsky most

Sadovaya ul.

Liteiyni

Mayakovskogo ul.

Vosstaniya ul.

Nekrasova ul.

Suvorovski

8 Liniya ul.

Moiseyenko ul.

Novgoradskaya

19 Pl. Iskusstv

Grechesky

Maloochinsky nab.

20

Zhukovskogo ul.

23

Mytninskaya ul.

24

25

Lomonosova ul.

22

Z. Rossisi

Bakunina

Lovaya ul.

Lomonosov Sq.

26

Moskovski Station

Nevsky

most A. Nevsky

30

21

Fontanka reky nab.

Zagorodny

A. Nevsky Pl.

29

Neva

Zvenigorodskaya ul.

Marata ul.

Obuchovsky

Vitebski Station

Ligovski

Ruzovskaya ul.

Oborony

oselsky ul.

Borovaya ul.

Tambovskaya ul.

Glinanaya ul.

Obvodnyi Canal nab.

Kechalova prot. ul.

to unwind and recharge, and just order rounds of appetizers. ✗ *24 ul. Karavannaya,* ☎ *812/315–3800. Rubles only.* ☉ *Daily noon–11.*

$$ Chaika. This lively, smoke-filled restaurant and bar is popular with young locals and expatriates alike. A German-Russian joint venture, it offers good, hearty northern German food and great German beer. The dark wood interior, with lots of booths, long tables, and paneling, is right out of Germany, and the food, except for such Russian delicacies as caviar, is dominated by dishes like frankfurters with sauerkraut. It's a great place to come on a rainy day for a piping hot bowl of French onion soup or Hungarian goulash. The system of taking orders is a bit odd: You're handed a punch card on entering, on which your waiter records your choices. When you leave you present it, not a bill, to the cashier. The staff seems studiously blasé but gets the job done. ✗ *4 Kanala Griboyedova,* ☎ *812/312–4631. Reservations not accepted.* ☉ *11 AM–3 AM. No credit cards; rubles only.*

$$ Chopsticks. It doesn't seem quite fair that the Grand Hotel Europe, among its other excellent offerings, also has the best Chinese food in town. With Chinese chefs and authentic ingredients (most supplies are imported), Chopsticks is in a league of its own. Its emphasis is on the sweet-and-sour dishes from the north, tangy but not too hot. If you crave American-style Chinese food, this is a gold mine. One word of advice: Don't count on nabbing one of its few tables if you just drop by; the cozy restaurant is always full. ✗ *1/7 Mikhailovskaya ul.,* ☎ *812/312–0072, ext. 6391. Reservations necessary. Dress: casual but neat. AE, MC, V.* ☉ *Daily 1–3, 6–11.*

$$ John Bull Pub. As easy to get to as it is on the nerves, this English pub serves Russian food in its dining hall and standard snacks at the bar. For a bowl of borscht, or just a foamy mug of beer and refuge from architectural overload, try this cozy inn. ✗ *79 Nevsky Prospect,* ☎ *812/164–9877. AE, MC, V.* ☉ *Daily noon–6, 7–2.*

$$ Literary Café. You may have encountered this slice of history on one of your walks. Famous as the site of Pushkin's last meal (it was a confectionery then), it's imbued with a melancholy air of the past. The old-fashioned dining rooms, adorned with white linen and old silver, draw a cultured crowd. You'll find only Russian food, but there's a lot to choose from. Service is the sore point: Waiters are frequently testy but still can't spoil the pleasantly hushed ambience. There's usually a small entrance fee, for the attendant classical musicians. ✗ *18 Nevsky Prospect,* ☎ *812/ 312–6057. Rubles only.* ☉ *Daily noon–4:30 and 7–11.*

$$ Na Fontanke. This restaurant's reputation rests on its status as St. Petersburg's first cooperative. When it opened in 1988, it met with immediate and resounding success, in large part because it faced little competition. Even though Na Fontanke is no longer the only place in town, reservations are still essential. Although the restaurant is right on the bank of the Fontanka (hence its name), there are no tables with a view of the city's canals: As in most Russian restaurants, all the windows are heavily draped. The one small dining room is elegantly decorated in blue and gold. The food is uninspired, but what it lacks in originality it does make up for in presentation. The menu is a mix of Russian and Continental dishes, emphasizing the former. The prix fixe dinner includes an array of Russian appetizers (cold cuts, herring, mushrooms in cream sauce in a pastry shell), a main course, ice cream, and coffee. The nightly entertainment is a fascinating—but loud—extravaganza of Gypsy music and dance. This is not the place for intimate dining and conversation, but it's not a bad choice for an authentic Russian meal. ✗ *77 reki Fontanka,* ☎ *812/310–2547. Reservations required. No credit cards. Rubles only.* ☉ *Daily 1–5, 7–11.*

$$ Petrostar. ★ This is another private restaurant aiming to create an exclusive image. The sign on the door—BY INVITATION ONLY—scares the casual customer away. The staff, however, would welcome a foreign visitor, who probably wouldn't understand the warning anyway, since it's in Russian. The Petrostar (Peter Star) actually comes close to achieving the high level of fine dining that it cultivates. Tuxedo-clad waiters provide polite and friendly service. The interior has been carefully remodeled (a beer hall occupied the space) in the tradition of "Old St. Petersburg." The main dining hall features wood-paneled ceilings, airy white drapes (which actually let the sunshine in), and cast-iron wall lamps. Entertainment in the evening varies but sometimes includes a Gypsy performance ensemble. The Petrostar proudly specializes in Russian and Ukrainian cuisines. Cold appetizers include black and red caviar, crab, and Georgian *satsivy* (spicy chicken in walnut sauce). The mushroom soup is excellent, and don't overlook the hot appetizer *pekantnaya* (ham slices stuffed with garlic and cheese). For your main course, try the excellent *Kievskaya kotleta* (chicken Kiev); the Petrostar's is about the best in the city. And best of all, when you're done with your meal, the staff will help you hail a cab home—a splendid service on a dark St. Petersburg winter night. ✕ *30 Bolshaya Pushkarskaya ul.,* ☎ *812/232–4047. Reservations required. Jacket and tie. No credit cards. Rubles only.* ☉ *Daily 1–midnight.*

$$ Sadko. This lively and comfortable restaurant-bar is another niche eating establishment of the Grand Hotel Europe, without any of its pomp and circumstance. Check your tie at the door and sit down for a refreshing (imported) draft beer and pizza. The blackboard menu, which changes daily, offers satisfying Western-style bar food, such as hamburgers, spare ribs, and pasta. The good food, fun atmosphere, and nightly entertainment, which usually features popular local performers and up-and-coming new bands, make this a good choice if you just want to kick back and settle in. You can also get a good view of life on the Nevsky Prospect. ✕ *1/7 Mikhailovskaya ul. (separate entrance from Grand Hotel Europe),* ☎ *812/119–6000, ext. 6390. Reservations accepted. AE, MC, V.* ☉ *Daily noon–1.*

$$ Shvabsky Domik. You can tell the food here is authentic by the crowds of German expatriates who keep coming back for the schnitzel and wurst. The simple decor, with heavy wood paneling and long wooden benches, makes for a relaxed and pleasant atmosphere. The waitresses, all in German national dress, aim to please and offer a pleasant change of pace from the usual harried service. Unlike most restaurants in St. Petersburg, advance reservations aren't necessary. Combine that with the quick service and location—right outside the Krasnogvardeiskaya subway station—and this becomes a good stop for a quick meal on those days when you haven't planned ahead. A German-Russian joint venture, the restaurant specializes almost exclusively in German cuisine, with a few Russian appetizers like blini with caviar or cabbage soup thrown in for variety. The kitchen produces its own homemade pretzels, the *Shvabski Brezel*. Wash down your sausage and sauerkraut with a cold mug of refreshing German draft beer, while you listen to the balalaika-strumming folk trio. ✕ *28/19 Krasnogvardeivsky Prospect,* ☎ *812/528–2211. Reservations accepted. AE, DC, MC, V.* ☉ *Daily 11 AM–1 AM.*

$$ Tandoor. This restaurant, specializing in the cuisine of northwest India, gets high marks across the board and is a good find for vegetarians. Among the many tandooris and excellent fish and meat dishes (try the lamb kurma or chicken tikka masala), you'll find plenty of paneer, lentil, and vegetable-only dishes. The friendly atmosphere is inviting, the service solicitous. Its location is good, too—at the foot of Voznesensky Prospect, which converges with Nevsky and Moskovsky prospects at the Admiralty. After touring St. Isaac's or the nearby Palace Square, you may want to drop by here. ✗ *2 Voznesensky Prospect,* ☎ *812/312–3886.* ⊙ *Daily noon–11.*

$ Austeria. This state-run restaurant inside the Peter and Paul Fortress dates from the reign of Peter the Great. Formerly an officer's club (hosteria), the restaurant offers Russian cuisine in an 18th-century setting. Handcrafted, cast-iron chandeliers provide the lighting, while the thick stone walls and fully draped windows create the somber atmosphere appropriate to a fortress. The cooking isn't exactly gourmet, but the appetizers and soups are consistently good, and prices are very reasonable. For starters, try the *Petrovsky shchi* (cabbage soup), served in a crock topped by a pastry shell. The kitchen does a good job with the St. Petersburg fillet, a local favorite served with a creamy mushroom sauce. Since this restaurant is still state-run, many items on the menu may not be available when you visit. The restaurant is rarely crowded, but since it closes for private parties or tourist groups, it's best to call ahead. It's located inside the fortress's outer fortification wall, a short walk to your left after entering through the Ivan Gate. The cast-iron sign above the entrance can be easy to miss. ✗ *St. John's Ravelin, Peter and Paul Fortress,* ☎ *812/238–4262. Reservations advised. No credit cards. Rubles only.* ⊙ *Daily noon–5, 6–midnight.*

$ Dom Arkhitektorov. Previously open only to members of the Architecture Union, this little-known restaurant is located in a beautiful 18th-century mansion just off St. Isaac's Square. The dazzling interior features carved oak paneling, ceiling paintings, brass chandeliers, and gilded window frames. Its astounding beauty has somehow remained a secret, and unlike other elegant dining establishments, the place is not swarming with tourists. The cuisine, unfortunately, is far less appealing than the decor. The kitchen offers simply prepared meat and fish appetizers, as well as standard Russian dishes. The house specialty, *Myaso po Arkhitektorsky,* is a beef dish baked in a mayonnaise sauce and topped with thinly sliced potatoes. This is obviously not gourmet food, but with interiors like these it doesn't matter. If you're nice to the friendly waitresses, they may let you take a peek upstairs at the oak-paneled library and gilded ballroom. ✗ *52 ul. Bolshaya Morskaya,* ☎ *812/311–4557. Reservations required. No credit cards. Rubles only.* ⊙ *Mon.–Sat. noon–4, 6–11.*

$ Hebei. This private enterprise in the Petrograd Side is one of the better options in the swelling ranks of the city's Chinese restaurants. The colorful wood carvings and Chinese lanterns adorning the entranceway make it hard to miss among the gloomy apartment buildings lining Bolshoi Prospect. The restaurant is located one flight up (bypass the dingy looking "Korean" café on the first floor). The interior, with its highly ornate ceiling decorations and lanterns, also has the wallpaper painted to look like brick and plastic-covered windows imitating stained glass you might expect from a Chinese restaurant—or a Russian one, for that matter. Service is friendly and the prices are reasonable, however. The chefs are Chinese, but the dishes keep to Russian presentation, since ingredients are from the local markets. An exception is the *Svetnyie Macaroni,* clear rice noodles imported from China and prepared with Chinese spices and whatever vegetables are in season. For your main course, try the house specialty, *Kura po Hebeiski* (Hebei chicken), or *Govyadino po Gunbao,* strips of beef prepared with soy sauce and vegetables (a real delicacy in these parts). ✗ *61 Bolshoi Prospect,* ☎ *812/234–1742. Reservations accepted. No credit cards. Rubles only.* ⊙ *Daily noon–4 and 5–midnight.*

$ Metropole. Centrally located near Gostinny Dvor and just off Nevsky Prospect, this faded, state-run restaurant was once one of St. Petersburg's finest. Today it faces stiff competition, and the kitchen is having trouble keeping up with the city's better-run and -funded ventures. The menu offers standard Russian fare, such as chicken Kiev and fried perch. The selection of *zakuski* (hors d'oeuvres) is good, but the main courses tend to be heavy on the sauces and fried potatoes. Where the Metropole has the city's shiny cafés beat is in atmosphere. Opened in 1898, it's the city's oldest restaurant, and its atmosphere can't be reproduced with modern decor—no matter how tasteful. Although it has clearly seen better days, the marble pillars, ceiling moldings, and crystal chandeliers still exude a sense of elegance. For a price, you can reserve one of the private balcony rooms (which accommodate up to 30 people) overlooking the main dining hall. Russian pop bands provide nightly entertainment. If you want to mingle and dance with the locals, ask for a table in the main hall. There is a limited selection of wine—but plenty of Russian vodka and champagne. Except for the unpleasant reception you might get from the grouchy man guarding the front door, service here is pleasant, although typically slow. ✕ *22 ul. Sadovaya,* ☎ *812/310–1845. Reservations advised. No credit cards. Rubles only.* ☾ *Daily noon–midnight.*

$ Saigon Neva. Don't be fooled by the name—you'll find nothing but Russian cooking at this pleasant restaurant located just a block off St. Isaac's Square. And don't be fooled by the finely remodeled interior. The Vietnamese partners in this newly opened private restaurant pulled out at the last minute, but the Saigon Neva opened anyway. It's a lovely, quiet place in which to take a break from the hustle and bustle of downtown St. Petersburg. The varying selection of Russian main dishes, although pleasantly prepared, is heavily laden with french fries and oily vegetables. The appetizers and soups are better. Try the house specialty, *Griby po Domashnemy* (homestyle mushrooms), served with a heavy sauce inside light pastry shells. If you like squid, you'll enjoy the *Stolichnyi Salat,* garnished with onions and radishes in a mayonnaise base. The chicken soup comes with a tasty open-faced grilled cheese sandwich. Where the Saigon Neva is ahead of the competition is in its soothing atmosphere, complete with background music that's quiet enough to allow conversation. ✕ *33 ul. Kazanskaya,* ☎ *812/315–8772. Reservations accepted. No credit cards. Rubles only.* ☾ *Daily 1–11.*

$ Tbilisi. One of St. Petersburg's first cooperatives, the Tbilisi was immediately besieged by hungry crowds eager for a decent restaurant, and it made it into just about every guidebook on the city. Today it is definitely the worse for wear. In addition to the thick clouds of smoke, its sometimes shady clientele makes for a seedy atmosphere, especially in the evenings. During the day, however, it's a great place to try some Georgian food (it's named after the capital of the former Soviet republic), provided loud music doesn't curb your appetite. Despite the rowdy crowds, the service is friendly. The food is much better than the atmosphere and reasonably priced. The *lobio* (butter beans in a spicy sauce), *satsivy,* and *kharcho* (a spicy meat soup) are the best in town. Lobio, served warm, is also available as a main course and is highly recommended. Don't forget to order *lavash* (Georgian bread) and *khachapuri* (cheese-filled fried dough). Georgian wine, German beer, cognac, and Soviet champagne (when available) are sold. Located near the Gorkovskaya subway station. ✕ *10 Sytninskaya ul.* ☎ *812/232–9391. Reservations advised. No credit cards.* ☾ *Daily noon–11. Rubles only (except for some alcoholic beverages).*

$ Tête-à-Tête. ★ As its name suggests, this exclusive private restaurant, which has just one small dining room, specializes in French cuisine. Tables are available only by advance booking, and the front door is bolted shut to keep unwanted customers from entering "off the streets." (If you have a reservation, ring the bell.) Although the chef is clearly not from Paris, the kitchen does a credible job of producing French dishes with locally procured ingredients. For starters, try the rich and creamy onion soup, or the *julienne s gribami,* served in a cream sauce with mushrooms and onions. The French menu also features *myaso po Milanski,* grilled beef wrapped inside a cheese omelet and served with a heavy mushroom cream sauce. The classically designed interior suits the restaurant's exclusive image well. In the evenings, the grand piano tucked away in the corner provides light background music. The fully draped windows and dim lighting further add to the intimate atmosphere. Just don't go in groups larger than four. ✕ *65 Bolshoi Prospect, near Petrogradskaya metro station,* ☎ *812/232–7548. Reservations required. Jacket and tie. No credit cards.* ◷ *Daily 1–5, 7–midnight. Rubles only.*

LODGING

St. Petersburg's hotel industry has undergone changes in recent years. Until the late 1980s, all of the city's hotels were controlled by Intourist, the Soviet tourist agency that enjoyed a monopoly over the tourist trade. Rates for foreign tourists were standardized, and there were few distinctions in service and facilities from one hotel to the next. Perestroika—and St. Petersburg's sudden rise in popularity as a tourist destination—changed this. The influx of tourists prompted foreign contractors to launch some renovation projects, with the result that two of the city's most prestigious hotels, the Grand Hotel Europe and the Astoria Hotel, reopened to luxury-class status after major reconstruction; a third, the Nevsky Palace Hotel, joined their ranks as a brand-new contender.

The choices are still limited, however. As in Moscow, but with fewer offerings, hotels fall into two groups, with a wide gulf in between. Since the least expensive way to come to Russia is on an organized tour, you are likely to land in one of the old Intourist standbys, whose quality has hardly improved. Most U.S. and British tour operators take advantage of the deeply discounted rates available to them at these hotels and usually place groups at the Moskva, the Pribaltiskaya, the Pulkhovskaya, or the St. Petersburg (formerly Leningrad). These hotels were built in the late 1970s and early '80s, though they look at least 30 years older. Their facilities are all similar to each others'. They would be considered inferior by Western standards. The service, though mildly unpredictable, is perfectly acceptable, however, provided you are not expecting royal treatment. The main reason to choose them is their vastly lower rates. You probably should opt for those with the best location for you, for in addition to their other inconveniences, only one or two are close to the major attractions.

If your surroundings don't affect you, and especially if you plan to have a car or easy access to group transport, you'll probably want to save on hotel rates and make do with one of the less expensive hotels. If you want insulation from the uglier sides of life here, however, plan to pay up in order to stay at accommodations where you can have it.

CATEGORY	COST*
$$$$	over $200
$$$	$140–$200
$$	$65–$140
$	under $65

All prices are for a standard double room for two, excluding service charge.

$$$$ **Astoria.** Reopened in 1991 after major reconstruction, the Astoria is actually two hotels: It interconnects with the old Angleterre, a hotel with enduring "fame" because it's where the much-loved poet Sergei Yes-

enin committed suicide in 1925. Originally built in the style Moderne in 1910–12, the Astoria was one of St. Petersburg's most renowned hotels before the 1917 Revolution. Its renovation by Finnish contractors was bitterly opposed by many residents, as plans to merge the two hotels called for the complete destruction of the original building where Yesenin died. The contractors won out, and their renovations produced a fine hotel: Not a trace of St. Petersburg's dusty streets can be found. The splendid interiors have been decorated using antiques retrieved from various museums. Adding to the hotel's attraction is its convenient location in the heart of downtown St. Petersburg, directly across the street from St. Isaac's Cathedral and a 10-minute walk from the Hermitage. The somewhat lackluster service, however, is disappointing, and standards of efficiency need polishing. Among the top three hotels here, however, this one is considerably (about $100) less expensive. ⊞ *39 Bolshaya Morskaya ul., ☎ 812/315–2676, 812/210–5757, 812/210–5010, or 812/210–5020, ℻ 812/315–9668. 436 rooms with bath. 2 restaurants, 2 cafés, bar, nightclub, fitness center with pool and sauna, business center, excursion bureau.*

$$$$ **Grand Hotel Europe.** This five-star hotel is without question the finest
★ in town. Reopened 1991 after extensive renovations, it offers the elegance of prerevolutionary St. Petersburg along with every modern amenity. Its stunning Baroque facade has been carefully restored, while the Art Nouveau interior, with its stained-glass windows and authentic antique furniture, brings back its past glory. The stylish and comfortable rooms, done in pleasing tones of mauve, cream, and gold, verge on luxurious. The hotel is operated as a Russian-Swedish joint venture and is managed by Reso Hotels of Sweden. The Russian staff has been carefully trained in European standards of excellence, and the service shines. The Swedish management has thought of everything: 24-hour room service, direct-dial international telephone, mail service via courier to Helsinki, and satellite TV and radio, with CNN and MTV programming. The central location can't be beat: Nevsky Prospect, the Hermitage, and the Square of the Arts are all within walking distance. If money is no object, this is the place to stay. ⊞ *1/7 Mikhailovskaya ul., ☎ 812/119–6000 or 812/329–6000; ℻ 812/119–6001, 812/329–6001, or 812/329–6002. 211 standard rooms with bath, 17 junior suites, 18 terrace rooms, 23 penthouse suites, 26 2-room suites, 4 executive suites, 2 deluxe suites. 4 restaurants, café, bar, nightclub, sauna, health club, banquet and conference facilities. Traveler's checks accepted. AE, MC, V.*

$$$$ **Nevsky Palace Hotel.** Sister to the Palace Hotel in Moscow, this modern and spacious five-star establishment was refashioned on the site of an old building but is completely new. The top-notch service caters to the business elite who are looking for no fuss and serious comfort. Well situated not far from the Moscow Rail Station, it's accessible to everything you're likely to want to see. ⊞ *57 Nevsky Prospect, ☎ 812/311–6366, satellite fax 812/850–1501. 287 rooms. 3 restaurants, coffee shop, 2 bars, business center, shopping arcade, conference rooms, sauna with dipping pool, exchange, service bureau. AE, DC, MC, V.*

$$$ **Olympia.** The Olympia is actually a Swedish ocean liner permanently moored at St. Petersburg's sea passenger terminal, situated on the western edge of Vasilievsky Island. Swedish-managed (by the firm that operates the luxurious Grand Hotel Europe), the hotel offers excellent service and many amenities (on par with a three-star Western hotel). Although the ocean liner underwent renovations (in Sweden) that doubled the size of the cabins, the accommodations are still cramped; it is a boat, after all. The interior decor is unimaginative, and every room has two sides that mirror each other, with two tiny, identical bathrooms.

With its low ceilings and brass railings lining the corridors, you never forget you're on a ship, although it rarely rocks, even in windy weather. Unusual for Russia, the hotel offers several no-smoking rooms. The isolated location is a drawback, but the hotel offers its guests complimentary shuttle service on the hour to the very centrally located Grand Europe Hotel. ☎ *Ploshchad Morskoi Slavy,* ☎ *812/119–6800, satellite* ☎ *873/137–0316,* FAX *873/119–6805, satellite fax 873/137–0317. 146 rooms with shower. Restaurant, 2 bars, satellite TV and telephone, sauna and fitness center, conference facilities, limited excursion bureau, mail service via courier to Finland. AE, DC, MC, V.*

$$$ Pribaltiskaya. Swedish-built but Soviet-designed, this huge 16-story skyscraper is frequently used for placing tourist groups. Opened in 1978, it was once considered the city's top hotel. The rooms are clean and all come with cable television (including CNN and MTV). The modest furnishings are adequate, although slightly worn. Its first major drawback is the location: Far out on the western tip of Vasilievsky Island, the hotel is a good 20-minute drive to downtown St. Petersburg, and the closest subway station is several bus stops away. The predominantly residential area offers rows and rows of benumbing Soviet-era highrises—but very few shops and restaurants. If you can stand the isolation, the views of the Gulf of Finland are phenomenal, especially at sunset (ask for a room on the western side of the hotel). Another disadvantage is its increasing appeal to unsavory crowds, which may particularly bother single travelers. One plus is the hotel's well-stocked "Baltic Store," where you can pick up bottled water, imported snack foods, and a fairly recent copy of the *International Herald-Tribune* or *USA Today.* ☎ *14 ul. Korablestroiteli,* ☎ *812/356–0263 or 1-800/537– 8483,* FAX *812/356–4496 or 812/356–0372.* ☎ *11 restaurants, 10 snack bars, 5 bars, bowling alley, sauna with dipping pool, banquet and conference facilities, pharmacy, post, parking, gift shop, excursion bureau, exchange bureau. Traveler's checks accepted. AE, V, MC.*

$$$ Pulkhovskaya. Opened in 1981, this Finnish-built hotel has withstood
★ heavy tourist traffic, and its attractive Scandinavian-designed interior is still surprisingly well maintained. Accommodations are on the same level as the Pribaltiskaya (*see above*), although the rooms are slightly cleaner and more attractive. Service is friendly and efficient by local standards. Unusual for a Russian hotel, the curtains and bedspreads actually match the upholstery; and the bathrooms, complete with Finnish plumbing, are relatively large. Again, the disadvantage here is location. The hotel is not near the city center and is convenient only to the airport; the subway is a 10-minute walk away, and the ride into town takes at least 20 minutes. But in contrast to the Pribaltiskaya's surroundings, the area around the Pulkhovskaya is much easier on the nerves. Mainly residential, it has plenty of shops and even a restaurant or two. The views from the rooms, though, can depress you: You have a choice of gloomy high-rises and smokestacks or the severe, very Soviet, Victory Square monument outside the hotel's main entrance. ☎ *1 Ploshchad Pobedy,* ☎ *812/264–5122, 812/264–5022,* FAX *812/264– 6396 or 812/264–5844. 850 rooms with bath, telephone, TV, refrigerator. 2 restaurants, 6 snack bars, 6 bars, beauty salon, 2 saunas and dipping pool, business center, excursion bureau, car rental, gift and souvenir shops. AE, DC, MC, V.*

$$ Moskva. The unimaginative and depressing decor at this enormous, visibly aging hotel is yet another prime example of Brezhnev-era design. Store up on patience before checking in, because the lackluster service can make even paying your bill a frustrating experience; the desk clerks spend more time at lunch and on the phone than they do serving guests. The dreary rooms and public areas show obvious signs of neglect, but the hotel management keeps making stabs at renovations. The hotel's reputation for seedy mobs hanging out at the main entrance seems to have improved. Perhaps because this is the best located of the Intourist hotels, many groups stay here, and while they may sometimes remind you of the crowds at Disneyland, you feel safe. Location is good here. It is literally on top of the subway and faces the entrance to the 18th-century Alexander Nevsky Monastery. This is at one end of Nevsky Prospect, which is still the center of town. Another plus is that rates are on the low end of the Moderate category. ⊡ *2 Ploshchad Alexandra Nevskovo,* ☎ *812/274–2115 or 812/274–2100,* FAX *812/ 274–2130. 770 rooms with bath. Restaurant, 7 snack bars, 5 bars, excursion bureau, exchange bureau (traveler's checks accepted), business center, souvenir and gift shops. AE, DC, MC, V.*

$$ **Okhtinskaya.** The location, directly across the river from the Baroque
★ Smolny Sobor, is great for views but terribly inconvenient if you ever plan on going anywhere by public transportation. St. Petersburg's museums and tourist attractions are all on the other side of the river, and the subway is several bus stops away. Canadian-built and opened in 1991, the hotel is now run as a French-Russian joint venture. Service is unusually friendly, and the rates are extremely reasonable. Although the interior features the usual marble-and-chrome decor, the public areas are cheery and bright and, most important, devoid of the ubiquitous slot machines. The rooms are clean and well appointed, with imported furnishings and pretty, flowered wallpaper. While almost all the rooms come with balconies, only the suites have full baths. Unfortunately only one room on every floor faces the cathedral, but the views of the urban landscape on this side of town are more refreshing than most. ⊡ *4 Bolsheokhtinsky Prospect,* ☎ *812/227–4438 or 812/227–3767,* FAX *812/227–2618. 204 rooms with bath or shower. 2 restaurants, snack bar, 2 bars, sauna, conference rooms, gift shop, grocery store. AE, DC, MC, V.*

$$ **St. Petersburg.** Formerly called the Leningrad, this aging hotel offers
★ both the best and worst views of contemporary St. Petersburg. While the rooms overlooking the Neva have magnificent vistas of the city's waterfront architecture, the other half face the depressing other side of the building. While this is definitely not the luxury hotel it once was, if you can land a waterfront room, it is the only place to stay during the White Nights. The Finnish-decorated interior is faded and the furnishings are a bit worn, but the rooms and public areas are clean, and overall, not nearly as shabby as the Moskva's. The vast lobby holds a host of stores, including souvenir and gift shops. The location, however, is good only for the views. The Finland Train Station and subway are within walking distance, but the route is unpleasant and takes you along a busy highway. ⊡ *5/2 Vyborskaya Naberezhnaya,* ☎ *812/ 542–9411 or 812/542–9123,* FAX *812/248–8002. 410 rooms with bath. 2 restaurants, 3 snack bars, 3 bars, sauna with dipping pool, excursion bureau, exchange bureau, business center, shops, conference facilities. DC, MC, V.*

$$ **Sovietskaya-Helen.** The first name says it all: This is a Soviet hotel with the typically slow and disgruntled service of a state-run enterprise. Yet another concrete-and-steel monstrosity, the hotel is in an attractive section of downtown St. Petersburg. While the location allows for some good views of St. Petersburg's canals, it's still a long walk to just about anywhere, including the subway. There are two buildings, both built in the late 1960s, but the "newer wing" (the part called Helen) was recently remodeled. All rooms in both wings are relatively clean and have decent views. But accommodations in the "new" wing are generally in better shape and come with Finnish furnishings (and higher

rates). ⌂ *43/1 Lermontovsky Prospect, For Sovietskaya:* ☎ *812/259–
2552 or 812/259–2652,* FAX *812/251–8890. For Helen:* ☎ *812/251–
4368 or 812/119–9385,* FAX *812/251–0859. 1,099 rooms with bath.
3 restaurants, café, 4 snack bars, 3 bars, sauna with dipping pool, business center, excursion bureau. No credit cards.*

$ **Gorny.** This unusual hotel is actually a renovated dormitory belong-
★ ing to the wealthy St. Petersburg Institute of Mining (Gorny Institute).
The rooms on the lower floors are reserved for foreign students studying Russian at the institute, while the upper floors have been painstak-
ingly renovated to meet hotel standards. Although the building itself,
a typical modern high-rise, is far from luxurious, the rooms are clean
and nicely appointed, with German furnishings and imported decor.
All the rooms are actually suites, with kitchen facilities available at the
end of the corridor. Again, the main drawback here is location: the western tip of Vasilievsky Island. The Gorny will, however, provide local
transportation as needed (for an additional fee). This is a good choice
for budget-minded tourists who want to get closer to real life in Russia without experiencing the hassles that go along with it. No one on
the staff speaks English all that well, but you can fax in English for a
reservation. ⌂ *15 Morskaya Naberezhnaya, Bldg. 3,* ☎ *812/218–8605
or 812/218–8681,* FAX *812/218–5463. 50 rooms with bath. 2 cafés.
Traveler's checks accepted. No credit cards.*

$ **Karelia.** Situated in a gloomy residential area dominated by monotonous
and crumbling high-rises, this former Intourist hotel is a prime example of Brezhnev-era architecture. Built for the 1980 Olympics, it looks
years older than it is. The lobby, decorated with gaudy, socialist-realist paintings depicting an outdated Leningrad, is dismal and smoky.
Service, however, is surprisingly friendly, and the rates are the best in
town. The double and triple rooms (no singles available) are adequate
and relatively clean, and the friendly floor attendants willingly address
complaints. While the decor is less than attractive (bedspreads, curtains, and carpets are all different colors), the furnishings have been
imported from Finland, and the beds are more comfortable than most.
Some rooms come with television, and all come with telephone and
balcony (and dreary views). For tourists on a budget who don't mind
long excursions on the city's unreliable trolleybuses, the hotel offers
bearable if far from luxurious accommodations. But if you're not
counting your rubles, stay elsewhere. ⌂ *27/2 ul. Tukhachevskovo,* ☎
812/226–3515, FAX *812/226–3511. 430 rooms with bath or shower.
Restaurant, 5 snack bars, 3 bars, casino, disco, post, pharmacy excursion
bureau, business center with satellite telephone and fax, sauna. Traveler's checks accepted. AE, DC, MC, V.*

THE ARTS AND NIGHTLIFE

The Arts

St. Petersburg's status as Russia's cultural capital is well deserved; its
cultural life is one of the city's top attractions. Except for the most
renowned theaters, tickets are easily available and ridiculously inexpensive. You can buy them at the box offices of the theaters themselves
and at theater kiosks (*teatralnaya kassa*) located throughout the city.
Central Box Office No. 1 is at 42 Nevsky Prospect (☎ 812/311–
3183; open daily 11–7). For performances at the Mariinsky Theater
(better known in the West by its Soviet name, Kirov) and the Mussorgsky
Theater of Ballet and Opera (also known as the Maly) you have two
choices: Pay the inflated rates charged by hotel excursion bureaus, or

buy a ticket from a scalper outside the theater just before the performance. The second route is invariably cheaper, although there's no guarantee that your seat will have a view of the stage.

Even if you're not staying at the Astoria Hotel, you're welcome to use their service bureau (☎ 812/210–5046) for booking theater tickets. Most hotels post performance listings in their main lobby. The two English-language newspapers, *Neva News* and *St. Petersburg Press,* will have theater and concert listings as will the quarterly English-language magazine *St. Petersburg Premier* or the monthly *St. Petersburg News.*

All sorts of special art performances are organized for the White Nights' Festival, held in the last two weeks of June. After that, most major theaters close down for the summer and start up again in mid-September.

Concerts

Classical music can be enjoyed all over the city. The famous **St. Petersburg Shostakovich Bolshoi Philharmonic** (2 ul. Mikhailovskaya, ☎ 812/110–4290) offers excellent performances in its concert hall on the Square of Arts, located in a former Nobleman's Club. Concerts are also given in the Philharmonic's **Maly Zal imeni Glinki** (Little Glinka Hall) around the corner (30 Nevsky Prospect, ☎ 812/312–4585). One of St. Petersburg's best-kept secrets is its lovely **Glinka Kapella Choral Hall** (20 Nab. Reki Moiki, ☎ 812/314–1159), where not only choral recitals but also symphonic, instrumental, and vocal concerts are held. The theater dates from the 1880s, and many famous musicians, including Glinka and Rimsky-Korsakov, have performed here.

For a relaxing evening of classical music in a prerevolutionary setting, try one of the concert halls in St. Petersburg's mansions and palaces. Performances are held regularly in the **Anichkov Palace Concert Hall** (39 Nevsky Prospect, ☎ 812/310–4822), **Beloselsky-Belozersky Palace** (41 Nevsky Prospect, ☎ 812/315–3821), **Bosse Mansion** (4-ya Liniya 15, ☎ 812/213–3488), and the **Smolny Cathedral and Convent** (3/1 Ploshchad Rastrelli, ☎ 812/311–3560).

Other major concert halls include the **Oktyabrski Bolshoi Concert Hall** (6 Ligovskii Prospect, ☎ 812/277–6960) and the **St. Petersburg Music Hall** (4 Alexandrovsky Park, ☎ 812/232–9201 or 812/233–0243).

Opera and Ballet

The world-renowned **Mariinsky Theater of Opera and Ballet** (1/2 Teatralnaya Ploshchad, ☎ 812/114–4344) should not be missed. Its elegant blue-and-gold auditorium has been the main home of the Russian ballet—the Kirov—since the 1880s. The lesser-known **Maly Theater of Opera and Ballet** (1 Ploshchad Iskusstv, ☎ 812/212–2040) also offers outstanding performances but at much lower prices. Operas are usually sung in Russian, and the repertoire is dominated by Russian composers.

Theater

St. Petersburg also offers some excellent dramatic theaters, but performances are almost exclusively in Russian. Even if you can't understand the dialogue, you may want to visit the famous **Bolshoi Drama Theater** (65 Nab. Reki Fontanki, ☎ 812/310–9242) or Russia's oldest theater, the elegant **Pushkin Drama Theater** (2 Ploshchad Ostrovskovo, ☎ 812/312–1545), where the repertoire is dominated by the classics.

Nightlife

Compared with Moscow, which is bursting at the seams with hot new night spots, St. Petersburg borders on tame. Yet it can still outdo its rival in trendiness. Maybe it's simply that St. Petersburg looks so arty, but it's always been considered the style capital and is also inarguably the home of Russian rock and roll. So when you're stepping out for the latest music, you will have a good time here. And do step out of an Intourist monolith if you're staying there. The floor shows that their clubs traditionally arrange are a deafening assault on the senses, so if you want something else, you'd better look well outside their doors for entertainment.

A note about security: Though media reports on increased crime in Russia exaggerate the situation, foreigners in this economically strapped country are easy prey for robbery and muggings. Use common sense and stay away from the sleazy bars and clubs where prostitution thrives and the main goal of guests seems to be to to reach a drunken bliss. If you plan to spend the evening outside your hotel, you'll be glad if you make arrangements for the trip home before setting out. Although there are virtually no after-dark hours during the White Nights, a too late-evening stroll down Nevsky Prospect may be an invitation to trouble.

Bars and Lounges

All the major hotels have bars and nightclubs, but except for the Astoria and Grand Hotel Europe, the local clientele is often of questionable intention and the atmosphere tends to get sleazy as the night wears on.

One of the better spots in town is **Sadko** (Grand Hotel Europe, 1/7 ul. Mikhailovskaya, ☎ 812/119–6000, ext. 6390). Nightly entertainment often features top local performers, such as the zany Sergei Kuriyokin, and a Russian reggae band. The crowds are mostly foreign tourists and Russian students, with a few *novy Russkis* mixed in. In the summer the hotel ship **Olympia** (Ploshchad Morskoi Slavy, ☎ 812/119–6800) has the outdoor White Nights Bar, which makes for enjoyable relaxation. **The Beer Garden** (86 Nevsky Prospect, ☎ 812/275–7620), the **Chaika** restaurant, or the **John Bull Pub** (*see* Restaurants, *above*) are good spots for a big mug of beer.

Casinos

Casino fever is lower in St. Petersburg than in Moscow and Kiev, but high rollers can still have fun. Some restaurants have their own casinos, as do the Hotels Astoria and Pribaltiskaya.

Full-out casinos are **Conti** (44 Kondratievsky, ☎ 812/540–1565) and **Casino 777** (7 ul. Malaya Konyushennaya, ☎ 812/311–3111).

Dance Clubs

For performance art, live rock, and the very trendy, there's **Art Clinic** (Pushkinskaya 10 commune); **Fish Fabrique,** at the same address, has a funky bohemian air. You can hear pop, techno, or reggae—or most likely, a concoction of all three—at **Domenico's** (70 Nevsky Prospect, ☎ 812/272–5717). That it takes its artiness seriously is reflected in its steep cover charge. Home to the Russian rave, **The Tunnel** used to be a fallout shelter, but it's definitely not for the already shell-shocked—but only the rough and tough. The noisy and lively **Wild Side** (12 nab. Bumazhnovo Kanala, ☎ 812/186–3466) accompanies its blasting music with lots of lights.

The nightclub on the fifth floor of the **Grand Hotel Europe** (☎ 812/210–3667) offers two dance floors, as well as a dazzling view of St. Petersburg's rooftops (jacket and tie required; cover charge). The

Russian-Swedish joint venture **Nevsky Melody** (62 nab. Sverdlovskaya, ☎ 812/227–2676) has a hopping dance floor and an erotic floor show that is definitely a matter of taste. This night spot is extremely popular with St. Petersburg's nouveaux riches.

Jazz, Rock, and Blues

To hear Russia's top jazz musicians, head for the St. Petersburg **Jazz Philharmonic Hall** (27 Zagorodny Prospect, near the Dostoevskaya metro station, ☎ 812/164–8565). Regular performances by the likes of world-renowned **Leningrad Dixieland Band** and **David Goloshchyokin's Ensemble** make this a favorite night spot. Serious jazz lovers will enjoy the fantastic atmosphere in this turn-of-the-century building. It makes for a classy night out. Some less emphatically highbrow jazz venues are the **New Jazz Club** (4 ul. Tavricheskaya, ☎ 812/275–6090)— which also hosts a Sunday blues night—and the **At the Art Café** (58 ul. Bolshaya Morskaya, 2nd floor, ☎ 812/510–4652), where you can mix your jazz with poetry and drama performances on Friday, Saturday, and Sunday.

The **Gora Club** (153 Ligovsky Prospect) showcases local rock bands. For heavy rock, try the small **Archwall Club** (10 ul. Pravdy). Rockabilly fans will find their fellows at the **Money Honey Saloon** (Dom 14, Apraksin Dvor), but pay heed: While the music may be good, the neighborhood is not.

ST. PETERSBURG ESSENTIALS

Arriving and Departing

By Boat

Cruise ships of the Baltic Line call at St. Petersburg. Cruises are available from Stockholm and Helsinki. For information on schedules and fares, contact their Helsinki office: 6 kluuvitaku, SF-00100, Helsinki, ☎ 358/90–665755.

The sea passenger terminal is on Vasilevsky Island at Morskoi Slavy Ploshchad (☎ 812/355–1310). The river passenger terminal is at 195 Obukhovskoi Oborony Prospect (☎ 812/262–1318).

By Bus

The Russian firm **Sovavto St. Petersburg** (☎ 812/298–1352, FAX 812/298–7760) offers daily departures to Helsinki from the following hotels: Astoria, Grand Hotel Europe, Pulkhovskaya, and Sovietskaya. The Finnish bus company **Finnord** (☎ 812/314–8951, FAX 812/314–7058) offers daily service to Vyborg, Lakhti, and Helsinki, leaving from the Sovietskaya Hotel.

By Car

You can reach St. Petersburg from Finland via the Helsinki–St. Petersburg Highway through the border town of Vyborg. To reach Moscow, take the Moscow–St. Petersburg Highway, which leaves the city near the Varshavsky (Warsaw) Railroad Station, close to Izmailovsky Cathedral.

Again, a word of warning about driving: Be aware of lines at fueling stations, the risk of car theft, and the lack of repair shops and replacement parts, added to the poor road conditions and maintenance. It's advisable not to drive.

By Plane

AIRPORTS AND AIRLINES

St. Petersburg is served by two airports, **Pulkhovo I** (domestic) and **Pulkhovo II** (international), located just 5 kilometers (3 miles) apart and 12 kilometers (7 miles) south of downtown St. Petersburg. The runways of the two Pulkhovos interconnect, so it's possible you could land at Pulkhovo I and taxi over to Pulkhovo II.

Compared to Moscow's Sheremetyevo II, Pulkhovo II is a breeze. It's small and well lit, with signs in Russian and English. Remember that on departure you will need to fill out a final customs declaration (available at all the long tables) before proceeding through the first checkpoint.

For domestic flight information, call 812/104–3822. For international information, call 812/104–3444.

Aeroflot (☎ 812/104–3444) offers direct flights to more than 20 countries out of Pulkhovo II. Other international airlines maintaining offices in St. Petersburg include **Balkan** (☎ 812/315–5030), **Delta** (☎ 812/311–5819), **Finnair** (☎ 812/315–9736), **Air France** (☎ 812/119–8252), **KLM** (☎ 812/104–3440), **Lufthansa** (☎ 812/314–4979), **Malev** (☎ 812/317–6380), and **Swissair** (☎ 812/314–5086).

BETWEEN THE AIRPORT AND DOWNTOWN

From Pulkhovo I, municipal bus No. 13 will take you to the Moskovskaya subway stop at the end of Nevsky Prospect; the stop at the airport is right outside the terminal. Tickets are sold on the bus, which runs every 40 minutes during the day and every 90 minutes at night. From Pulkhovo II, the service is less reliable and more inconvenient. If you have any luggage, the only realistic way to reach downtown St. Petersburg is by car. If you are traveling with a tour package, all transfers will have been arranged. Independent tourists are advised to make advance arrangements with their hotels for transfers from the airport. There are plenty of taxis available, but for safety reasons non-Russian speakers should not pick up a cab on their own. Foreign tourists, especially arriving passengers at train stations and airports, are prime crime targets. Cab fare from the airport will depend entirely on your negotiating skills; the range is $10 to $50. The airport is about a 40-minute ride from the city center.

By Train

Train travel is by far the most convenient and comfortable mode of travel in Russia. St. Petersburg has several train stations, the most important of which are **Finlandsky Vokzal** (Finland Station), for trains to Finland; **Moskovsky Vokzal** (Moscow Station), at Ploshchad Vostania, off Nevsky Prospect, for trains to Moscow and points east; **Varshavsky Vokzal** (Warsaw Station) for trains to the Baltic countries; and **Vitebsky Vokzal** (Vitebsk Station) for trains to Ukraine and points south. All the major train stations have a connecting subway stop, so they are easily reached by public transportation.

There are several trains daily from Moscow to St. Petersburg, the most popular of which is the **_Red Arrow,_** a night train that departs Moscow at 11:55 PM and arrives in St. Petersburg at 8:25 AM the next day. During the day travelers prefer the high-speed **_Avrora,_** which makes the trip in less than six hours. There are two trains daily to and from Helsinki; the trip takes 6½ hours.

For information on train arrival and departure schedules, call 812/168–0111. Train tickets may be purchased through the tourist bureau in your hotel or at the Central Railway Agency Office at 24 Kanal Griboyedova (off Nevsky Prospect, adjacent to the Kazan Cathedral), ☎ 812/162–3344. Tickets for anything other than same-day departures are *not* for sale at the train stations.

A reminder about train travel: You must travel on an Intourist train ticket or risk being fined by the railway. As a foreigner you pay the special higher price for train travel and, in return, usually get above-average service (the best trains are still reserved for foreign tourists).

Very long-distance travelers should be aware that trains can often lack heat and hot water, a result of feuds between rail administrations in different republics. To avoid discomfort, be sure to bring along some drinking water whenever traveling by train. You are also advised to have your own supply of toilet paper.

Getting Around

Although St. Petersburg is spread out over 650 square kilometers (150 square miles), most of its historic sites are concentrated in the downtown section and are best explored on foot. Most of the historical sites are not well served by the extensive public transportation system, so be prepared to do a lot of walking.

By Bus, Tram, and Trolley

Surface transportation operates on the honor system: Upon entering, you validate your ticket by punching it in one of the machines on the wall of the vehicle. You can purchase strips of tickets at subway stops and kiosks throughout the city or, sometimes, from the driver after you have boarded. The ticket is valid for one ride only; if you change buses you must pay another fare. Buses, trams, and trolleys operate from 5 AM to 1 AM, although service in the late evening hours and on Sundays tends to be unreliable.

St. Petersburg has an elaborate surface transportation system, but in contrast to the subway, service has greatly deteriorated in recent years. Vehicles tend to be dilapidated and extremely overcrowded during rush hours. People with claustrophobia should avoid them. In the last years of the Soviet regime, Russia depended on Hungary for buses, but in today's economic order, they are no longer forthcoming. It is not uncommon to ride a bus with holes in the ceiling and doors that will not close due to constant overcrowding, or that keels to the side when turning corners like a sailboat on rough seas.

By Subway

Although St. Petersburg's metro does not boast the elaborate design and decoration of the Moscow subway, its beauty and convenience are still great. And despite economic hardships, St. Petersburg has managed to maintain efficient service. The only drawback to the system, which is simple to use and inexpensive as well, is that the stops tend to be far apart.

To use the subway, you must purchase a token (available at stations) and insert it upon entering into the slot at the turnstile. The fare is the same regardless of distance. Alternatively, you may purchase a pass valid for the entire month and good for transport on all modes of city transportation. The cost is insignificant and well worth the convenience if you plan to use the subway a lot. The subway operates from 5:30 AM to 1 AM and is best avoided during rush hours. Stations are deep underground with long escalator rides. Some of them have encased land-

St. Petersburg Metro

Parnasskaya

Prospekt
Prosveshcheniya

Komsomolskaya

Ozerki

Grazhdansky
Prospekt

Udelnaya

Akademicheskaya

Pionerskaya

Politekhnicheskaya

Chyornaya
Rechka

Ploshchad
Muzhestva

Staraya
Derevnya

Petrogradskaya

Lesnaya

Krestovsky
Ostrov

Gorkovskaya

Vyborgskaya

Chkalovskaya

Ploshchad
Lenina

Primorskaya

Sportivnaya

Chernyshevskaya

Vasileostrovskaya

**Gostinny
Dvor**

Nevsky Prospekt

Pl. Vosstaniya

Mayakovskaya

Ploshchad Mira

Dostoyevskaya

Sadovaya

**Pl. Aleksandra
Nevskovo**

Vladimirskaya

Krasnogvardeyskaya

**Tekhnologichesky
Institute**

Puskinskaya

Ligovsky
Prospekt

Ladozhskaya

Frunzenskaya

Prospekt
Bolshevikov

Balktiyskaya

Moskovskiye
Vorota

Narvskaya

Electrosila

Ul. Dybenko

Kirovsky
Zavod

Park
Pobedy

Avtovo

Moskovskaya

Yelizarovskaya

Leninsky
Prospekt

Zvyozdnaya

Narodnaya

Lomonosovskaya

Prospekt
Veteranov

Kupchino

Proletarskaya

Obukhovo

Rybatskoye

ings so that entry is possible only after the train has pulled in and the secondary doors are opened.

By Taxi

Although taxis roam the city quite frequently, it is far easier—and certainly safer—to order a cab through your hotel. Fares vary according to the driver's whim; you are expected to negotiate. Foreigners are always charged much more than Russians, and tourists tend to be gouged. If you speak Russian, you can order a cab by dialing 312–00–22. There is sometimes a delay, but usually the cab arrives within 20–30 minutes. If you order a cab this way, you pay the official state fare, which turns out to be very reasonable in dollars, plus a fee for the reservation. Drivers will appreciate and expect a tip of at least 20%. If you hail a cab on the street, expect to pay the ruble equivalent of at least $5.

Tourists should take the same precautions when using taxicabs in St. Petersburg as in Moscow.

Guided Tours

A host of private tour agencies have arisen in the past few years, primarily because tourism is seen as an easy source of foreign currency. Keep in mind that whatever the price quoted for a tour, it may very well be negotiable. In addition to the private agencies, every major hotel has a tourist bureau through which individual and group tours can be booked.

St. Petersburg Tourist Company (formerly Intourist) offers group or individual excursions to all of the major sites and suburban palaces. City tours start daily at 10 AM. For more information, call 812/315–5129 or fax 812/315–5554.

The **St. Petersburg City Excursion Bureau** (56 Krasnovo Flota nab., ☎ 812/311–4019, FAX 812/311–8666) arranges sightseeing trips throughout the city. Specially tailored tours can be made through **Peter the Great Person-to-Person Tours** (16 Dmitrovsky per., ☎ 812/311–8019, FAX 812/526–6624) or by **Staraya Derevnya** (72 ul. Savushkina, ☎ 812/239–0000).

Important Addresses and Numbers

Consulates

United States (15 Furstadtskaya, ☎ 812/275–1701, 812/274–8568, or 812/274–8689). **Canada** (32 Malodetskoselsky Prospect, ☎ 812/119–8448). **Great Britain** (5 Ploshchad Proletarskoi Diktatury, ☎ 812/119–6036).

A word of warning: Phone lines to the U.S. Consulate are constantly busy. It may take hours of persistent dialing to get through.

Emergencies

Fire (☎ 01), **police** (☎ 02, Russian speakers only), **ambulance** (☎ 03, Russian speakers only).

HOSPITALS AND CLINICS

Medical facilities in St. Petersburg still are poorly equipped and short on supplies. As in the other cities, it is recommended that tourists seek emergency medical help at Western-style clinics. The **American Medical Center** offers 24-hour comprehensive care; it is located at 77 nab. reki Fontanka, ☎ 812/119–6101; fax 812/119–6120. **The Medical Centre for Foreigners** has been around for years as the St. Petersburg Polyclinic No. 2 (22 Moskovsky Prospect, ☎ 316–6272; fax 812/292–5939, open weekdays 9–9, Sat. 9–3). While care is still below Western standards, the facilities are clean and foreign medicines are available. A doctor is on call 24 hours a day.

If you are unfortunate enough to be hospitalized while in St. Petersburg, you will probably be placed in **Hospital No. 20** (21 ul. Gastello, ☎ 812/108–4808 or 812/108–4066).

DENTISTS
Several private dental practices operate in St. Petersburg. In an emergency, you could ask your hotel for a referral, or try one of the following private clinics: **St. Petersburg Polyclinic No. 2** (22 Moskovsky Prospect, ☎ 812/316–6272), **Dental Polyclinic No. 3** (21-ya Liniya, ☎ 812/213–7551 or 812/213–5550), **Dental Center** (10-ya Sovetskaya, ☎ 812/274–6480), or **Nordmed** (12/15 ul. Tverskaya, ☎ 812/110–0654 or 812/110–0401).

English-Language Bookstores
For English-language publications, try St. Petersburg's largest bookstore, **Dom Knigi** (House of Books), at 28 Nevsky Prospect. The selection is nothing to write home about, but it's still the biggest bookstore in town and fun to see. **Planeta,** at 30 Liteiny Prospect, has a selection of imported books, too. A limited selection of outdated English-language guidebooks on various parts of the former Soviet Union is available at **Akademkniga** (57 Liteiny Prospect) and **Iskusstvo** (52 Nevsky Prospect). American and British paperbacks, newspapers, and magazines are on sale in hotel gift shops.

Pharmacies
Most pharmacies in St. Petersburg close by 8 or 9 PM. However, **Petro-Farm** (22 Nevsky Prospect, ☎ 812/164–4410) has a pharmacist on call 24 hours a day.

Pharmacies that regularly stock imported and Western medicines are **Pharmacy Damian** (22 Moskovsky Prospect, ☎ 812/110–1744); **Petro-Farm** (also at 83 Nevsky Prospect, ☎ 812/277–7966); and **Pharmadon** (5 Nevsky Prospect, ☎ 812/312–7078).

Travel Agencies
For international travel help, **American Express** operates an office in the Grand Hotel Europe (1/7 ul. Mikhailovskaya, just off Nevsky Prospect, ☎ 812/315–7487). Besides ticketing, here you can also replace lost traveler's checks and credit cards or take out a cash advance (in traveler's checks only). The office does not have an automated teller machine, and due to limited availability of cash, it is not always possible to cash your traveler's checks for dollars. ⊙ *Weekdays 9–5.*

Avista Tours (7 ul. Millionaya, ☎ 812/275–6635) arranges international bookings. **EPOL Travel Agency** (61 Liteiny Prospect, ☎ 812/279–5060, FAX 812/279–5066) can arrange train and plane tickets as well as customized tours throughout Russia. **Griphon Travel** has a desk at the Moskva Hotel (☎ 812/274–0022), where they can take care of air tickets throughout the CIS as well as abroad.

Where to Change Money
Inkombank, 41 ul. Komsomolska (☎ 812/542–3611); **St. Petersburg Bank,** 16 Voznesensky Prospect (☎ 812/314–6095); **Industry and Construction Bank,** 38 Nevsky Prospect (☎ 812/110–4958).

Again, your hotel is more convenient; all of them also have exchange bureaus, which are generally open from 9 AM to 6 PM with an hour's break for lunch in the afternoon.

Visitor Information

You may consult the **St. Petersburg Council for Tourism**, whose head office is at 3 ulitsa Italianskaya, ☎ 812/314–8786 or 812/110–6739; FAX 812/110–6824 or 812/311–9381.

But your most expeditious route is your hotel, for virtually all of them have established tourist offices for their guests. These offices, which provide a wide variety of services, will help you book individual and group tours, make restaurant reservations, or purchase theater tickets. Even if you are not a hotel guest, you are usually welcome to use these facilities, provided you are willing to pay the hefty fees (charged in foreign currency only) for their services.

4 Kiev

By Lauri del
Commune

THINK OF YOUR TRIP TO KIEV as a journey by time machine that will transport you back to the earliest mo-
ments of Ukrainian-Russian history. Kiev (in Ukrainian,
Kiyv) is known as the mother of Russian cities, for it was here, around
the end of the 9th century, that the Eastern Slav lands collectively called
Rus were first unified. The city of Kiev itself was reportedly founded
near the end of the 5th century by a family for whose eldest brother,
Kii, it was named. For the next 1,500 years it was a center of unceas-
ing activity in trade, religion, and politics. Today it is a bustling modern metropolis—the capital of independent Ukraine—beginning a new
chapter in its identity but still closely tied to its ancient past and founding role in the development of Russian culture.

Between the 10th and 12th centuries Kiev flourished as the capital of Rus.
After Christianity became the official religion in 988, Kiev became one
of the most significant points of religious exchange and learning in the
ancient empire. A gradual decline began in the late 1100s, ending abruptly
in 1240, when the city was razed to the ground by Mongol invaders. Thereafter, until 1991, Kiev was the capital of an independent nation for only
brief periods. Freed from the Mongol yoke in the 14th century, it fell under
the rule of the Lithuanians and then the Poles. In 1654, choosing the lesser
of two evils, Ukraine joined the Russian empire.

Much of what is known of Kiev's early history comes from the *Primary Chronicle,* written in the 11th–12th centuries by monks at Kiev's
Monastery of the Caves. It was there that Nestor first wrote of the "three
brothers . . . Kii lived upon the hill where the Borich trail now is; and
Shchek dwelled upon the hill now named Shchekovitza; while on the
third resided Khoriv, after whom this hill is named Khorevitsa. They
built a town and named it Kiev after their oldest brother." (The founding family also had a sister named Lybid, but her legacy today seems
to be an eponymous hotel, not a city.) Archaeological findings confirm
that there was indeed a settlement called Kii around the end of the 6th
century, and the hills still exist. You will see them and the golden
domes of Kiev's ancient churches rising above the green expanses that
carpet the hilly terrain and vast plains.

The city has always had its full share of violence and bloodshed, which,
along with its ancient glory, is an essential key to understanding today's
Kiev. In the aftermath of the Bolshevik Revolution and the ensuing civil
war, Kiev saw bitter fighting that pitted brother against brother. The
city suffered heavy losses and was nearly destroyed again during World
War II, when it was captured and held by German forces for almost
800 days. Liberated by the Soviet army, Kiev again suffered terribly under
Red recapture, when many Ukrainians were perceived as Nazi collab-
orators—sometimes merely because the city had been occupied by the
Germans. Postwar punishment escalated as Stalin's notorious purges,
intense in the Ukraine starting in the 1930s, were translated into camp
deportations, land collectivizations, and executions. After Stalin's death
in 1953, three decades of enforced Russification took hold, with
Ukrainian educational, governmental, and social institutions being
made to fit the Soviet mold. In 1986, the Ukraine suffered the tragedy
of Chernobyl when one of its nuclear power reactors, just 104 kilometers
(65 miles) north of the city, exploded, spewing radioactive materials into
the air and into the city's water supply. Scientists affirm that Kiev is now
safe for visitors, but residents will feel the effects of the accident for decades
to come. As the former USSR began to founder in the late 1980s, so

did much of its authority over the Ukrainian state. In 1991, the Ukrainian parliament rejected Soviet Russian hegemony altogether, by declaring itself a fully independent nation and electing its own president.

The Ukrainian capital straddles the wide Dnieper River. To the east lie the steep hills of Old Kiev, while to the west you will find the newly developed regions of the low-lying left bank. The political and industrial center of modern Ukraine, Kiev displays both the tranquillity of its ancient past and the agitation of a newly independent nation grappling with the political and economic problems of moving ahead as an autonomous nation.

EXPLORING

Tour 1: The Khreshchatik and Kiev's Art Museums

Numbers in the margin correspond to points of interest on the Kiev map.

★ This tour takes you along Kiev's main thoroughfare—the **Khreshchatik**—and to the city's most important art museums. It might be tempting to begin your exploration with the city's many monuments to ancient history, but the Khreshchatik is the best place to gain a sense of today's Kiev. The avenue's role as the city's cultural center and main shopping district invites comparison with St. Petersburg's Nevsky Prospect. Kievans themselves like to think of it as a Ukrainian Champs-Elysées. It is lined with monumental high-rises, many in the Stalinist architectural style, interspersed with broad strips of green lanes and parks. As thoroughfares go, the Khreshchatik is quite short—just 1.6 kilometers (less than a mile) long. It is located in a valley and runs along the lines of a deep ditch that once occupied the site. Hills rise steeply along both sides, especially to the south. The Khreshchatik was almost completely destroyed during World War II and was rebuilt at twice its original width. The street's name may come from the dried-up riverbed that once ran through the valley. The river was called Khreschata (meaning crisscrossed), for the valley was crossed by numerous ravines. Other possibilities are that the name derives from the word *khreshchennya,* meaning "baptism," or from *khrest,* which means "cross." The street leads to the site in the Dnieper River where, according to legend, the people of Kiev were baptized en masse in 988.

❶ The tour begins at **Lenkomsomol Square,** at the eastern end of the Khreshchatik. If the current frenzy of name-changing continues, this square will soon be known by another name. But surely it will not be returned to its former name, Stalin Square. You can reach it by taking the subway to **Maidan Nezalezhnosti.** Take a right as you exit the stop, and go all the way to the end of the Khreshchatik (you will already be on it when you emerge). Lenkomsomol Square marks the end of the Khreshchatik, and other main streets radiate from it. Standing in front of the Hotel Dnipro, to the near left alongside the rectangular, all-white building that was the short-lived Lenin Museum (*see* Tour 2, *below*) **vulitsa Trokh-Svyatitelska** (Three Saints Street) leads up a steep incline to the famous St. Andrew's Cathedral (*see* Tour 3, *below*). **Vulitsa Mikhaila Grushevskovo** to the right leads to the Pechersk district and the ancient Monastery of the Caves (*see* Tour 4, *below*). **Volodimirski Spusk,** diagonal from the hotel, leads down to the riverbank.

❷ Take the underpass that goes beneath the square to cross to the opposite side. The yellow building here is the **Hall of Columns,** built in 1882. The former meeting place of the prerevolutionary Merchants' Assem-

bly, it is now home to Kiev's Philharmonic Society. Climb the broad stairway next to it, which will wind its way up alongside a park. At the top, head toward the back. You will soon be greeted by a huge steel rainbow, which is the Monument Commemorating the 325th Anniversary of the Reunion of Russia and Ukraine. The union is over now, of course, but the monument remains. Erected in 1982, the gigantic arch has five sections representing the Earth's continents, and the proletarian figures with a bas-relief depict Russo-Ukrainian brotherhood. You may prefer to concentrate on the splendid view behind it of the wide Dnieper, the long bridges that span its islands, and the vast plains of the left bank.

As you enjoy the view, look across the ravine to your immediate left. ❸ There you will see **Volodimirska Girka** (Vladimir Hill) and the **Monument to the Baptism of Russia.** The 20-meter (66-foot) monument shows Prince Vladimir—the pagan ruler who brought Christianity to Russia—dressed as a Russian warrior and holding a cross in his right hand. The pedestal, shaped like a Russian chapel, is engraved with the ancient seal of Old Kiev. Erected in 1853, the bronze statue was designed by Vasily Demut-Malinovsky, a St. Petersburg sculptor, and was cast by Peter Klodt, creator of the famous horse statues adorning St. Petersburg's Anichkov Bridge.

Return now to Lenkomsomol Square and turn left to go up vulitsa Mikhaila Grushevskovo. The attractive mauve stone building on the corner is the National Parliamentary Library. The street just beyond it leads to the **Central Park of Culture and Rest,** where Kiev's Dynamo Stadium is located. Keep to the right of this street and, going up another block ❹ further, you'll find the **Museum of Ukrainian Art.** Its huge granite steps are flanked by a pair of lions. Opened in 1899, it originally housed Kiev's Museum of Antiquities and Art. In 1936 the exhibits were moved to another location, and the present museum, devoted to Ukrainian art from the 12th to early 20th centuries, was opened. *6 vul. Mikhaila Grushevskovo,* ☏ *044/228–6482.* ⏱ *Mon.–Thurs., weekends 10–6.*

The museum's 21 halls house a wonderful collection of Ukrainian paintings, sculptures, and drawings as well as religious art. The rich collection of icons, located on the first floor, includes the 12th-century St. George with scenes from his life and the 14th-century Virgin Hodegetria, brought here from the town of Lutsk. The 18th-century Intercession is interesting for its portrait of Bogdan Khmelnitsky, the hetman who led the revolt that liberated Ukraine from Polish rule. The first-floor exhibits also contain fine examples of Ukrainian portrait and landscape paintings from the 17th to the 19th century, including Vasily Tropinin's *Girl from Podolia* and Taras Shevchenko's *Self-Portrait.* Several well-known works by Nikolai Pimonenko, including his *Wedding in Kiev* and *Victim of Fanaticism,* are also on display. The second-floor exhibits are devoted to modern Ukrainian art. Strongly influenced by Soviet propaganda and the demands of socialist realism, the works here are interesting primarily as a sociopolitical statement.

Leaving the museum, return again to Lenkomsomol Square to begin a tour of the Khreshchatik itself. Most of the architecture here dates from the 1950s and '60s, with a few exceptions at the beginning of the street. On the right-hand side stand the former **St. Petersburg Bank** (No. 8) and the former **Volzhsko-Kamsky Bank** (No. 10), both built at the turn of the century.

TIME OUT   The **Konditerska** across the street (5 Khreshchatik) has a stand-up café where you can have coffee or tea and pastry. Kiev has always been known for its delicious cakes, and you will find Kievans lining up here to buy them. If you're looking for a place to sit down, you can stop by the **Dnipro Hotel,** back at the corner with Lenkomsomol Square, where you can have a cup of coffee or a draft beer at the lobby bar.

5 One block from Lenkomsomol Square, the Khreshchatik meets **Maidan Nezalezhnosti** (Independence Square), to which you came by subway. In Yaroslav's day the southeastern gates of the high defensive wall surrounding the city stood near here, at the bottom of vulitsa Zhitomirska (to your right, beyond the fountains). During the communist regime, this broad, sprawling square was named in honor of the October Revolution, and a huge, red granite statue of Lenin once stood on the terrace (to your left) across the street.

Towering above the square on the left, fronted by a series of broad steps, is the **Moskva Hotel,** built in the early 1960s and designed after the Moscow original. If you're feeling energetic, climb up vulitsa Institutska, which runs alongside the hotel. Crowning the hill, at No. 5, is a prerevolutionary building with a Classical colonnade. Built by the architect Vikenty Beretti in the early 1840s, it was originally a finishing

6 school for young ladies of the nobility. Today it is the **Palace of Culture,** one of the city's largest concert halls.

The building below and to the right as you face the hotel is the **Tchaikovsky Conservatory,** a restored version of the 1899 original. Look across the street at the large and elaborate building on the opposite corner. It is Kiev's main **post office.** If you turn left onto the street that skirts the conservatory's right side, you will be on vulitsa Karla Marksa, a lovely side street with a cinema, small park, and shops. Not far away, it is bisected on the right by Zamkovetskaya vulitsa. Take a right onto it.

This is a very pleasant area to browse and shop, and you will find many boutiques and cooperatives. To get back to the Khreschatik, go through one of the "passages," unmarked lanes that lead through the large arches linking sections of the long, connected buildings that front this part of the Khreshchatik.

Back on this main street, heading away from Maidan Nezalezhnosti, the next block contains several large department stores and administrative buildings, including the imposing Office of the President of Ukraine. Cross to the right-hand side via one of the underground crossings. At the very end of the Khreschatik, one of the city's few surviving statues of Lenin marks the beginning of **Bulvar Tarasa Shevchenka,** named in honor of the 19th-century Ukrainian poet and artist.

TIME OUT At No. 2 you will find a cornucopia of hard-currency shops and restaurants, including the **Arlechino Pizzeria** (☎ 044 225–0271). Take a break here before you head into the heart of Kiev's museum district. It's a cheery spot, and their array of pizzas and drinks will refresh you. They have take-out service, too.

7 Walk two blocks up the boulevard, and on your right, at the corner with vulitsa Repina, is the **Taras Shevchenko State Museum.** If you have spent any time in Ukraine, you have probably heard about this beloved national hero. Born into serfdom in 1814, he became one of the nation's greatest artists and poets, as well as a leader in the fight against serfdom. A member of the secret Society of Sts. Cyril and Methodius, which opposed serfdom, he was arrested in 1847 and spent more than 10 years in internal exile. In failing health when he returned, he died four years later, at the age of 47. At the age of 16 he had gone to St. Petersburg, where he quickly gained recognition for his artistic abilities, despite his lack of formal training. Art critics encouraged him to enter the St. Petersburg Academy of Arts, but first he had to purchase his freedom from his owner. The artist Karl Bryullov came to his aid, auctioning his portrait of the Russian poet Vasily Zhukovsky and donating the proceeds to Shevchenko. The portrait is now one of the museum's 4,000 exhibits. Also on display are more than 800 literary and artistic works by Shevchenko, as well as many of his personal effects. *12 Bulvar Tarasa Shevchenka,* ☎ *044/224-2556.* ⊗ *Tues.–Sun. 10–6.*

⑧ Turning left onto vulitsa Repina, you'll come to Kiev's **Russian Art Museum,** one of the largest repositories of Russian art outside Moscow and St. Petersburg. The building was built in the 1880s and belonged to the wealthy Tereshchenko family. The museum was founded in 1922 on the basis of the Tereshchenko collection and other private collections confiscated and nationalized by the Soviet government. The splendid interiors were designed by Robert Friedrich Meltzer, known for his work in the Winter Palace in St. Petersburg. The fine collection includes masterpieces from the 12th to the 20th century. *9 vul. Repina,* ☎ *044/224-6218.* ⊗ *Mon., Tues. noon–8; Wed., Fri.–Sun. 10–6.*

The permanent exhibits are on the second floor; the gallery on the first floor is reserved for temporary exhibits. Tickets for the two sections are sold separately. The outstanding collection of religious art is contained in the first two galleries on the second floor. Here you'll find icons from the Novgorod, Rostov-Suzdal, and Moscow schools, including a 12th-century icon from Novgorod of the Russian saints Boris and Gleb. Russian 18th-century portrait art is also represented by Vasily Borovikovsky's *Portrait of Vera Arsenyeva* as well as by Dmitry Levitsky's *Unknown Woman in Blue* and his portrait of Catherine the Great. Most important is the museum's extensive collection of works from the 19th century, such as Vasily Tropinin's *The Gamblers,* Vasily Perov's *God's Fool,* and Victor Vasnetsov's *Three Tsarevnas of the Underground Kingdom.* There are also many fine landscapes by Isaac Levitan and the seascape painter Ivan Aivazovsky. The World of Art Movement (*Mir Isskustva*) is represented by works of Serov, Korovin, and Benois. The last exhibit hall contains an interesting display of 18th–20th century china, porcelain, and glass, including plates produced in St. Petersburg in the early 1920s.

Just a few doors down the street is yet another important art museum, **⑨** the **Museum of Western and Oriental Art.** Like the Russian Museum, it was founded after the Bolshevik Revolution on the basis of a private collection. It is housed in the former mansion of the well-known archaeologist Bogdan Khanenko, who started the collection in the 1870s. The holdings include a rich collection of Corinthian and Attic painted vases from the 3rd to 4th century, found in digs in the Black Sea area, as well as terra-cotta statuettes (400 BC) and Roman sculptural portraits of the 2nd century. There are also several Byzantine icons dating from the 6th and 7th centuries. The section devoted to Western European art includes Italian Renaissance and Baroque art and works from the golden age of Spanish Art. Velázquez's *Portrait of the Infanta Margarita,* a highlight of the collection, was a study for a large formal portrait now housed in Madrid's Prado. Flemish and Dutch schools of the 15th–18th centuries are also represented. Unfortunately, the museum was closed in 1993 for major restoration work and is not scheduled to reopen until at least 1998. Its holdings may be moved to other locations; for information, call the museum. *15 vul. Repina,* ☎ *044/224-6162 or 044/225-0206.*

⓾ Bordering vulitsa Repina to the north is **Taras Shevchenko Park.** In its center stands a statue of the Ukrainian classical writer, erected in 1939 on the 125th anniversary of his birth. It replaced an earlier statue of the deposed Russian czar, Nicholas II. On the opposite side of the park,

⑪ on vulitsa Volodimirska, stands the bright red building of **Kiev University** (also known as Shevchenko University), Ukraine's most prestigious institution of higher education. Built in 1837–43, this is another Classical structure created by Vikenty Beretti. The long central facade is adorned by an eight-columned portico in the Ionic style. Completely destroyed during World War II, the building has been restored to its original appearance. According to legend, the building acquired its unusual color in 1901, when Czar Nicholas II ordered it doused in bright red in retaliation against rebellious students who refused to comply with the draft. The color was supposed to embarrass them and intimidate others.

To the south (to your left as you face the university) vulitsa Volodimirska intersects **vulitsa Lva Tolstovo** (Leo Tolstoy Street). Turn left at the corner and walk to the end of the street. The street ends at **Ploshcha Lva Tolstovo** (Leo Tolstoy Square), where it intersects vulitsa Chervonoarmiiska.

If you continue down vulitsa Chervonoarmiiska, you will come out at the western end of the Khreshchatik. Here, on Bessarabska Ploshcha,

⑫ you will find Kiev's first indoor market, the **Kriti Rynok.** Designed by Heinrich Gay and completed in 1912, the market, in Art Nouveau style, was established on this site for Bessarabian (Moldovan) merchants who came to trade in Kiev. Today it is Kiev's most important market, and inside the domed building you'll find rows of private farmers selling fruit, meat, and vegetables, as well as an occasional Ukrainian souvenir. In a separate section on the market's far side, you'll find the glass-enclosed dairy section. Ukrainian matrons, bedecked in neat caps or kerchiefs and smocks, dole out generous samples of their freshly made cheeses, including the sweet *tvorog,* and sour cream. Once you venture in, each vendor will try to persuade you that only her product is worthy of you. Your tour of the Khreshchatik area ends here; to reach the subway you can either walk down the street to Maidan Nezalezhnosti or return to Lev Tolstoy Street, where there is a subway station of the same name.

Tour 2: St. Sophia's and the Upper Town

This tour takes you through the hilly section of the **Verkhny Gorod** (Upper Town), also known as Old Kiev, where you will find the surviving monuments of Kiev's ancient past. The tour begins at the **Zoloti**

⑬ **Vorota** (Golden Gate), located just outside the subway station of the same name. When you exit the subway, you'll find yourself at the back side of the Golden Gate. In Yaroslav's day it served as the main entrance into the city, which was surrounded by a high defensive wall. Walk around to the front. Of the original gates, only the two parallel walls supporting the main entrance remain. The reconstructed version before you was completed in 1982, to coincide with celebrations of the city's 1,500th anniversary. Today the pavilion houses a museum of ancient Russian architecture, which is open only in summer. *48A Yaroslavov Val,* ☎ *044/224–7068.* ☉ *Mar.–Nov., Mon.–Wed. and Fri.–Sun. 10–6.*

Built in 1037 by Yaroslav the Wise, the original Golden Gate, inspired by the gates of Constantinople, was famous throughout Europe. Covered by beaten gold and other precious metals, it was topped by a tiny

Church of the Annunciation. According to legend, it was through the Golden Gate that Batu Khan entered the city after the Mongols captured Kiev in 1240. Four centuries later, in 1648, Bogdan Khmelnitsky (the Cossack hetman who led the Ukrainian liberation movement), rode triumphantly through these gates after freeing the city from its Polish captors.

★ ⑭ We will follow the path of Yaroslav and his contemporaries, down the road leading to the city's oldest church, **Sofiisky Sobor (St. Sophia's Cathedral)**. Walk down vulitsa Zolotovoristska, which begins directly across the street from the entrance to the Golden Gate. Bear right at the end of this short street, onto vulitsa Reitarska, which will soon come out onto vulitsa Volodimirska. The entrance to St. Sophia's is just a few steps down to your left. Today the complex of buildings and churches that make up St. Sophia's is a museum. In addition to the cathedral itself, on display are models of ancient Ukrainian and Russian towns, as well as local archaeological discoveries. You'll enter the complex through the Southern Gate Tower, following the path directly in front of you to reach the cathedral entrance. Tickets are sold at the kiosk to your right, just before you reach the cathedral. *24 vul. Volodimirska,* ☎ *044/228–6152.* ☉ *Mon.–Wed., Fri.–Sun. 10–5.*

Dedicated in 1037, St. Sophia's (also known as the Cathedral of Holy Wisdom) was built by Prince Yaroslav the Wise in gratitude for winning a battle against the Pechenegs, an invading tribe from the east. Prince Yaroslav, the Peter the Great of Kievan Rus, looked not west but south for inspiration, basing his cathedral on the Hagia Sophia of Constantinople. Over the centuries, the Cathedral of St. Sophia acquired an importance far exceeding its religious role: It was not only the seat of the metropolitan but also the center of political and social life in Kievan Rus. It housed the nation's first library, whose rich collection included manuscripts from Europe and Greece. It was the site of cultural events, and it was here that princes were crowned and foreign ambassadors received.

At first glance you may wonder how the cathedral's helmet-like cupolas could possibly adorn the city's oldest church. The church was reconstructed on several occasions, and its present exterior owes much to the era of Ukrainian Baroque. The original design, strongly influenced by Byzantine architecture, also contained elements of Ukrainian wooden architecture. The huge, five-aisled church originally had 13 cupolas and was built in the shape of a Greek cross. The main cupola in the center represented Christ; the surrounding cupolas depicted the 12 Apostles. After the death of Yaroslav (who is buried inside) in 1054, the northwestern tower was added and a vault was built for his tomb. Badly damaged during the Mongol invasion and further destroyed by the Poles and Lithuanians, the cathedral lay in ruins until after the reunification of Ukraine and Russia in 1654, when restoration began. In the early 18th century, on orders from Peter the Great, the cathedral was reconstructed and the six additional domes (for a total of 19) were added.

In contrast to the exterior, much of the 11th-century interior has been preserved. It is richly decorated with mosaics and frescoes, many of which date from the 11th and 12th centuries. One curious feature of the fresco work is the use of secular subjects. Frescoes depicting hunting scenes, wild animals, court jesters, and musicians afford a glimpse of everyday life in Kievan Rus. The spiral staircase of the towers, whose entrance was once located outside the cathedral, led to the choir loft, where Yaroslav and his family sat during services.

Continue now to the central nave, whose walls, ceilings, and pillars are decorated with colorful mosaics and frescoes. You will be immediately struck by the golden glow of the central dome. Peering down at you is an 11th-century mosaic of Christ as the Pantokrator; his portrayal as Father, Son, and Holy Ghost was influenced by Byzantine traditions. The vault of the main apse is adorned by a beautiful mosaic of the Orant Virgin. Because this mosaic has survived intact after centuries of abuse and reconstruction, it has become known as the Indestructible Virgin. The magnificent gilded iconostasis in front of the altar was erected in 1747; it was partially dismantled in the 19th century, and only the lowest of the three original tiers remains.

In addition to religious themes, the frescoes include portraits of Yaroslav and his family. Considering that Yaroslav was alive when they were painted, the portraits are highly unusual for church decoration. A portrait of his four daughters, including Anna, the future queen of Henry I of France, are on the southern wall, while four of his sons are depicted on the northern wall. Fragments of portraits of Yaroslav himself and his wife, Irina, their eldest daughter, Elizabeth (later queen of Norway), and their eldest son, Vladimir, are on the western wall.

Yaroslav's marble sarcophagus is in the northeast chapel, to the left of the central nave as you face the iconostasis. The tomb, which weighs six tons, dates from the 5th or 6th century. It was brought from Greece, and its carved decoration includes such early Christian symbols as palms, cypresses, fishes, and grapevines.

Leaving the cathedral, walk around to the back. To your left stands a four-story, stone bell tower, painted azure with white trim. This is a fine example of Ukrainian Baroque; the lush ornamentation includes the double-headed eagle of the Romanov dynasty. Measuring 76 meters (249 feet), the bell tower was erected between 1744 and 1752; the fourth story and gilded cupola were added in 1852.

Head back in the direction of the main entrance to the cathedral grounds. To your left, just before you reach the ticket booth, is the 18th-century refectory, which houses archaeological and architectural displays. Its finds include the sarcophagus of Princess Olga, which once stood in the 10th-century Tithe Church (*see* Tour 3, *below*) destroyed by the Mongols. The model panoramas of Kiev in the 10th–12th centuries will give you an idea of what the city looked like before it was razed to the ground by Mongol invaders.

TIME OUT If you're not disturbed by the obligatory cats on the windowsills, you can sit down and have a coffee or hot cocoa at the **Kulinaria** on the corner of Volodimirska and Reitarska vulitsa (to your right as you exit the cathedral through the southern gate). The coffee is very sweet and heavily diluted with milk. Pastries and cakes are sometimes available, as well as sausages and champagne.

🟑 As you leave the St. Sophia complex, turn left onto Volodimirska vulitsa. The street opens onto **St. Sophia Square,** which until recently was named in honor of Bogdan Khmelnitsky, whose equestrian statue stands in the square's center. Khmelnitsky (1595–1657) led the Ukrainian people in the war of liberation against Poland and later pushed for reunification with Russia. The statue stands on this site where the residents of Kiev gave their hero a triumphant welcome. Paid for primarily by public conscription, it was designed by a well-known St. Petersburg sculptor, Mikhail Mikeshin, and was erected in 1888. The hetman bestrides a rearing horse that towers above a red-granite pedestal. In the distance above the trees, to your far left, is St. Andrew's Cathedral (*see* Tour 3, *below*).

Follow the street running down the right-hand side of the square, with the statue to your left and a small strip of park to your right. Before you leave the square, pause for a moment for another look at St. Sophia's, whose massive bell tower and helmet-shaped cupolas dominate the square. You are now on **Volodimirski Proizd;** the strip of park bordering the street to your right is dotted with sculptures of pagan gods. Walk the length of the street, approximately three blocks, and ⑯ you will come to **Mikhailivska Ploshcha** (**St. Michael's Square**).

Bordering the square to your left is the massive, very Soviet structure of the former Central Committee of the Ukrainian Communist Party. It was built in 1937, and its cold and severe facade recalls the dark days of Stalinism. Today it houses the Ministry of Foreign Affairs of the Ukraine. The square takes its name from the Mikhailovsky-Zlatoverkhy Monastery (St. Mikhail Monastery of the Golden Roof) that was founded on this site in 1051; its cathedral, built by Prince Sviatopolk in 1108, was the city's second most important house of worship after Sofiisky Sobor. It survived the brutal Mongol invasions and the years of Polish and Lithuanian rule—but not the Soviets. In 1936 it was destroyed to make way for the Central Committee building. Because St. Mikhail was considered the city's patron saint, many Kievans find a connection between the monastery's destruction and subsequent disasters that have struck the city such as Germany's World War II occupation and the Chernobyl nuclear accident. Now that the monastery has been restored, it is hoped that Kiev's patron saint will spare the city any further misfortune.

Turn right off the square, onto vulitsa Trokh-Svyatitelska (Three Saints' Street). At the left-hand corner (with your back to the square) stands ⑰ the 18th-century **Refectory,** the only building of the 11th-century monastery to have been spared destruction. The stone church, with its single wooden cupola, was built in 1712. Like many churches in the former Soviet Union, it was turned into a museum after the Bolshevik Revolution. Little remains of its original interior, and, like the rest of the monastery, the building had to be restored. With the recent religious revival, the museum was closed and the refectory now belongs to the Ukrainian Orthodox Church. Services are held daily at 7 AM and 5 PM.

Continue on Three Saints' Street, walking away from St. Michael's Square. The street soon turns down a steep incline, which ends at Lenkomsomol Square. To your right as you head down the steep hill is the Catholic **Church of St. Alexander** (1817–1842), renovated in 1994 by Polish contractors. To your left, at the bottom of the hill, was Kiev's obligatory but short-lived Lenin Museum, erected in 1982. In 1991, the museum was closed and converted into the **Ukrainina Dim** (Ukrainian House of Culture). It contains temporary displays on Ukrainian culture, from food to dress. *2 Khreshchatik.* ⊘ *Tues.–Sun. 11–6:30.*

The square marks the beginning of Kiev's main thoroughfare, the tree-lined Khreshchatik (*see* Tour 1, *above*). The subway is just one block away, to your right as you enter the square from Three Saints' Street.

Tour 3: St. Andrew's Cathedral and the Podol

★ This tour takes you to the magnificent **Andreyivsky Sobor** (St. Andrew's Cathedral), situated on a high bluff overlooking the Dnieper, and then down the steep incline to the **Podol,** the old trading quarter, on the lower right bank. Although settlement of the Podol dates from Kiev's earliest days, none of the original architecture survives; the Mongol invasion obliterated the original wooden settlement. Rebuilt in the 17th and 18th centuries, the Podol burned to the ground in 1811 after a three-day fire. Its charm today lies in the rectangular pattern of its streets, lined with 19th-century apartment buildings and trading arcades, and the glorious views of St. Andrew's Cathedral towering above.

⑱ Begin your tour at the **Ploshcha Poshtova** subway stop. To reach the bluff on which St. Andrew's sits, take the funicular (cable car), built in 1905. Its entrance is at the bottom of the hill, just outside the subway. The ride up, which takes only a few minutes, gives you an excellent view of the city. When you reach the top, walk straight to the square ahead of you and take a right onto vulitsa Desyatinna, which will lead you directly to St. Andrew's. On your right, you will pass again the monolithic Ukrainian Ministry of Foreign Affairs building, formerly the seat of the Communist Central Committee here (*see* Tour 2).

Vulitsa Desyatinna is named for the **Desyatinna Tserkva** (Tithe Church) that once stood at the end of the street. Founded in 989 as the Church of the Holy Virgin, it became known as the Tithe Church because Prince Vladimir the Great, father of Yaroslavl the Wise, gave one-tenth of his income toward its maintenance. During the Mongol invasion, women and children took refuge inside its massive stone walls. But the roof collapsed under the weight of the fiery blows, killing everyone inside. If you turn left at the end of the street and walk a few hundred feet up vulitsa Volodimirska, you will find the outline of its foundation, which was been reconstructed with red quartz. Desyatinna itself is a very attractive street, now home to the British embassy and the Ukrainian president.

⑲ To your right as you reach the end of vulitsa Desyatinna stands **St. Andrew's Cathedral.** A fine example of Ukrainian Baroque, its green, blue, and gold cupolas light up the skies above Kiev's sweeping hills and the gently flowing Dnieper. It was designed by the Italian architect Bartolomeo Rastrelli, who built so many of St. Petersburg's masterpieces. Its site, on the highest point of Old Kiev, was allegedly chosen because it was here that the Apostle Andrew, who first preached the Gospel in Kievan Rus, erected a cross.

The church was built at the behest of Peter the Great's pious daughter Elizabeth, who visited Kiev in 1744. Construction of the monumental cathedral proved a complicated task due to the hilly terrain—the foundation is 15 meters (50 feet) deep—and was completed in 1752. The church was not consecrated until 1767.

St. Andrew's stands on a platform above a broad flight of steps. The proportions are perfect, and the elegant interior is monumental and striking. Its three-tiered iconostasis, whose red-velvet background accentuates the gilded wooden carvings and sculptures, is the work of the Russian painter Alexei Antropov and the Ukrainian artist Grigory Levitsky. Unfortunately, the church has been closed for interior renovation since 1991 and will not reopen until at least 1996. Although you cannot go inside, don't be dissuaded from visiting the site, however, for a view of its elaborate exterior alone is worthwhile, and you can see the church quite close up. *33 Andriivsky Uzviz,* ☎ *044/228–5861.* ☉ *Mon., Tues., Thurs.–Sun. 10–6; May–Sept., also Wed. noon–8.*

When you are done basking in the glories of St. Andrew's, begin your walk down the cobblestone incline of Andriivski Uzviz. This picturesque street, lined by cafés, art galleries, and small museums, is home to many artists; you'll see them offering their work for sale. In look and spirit, the area evokes Montmartre in its earlier days. As you descend the hill, you'll come to sets of twisting iron steps. They will take you to lookout platforms affording fantastic views of Kiev old and new, with its rows of Soviet-made apartment buildings, the ubiquitous heavy cranes idle alongside them, the colored, older buildings of the Podol merchant district, and the bright tops of small churches glistening like drops of gold throughout, with the lovely Dnieper benignly winding its way down the middle. The first sloping hill to your left is **Zamkova Gora,** also known as Kiselyovka Mount. It is believed that this is the hill mentioned in the ancient chronicles in connection with Kii, who with his two brothers founded the city of Kiev around the end of the 6th century. At No. 22, on the left-hand side of the street, is the newly opened (1994) Museum of Kiev's Podol. It holds displays about the history and architecture of the district, and this street in particular, using documents, photographs, and reconstructions, with its signs in Ukrainian and Russian. ☎ 044/416–0398. ☉ *Daily noon–8.*

TIME OUT   Andriivski Uzviz, with its cafés and art salons, is the heart of Kiev's artist community. **Svitilitsa,** at No. 13A, is a popular hangout for writers and artists. Join them for some Turkish coffee or a shot of vodka. Pastries and small sandwiches are also available. The interior is reminiscent of a peasant cottage, with Ukrainian embroidery, a tile stove, and wooden picnic tables.

At No. 13 Andriivski Uzviz, on the right, readers of Bulgakov will be **㉑** thrilled to find the seven-room **Bulgakov Museum,** which was the family home of Mikhail Bulgakov, the renowned Russian writer whose satirical works were long suppressed by the Soviet regime. He lived here from 1906 to 1916 and again in 1918 and 1919, and it provides the setting of his first major work, the novel *The White Guard.* For years the house stood unmarked, but today it has been lovingly redone. On exhibit are rooms that are either made to look as they did when he lived there (with the effect heightened by displays of personal items, such as his familiar spectacles) or as he described them in his writings. A pleasingly ghostly air pervades, too, for the rooms are virtually all-white, in homage to the novel's theme. A terrific blend of the imaginative and the factual, the museum will be most appreciated by those who have read Bulgakov's work. All visitors are shown through with their own guide; you should ask for one who speaks English though there may not be one everyday. *13 Andriivskii Uzviz,* ☎ *044/416–5254.* ☉ *Mon., Tues., Thurs.–Sun. 10–6.*

When you reach the bottom of the hill, turn right onto Borichiv tik and then, not too much further, left onto vulitsa Andriivska. At the end of this short street is busy vulitsa Petra Sagaidachnovo; at this point you can turn right to return to the subway at Poshtova Ploshcha, just a few blocks away. To continue your excursion on through the Podol, however, turn left. This busy shopping district is very different from the Khreshchatik, which is dominated by the monumental architecture of the Stalinist era. Before the revolution, the Podol was inhabited by merchants and craftsmen. A stroll through its quaint, narrow streets gives you a sense of Old Kiev.

㉑ After one long block, you will enter the broad **Kontraktova Ploshcha** (Contract Square). This is only the first side of it. Straight across from you is the long, white **Gostinny Dvir** shopping arcade that splits the square down the middle. Originally built in 1809, it was destroyed in the 1811 fire and rebuilt in 1833 by the prominent Ukrainian architect Andrei Melensky. The arcade is similar to Moscow's GUM and St. Petersburg's Gostiny Dvor, but much smaller. Walk beyond it and you will be on the second side of the square. The statue in the center is of the 18th-century Ukrainian poet and philosopher Grigory Skovoroda. At the far corner of the square stands the **Kontraktovy Dom** (Contract House), for which the square is named. An interesting example of the Classical style, it was built in 1817 expressly as a headquarters for negotiating and signing agreements with foreigners. In dire need of reconstruction, which seems to have been abandoned, it still provides a hint of its past grandeur.

Cross vulitsa Sagaidachnovo (the large street that runs in front of the square), backtracking slightly to the north end of Contract Square. Turn left onto vulitsa Illinska, heading in the direction of the river. Three blocks down the street, at the corner of vulitsa Pochaininska (just before you reach the harbor), stands the 17th-century **Illinska Tserka** (St. Elias Church). Its history actually dates from Kiev's earliest days. According to legend, the first wooden church built on this site was erected by Askold (Rurik), the Kievan prince who was murdered by his rival from Novgorod, Prince Oleg, in 882. The present white-stone church, which holds services daily at 5 PM, was built in 1692.

Now return to Contract Square and turn right again onto Sagaidachnovo. The rectangular building on the right is the former **Kievo-Mogilianksa Academy.** It was founded in the late 17th century inside the walls of the now destroyed Bratsky Monastery. In 1701 Peter the Great turned it into the Kiev Academy, which became one of the largest and most prestigious institutions of higher learning in all of Russia and Ukraine. Many famous scholars worked here, including the Russian scientist Mikhail Lomonsov, the composer Dmitry Bortnyansky, and the Ukrainian philosopher Grigory Skovoroda. Today the building houses a branch of the central library of the Ukrainian Academy of Sciences.

Take a right onto vulitsa Spaska, which begins across from the Contract House. On the first sidestreet on the left, you'll see a 19th-century yellow-brick building with a rectangular tower. Formerly a fire station, the building is now the **Chernobyl Museum.** Opened on April 25, 1992, on the sixth anniversary of the Chernobyl accident, the museum houses a somber exhibit depicting the accident and its horrifying aftermath. On display are the personal effects of the young soldiers who died as a result of their heroic efforts to put out the fire. Above the exhibit hangs a clock, permanently set at 1:23 AM, the time the explosion occurred. A reminder of the secrecy that shrouded the event is found in the display case containing newspaper clippings from around the time of the accident. The first official announcement by Soviet authorities, not issued until April 29, consists of just three short lines: "An accident occurred at the Chernobyl Atomic Power Plant. Measures are being taken to rectify the damage. The injured are being cared for." Other exhibits contain photos of Kiev's May Day celebrations and parade, after which residents were instructed to stay indoors and keep their windows tightly closed. Another display contains graphic photos of the dying, as well as mutilated animals and children born after the accident. The displays are supplemented with videos and documentary films. Entrance and guided tours (in Russian or Ukrainian) are free. *1 Provulok Zhorevii,* ☎ *044/417–5422.* ☼ *Mon.–Sat. 10–6. Closed last Mon. of month.*

TIME OUT If you're up for some hearty Ukrainian cooking, stop by the **Spadshchina** (8 vul. Spaska, ☎ 044/417-0358), just one block to your right off Kontraktova Ploshcha. Ask for a table in the back room, where you can rest in a comfy private booth. The specialty is *Kotleta Spadshchina,* fried chicken rolled in bread crumbs. The *vareniki,* filled with meat, potatoes or cabbage, are also homemade. ⊙ *Daily noon–5, 6–11. Ukrainian coupons only.*

Return again to vulitsa Petra Sagaidachnovo (the continuation of which is called Mezhigirska vulitsa). A short walk down this block of decaying buildings brings you to vulitsa Khoreva. Turn left and walk one block. At the corner of Kostyantinivska vulitsa stands an 18th-century, white-stone building. This was **Peter the Great's headquarters** in 1706, when he prepared his attack on the Swedes, who had advanced to within 40 kilometers (25 miles) of Kiev. The building is not open to the public.

Continuing up vulitsa Khoreva, will you reach the oldest surviving building in the Podol, the **Nikolai Pritiska Tserka** (Pritisko-St. Nicholas Church). The modest, white-stone church, which bears just two cupolas, was built in 1631 and is similar in design to Ukrainian wooden cathedrals. Closed during the Soviet era, it was recently returned to the Ukrainian Orthodox Church and is open for services on Saturdays at 9 and 5, and Sundays at 10.

Turn left onto vulitsa Pritisko-Mikilska, and a few steps will bring you to the **Florivski Monastir** (St. Flor's Convent). The area may be swarming with uniformed soldiers, because directly across the street is the headquarters of the Ukrainian National Guard. The convent, whose history dates from the 16th century, miraculously survived the antireligious campaigns of the Stalin era and remained open under Soviet rule. Enter the convent through the bell-tower gates, designed by Andrei Melensky (who also built the shopping arcade on Contract Square) in the 1830s. To your right stands the **Voznesenska Tserka** (Church of the Ascension), the convent's main cathedral and the only functioning church left on its territory. Built in 1732, it suffered severely in the Podol fire of 1811, when the original iconostasis was destroyed. Tourists are not overly appreciated here, so to avoid a bitter scolding from the elderly women at prayer, leave your camera in your bag and your hands outside your pockets. To the right of the cathedral is a well at which you will see people lining up with glass jars. The water, which comes from an underground spring, is thought to have medicinal powers.

Just outside the convent walls, to your left as you exit through the bell tower, stands Kiev's very first apothecary, which dates from 1728. Restored to its original appearance, the building contains a functionary pharmacy, as well as a museum devoted to the history of medicine. The unusual exhibits, obviously compiled during the Soviet era, include a room decorated with authentic church icons and devoted to the "Christian Era" of medicine. The museum is open only for group excursions, which can be arranged by calling in advance (you'll have to provide your own interpreter). *7 vul. Pritisko-Mikilska, ☎ 044/416–2437. ⊙ Tues.–Sun. 9–4.*

Look up to the bluff as you leave, and you'll see soaring St. Andrew's, dominant against the sky. To reach the subway again, retrace your steps to Peter the Great's house. Turn right onto vulitsa Kostyantinivska. The entrance to the subway station Kontraktova Ploshcha is just a few steps away, on the left-hand side of the street.

Tour 4: Monastery of the Caves and World War II Museum

★ ㉗ If time permits, set aside an entire day for the fascinating **Kievo-Pecherska Lavra** (**Monastery of the Caves**). It is not only a functioning monastery, with miles of mazelike underground tunnels containing nu-

---

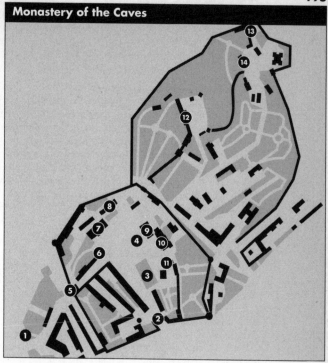

Monastery of the Caves

Annozachatievska Church, **14**

Dalnyie Pechery (Distant Caves), **13**

Economic Wing, **6**

Khrestovozdvizhenska Church, **12**

Microminiatures Exhibit, **11**

Museum of Historical Treasures, **7**

Museum of Ukrainian Books and Printing, **8**

Refectory Church, **9**

State Museum of Ukrainian Folk Art, **10**

Trinity Gate Church, **2**

Tserka Spas-na-Berestove, **1**

Uspensky Sobor, **4**

Velika Lavskra Dzvinitsa (Great Belfry), **3**

Vsikhsvyatska Tserka, **5**

merous churches and ancient crypts, but also houses some of Kiev's richest museums. Among them are the Museum of Historical Treasures (the Ukrainian equivalent of Moscow's Armory or the Gold Rooms in the Hermitage), the Museum of Ukrainian Decorative and Applied Art, and the Museum of Ukrainian Books and Printing.

A *lavra* is a monastery of the highest order. The Monastery of the Caves received this honored title in 1598, but its history goes back much farther. It was founded in 1051 by a monk named Antony and his follower, Theodosius. They chose this hilly site, on the banks of the Dnieper, for its natural caves (in Ukrainian, *pechery*, hence the name). The monks lived in underground cells and were also buried in them. The cool temperatures and humid atmosphere of the caves allowed their bodies to mummify; even today their bodies allegedly remain almost perfectly preserved. At the time of the monastery's foundation, this appeared to be a miracle, enhancing the monastery's prestige in a land where Christianity had been adopted less than a century earlier.

From the 11th to the early 13th century, the Pechersky Monastery was the ecclesiastical center of the Orthodox Church in Kievan Rus. Like the city of Kiev, its demise came with the Mongol invasion of 1240. Its religious life revived in the 15th century, but it wasn't until the 18th century that the monastery began to prosper again. It became the site of imperial pilgrimages, and Peter the Great financed much new construction. Many of its churches as well as the surrounding fortification wall, date from this time. By the mid-18th century the monastery was so wealthy that it owned several villages, 80,000 serfs, and three glassworks. It suffered the same fate as many churches after the Bolshevik Revolution; in 1927 it was closed and converted into a museum.

With the advent of perestroika and the religious revival in Russia and Ukraine, the monastery was returned to the church in 1987, on the anniversary of 1,000 years of Christianity in Rus. Parts of the grounds are still functioning as a museum, but the two sets of caves and their many churches are once again open for worship.

The monastery is situated on two hills divided by a shallow valley; it has two distinct sections. The **Verkhnya Lavra** (Upper Lavra) is situated on the highest hill and is surrounded by its own fortification wall. On the lower hill lies the Territory of the **Dalnyie Pechery** (Distant Caves). The **Blizhnyie Pechery** (Near Caves) are located in the gully between them. To reach the monastery, take the subway to Arsenalna. When you exit, cross the street and take Trolleybus 20 two stops. You will see the whitewashed walls of the fortification across the street. Walking south, follow the wall until you reach the entrance, a few hundred feet down the street. *21 Sichnevovo Povstannya,* ☎ *044/290–6646.* ☉ *Wed.–Mon. 9:30–6.*

Before you begin your excursion of the monastery, you may want to stop by the **Tserka Spas-na-Berestove** (Church of the Redeemer in the Birchwood), located just outside its walls. Follow the road directly across the street from the trolley-bus stop, running along the northern edge of the fortification walls. The road will lead you directly to the church. It was built in the early 12th century by Prince Vladimir Monomakh as a burial place for the princes of Kiev. The founder of Moscow (and Monomakh's son) Yuri Dolgoruky was buried here in 1157. The church is built in the characteristic style of the time: a cross dome with six pillars. Its eastern wing, which faces the Dnieper, was added in 1640–44. In 1947, on the 800th anniversary of the founding of Moscow, a marble sarcophagus was installed here in memory of Yury Dolgoruky. It was recently returned to the Ukrainian Orthodox Church; it is open for viewing daily 9:30–1:30 and 2–6.

Continuing to the monastery, you will enter the grounds of the Upper Lavra through the archway of the **Trinity Gate Church,** which is crowned by a gilded cupola. Built in 1108, it once doubled as a watchtower. The majestic blue-and-gold exterior dates from the 18th century. The interior is decorated with colorful frescoes and a beautiful wooden iconostasis.

The ticket office is in the kiosk to your left before you enter; here you will buy tickets for all the exhibits and museums on the monastery's territory, except for the Museum of Historical Treasures, the Bell Tower, and the Caves, where you will purchase a candle in lieu of a ticket. To your right, as you first come in, is a long white building, the former Monks' Dormitories. This building houses small exhibits of Ukrainian icon painting (17th–19th centuries), portraits from the Kiev Monastery (18th–19th centuries), and religious manuscripts. They are interesting, but if you are short on time, pass them by, for there is much to see. The passageway to your left, through the archway, leads to the St. Nicholas Church, which houses an exhibit of 17th-century Western European graphic art. *Exhibits open Wed.–Mon. 9:30–6, with 30-min lunch break between 12:30 and 2.*

Going forward, past these exhibits, you reach the **Velika Lavskra Dzvinitsa** (Great Belfry). Great is the right name for it; in its day it was Russia's tallest structure. The present belfry, which reaches a height of 96.5 meters (317 feet), was built in the 18th century to replace a wooden version that had burned down in 1718. It was designed by the German architect Gottfried Schädel, who was dispatched from St.

Petersburg. Each of the four tiers is of a different design, with Doric columns on the second level, Ionic on the third, and Corinthian on the fourth. It is under reconstruction, but the belfry is open to visitors. You buy a ticket at the foot of it. From the top you'll get a marvelous view of the monastery, the rolling hills, and the Dnieper. But the wooden stairs are somewhat rickety, and every once in a while you see a piece of sky shining through the holes.

In the square in front of the Bell Tower are the ruins of the **Uspensky Sobor** (Assumption Church). Built in the 11th century, the huge stone cathedral was, like St. Sophia's, influenced by Byzantine architecture. It became a center of ecclesiastical learning and was the monastery's most important cathedral between the 11th and the 13th centuries. Like the rest of the monastery, it was destroyed during the Mongol invasion and rebuilt in 1470. The restored church, which burned in the same fire of 1718 that took the Bell Tower, was rebuilt again in the 1720s. The church was destroyed for the last time during World War II, when it was blown up by the Nazis.

Follow the pathway as it curves around the ruins, and it would lead to the five-domed **Vsikhsvyatska Tserka** (All Saints' Church), which was built over the northern gate at the end of the 17th century. Its ornate design is considered a pure example of Ukrainian Baroque. Like the Trinity Gate Church, it also served as a watchtower on the fortification wall.

Before you would reach it, you get to the "**Economic Wing**"; at the window to your left, just beyond the entrance to the building, tickets are sold to the **Museum of Historical Treasures.** The museum is located in the building next to it (to the right), which formerly housed the monastery's bakery. The museum is not open to groups, but if you are patient, after a short wait enough people will gather to form a group tour. If you call ahead, you can request a tour in English. ☎ *044/290–1396.* ☾ *Wed.–Mon. 10–5 (lunch break 1–1:45).*

The tour begins on the second floor, with the museum's collection of Scythian gold found in archaeological digs along the coast of the Black Sea. The highlight of the collection is a massive gold chest ornament, decorated with scenes from everyday Scythian life in the 4th century BC. One of the rooms contains the tomb of a Scythian princess and her baby, found in an ancient settlement in the Black Sea area. The skeletons of the princess and her child are arranged as they were buried, surrounded by gold and priceless jewelry. The museum's coin collection includes the first metal coins produced in Kievan Rus, which were introduced in the 10th century.

Next door, in an adjoining building (to your left as you exit), is the **Museum of Ukrainian Books and Printing.** It is housed in the monastery's former printing shop, where Russia's first printing press was established. The collection includes manuscripts dating from the 12th century and features ornately designed, jewel-encrusted volumes. ☾ *Wed.–Mon. 10–6.*

Exit left from the museum's courtyard and walk straight down the short path to the *vidovaya* (lookout) platform. It offers a spectacular view.

As you leave the platform, turn left, back in the direction of the Great Bell Tower. On your left is the large **Refectory Church,** built at the end of the 18th century and attached to the Metropolitan's House. The church is open for viewing as a museum, but it is also a functioning church (services at 7 AM and 5 PM). It's worth a quick look inside; the gilded interiors were designed by the Russian architect Alexei Schusev. Outside the church are the graves of the Cossack leaders Ivan Iskra and Vasily Kochubei, who were executed by Ivan Mazepa in 1708.

The former Metropolitan's House now contains the **State Museum of Ukrainian Folk Art.** The entrance is to your left, a few steps up the path from the Refectory Church. Its extensive exhibits are housed on two floors and date from the 16th to the 20th century. An entire room is devoted to folk dress and another to bedspreads. Also on display are embroidered linens, handicrafts, pottery, wood carvings, and ceramics. A highlight of the collection is the *krashanki,* delicately painted Easter Eggs. ☎ 044/293–9442. ☯ Wed.–Mon. 10–5:45.

The last stop on the tour of Upper Lavra museums is the fascinating exhibit of "microminiatures," art so tiny that it can be seen only with a microscope. This is a strange place for an exhibit of art that clearly belongs to the modern age of technology (its establishment here was probably the decision of a Soviet bureaucrat), but it is interesting all the same. The creator of the work is Nikolai Syadristy, a contemporary artist who has received many awards for his unusual medium. The works on display include a portrait of Ernest Hemingway engraved on a pear seed; a glass portrait of the Russian balalaika virtuoso Vasily Andreyev (complete with balalaika and case), which is set inside a poppy seed; and the world's tiniest book (0.6 sq. mm.), which is engraved with Taras Shevchenko's portrait. The entrance to the exhibit is across the pathway from the Metropolitan's House, to your left as you exit the museum. ☯ Wed.–Mon. 10–6.

Leave the Upper Lavra and its museums to begin your visit of the cave sites by returning to the pathway, keeping the Great Bell Tower to your left, and starting down the hill. Just past the viewing platform, the road twists and curves down a steep incline. Follow it as it goes to the right, through the iron gates marking the boundary of the Upper Lavra, and soon the road shoots off to your left, leading down, again steeply, to the **Blizhnyie Pechery (Near Caves),** which are also sometimes called St. Anthony's Caves. Instead of a ticket, you'll purchase a candle outside the entrance.

After you buy a candle, you'll enter a courtyard of green-and-white church buildings, abutted by a botanical park on the right. Walk toward the far end, where you will see a clock and short bell tower, and past which you can look over the parapet for more breathtaking views of Kiev. To your left, next to the **Khrestovozdvizhenska Church** (Church of the Exaltation of the Cross) is the entrance to the Near Caves. Join the line for the next small group that will be ushered in, and buy a candle inside, if you were unable to do so before.

The passageways of the caves run about ½ kilometer (⅓ mile), but the visitors' route does not take you into every nook and cranny. Inside there are 73 tombs and three underground churches. Icons and fragments of 18th-century frescoes cover the walls. Many important historical figures are buried here, including Antony, the monastery's founder; Nikon and Nestor, the monks who authored the *Primary Chronicle;* Alimpy, thought to be Kievan Rus's first icon painter; and other revered monks. The caves are open every day, with a break from 11:30 to 1, but close when it rains, due to flooding. Sometimes they reopen after just a few hours, so it may be worth waiting around.

To reach the **Dalnyie Pechery (Distant Caves),** follow the covered gallery, which begins across the courtyard from the Church of the Exaltation of the Cross. It is a very long passageway. If it is closed you can take the longer route, walking back up the hill to the path along the Upper Monastery fortification wall. Turn left, and keep walking until you reach the second road branching off to the left. It will lead you to the territory of the Distant Caves, also known as St. Theodosius' Caves. Here the entrance is actually through the **Annozachatievska Church** (Church of the Conception of St. Anne). Again, you will purchase a candle from the monk before you start. These caves are the older of the two; they contain 47 tombs and another three churches, all of which date from the 12th century. As you make your way, along the walls you'll see the covered remains of the mummified monks, buried in or near the cells where they prayed during their lifetime.

Unless you are an expert in early Russian church history, you don't need to be particular about which set of caves you see. The experience, which can be rather spooky, is similar in both. You'll follow a twisting path through the cool interiors of the underground labyrinth. Often the only light comes from your candle and threatens to go out in the damp drafts that waft below. Of the two, the Distant Caves are on the sharpest incline, but it is not advisable for people with serious conditions of the heart, lungs, or legs, or pregnant women, to go into either one. Women will be asked to cover their head, and short skirts, pants, or all-black clothing (except for the monks, it seems!) may bar you from entry.

To leave, walk back up the hill to the road along the fortification wall of the Upper Lavra. Continue climbing the incline as it leads up the hill to your left; at the top you will find the stop for Trolleybus 20, which will take you back to the subway (three stops). You'll find snack booths outside the monastery walls, if you want a coffee or soda before going on your way.

You may want to stop by the **Museum of the Great Patriotic War** (World War II), located on the hillside to the south of the monastery (to your left). This museum is topped by a gigantic steel statue called *Mother Russia*. It is 72 meters (236 feet) high, and it dwarfs the monastery domes on the riverbank. Its construction was controversial; it is a gaudy, oversize structure typical of the wasteful spending of the Brezhnev era. It looks very strange and inappropriate after an excursion through the ancient monastery, but it, too, is representative of Kiev's past—albeit more recent.

The museum contains several sections, the most recent of which is devoted to the Afghan War (in the building to your right as you walk down the terrace leading to the *Mother Russia* statue). The building is surrounded by an open-air museum of Soviet artillery, planes, helicopters, and military jeeps. The somber exhibits display the uniforms and medals of the war dead, as well as their letters home and the death notifications sent to their families. Soviet propaganda photographs of smiling Afghan children hang on the walls. Russian pop songs written about the war in Afghanistan add to the emotional effect.

The exhibit to World War II located in the base of the statue has also recently been updated. The theme of the museum is the devastating effect of war on children. The main exhibit shows how children suffered during World War II, with photos and letters from Ukrainian children deported to Germany, as well as the concentration-camp garb of babies. The central dome of the statue is inlaid with a huge mosaic, which is eerily reminiscent of a religious icon. The mosaic is in the shape of a five-pointed red star with the words USSR–VICTORY. *44 vul. Sichnevovo Povstannya.* ☎ *044/296–2889.* ☉ *Tues.–Sun. 10–6.*

Excursion: Folk Architecture Museum

This open-air museum of peasant homes is set in a vast field dotted with cottages, windmills, and wooden churches. Located near the village of Pirogova, it is a lovely place to spend a hot summer day. A visit in winter, however, or on one of Kiev's wet and rainy spring days, can be dispiriting: the buildings are far apart and a visit involves a lot of walking along dirt (or muddy) roads. The museum administration organizes a variety of festivals and special events throughout the year, including Ukrainian Independence Day (August 24) and the festive Ivan Kupallo Day (June 6), a celebration of midsummer night that dates back to Kiev's pre-Christian era. The 17th-century wooden church transferred here from the village of Doroginka now holds services on church holidays, and weddings are occasionally performed here. To find out what's going on, call the museum. You can reach it by public transportation, although a guided excursion is advised, since there are few signs in English explaining the exhibits. Both Intourist-Kievska and the Slavutich excursion bureau (*see* Guided Tours *in* Kiev Essentials, *below*) offer tours. To reach the museum, take the subway to Lybedskaya. From there take Trolleybus 11 to the VDNKh stop and transfer to bus 24. *Village of Pirogova,* ☎ *044/266–5542.* ☉ *Winter, Thurs.–Tues. 10–4; summer, Thurs.–Tues. 10–5.*

The museum occupies a territory of 120 hectares (297 acres), and its nine sections cover various regions of Ukraine from the 18th–20th centuries. Each section re-creates a Ukrainian village, with thatch-roof white-washed cottages, windmills, wells, and wooden churches, most of which were brought from the region on display. The cottages are furnished and arranged to show how people actually lived and feature authentic household objects, including wooden utensils and cast-iron pots, embroidered linens, and wooden furnishings. The last section shows the architecture and lifestyle typical of a modern Ukrainian village.

What to See and Do with Children

A ride up Kiev's **cable car** (*Funikuler, see* Tour 3, *above*) will give any child a thrill. The cars run on the same schedule as the subway, and the cost one-way is slightly less than the fare for a ride on a subway. On Sunday the rides are free.

There is no better way to spend a hot summer day than **cruising** the **Dnieper.** Excursion boats ply the river from late spring to early fall, leaving from pier No. 3 at the River Passenger Terminal (subway Ploshcha Poshtova). Check for excursions with your travel bureau.

The **Kievsky Circus** (1 Ploshcha Peremogi, ☎ 044/216–3856) has been a favorite outing for children since 1959. Further details and tickets are available at all hotel information desks.

All children will enjoy Kiev's two puppet theaters: **City Puppet Theater** (12 vul. Lunacharskovo, ☎ 044/517–4237 or 044/517–0269) and the **Puppet Theater** (13 shota Rustaveli, ☎ 044/220–9065, which is also an active synagogue again (having been made into a puppet theatre under the communists).

Kiev's **Zoo** (32 Prospect Peremogi, ☎ 044/274–6054) is easy to reach by subway (Politekhnicheska Institute Station). It's open all year (daily 9–6, closed Mon.), though it keeps shorter hours in the winter.

The Museum of Folk Architecture (*see* Excursion, *above*) is both fun and educational for young ones, with the added advantage of letting them stretch their legs. It's best to go in the good-weather months, however.

Off the Beaten Path

Askold's Grave

This memorial to Kiev's ancient past is located in a picturesque park not far from the Park of Glory and World War II Tomb of the Unknown Soldier. Askold (also known as Rurik) was the legendary Varangian (Viking) prince who ruled Kiev during the second half of the 9th century. According to the ancient chronicles, he was murdered by the Novgorodian Prince Oleg, who seized Kiev in 882. Legend has it that Askold was buried on this hillside site overlooking the Dnieper River. A wooden church, dedicated to St. Nicholas, was built above his tomb but was later moved to the Monastery of the Caves. In 1810 a small Classical rotunda church was built on the gravesite to a design by the architect Andrei Melensky, and in 1936 a colonnade was added to protect it. You can reach Askold's grave by taking the subway to Arsenalna Station and walking south (left as you exit the subway) until you reach Dneprovskii Spusk, which slopes off to your left. Follow the road down the incline, and the rotunda will appear in the distance to your left.

Babi Yar

★ There was a time when Babi Yar was just another pretty ravine on the outskirts of town. World War II changed that. In September 1941, the German occupying forces ordered Kiev's 33,700 Jewish residents to gather their belongings and march to Babi Yar. Thinking they would be transported to another location, the men, women, and children did as they were told and lined up along the edge of the ravine. Nazi firing squads proceeded to execute them, and their bodies toppled into the ravine below. Throughout the Nazi occupation Babi Yar was used for mass killings. In all, over 100,000 people were killed here, including partisans and members of the Soviet underground. In 1976 a monument was erected on the site, with the official cumbersome title of **Monument to Soviet Citizens, Soldiers, and Officers, Prisoners of War, Who Were Tortured and Killed by the Nazi Invaders in 1941–43.** Although Soviet officials denied for decades that Jews had been a specific target of the Nazis, the dramatic monument—crowned by the figure of a young mother—is a moving testament to their suffering. To reach Babi Yar, take Trolleybus 16 or 18 from Maidan Nezalezhnosti (No. 16 stops across the street, at the bottom of vulitsa Zhitomirska; No. 18 stops at the bottom of Sofiska vulitsa). The trip takes 30–40 minutes; Babi Yar is located just past the tall television tower.

Kirilovska Tserkva (St. Cyril's Church)

Even if you are sated with church architecture, the trip to this magnificent 12th-century cathedral, located at the northwestern end of the Podol, is well worth it. Inside, more than 800 square meters (8,600 square feet) of medieval frescoes have been preserved. The church was once attached to the St. Cyril Monastery, founded in 1140 by Vsevolod II, prince of Chernigov, a pretender to the Kievan throne. Sviatoslav Vsevolovich, a hero in the ancient Russian epic, *The Lay of Igor's Campaign,* was buried here in 1194. Badly damaged during the Mongol invasion, the church has been rebuilt several times. Its present Baroque exterior dates from the 18th century, when it was reconstructed by Alexander Beretti. Restoration of the frescoes was entrusted to the art historian Adrian Prakhov. Among his apprentices was Mikhailo Vrubel, at that time an unknown artist from St. Petersburg. Vrubel's distinctive Symbolist brush is evident in the paintings on the marble altar screen and in the figures of the Holy Virgin and St. Cyril on the iconostasis. Like many churches in the Soviet Union, St. Cyril's was closed after the Bolshevik Revolution and opened as a museum in 1929. To reach the church, take Trolleybus 18 from Maidan Nezalezhnosti (the trolleybus stops across the street, at the bottom of vulitsa Sofiskaya) to the stop Stadion Spartak. The ride takes about 40 minutes. *12 Oleni Teligi,* ☎ *044/435–1126.* ☉ *Mon.–Thurs., weekends 10–5:30.*

Mariinsky Dvorets (Maria's Palace)

If you are coming from St. Petersburg, this lovely blue-and-cream palace will probably bring back memories of the imperial summer estates, and with good reason. Like St. Andrew's Cathedral (*see* Tour 3, *above*), the palace was commissioned by Empress Elizabeth during her 1744 visit to Kiev. It was designed by her favorite architect, Bartolomeo Rastrelli, and was built between 1750 and 1755 under the direction of the Moscow architect Ivan Michurin. Styled after Rastrelli's Razumovsky Palace in Perovo (near Moscow), it is a lovely mixture of Ukrainian and Russian Baroque. The main building faces an open courtyard surrounded by an elaborate wrought-iron fence. Corinthian columns and sculptures adorn the main entrance. The park facade is even more impressive: Balustrades decorated with vases and sculptures of lions lead majestically down to the formally landscaped park, also designed by Rastrelli. Unfortunately, only the main facade is open for viewing; the building now houses offices of the Ukrainian government and is closed to the public.

Before the 1917 Revolution, the palace was used as the residence for visiting members of the imperial family. It has undergone many reconstructions. In 1819 the upper, wooden floor of the main building burned. It was rebuilt in the 1870s, in preparation for an impending visit from Czar Alexander II and his wife, Maria, for whom the palace is now named. Severely damaged during World War II, it has been faithfully restored to its original appearance. To reach the palace, take the subway to Arsenalna Station. When you exit, do not cross the street. Take Trolleybus 20 one stop. The palace is a short walk to your left through a small park.

Volodimirsky Sobor (St. Vladimir's Cathedral)

Commissioned in 1862, this elaborate neo-Byzantine cathedral was supposed to have been finished in time for the 900th anniversary of Russia's conversion to Christianity. A series of construction problems delayed its completion, and the celebrations (in 1888) came and went before the cathedral was finally consecrated in 1896. Construction was begun by Ivan Strom and finished by Alexander Beretti, with several other architects working on the cathedral in the meantime. Frequent changes in design resulted in a diversity of styles. The highly ornate exterior is a strange and not particularly attractive mix of Baroque and Byzantine; the interiors, however, are splendid, with frescoes, icons, and murals created by some of Russia's most prominent artists, including Nesterov. The work was supervised by the art historian Professor Adrian Prakhov, who was also in charge of the restoration of St. Cyril's Church (*see above*). Among the historical figures depicted are Prince Vladimir (the pagan ruler who brought Christianity to Russia), Princess Olga, Alexander Nevsky, and Monk Nestor (coauthor of the *Primary Chronicles*). *20 Bulvar Tarasa Shevchenka, across from Universitet subway station,* (☎ *044/225–0362). Services daily Mon.–Sat. 9 AM, 6 PM.*

Sightseeing Checklist

This list includes attractions covered in the preceding tours as well as additional attractions described for the first time.

Churches, Monasteries, and Convents

Church of the Redeemer in the Birchwood (*see* Tour 4)
Church of the Tithe (Desyatinna Tserkva, *see* Tour 3)
Monastery of the Caves (Kievo-Pecherska Lavra, *see* Tour 4)
Pritisko-St. Nicholas Church (Nikolai-Pritiska Tserkva, *see* Tour 3)
Refectory Church of Mikhailovsky-Zlatoverhy Monastery (*see* Tour 2)
St. Alexander's (*see* Tour 2)
St. Andrew's Cathedral (Andreyivsky Sobor, *see* Tour 3)
St. Cyril's Church (Kirilovska Tserkva, *see* Off the Beaten Path)
St. Elias's (Illinska Tserkva, *see* Tour 3)
St. Flor's Monastery (Florivskii Monastir, *see* Tour 3)
St. Nicholas's (House of Organ and Chamber Music, *see* Arts and Nightlife)
St. Sophia's Cathedral (Sofiisky Sobor, *see* Tour 2)
St. Vladimir's Cathedral (Volodimirsky Sobor, *see* Off the Beaten Path)
Vydubetsky Monastery. Founded in 1070 by Prince Vsevolod, son of Yaroslavl the Wise, this monastery was largely destroyed by a landslide in the 15th century. A section of St. Michael's Cathedral (1077–88) remains, including a fragment of a 12th-century fresco of the Last Judgment. Also on the monastery grounds is St. George's Church (1696–1791), a five-domed masterpiece of Ukrainian architecture. You can reach the monastery, which is in botanical gardens, by tram from Arsenalnaya or Dneiper subway stations. *5 km (3 mi) s. of Monastery of the Caves, on bank of Dnieper.*

Historical Buildings and Sites

Askold's Tomb (*see* Off the Beaten Path)
Babi Yar (*see* Off the Beaten Path)
Contract House (Kontraktovy Dom, *see* Tour 3)
Gostinni Dvir (*see* Tour 3)
Kievo-Mogilianska Academy (*see* Tour 3)
Kiev University (*see* Tour 1)
Kriti Rynok (*see* Tour 1)
Maria's Palace (Mariinsky Dvorets, *see* Off the Beaten Path)
Zoloti Vorota (Golden Gate, *see* Tour 2)

Monuments and Statues

Bogdan Khmelnitsky Monument (*see* Tour 2)
Magdeburg Law Column. Designed by the Ukrainian architect Andrei Melensky, this monument was completed in 1808 and honors Kiev's right to self-government. *In Khreshchaty Park, at bottom of Volodimirska Girka.*
Monument to the Baptism of Russia (*see* Tour 1)
Monument Commemorating the 325th Anniversary of the Reunion of Russia and Ukraine (*see* Tour 1)
Monument to the Dynamo Soccer Team (at the Republican Stadium, *see* Spectator Sports)
Mother of Russia Monument (*see* Tour 4)
Skovoroda Monument (*see* Tour 3)
Taras Shevchenko Monument (*see* Tour 1)
Tomb of the Unknown Soldier of World War II. An eternal flame burns in memory of soldiers lost during the war. *In Vechnoi Slavy (Eternal Memory) Park, 1 trolleybus stop s. of Arsenalna subway station.*

Museums

Apothecary Museum (*see* Tour 3)
Bulgakov Museum (*see* Tour 3)
Chernobyl Museum (*see* Tour 3)
Folk Architecture Museum (*see* Excursions)

Historical Museum. The museum's extensive exhibits cover the history of Kiev from prehistoric times to the present. The section on Kievan Rus is particularly interesting. Also on display are examples of Ukrainian folk art from the 17th to the 20th century. *2 vul. Volodimirska,* ☎ *044/ 228–4864 or 044/228–2924.* ◔ *Mon., Tues., Thurs.–Sun. 10–5.*

History of Kiev Museum. Situated in the Klovsky Mansion, this museum was designed in the 1750s by the serf-architect Stepan Kovnir. *8 vul. Pilila Orlika,* ☎ *044/293–6071.* ◔ *Mon.–Thurs., Sat., Sun. 10– 5. Closed last Thurs. of month.*

Lesya Ukrainka Museum. This is a memorial museum to the well-known Ukrainian poetess Lesya Ukrainka. *97 vul. Sagaidachnovo,* ☎ *044/220– 1651.* ◔ *Mon.–Sat. 10–5.*

Museum of Historical Treasures (*see* Tour 4)
Museum of Ukrainian Books and Printing (*see* Tour 4)
Museum of Ukrainian Folk Art (*see* Tour 4)
Museum of Western and Oriental Art (*see* Tour 1)

Natural Science Museum. This is four museums in one: the Archaelogical Museum, the Botanical Museum, the Geological Museum, and the Zoological Museum. *15 vul. Bogdana Khmelnitskogo,* ☎ *044/224– 9383.* ◔ *Fri.–Tues. 10–4:30.*

Russian Art Museum (*see* Tour 1)

Shevchenko Memorial Museum. The personal effects and literary manuscripts of Taras Shevchenko are on display in the house where the Ukrainian writer lived in 1846. *8a Shevchenko Pereulok,* ☎ *044/ 228–3511.* ◔ *Sat.–Thurs. 10–5.*

Shevchenko State Museum (*see* Tour 1)
Ukrainian Art Museum (*see* Tour 1)
Ukrainian Cultural Center (Ukrainina Dim, *see* Tour 2)
Museum of the History of the Great Patriotic War (*see* Tour 4)

Parks and Gardens

Kiev has miles of beautiful parkland. The right bank of the Dnieper is lined with a series of adjoining parks, beginning with **Volodimirska Girka** (*see* Tour 1), which runs into **Khreshchaty Park.** That in turn runs into the **Park of Askold's Grave,** which later becomes the **Vechnoi Slavy (Eternal Memory) Park.** Collectively, they are called **Central Park.** The entrance to Khreshchaty Park is at Lenkomosol Square; Eternal Memory Park can be reached by taking the subway to Arsenalna Station. From there it is one stop south on any trolleybus.

Academy of Sciences Botanical Garden. This park is situated on the banks of the Dnieper River and covers 180 hectares (445 acres). It can be reached by tram from the Arsenalna and Dnieper subway stations.

Fomin Botanical Garden. This park in the center of town was laid out in 1841. It is named after Alexander Fomin, a botanist and director here in the 1920s. The entrance is near the Universitet subway station.

Gidro Park. This pretty park on an island near the left bank is a popular spot in summer for boating and bathing. To reach it, take the subway to the Gidro Park Station.

Trukhanov Island. There are several parks with outdoor recreational facilities on this island in the Dnieper. The beach is crowded with sunbathers in summer. You can reach the island via the pedestrian footbridge, south of the main river terminal (Ploshcha Poshtova subway station).

Zoo (*see* What to See and Do with Children)

SHOPPING

You don't go to Kiev to shop, but still, to avoid frustration, think of shopping here as a way to acquaint yourself with the challenges facing Ukrainian citizens as their government tries to reform the economy. The old classification of stores by what they sell has been thrown out, and the stores themselves are in the process of rearranging themselves. Economic "reform" allows people to resell goods purchased in state-run stores—an activity once considered a capital crime. As a result, the streets are lined with makeshift kiosks offering a hodgepodge of goods, from caviar to nylons, and you'll often find an incongruous mix of items. Every subway station has several bookstands, where the selection is much better than it is in even the largest bookstores (you may even come across a book in English). The shopping center has traditionally been and remains the Khreshchatik, although you'll probably find just as much for sale in the streets and in all the new shops as you will in the huge department stores along its path.

There are two categories of shops: those operating for Ukrainian "coupons" and those that accept only foreign currency. The coupon was originally introduced in 1990 as a ration card. When prices in Russia and other republics started escalating, they remained relatively stable in Ukraine. To prevent people from buying up all of Ukraine's goods for resale in other republics, the government started paying Ukrainians in coupons instead of rubles. At first the "coupon" applied only to basic consumer goods and grocery-store items, but over time more and more stores stopped accepting rubles. Eventually the coupon acquired the status of a national currency. The government plans to phase out this "intermediate" currency and replace it with a convertible one called the grivna. The value of coupons, which look more like Monopoly money than rubles, plummets daily, and they are barely worth the paper they are printed on. Goods for sale for coupons are usually incredibly inexpensive, thanks to the advantageous exchange rate against the dollar.

Department Stores

Kiev's largest department store, the TsUM Central Department Store, is located just off the Khreshchatik (2 vul. Bogdana Khmelnitskovo, ☎ 044/224–9505. The huge **Ukraina** (1 Ploshcha Peremogi, ☎ 044/274–6017) is close to the Libid Hotel. To reach it, take any bus or trolleybus heading down the hill from the Universitet subway station. **Ditiachi Svet** (3 Maliashka, ☎ 044/559–2170) is the children's department store.

Hard-Currency Stores

The dollar stores sell a wide variety of goods, often a mix of foodstuffs and large consumer items, such as imported TVs, VCRs, or even cars.

Candor (vul. Spaska, ☎ 044/416–1308) sells shoes, boots, cosmetics, TVs, washing machines, batteries, bottled water, coffee and tea, cigarettes, and liquor.

Nika Group Stores (2 bul. Tarasa Shevchenka, ☎ 044/225–0271) is a collection of shops that includes a large supermarket (with imported cheese and fresh bread sections), a clothing emporium, and an office-supply store that stocks foreign reading material.

Seagram (4 vul. Karla Marksa) is perhaps the world's most luxurious liquor store, offering premium wines and liquors from around the world.

Slavuta (14 vul. Gorkhovo, ☎ 044/227–8464) is a hard-currency grocery with a good selection of imported foods, including frozen pizza, spaghetti, cereal, crackers, bottled water, coffee, canned goods, wine, beer, and alcohol. AE credit cards and traveler's checks are accepted.

Steilmann (14 vul. Chervonoarmiiska) sells men's and women's western clothing, shoes, and accessories.

Kashtan Stores

The Ukrainian variant of the state-run stores catering to tourists and operating only for dollars called Beriozkas (birch tree) in Russia are named for Ukraine's national tree: the **Kashtan** (chestnut). In these changed times, however, such stores are not really different from the hard-currency shops (*above*). The largest Kashtan store (24/26 Bulvar Lesi Ukrainki, ☎ 044/295–6127) sells souvenirs, snacks, food, clothing, and electronics.

Specialty Stores

Art Shops and Galleries

This is one area where Kiev has lots to offer. **Andriivskii Uvziv,** the twisting and winding street leading down the steep incline from St. Andrew's Cathedral, is lined with art shops and galleries that sell works in all price ranges. Even if you're not in the market for Ukrainian art, you'll enjoy browsing.

Gallery Taras (4 Kontraktova Ploshcha, in the Podol Shopping Arcade, ☎ 044/416–2531) sells contemporary paintings and a small selection of Ukrainian handicrafts.

Gallery Triptych (34 Andriivskii Uzviz, ☎ 044/416–4453), owned by an association of well-known Kievan artists, sells paintings, handcrafted jewelry, embroidered vests, pottery, graphic art, and textiles.

Gonchari (10A Andriivskii Uzviz, ☎ 044/416–1298) has a wide selection of pottery, including teapots of all shapes and sizes, teacups, chess sets, and ceramic animals.

Tsentralny Khudozhni Salon (27 vul. Bogdana Khmelnitskovo, ☎ 044/224–1660) is a former central art salon and sells a variety of handicrafts.

Tvorchistvo (34A Andriivskii Uzviz, ☎ 044/228–3953) sells handcrafted Ukrainian souvenirs at very reasonable prices.

Virobi Maistriv Ukraine (15 Khreshchatik, Passage, ☎ 044/228–5652) features an excellent selection of handmade items from Ukrainian artists.

Souvenir Stores

The state-run **Ukrainian Souvenir** (23 vul. Chervonoarmiiska, ☎ 044/224–8516) has a surprisingly good selection of Ukrainian woodcrafts, tablecloths, bedspreads, and embroidered blouses. **Krystal** (5A vul. Lva Tolstovo, ☎ 044/227–3703) sells crystal and glass products, which make pretty gifts to bring home. The **House of Gifts** (5 bul. Lesi Ukrainki, ☎ 044/224–0590) showcases all manner of goods made only in Ukraine. The second remaining **Kashtan** store, at 2 bul. Tarasa Shevchenka (☎ 044/224–7053) sells only gold and silver jewelry, created by artists from either Ukraine or other nations in the CIS. When you're visiting the Monastery of the Caves, you might want to stop by the **Ukrainian Folk Art Shop** (Building No. 5 in the Upper Lavra, ☎ 044/290–1249).

Street Markets

Kiev's largest farmers' market is the **Kriti Rynok** on Bessarabska Ploshcha at the western end of the Khreshchatik. Inside the domed building you'll find rows of private farmers selling fresh fruit and vegetables, cheeses, and fine cuts of meat; Ukrainian souvenirs are occasionally sold. Be aware that you are expected to bargain. There is also the **Volodirmirska** market at 115 Gorkovo vul. and the **Lukianivsky** market located at 1 Melnikova vul.

SPORTS AND FITNESS

Participant Sports

If you're a fitness fanatic, you'll have a hard time in Kiev, especially in winter. None of the major hotels has a fitness center. The Intourist Hotel's small pool, attached to its sauna, is too small to satisfy lap swimmers.

Access to Kiev's public indoor athletic facilities is restricted, just as it is in Moscow and St. Petersburg. The prerequisite "doctor's certificate" attesting to your good health would probably take more time to obtain than you plan to spend in Kiev. If you are visiting in summer, you're in luck, since the outdoor facilities are open to everyone.

Boating and Swimming

You can rent boats at Kiev's **Gidro Park,** which is easily reached by subway (Gidro Park Station); there is also a nice beach here. The most popular beach by far is on **Trukhanov Island,** which is connected to the right bank by a pedestrian footbridge (south of the main river terminal, Ploshcha Poshtova subway station).

Jogging

You are welcome to try any of the city's parks, and you will probably feel comfortable on many of its wide, tree-lined streets—at least if you can take the hills. You can also see if the tracks at either the **Central Republican Stadium** (55 vul. Chervonoarmiiska) or **Dynamo Stadium** (3 vul. Mikhaila Grushevskovo) are free on days when there are no scheduled sports events.

Skiing and Skating

In winter you can rent skates and cross-country skis at the park on Trukhanov Island.

Tennis

There are public tennis courts in the park on Trukhanov Island.

Spectator Sports

Tickets to athletic events are sold at the sporting arena prior to the game, but popular events, especially soccer games, sell out far in advance. You may want to ask your hotel's excursion bureau for assistance in obtaining tickets. Kiev's main **ticket office** for sporting events is at 16 vulitsa Chervonoarmiiska (☎ 044/225–3258 or 044/224–8234).

Hockey

Hockey is second in popularity only to soccer among Kievans. The home team, Kievskii Stroitel, plays at the **Central Republican Stadium** on vulitsa Chervonoarmiiska (☎ 044/221–5775). The season is from October through March.

Soccer

Soccer is a national pastime, and Kiev's Dynamo team, along with its main rival, Moscow's Spartak, is one of the two most popular in the former Soviet Union; it has won several Soviet and European championships. You can watch them in action from March through September at the **Dynamo** (3 vul. Mikhaila Grushevskovo, ☎ 044/229–5252). The stadium, which seats 100,000, was built in 1941 but was not opened until after World War II. There is a monument here in honor of the Dynamo Soccer Team, which was forced to play against the Nazis—and then was shot for winning.

DINING

Compared with St. Petersburg and Moscow, dining in Kiev is, simply put, provincial, and before Ukraine's declaration of independence in 1991 the situation was downright bleak. Although Ukraine was always considered the breadbasket of the Soviet Union, its capital had only a handful of decent restaurants, located primarily in hotels catering to foreign tourists. The cuisine here differs little from the bland, meat-laden dishes offered in the state-run hotels of Moscow and St. Petersburg. The overall situation in Kiev is slowly improving, however. The establishment of several foreign embassies and the influx of Western businesspeople have spurred the opening of more sophisticated establishments, though unfortunately, if you're looking for traditional Ukrainian cuisine, you're not likely to find it in these places. The menus tend to cater to the city's growing expatriate community, which long ago had its fill of chicken Kiev. Prices, too, are high, not only because there are more foreigners than restaurants but also because many of the supplies are often imported.

As in Moscow and St. Petersburg, dining out requires planning. Reservations are almost always essential in the evenings and are advised even during the day. Most restaurants close in the afternoon for a "dinner break," and some are open only in the evenings. You are unlikely to meet "typical" Kiev residents by dining out. The current inflation rate and plummeting value of the Ukrainian coupon make a restaurant meal a luxury that few Kievans can afford.

Like their languages, the cuisines of Russia and Ukraine differ only slightly; both concentrate on meat-and-potato dishes, usually served with heavy sauces. Mushrooms, served in a variety of forms, are a favorite in both countries. Both Russians and Ukrainians love to smother their dumplings and potatoes with *smetana,* a rich sour cream. Despite these similarities, Ukrainian cuisine does have its specialties. One, of course, is the famous *Kievskaya kotleta* (chicken Kiev), which is very tricky to make. If prepared correctly, a fountain of butter spurts out of the fried chicken breast when pierced with a fork. Another Ukrainian specialty is *vareniki,* boiled dumplings filled with *tvorog* (a sweet cottage cheese), potatoes, mushrooms, cabbage, or meat. Ukrainian *borscht,* beet soup served with a huge dollop of *smetana,* is usually accompanied by *pampushki,* hot rolls dripping in garlic butter.

CATEGORY	COST*
$$$$	over $50
$$$	$35–$50
$$	$15–$35
$	under $15

*per person, excluding drinks and service

What to Wear

Dress at the restaurants listed below is casual, unless noted otherwise.

$$$$ **El Dorado.** If you'd rather be anywhere but in Kiev, seek out this ritzy restaurant and bar, tucked away in a cellar off Bessarabska Square. Its modern decor features a high-tech lighting system that re-creates a star-lit night through the restaurant's crystal-studded ceiling. The Ukrainian owner caters to Kiev's foreign business community and its fat expense accounts. The menu features traditional European cuisine, such as smoked duck breast and roasted lamb. The prix fixe dinner changes weekly and includes appetizer, soup, main course, and dessert. Although the business-oriented clientele can make for a rather stuffy atmosphere, things turn lively after the kitchen closes. Unlike most establishments in Kiev, the bar stays open until the last patron leaves. ✕ *13 vul. Chervonoarmiiska,* ☎ *044/244–2921. Reservations advised. Jacket and tie. AE. Hard currency only: American Express traveler's checks or cash. Lunch daily noon–3, dinner daily 7–10:30, bar open daily until 2 AM. No Sun. lunch.*

$$$$ **Napoleon.** This extravagently ornate restaurant must be Kiev's challenge to Paris. If you can cope with its overly opulent interior (ivory-hued and wood-inlaid walls, marble floors, an abundance of crystal and silver) you'll find attentive and serious service and very good food. Dressed in full Empire regalia, the waiters proffer a heavy, 14-page menu (with English translation) and are happy to walk you through it. A melange of cold dishes like aspics, poached fish, and various kinds of caviar is followed by salads, hot appetizers, and a series of wonderful soups. You may want to try the Marseilles fish soup or the consommé with apples. Then there are more than 25 meat courses, from beef in burgundy sauce to chicken fricassee to beef tongue with nuts. You may prefer one of the fish dishes, however, all of which are excellently prepared. Lighter appetites can opt for omelets, but make up for it by ordering mousse or cake with fruit for dessert. The string quartet tends to overwhelm the room but plays beautifully nonetheless. Lest it all sound too serious, the well-laid table also includes a pack of tic tac and pieces of bubblegum! ✕ *16 Shota Rustaveli,* ☎ *044/221–5597. Reservations advised. Jacket and tie. Credit cards and U.S. dollars.* ☉ *Daily 10 AM–midnight.*

$$$
★ **Apollo.** One of the main restaurants catering to the city's foreign community, this Swiss-Ukrainian joint venture has set a standard for fine dining in Kiev. The beautifully restored interior, with ceiling paintings from the 19th century, Greek statues, and high-back wooden chairs, creates an elegant atmosphere far removed from the hustle and bustle of the nearby Khreshchatik. The service, like the interior, is elegant, and the formally dressed waiters have clearly been trained to meet European standards of excellence. Thanks to its Swiss partners, the restaurant imports 80 percent of its supplies, allowing it to offer truly European cuisine. For starters, try the quiche Lorraine, prepared in a light cream sauce and served in a delicate pastry shell, or the creamy broccoli soup. The light mushroom omelet makes for a nice break from meat-laden Ukrainian cuisine. But if you're a meat lover, you won't be disappointed by the steak fillet, served with melted cheese and mushrooms and accompanied by Italian green noodles. The dessert menu features fruit salad—a rare find in this city—made of mango, kiwi, pineapple, and bananas. On Sundays the restaurant offers a popular champagne brunch. Good wine list. ✕ *15 Khreshchatik, passage,* ☎ *044/229–0437. Reservations advised. Jacket and tie. AE, DC, MC, V. Hard currency only.* ☉ *Daily noon–3, 5–11; bar open until 1 AM.*

$$$ Italia. If you prefer spaghetti bolognese to chicken Kiev, come to this centrally located spot for anything but Ukrainian cuisine. The restaurant offers a taste of Western Europe in a post-Soviet setting. With the no-frills atmosphere still a bit haunted by the state-run "dietetic cafeteria" that once occupied the space (watercolors of faraway Italy decorate the walls, but the modest decor, disco lighting, and simple furnishings place you firmly in the former Soviet Union), it's comfortable nonetheless. The extensive menu offers several kinds of pizza, a wide variety of traditional meat dishes, as well as spaghetti, lasagna, and other pasta. For the full effect, order a bottle of imported Chianti from the extensive wine list, and top off your meal with a strong espresso and Italian ice. ✕ *8 vul. Prorizna,* ☎ *044/224–2054. Reservations advised. No credit cards. Hard currency or coupons. No traveler's checks.* ◷ *Daily 1 PM–2 AM.*

$$ Dnipro. Centrally located at the eastern end of the Khreshchatik, on the second floor of the Dnipro Hotel, this used to be the best restaurant in town. With the recent opening of cooperatives and Western-run joint ventures, it now faces some stiff competition, but it's still the best of the hotel restaurants. Heavy chandeliers, high ceilings, and the view onto Lenkomsomol Square make for a relatively pleasant atmosphere. You can opt for the buffet dining room if you want a slightly lower bill and a sample of various decent dishes. In the main dining room, the service is polite and formal although a bit slow. The kitchen offers a wide selection of standard Ukrainian and Russian dishes, but only half the items listed are ever available at any time. The food is not particularly imaginative, and the main courses come loaded with greasy fried potatoes. Therefore, it might be best to stick to staples like beef stroganoff. As is often the case, the appetizers and soups fare much better than entrees and the restaurant serves an excellent Ukrainian borscht, chock-full of fresh vegetables. ✕ *1/2 Khreshchatik,* ☎ *044/229–8160. Reservations accepted only in person and only for same day. No credit cards. Ukrainian coupons.* ◷ *Daily 8–noon, 1–5, 6–11.*

$$ Slavuta. This low-key, casual place is another favorite of Kiev's expatriate community. The modest menu features mainly chicken and fish dishes, including several of Finnish origin. The dark interior, with imitation stained-glass windows and trompe l'oeil brick walls, seems right out of a latter-day Monastery of the Caves. Compared to the city's other hard-currency establishments, the prices are reasonable, and the restaurant's central location keeps the crowds coming back. ✕ *14 vul. Gorkhovo,* ☎ *044/227–6484. Reservations advised. AE. U.S. dollars or German marks.* ◷ *Daily noon–midnight.*

$ Gostinny Dvir. Located in the heart of the Podol, in the 19th-century
★ merchant's arcade, this lively restaurant specializing in traditional Ukrainian cooking is the perfect place to top off a day of sightseeing. The interior is warm and inviting, with high arched ceilings decorated with Roman motifs and brass chandeliers. The friendly waitresses, dressed in colorful Ukrainian costumes, will insist that you eat every bite—which shouldn't be too hard, because the food is excellent. Start off with a spicy bowl of Ukrainian borscht, which comes with *pampushki*, piping hot rolls topped with finely diced garlic and dripping with garlic butter. The *Gribi v Smetanoi Sousi*, the local version of mushrooms in cream sauce, is a tasty appetizer. For your main course, try the house specialty, *Vareniki z Kartopleyu*, boiled dumplings filled with potatoes and topped with crisp, butter-fried onions. The slightly sweet *Varenki z Sirom* come filled with tvorog. Great food and atmosphere make this restaurant attractive as well to local residents, so chances are you won't be completely surrounded by foreigners. ✕ *4 Kontraktova Ploshcha,* ☎ *044/416–2271. Reservations advised. No credit cards.* ◷ *Daily noon–5, 7–11. No Mon. dinner. Ukrainian coupons only.*

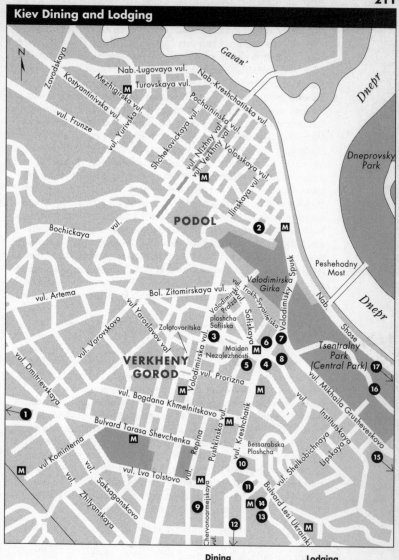

Dining
Apollo, **6**
Dnipro, **7**
El Dorado, **10**
Gostinny Dvir, **2**
Italia, **5**
Kureny, **16**
Napoleon, **11**
Skhodi, **3**
Slavuta, **9**

Lodging
Bratislava, **17**
Dnipro, **7**
Intourist, **14**
Khreshchatik, **4**
Libid, **1**
Mir, **12**
Moskva, **8**
Rus, **13**
Salyut, **15**

$ **Kureny.** If you are a summertime visitor to Kiev, you may find this enjoyable as an excursion as well. It is an open-air restaurant near the river, and it's laid out like a tiny Ukrainian village. The staff is in folk costume, and both the decor and food are traditional. ⌧ *4 Parkova Aleya,* ☎ *044/293–4062. Reservations advised. Coupons only.* ⊙ *Noon–midnight.*

$ **Skhodi.** Better known by its Russian translation, *Lesnitsa,* this popular restaurant gets its name from the long stairway leading down into its dark premises, formerly used as an all-purpose storage room by the Ukrainian Architecture Union. Although a modest attempt has been made to pretty it up with wall mirrors and fake flowers, the dust still hasn't settled. But what the restaurant lacks in modern decor, it makes up for in lively atmosphere and excellent food. The dishes are all prepared from products purchased daily at the local markets. The menu features traditional Ukrainian fare, such as *Kievskii Bitok,* fried pork rolled in flour and served with a plate of vegetables and french fries. For starters, try the *Salat Kashtan,* a mayonnaise-based salad made of finely diced roast beef, pickles, hard-boiled egg, peas, and carrots. The borscht is always tasty. To add to the pleasure, the service shines. For local color and wholesome Ukrainian food, this is just the place. ✕ *7 vul. Borisa Grichenka,* ☎ *044/229–8629. Reservations advised. No credit cards. Ukrainian coupons only.* ⊙ *Daily noon–4, 7–11, except Sundays.*

LODGING

The building boom that has taken Moscow and St. Petersburg by storm has so far bypassed the Ukrainian capital. Even at the height of perestroika, when the Soviet Union suddenly became a hot new destination, Kiev was never besieged with tourists. As a result, accommodations are limited to the old Intourist standbys, which are primarily of modern construction, heavy on chrome and cement, and light on character. There are no grand, prerevolutionary hotels or new luxury ones—even though you may feel that you are paying near-luxury prices, considering what you get. And although you'll find that staff members exude hospitality, the service in general is still redolent of Soviet inefficiency. But thanks to the growing demands of foreign businesspeople, improvements are slowly being made.

Tourist groups are usually placed at one of Intourist's three-star hotels: the **Libid, Rus,** or **Intourist.** Although standards here fluctuate greatly, all provide adequate, if not exactly sightly, accommodations. Bring your patience and be prepared for a few unexpected touches. Shower curtains and sink stoppers are not standard issue. Not all rooms come with telephone and television, but most of them have refrigerators.

All prices are quoted in U.S. dollars; with only rare exceptions, hotels require payment in foreign currency or by credit card and do not accept Russian rubles or Ukrainian coupons.

CATEGORY	COST*
$$$$	$150–$180
$$$	$100–$150
$$	$50–$100
$	under $50

All prices are for a standard double room for two, excluding service charge.

$$$$ **Intourist.** Built by Polish contractors, this huge complex overlooking
★ the gigantic sport stadium is Kiev's newest hotel. Although the dark
lobby features the usual marble decor, the rooms are pleasant and nicely
appointed. All of them come with refrigerator, television, and telephone,
and the higher floors feature balconies with superb views of the city.
Popular with businesspeople, all of the suites have been leased as offices. The business center on the first floor offers satellite communi-
cations with direct dialing abroad. The only major drawback is the hilltop
location: You'll have to put on your hiking shoes to reach the subway,
since the closest stop is a 10-minute trek down the steep hill. ☎ *12
Gospitalna vul.,* ☎ *044/220–4144,* ℻ *044/220–4568. 350 rooms with
bath. Restaurant, foreign-currency snack bar, casino, foreign-currency
souvenir shop, excursion bureau, exchange office, sauna with dipping
pool. AE, DC, MC, V.*

$$$$ **Rus.** Situated next door to the new Intourist Hotel, this high-rise has smaller
rooms and a less appealing interior. The walls with their dark floral paper
don't match the faded orange curtains, and the chairs are upholstered
with the same carpeting material as the floors, and neither is particularly clean. All rooms come with telephone, television (local stations only),
and refrigerator. The staff is professional and courteous. Thanks to good
relations with the Intourist, guests can use the sauna next door. The views
here are just as good, and the walk to the subway just as exhausting. ☎
4 Gospitalna vul., ☎ *044/227–8594 or 044/220–4255,* ℻ *044/220–
4396. 477 rooms with bath. 3 restaurants, 2 foreign-currency bars, 3
snack bars, exchange bureau. AE, DC, MC, V.*

$$$ **Dnipro.** Conveniently located at the eastern end of the Khreshchatik,
★ this hotel is one of the city's most popular, particularly for business
travelers and groups. It's an organizing site for conferences and quite
user-friendly for those with business needs. All the major tourist sites
are easily accessible by public transportation, and the Philharmonic Con-
cert Hall is just across the street. The interior is typically unimagina-
tive for a Soviet-built hotel, but the friendly staff does its best to
brighten up the place with flowers and plants. The rooms are clean
and pleasant, and all have television and telephone. The double rooms
have nice views onto the square below, but the singles all face the back
alley. The second-floor restaurant is the best of the city's hotel restau-
rants. ☎ *1/2 Khreshchatik,* ☎ *044/229–8287,* ℻ *044/229–8213.
180 rooms with bath. Restaurant, 3 banquet halls, 3 foreign-currency
bars, excursion bureau, exchange bureau. AE, DC, V.*

$$$ **Khreshchatik.** Another hotel with a good location, this one is named
after Kiev's main street. Less than 10 years old, it has comfortable and
spacious rooms, including suites. Located amid various international
airline offices, it is popular with tourists. ☎ *14 Khreshchatik,* ☎ *044/
229–7339. 2 restaurants, bar, sauna. Credit cards.*

$$$ **Salyut.** Yet another Soviet concrete monstrosity, this circular high-rise
looks like a spaceship fuselage but is really one of Kiev's finest hotels.
It, too, is popular with businesspeople. For the tourist, it is within walk-
ing distance of the Monastery of the Caves. The rooms are relatively
large, and some offer glorious views of the Dnieper and the golden cupo-
las of the monastery's churches. The furniture is slightly worn, but the
overall atmosphere is light and cheerful. Throw rugs cover the indus-
trial carpeting, and flowered wallpaper and framed dried flowers re-
place the usual stucco green walls. All rooms come with direct-dial
telephone, cable television (including CNN), refrigerator, and balcony.
Service is excellent by local standards. ☎ *10 vul. Sichnevovo Povstannya,*
☎ *044/290–6130,* ℻ *044/290–7270. 110 rooms with bath. Restau-
rant, snack bar. Traveler's checks accepted. AE, MC, V.*

$$ **Libid.** If you're on a tour arranged through any of Intourist's retooled groups, you may very well land in this cement block. Although it advertises a central location, the walk to the subway is a 20-minute climb up a steep hill. Opened in the early 1970s, the hotel offers the cement-and-steel decor of Brezhnev-era architecture, with plywood furnishings and green stucco walls. Only half the rooms come with television, but they all come with industrial carpeting stained from years of overuse and undercleaning. You may also find the mob of taxi drivers hanging around the main entrance a bit unpleasant. The service doesn't exactly shine, but it certainly beats the decor and atmosphere. ⊞ *Ploshcha Peremogi,* ☎ *044/274–0063,* FAX *044/224–0578. 280 rooms with bath. 14 suites. Restaurant, bar, exchange bureau, excursion bureau. AE, MC, V.*

$$ **Moskva.** Located just off the Khreshchatik, this 16-story high-rise towers on the steep hill above Kiev's main thoroughfare. Its monumental design reeks of Stalinism, though the hotel was built in the early 1960s. The rooms are spacious, with high ceilings and thick walls, but the place could use some sprucing up. Nevertheless, standards of cleanliness are higher than at the Libid, and the overly friendly floor attendants will be more than willing to respond to any complaints. Some rooms come with balconies offering grand views of the city. A telephone and television in every room just about exhausts the list of modern amenities. The main lobby is lined with souvenir kiosks selling such imported goods as Polish cosmetics and American bubblegum. Slot machines in a back room off the main entrance attract a seedy crowd that fills the lobby with cigarette smoke. This is obviously not the place for luxury accommodations, but it does offer local color and a good location. *4 vul. Institutska,* ☎ *044/229–0347,* FAX *044/229–1353. 360 rooms with bath. Restaurant, 3 snack bars, sauna with dipping pool, excursion bureau. No traveler's checks or credit cards.*

$ **Bratislava.** This low-budget hotel is a good choice if you don't mind
★   roughing it and being far from the city center. It's located on the left bank 11 kilometers (7 miles) from downtown Kiev, with the metro about 10 minutes away, though the ride (above-ground) takes you through pretty Gidro Park. The modest rooms have telephones and small balconies, but no television. The hotel's official rating is lower than the Libid's, but the rooms are cleaner and the atmosphere is far more pleasant. Missionary groups like to stay here. Single accommodations are not available. *1 vul. Andreya Malyshka,* ☎ *044/559–7570,* FAX *044/559– 7788. 347 rooms with bath. Restaurant with adjoining banquet halls, 2 bars, snack bar, excursion bureau. No traveler's checks or credit cards.*

$ **Mir.** Formerly owned by Sputnik, the Soviet youth tourist agency, this very basic hotel is essentially a youth hostel and far from the city center and accessible public transportation. Considering its super low rates, though, the accommodations are quite decent, and all rooms come with television and telephone. However, water-pressure problems make a hot shower next to impossible. The lobby's slot machines and all-night bar attract large numbers of the city's youth. *70 Prospekt 40-richchya zhovotnya,* ☎ *044/268–5600. 216 rooms with bath. Restaurant (for groups only), 3 snack bars, casino, sauna with dipping pool. Ukrainian coupons only. No credit cards.*

THE ARTS AND NIGHTLIFE

Kiev's cultural life is as rich as its ancient past, and the city boasts numerous theaters and concert halls. Except for popular ballet performances at the elegant Opera House, tickets are easy to come by and not expensive. The excursion bureau at your hotel will obtain tickets for you, but if you want to avoid their fee, which is often 10 times as much as the ticket itself, go directly to the theater's ticket office or to one of the ticket kiosks scattered throughout the city. They post available tickets in the window, together with a full schedule of upcoming events.

For the latest in pop and folk music, check out the underground passageways of the subway stations on the Khreshchatik. Spontaneous performances of music and dance are given in these cavelike premises night and day, and crowds make the lively events hard to ignore.

The Arts

Concerts

The **House of Organ and Chamber Music** (77 vul. Chervonoarmiiska, ☎ 044/269–5678), located in the former St. Nicholas Catholic Church, which was built at the turn of the century in the German-Gothic style.

International Center of Culture and Arts (1 Institutsky, ☎ 044/228–7491) Kiev's largest concert hall is located in a 19th-century finishing school for daughters of the nobility.

Philharmonic Concert Hall (Volodimirsky uzviz, ☎ 044/229–6251). Classical music concerts are performed in the former Merchant's Hall, built in 1882.

Ukrainian Palace of Culture (103 vul. Chervonoarmiiska, ☎ 044/268–9050). Contemporary ballet, musicals, and operas are featured here.

Drama

Lesya Ukrainka Russian Drama Theater (5 vul. Bogdana Khmelnitskovo, ☎ 044/224–4223 or 9063). Although the theater is named for a famous Ukrainian poetess, the repertoire is strictly Russian. Foreign dramas are occasionally performed, but only in Russian.

Ivan Franko Ukrainian Theater (3 ploshcha Ivana Franka, ☎ 044/229–5991). Here you'll find Ukrainian classical and contemporary dramas, but only in Ukrainian.

Opera and Ballet

The **Taras Shevchenko Opera and Ballet Theater** (50 vul. Volodimirska, ☎ 044/224–7165 or 044/229–1169), built in 1901, offers fine performances of Russian and Ukrainian operas and ballets in a gilded auditorium. The **State Operetta Theater** (53/3 vul. Chervonoarmiiska, ☎ 044/220–8754 or 044/227–2241) stages Ukrainian musical comedies. Also try the **Tchaikovsky Conservatory** (1/3 vul. Karla Marksa, ☎ 044/229–0792).

Nightlife

As in most cities in the former Soviet Union, nightlife centers around the city's restaurants and hotels, with their dining and dancing extravaganzas, which are usually not to the tastes of British and North American tourists. The only full-fledged bars are located in hotels catering to tourists; the **Dnipro, Intourist,** and **Rus** have lively lobby bars. For late-night action, the best place is the snazzy **El Dorado** (*see* Dining), whose bar stays open until the last customer leaves. For quiet late-night conversation, the **Apollo** bar offers a rare haven from rowdy crowds in the hotel bars. Around town, small café-bars are increasing, and they stay open late. Casinos are sprouting like mushrooms, and you'll find advertisements for them everywhere. While you might get a kick out of these bits of Las Vegas, don't fool yourself or underestimate the atmosphere. It's not a good idea to play too loose or friendly or, of course, to deal in too much cash. If you're in the mood, however, you can check out **Casino Club First** in the Hotel Intourist (☎ 044/220–1978, open daily 8 PM–4 AM), **Playoffs International** in the Hotel Libid (☎ 044/221–7674), **Club Flamingo** in the Mir Hotel (☎ 044/264–9203, open daily 24 hours), or **Casino Split** (6 Prorizna, ☎ 044/228–5877, open daily 7 PM–4 AM).

KIEV ESSENTIALS

Arriving and Departing

By Boat

Kiev is a river city, and there is passenger service to several other cities on the Dnieper and the Black Sea, into which it runs. The River Terminal is located at Poshtova Ploshcha (for which there is a subway stop of the same name). For tickets, you can go there in person, or you may inquire at your service bureau.

By Car

It is possible to drive to Kiev from Moscow (via the M4 Highway through Orel) or from Poland, Slovakia, the Czech Republic, and Hungary. Be aware, however, that roads are poorly maintained, repair shops are few and far between, and there is a possibility of fuel shortages.

By Plane

AIRPORTS AND AIRLINES

Visitors arriving at Kiev's **Borispol International Airport** (☎ 044/295–6701), located 29 kilometers (18 miles) east of Kiev, are in for a pleasant surprise. The airport, in a priority project, has been completely renovated to modern standards and is clean, well-lighted, and easy to navigate, with a large terminal and signs in English as well as Ukrainian.

After you disembark, before passport control, you may obtain a visa if you have arrived without one and possess the proper documents. (For details, see Passports and Visas *in* the Gold Guide.) Baggage carousels are located just beyond passport control. Here you will also complete a customs declaration and exit via Customs in the adjacent room. You should be meticulous in declaring all goods of value, including personal items such as jewelry and cameras.

Some domestic flights depart from the small **Zhulyany** airport (☎ 044/272–1201 or 044/272–1202) located on the city outskirts.

The international Ukrainian carriers are **Air Ukraine** (☎ 044/216–7040) and **Ukraine International** (☎ 044/216–6730, 044/224–2905, or 044/296–7455). Each flies between several European capitals, and Air Ukraine also has routes to the U.S. and Canada. From Russia, you can use **Aeroflot** (☎ 044/274–5223) or **Transaero** (☎ 044/224–8748), which has more flights, including four daily between Moscow and Kiev. Airlines from other countries include **Air France** (☎ 044/296–7050 or 044/229–1395), **Austrian Airlines** (☎ 044/212–2592 or 044/296–7454), **Balkan Bulgarian Airlines** (☎ 044/229–7203), **CSA Airlines** (☎ 044/228–0296), **Finnair** (☎ 044/296–7240), **KLM** (☎ 044/268–9023), **LOT Polish Airlines** (☎ 044/228–7150), **Lufthansa** (☎ 044/296–7686 or 044/229–6297), and **Malev Hungarian Airlines** (☎ 044/296–7453).

BETWEEN THE AIRPORT AND DOWNTOWN

It is best to have made advance arrangements for your transfer from the airport, particularly as it is outside Kiev's city limits. If you have flown Air Ukraine, you may use their coach service between the airport and the Rus Hotel, by booking a ticket at the same time as your plane ticket; business-class passengers and babies (under 2) may use this service for free; space on the coach is not guaranteed without an advance reservation.

There is also an express bus service—**Polet**—that will take you to Ploshcha Peremogi in the center of town. Departures are scheduled every 20 minutes. The ride takes one hour. Taxis and private cars are available, and you will no doubt encounter a mob of drivers as you exit, but it is up to you to decide if this is the best way to get into Kiev.

By Train

Train is by far the most convenient mode of traveling to other points in the CIS. There are several overnight trains daily to and from Moscow; the trip takes about 12 hours. There is also a daily train to St. Petersburg, but the ride is 30 hours long. The train station is located at 1 Vokzalnaya Ploshcha (☎ 044/233–1111); there's a connecting subway station (Vokzalnaya), so it is easily accessible by public transportation. For information on arrival and departure schedules, call 044/223–3306. The ticket office is at 38 vul. Shevchenko, but it's easiest to buy them through the service bureau of your hotel.

Trains can lack heat and hot water. In general, they are likely to be less comfortable than those between Moscow and St. Petersburg, for instance. Bring along some drinking water and light snacks. Also be aware that unless you and your group have purchased tickets to an entire compartment, there can be up to four travelers per wagon-car, and there is no segregation by sex on overnight trains. Your trainmates, if male, are also likely to consume several bottles of alcohol until journey's end. Courteous behavior is always proclaimed the standard—but heavy drinking is common—so consider what you want from a train trip before you get a ticket. There is no official border check between Ukraine and Russia, but Russian officials occasionally check the documents of foreign passengers upon arrival in Moscow and St. Petersburg. Traveling to Russia without a valid Russian visa carries a fine of up to $300.

Getting Around

Kiev is divided into 12 districts, but most of its historical sites are concentrated in the **Verkhny Gorod** (Old Town), **Podol** and **Pechersk** districts, and along the **Khreshchatik,** the principal thoroughfare. Although the main tourist attractions are far apart, they are all easily reached by subway.

By Bus, Tram, and Trolley

Buses, trams, and trolleys operate on the honor system. Upon entering, you validate your ticket by canceling it, using one of the machines on the wall of the vehicle. You can purchase tickets at yellow kiosks throughout the city (but not from the driver). The ticket is valid for one ride only; if you change buses, you must pay another fare. Buses, trams, and trolleys operate on the same schedule as the subway, although service in the late evening hours and Sundays tends to be unreliable.

Kiev has an extensive surface transportation system, but fuel shortages have led to cutbacks on many routes, so service may be somewhat slower than in Moscow or St. Petersburg. However, the vehicles here are in much better condition. During rush hours the word "crowded" acquires new meaning, as passengers squeeze into already jam-packed trams and trolleys.

By Car

Car rental is limited, and it is recommended that you stick to public transport. If you do opt to drive, you will at least find the roads much easier to navigate than those in the larger Russian cities. **Nikita** (9A Seratymovyela, ☎ 044/550–3226) and **Prostor** (23 Lvivska, ☎ 044/450–9261) both rent to tourists. You will need a valid driver's license, an international license, and a credit card.

By Subway

It pales by comparison with the elaborate and extensive metro of Moscow and St. Petersburg, but Kiev's subway system is efficient and well maintained. Three lines radiate from the Khreshchatik, connecting the city's historical center to the newer residential districts on the left bank of the Dnieper.

Purchase a token and insert it into the slot at the turnstile. Tokens are available at all stations. The fare is the same regardless of distance. If you are in Kiev at the beginning of the month, you may choose to purchase a monthly pass, good on all public transportation. They go on sale at the end of the month and are available through the first week. The subway operates from 5:30 AM to midnight and is best avoided during rush hour, when trains can be very crowded.

By Taxi

Official taxis roam much more frequently here than in Moscow and St. Petersburg. You will see them at most major sites, or you may wave them down on the street, where you should negotiate a price before getting in. To order a cab by phone, call 058. All the major hotels offer car service, available at inflated prices.

Guided Tours

Intourist-Kievska (12 vul. Gospitalna, in the Hotel Intourist, ☎ 044/224–7345) is the Ukrainian branch of the defunct Intourist. It will arrange excursions to any site in or around Kiev. It will also assist you with travel and hotel arrangements to other cities in Ukraine.

The city excursion bureau **Slavutich** (22 vul. Sichnevovo Povstannya, ☎ 044/290–8680) also offers excursions in and around Kiev on virtually any theme (historical, architectural, etc.). The agency can provide English-speaking guides and translators and assistance in booking low-budget accommodations.

Sputnik (4/6 Desyalynna, ☎ 044/212–2586) is another full-service agency that can arrange excursions as well as travel ticketing. Ask for English-language guides and programs.

Important Addresses and Numbers

Emergencies

Fire (☎ 01), **police** (☎ 02), **ambulance** (☎ 03). As in Moscow and St. Petersburg, you are unlikely to get an English-speaking operator if you call these emergency numbers. Medical facilities are far below world standards, and Kiev is plagued by even more shortages in basic medical supplies and equipment than can afflict Moscow and St. Petersburg. In a true emergency, evacuation to Finland or Western Europe should be considered.

The U.S. Embassy suggests calling the **Lifeline Medical Clinic** (☎ 044/553–7416), located at St. Andrew's School. The Ukrainian staff works under the instruction of U.S. doctors; U.S. missionary workers there include hospital adminstrators and a nurse.

For referrals to Ukrainian facilities you may also call **Ukrainian Medical Services** (☎ 044/440–6344), a 24-hour service with English-speaking operators. They can make arrangements for you and send a doctor, ambulance, and interpreter as necessary. Be prepared to pay any medical costs up front and in cash (US$).

In all likelihood, further clinics, such as an American Medical Center like the one in Moscow, will open no later than 1996. If you call an ordinary ambulance (03), you will probably end up at **the Emergency Care Center** (1/29 vul. Mechnikova, ☎ 044/224–7364). It enjoys a good reputation, partly because foreigners have always been sent here for treatment.

Dental care is available at this center as well (☎ 044/227–9240). You may also try **Cabot Dental Services,** which has two locations. The first is on vul. Chkalova, across from the German embassy (☎ 044/244–4682 or 044/219–1679) and is open weekdays 9–9, Sat. 9–2. The second is at 9 Khmelnitskogo St. (☎ 044/224–0468), open weekdays 9–9, Sat. 9–6.

English-Language Bookstores

Druzhba (30 Khreshchatik, 044/224–0373) and **Inostrannaya Kniga** (48 Chervonoarmiiska, ☎ 044/227–0088) have English-language sections, but the selection is meager, and bookshelves are usually lined with Ukrainian souvenirs. The art-book shop **Mistetstvo** (24 Khreshchatik, ☎ 044/228–2526) has the best selection of the state-run stores. You'll find an occasional guidebook or art book on Kiev in street kiosks and in the cavelike passageways of the subway (a favorite spot for budding entrepreneurs). American and British newspapers and magazines (*USA Today, Financial Times, Wall Street Journal*) are available at the lobby kiosks of the hotels Dnipro, Intourist, and Rus.

Pharmacies

Drugs and medicines are not necessarily readily available in Kiev. The foreign-currency pharmacies **Farma** (3 vul. Prorizna, ☎ 044/228–2871), **Shance** (15 Kreshatik, ☎ 044/228–3249), and **Pharmacie** (67 vul. Chkalova, ☎ 044/216–4562) are generally better stocked than the state-run pharmacies operating for Ukrainian coupons. For payment in coupons, **Biocon** operates two pharmacies out of district hospitals—Starokiev (100 Saksahanskoho, 1st fl., ☎ 044/228–1518) and Moskovsky (104 vul. Chervonoarmiiska, 1st fl., ☎ 044/212–8293). They stock Western medicine and are open also on Saturday 9–3.

Where to Change Money

All of the major hotels have exchange bureaus, which are generally open from 9 to 6, with an hour break for lunch.

You may also use some of the Ukrainian banks, including **Ukrinbank** (26 Bulvar Lesi Ukrainski, ☎ 044/294–6009) or **Inko Bank** (10/2 vul. Mechnikova, ☎ 044/290–7130), which also accepts American Express traveler's checks. **Dendi** Currency Exchange points can be found throughout the city (3 Bulvar Khmelnitskovo, ☎ 044/228–6595). The hotel **Lybid** (☎ 044/221–7731) can handle transactions involving most credit cards as well as American Express and Thomas Cook traveler's checks, and can also arrange Western Union money transfers.

Visitor Information

The closest thing Kiev has to a tourist information bureau is the former Ukrainian branch of Soviet Intourist, now known as **Intourist-Kievska** (12 vul. Gospitalna, in the Hotel Intourist, ☎ 044/224–7345 or 044/225–3243). You can also obtain tourist information at the excursion bureaus of major hotels, or consult one of the three agencies listed below. Most of the printed materials available are outdated, Soviet-produced booklets, which are heavy on propaganda and scant on information, but this is beginning to change.

Embassies

United States (10 vul. Yuria Kotsyubinskovo, ☎ 044/244–7344, FAX 044/244–7350), **Canada** (31 Yaroslaviv Val, ☎ 044/212–2235, FAX 044/225–1305), and **United Kingdom** (9 Desyatinna vul., ☎ 044/228–0504, FAX 044/228–3972).

English-Russian
Vocabulary

ENGLISH-RUSSIAN VOCABULARY

Although we have tried to be consistent about the spelling of Russian names in this book, we find the Soviet authorities are not consistent about transliteration of the Cyrillic alphabet into our familiar Latin letters. In Moscow, for example, Intourist spells a street name "Chaikovsky," but in St. Petersburg it's "Tchaikovsky." We've tried to stick to internationally recognized U.S. and British systems of transliteration, but don't be surprised if you occasionally come across differences like Chekhov and Tchekov, Tolstoy and Tolstoi, Baykal and Baikal, Tartar and Tatar, rouble and ruble—to say nothing of icon and ikon!

We give here some hints on the vital matter of reading Russian signs and on pronunciation, as well as a general English-Russian tourist vocabulary. Reading street names is probably the most important use for even a small knowledge of the Cyrillic alphabet. To help you, a word or two about how they work in Russian. Many Russian streets and squares are named after *people,* but the people's names may appear in different spellings—often they are made into adjectives. Suppose we have a street called Pushkin street, after the poet. The word street, ULITSA in Russian, is feminine (all Russian nouns have a gender; masculine nouns usually ending consonants, feminine in "a" and neuter in "o" or "e"). So you will see the street name as *Pushkinskaya ulitsa,* a feminine form of Pushkin. Pushkin Avenue would be *Pushkinsky Prospekt* in Russian (the word for avenue is masculine). Pushkin Chaussée would be *Pushkinskoye Shosse* (Chaussée is neuter). Don't be worried if you see one of these signs when our guide tells you you are on *Pushkin* street, avenue, etc.—it's the same thing! Almost every Soviet town has its *Leninsky Prospekt*—Lenin Avenue. As a general rule, once you have deciphered the first few letters, you will recognize the name—don't worry about the ending!

Another common way of naming streets is to say, for example, "Street of Pushkin," "Avenue of Lenin," etc.—*Ulitsa Pushkina, Prospekt Lenina* and so on. Here again, the *name* is easy to spot—its ending is not a spelling mistake, just a genitive case form of Pushkin, Lenin, etc. If you do get lost, most passers-by will understand if you ask for a street by its English name.

We owe a debt of gratitude to the Government Affairs Institute, Washington, D.C., for their permission to reproduce the Tables of the Russian Alphabet which follow.

THE RUSSIAN ALPHABET

А а	И и	С с	Ъ ъ
Б б	Й й	Т т	Ы ы
В в	К к	У у	Ь ь
Г г	Л л	Ф ф	Э э
Д д	М м	Х х	Ю ю
Е е	Н н	Ц ц	Я я
Ё ё	О о	Ч ч	
Ж ж	П п	Ш ш	
З з	Р р	Щ щ	

The Sound of Russian

Category 1: Russian Consonants that Look and Sound like English

Russian Letter (Capital)	Russian Letter (Small)	English Letter
Б	б	b
К	к	k
М	м	m
Т	т	t
З	з	z

Category 2: Russian Consonants that Look Different from Their English Equivalents

Russian Letter (Capital)	Russian Letter (Small)	English Letter
Д	д	d
Ф	ф	f
Г	г	g
Л	л	l
Н	н	n
П	п	p
Р	р	r
С	с	s
В	в	v
Й	й	y

Category 3: Russian Consonants that Have No English Equivalents

Russian Letter (Capital)	Russian Letter (Small)	Sound
Ч	ч	ch
Х	х	kh
Ш	ш	sh
Щ	щ	shch
Ц	ц	ts
Ж	ж	zh
	ь	soft sign

The Russian Vowels

Russian Letter (Capital)	Russian Letter (Small)	Sound
А	а	ah
Я	я	yah
Э	э	eh
Е	е	yeh
Ы	ы	ih
И	и	i (ee)
О	о	oh
Ё	ё	yo
У	у	u (oo)
Ю	ю	yu

EVERYDAY WORDS AND PHRASES

The most important phrase to know (one that may make it unnecessary to know any others) is: "Do you speak English?" — *Gavaree'te lee vy pa anglee'skee?* If the answer is "Nyet," then you may have recourse to the lists below:

Please	Пожа́луйста	pazhah'lsta
Thank you	Спаси́бо	spasee'ba
Good	Хорошо́	kharasho'
Bad	Пло́хо	plo'kha
I	Я	ya
You	Вы	vy
He	Он	on
She	Она́	anah'
We	Мы	my
They	Они́	anee'
Yes	Да	da
No	Нет	nyet
Perhaps	Мо́жет быть	mo'zhet byt
I do not understand	Я не понима́ю	ya ne paneemah'yoo
Straight	Пря́мо	pryah'ma
Forward	Вперёд	fperyo't
Back	Наза́д	nazah't
To (on) the right	Напра́во	naprah'va
To (on) the left	Нале́во	nale'va
Hullo!	Здра́вствуйте!	zdrah'stvooite!
Good morning!	До́брое у́тро!	do'braye oo'tra!
Good day (evening)!	До́брый день (ве́чер)!	do'bree den (ve'cher)!
Pleased to meet you!	О́чень рад с ва́ми познако́миться!	o'chen rat s vah'mee paznako'meetsa!
I am from USA (Britain)	Я прие́хал из США (Англии)	ya preeye'khal eez sshah' (ah'nglee ee)
I speak only English	Я говорю́ то́лько по́-англи́йски	ya gavaryoo' to'lka pa anglee'skee
Do you speak English?	Говори́те ли вы по-англи́йски?	gavaree'te lee vy pa anglee'skee?
Be so kind as to show (explain, translate)	Бу́дьте добры́ по-кажи́те (объясни́те, переведи́те)	boo'te dobry' paka-zhee'te (abyasnee'te, perevedee'te)
Excuse my poor pronunciation	Извини́те моё плохо́е произноше́ние	eezveenee'te mayo'pla-kho'ye praeeznashe'nye
I beg your pardon	Прости́те	prastee'te
I want to post a letter	Мне ну́жно отпра́вить письмо́	mne noo'zhna atprah'-veet peesmo'
Postcard	Почто́вая ка́рточка	pachto'vaya kah'rtachka

DAYS OF THE WEEK

Monday	Понеде́льник	panede'lneek
Tuesday	Вто́рник	fto'rneek
Wednesday	Среда́	sredah'
Thursday	Четве́рг	chetve'rk

Friday	Пя́тница	pyah'tneetsa
Saturday	Суббо́та	soobo'ta
Sunday	Воскресе́нье	vaskrese'nye
Holiday, feast	Пра́здник	prah'zneek
Today	Сего́дня	sevo'dnya
Tomorrow	За́втра	zah'ftra
Yesterday	Вчера́	vcherah'

NUMBERS

How many?	Ско́лько?	sko'lka?
1	оди́н	adee'n
2	два	dva
3	три	tree
4	четы́ре	chety're
5	пять	pyat
6	шесть	shest
7	семь	sem
8	во́семь	vo'sem
9	де́вять	de'vyat
10	де́сять	de'syat
11	оди́ннадцать	adee'natsat
12	двена́дцать	dvenah'tsat
13	трина́дцать	treenah'tsat
14	четы́рнадцать	chety'rnatsat
15	пятна́дцать	pyatnah'tsat
16	шестна́дцать	shesnah'tsat
17	семна́дцать	semnah'tsat
18	восемна́дцать	vasemnah'tsat
19	девятна́дцать	devyatnah'tsat
20	два́дцать	dvah'tsat
30	три́дцать	tree'tsat
40	со́рок	so'rak
50	пятьдеся́т	pyadesyah't
60	шестьдеся́т	shezdesyah't
70	се́мьдесят	se'mdesyat
80	во́семьдесят	vo'semdesyat
90	девяно́сто	deveno'sta
100	сто	sto
1000	ты́сяча	ty'syacha

INFORMATION SIGNS

Toilet (Gentlemen) (Ladies)	Туале́т (М) (Ж)	tooale't
No smoking!	Не кури́ть!	ne kooree't!
Taxi rank	Стоя́нка такси́	stayah'nka taksee'
Entrance	Вход	fkhot
Exit	Вы́ход	vy'khat
No exit	Вы́хода нет	vy'khada net
Emergency exit	Запасно́й вы́ход	zapasnoi' vy'khat
Stop!	Стоп!	stop!

Drinks

cold water	холо́дной воды́	khalo'dnoi vady'
mineral water	минера́льной воды́	meenerah'lnoi vady'
grape, tomato juice	виногра́дного, тома́т- ного со́ка	veenagrah'dnava, tamah'tnava so'ka
whisky, vodka	ви́ски, во́дка	vee'skee, vod'ka
liqueur	ликёр	leekyo'r
lemonade	лимона́д	leemanah't
beer	пи́во	pee'va
tea, coffee, cocoa, milk	чай, ко́фе, кака́о, молоко́	chai, ko'fe, kakah'o, malako'
fruit juice	сок	so'kee

Meat

steak	бифште́кс	beefshte'ks
roast beef	ро́стбиф	ro'stbeef
veal chops	отбивну́ю теля́чью котле́ту	atbeevnoo'yoo telyah- chyoo katle'too
pork chops	свину́ю котле́ту	sveenoo'yoo katle'too
ham	ветчину́	vecheenoo'
sausage	колбасу́	kalbasoo'

Poultry

chicken	цыплёнка	tsyplyo'nka
hazel-grouse	ря́бчика	ryah'pcheeka
partridge	куропа́тку	koorapah'tkoo
duck	у́тку	oo'tkoo

Fish

soft caviar	зерни́стой икры́	zernee'stoi eekry'
pressed caviar	па́юсной икры́	pah'yoosnoi eekry'
salmon	лососи́ны	lasasee'ny
cold sturgeon	холо́дной осетри́ны	khalo'dnoi asetree'ny

Vegetables

green peas	зелёный горо́шек	zelyo'nee garo'shek
radishes	реди́ску	redee'skoo
tomatoes	помидо́ры	pameedo'ry
potatoes	карто́шка	**karto'shka**

Desserts

cake	пиро́жное	peero'zhnaye
fruit	фру́ктов	froo'ktaf
pears	груш	groosh
mandarines	мандари́нов	mandaree'naf
grapes	виногра́ду	veenagrah'doo
bananas	бана́нов	banah'naf

white and rye bread	бéлый и чёрный хлеб	be'lee ee cho'rnee khlep
butter	мáсло	mah'sla
cheese	сыр	syr
soft-boiled eggs	яйца всмя́тку	yai'tsa fsmyah'tkoo
hard-boiled eggs	яйца вкруту́ю	yai'tsa fkrootoo'voo
an omelette	омлéт	amle't

SHOPPING

Description

good	хорóший	kharo'shee
bad	плохóй	plakhoi'
beautiful	краси́вый	krasee've
dear	дорогóй	daragoi'
cheap	дешёвый	desho'vee
old	стáрый	sta'ree
new	нóвый	no'vee

Colors

white	бéлый	be'lee
black	чёрный	chyo'rnee
red	крáсный	krah'snee
pink	рóзовый	ro'zavee
orange	орáнжевый	arah'nzhevee
yellow	жёлтый	zho'ltee
brown	кори́чневый	karee'chnevee
green	зелёный	zelyo'nee
light blue	голубóй	galooboi'
blue	си́ний	see'nee
violet	фиолéтовый	feeale'tavee
grey	сéрый	se'ree
golden	золотóй	zalatoi'
silver	серéбряный	sere'bryanee

In the shop

Baker's	Бу́лочная	boo'lachnaya
Confectioner's	Конди́терская	kandee'terskaya
Food Store	Гастронóм	gastrano'm
Grocer's	Бакалéя	bakale'ya
Delivery Counter	Стол закáзов	stol zakah'zaf
Wine and Spirits	Ви́на—коньяки́	vee'na — kanyakee'
Fruit and Vegetables	Овощи—фру́кты	o'vashshee — froo'kty

INDEX

Index

NOTES

NOTES

NOTES

NOTES

NOTES

NOTES

Fodor's Travel Publications

Available at bookstores everywhere, or call 1–800–533–6478, 24 hours a day.

Gold Guides

U.S.

Alaska

Arizona

Boston

California

Cape Cod, Martha's
Vineyard, Nantucket

The Carolinas & the
Georgia Coast

Chicago

Colorado

Florida

Hawaii

Las Vegas, Reno,
Tahoe

Los Angeles

Maine, Vermont,
New Hampshire

Maui

Miami & the Keys

New England

New Orleans

New York City

Pacific North Coast

Philadelphia & the
Pennsylvania Dutch
Country

The Rockies

San Diego

San Francisco

Santa Fe, Taos,
Albuquerque

Seattle & Vancouver

The South

U.S. & British Virgin
Islands

USA

Virginia & Maryland

Waikiki

Washington, D.C.

Foreign

Australia &
New Zealand

Austria

The Bahamas

Bermuda

Budapest

Canada

Cancún, Cozumel,
Yucatán Peninsula

Caribbean

China

Costa Rica, Belize,
Guatemala

Cuba

The Czech Republic
& Slovakia

Eastern Europe

Egypt

Europe

Florence, Tuscany
& Umbria

France

Germany

Great Britain

Greece

Hong Kong

India

Ireland

Israel

Italy

Japan

Kenya & Tanzania

Korea

London

Madrid & Barcelona

Mexico

Montréal &
Québec City

Moscow, St.
Petersburg, Kiev

The Netherlands,
Belgium &
Luxembourg

New Zealand

Norway

Nova Scotia, New
Brunswick, Prince
Edward Island

Paris

Portugal

Provence &
the Riviera

Scandinavia

Scotland

Singapore

South America

South Pacific

Southeast Asia

Spain

Sweden

Switzerland

Thailand

Tokyo

Toronto

Turkey

Vienna &
the Danube

Fodor's Special-Interest Guides

Branson

Caribbean Ports
of Call

The Complete Guide
to America's
National Parks

Condé Nast Traveler
Caribbean Resort and
Cruise Ship Finder

Cruises and Ports
of Call

Fodor's London
Companion

France by Train

Halliday's New
England Food
Explorer

Healthy Escapes

Italy by Train

Kodak Guide to
Shooting Great
Travel Pictures

Shadow Traffic's
New York Shortcuts
and Traffic Tips

Sunday in New York

Sunday in
San Francisco

Walt Disney World,
Universal Studios
and Orlando

Walt Disney World
for Adults

Where Should We
Take the Kids?
California

Where Should We
Take the Kids?
Northeast

Special Series

Affordables
Caribbean
Europe
Florida
France
Germany
Great Britain
Italy
London
Paris

Fodor's Bed & Breakfasts and Country Inns
America's Best B&Bs
California's Best B&Bs
Canada's Great Country Inns
Cottages, B&Bs and Country Inns of England and Wales
The Mid-Atlantic's Best B&Bs
New England's Best B&Bs
The Pacific Northwest's Best B&Bs
The South's Best B&Bs
The Southwest's Best B&Bs
The Upper Great Lakes' Best B&Bs

The Berkeley Guides
California
Central America
Eastern Europe
Europe
France
Germany & Austria
Great Britain & Ireland
Italy
London
Mexico

Pacific Northwest & Alaska
Paris
San Francisco

Compass American Guides
Arizona
Chicago
Colorado
Hawaii
Hollywood
Las Vegas
Maine
Manhattan
Montana
New Mexico
New Orleans
Oregon
San Francisco
Santa Fe
South Carolina
South Dakota
Southwest
Texas
Utah
Virginia
Washington
Wine Country
Wisconsin
Wyoming

Fodor's Español
California
Caribe Occidental
Caribe Oriental
Gran Bretaña
Londres
Mexico
Nueva York
Paris

Fodor's Exploring Guides
Australia
Boston & New England
Britain
California
Caribbean
China
Egypt
Florence & Tuscany
Florida
France
Germany
Ireland
Israel
Italy
Japan
London
Mexico
Moscow & St. Petersburg
New York City
Paris
Prague
Provence
Rome
San Francisco
Scotland
Singapore & Malaysia
Spain
Thailand
Turkey
Venice

Fodor's Flashmaps
Boston
New York
San Francisco
Washington, D.C.

Fodor's Pocket Guides
Acapulco
Atlanta
Barbados

Jamaica
London
New York City
Paris
Prague
Puerto Rico
Rome
San Francisco
Washington, D.C.

Rivages Guides
Bed and Breakfasts of Character and Charm in France
Hotels and Country Inns of Character and Charm in France
Hotels and Country Inns of Character and Charm in Italy

Short Escapes
Country Getaways in Britain
Country Getaways in France
Country Getaways Near New York City

Fodor's Sports
Golf Digest's Best Places to Play
Skiing USA
USA Today The Complete Four Sport Stadium Guide

Fodor's Vacation Planners
Great American Learning Vacations
Great American Sports & Adventure Vacations
Great American Vacations
National Parks and Seashores of the East
National Parks of the West

Your guide to a picture-perfect vacation

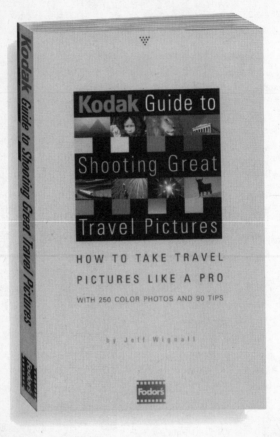

Kodak and Fodor's join together to create the guide that travelers everywhere have been asking for—one that covers the terms and techniques, the equipment and etiquette for taking first-rate travel photographs.

The most authoritative and up-to-date book of its kind, **The Kodak Guide to Shooting Great Travel Pictures** includes over 200 color photographs and spreads on 100 points of photography important to travelers, such as landscape basics, under sea shots, wildlife, city street, close-ups, photographing in museums and more.

$16.50 ($22.95 Canada)

At bookstores everywhere, or call 1-800-533-6478.

Fodor's. The name that means smart travel.™